Reconstruction in the South

Second Edition

Edited and with an introduction by

Edwin C. Rozwenc
Amherst College

D. C. HEATH AND COMPANY
Lexington, Massachusetts   Toronto

Published simultaneously in Canada.

Printed in the United States of America.

International Standard Book Number: 0-669-82735-5

Library of Congress Catalog Card Number: 72-5148

CONTENTS

III COUNTER RECONSTRUCTION

IV JUDGMENTS AND REFLECTIONS

INTRODUCTION

Reconstruction of the Union after the American Civil War was a crisis-laden experience that generated vast quantities of bitterness, hatred and frustrated hope, and left succeeding generations of Americans with a fractured historical memory. As a result, the Reconstruction era has given rise to a variety of scenarios in the writing of American history.

For some Americans, historians among them, the Reconstruction era was a dark and tragic interlude of military coercion that had to be abandoned before Americans of the North and the South could once again be truly reunited. For other Americans, including historians, the Reconstruction has been looked upon as a shameful episode of vindictive and corrupt rule by carpetbaggers and ignorant black freedmen that justifies continued Southern alienation from the rest of America. For still other Americans, historians among them, the failures of Reconstruction are another proof of the suffocating limits of the liberal tradition in America. Closely allied to these in their sense of the past are those black and white Americans who regard the Reconstruction experience as proof positive of the ineradicable racism of white Americans.

It may be somewhat lurid to refer to Reconstruction historiography as a "dark and bloody ground" but one must admit that it has been a field where historians have not flinched from proclaiming varied forms of moral indignation. The student of history, therefore, often feels that his interpretative options are severely reduced by the controversies of Reconstruction historiography. The only course that seems personally satisfying is to embrace a historical justification that serves his present politics. And much of the current discussion about the question "What is the use of history?" seems to bestow a blessing on such a use of history.

But there is a persistent heresy that lingers among historians despite incessant efforts to extirpate it. This is the belief that the study of history is a search for truth about the past—that the historian should cultivate a sense of the past that is somehow free of the need to justify or moralize without thereby becoming insensitive to the moral dimensions of the events he is explaining.

A serious historian needs to remain open to questions even about his most passionate political and moral convictions. Indeed, one might argue that the possibility of conducting a search for historical truth is usually enhanced when contending historical interpretations are being offered to us. To a very important degree, the intellectual strength of history becomes fully engaged only when the historian confronts conflicting interpretations of the past. Conflicting interpretations constitute a cognitive crisis for the historian—one that calls upon him to engage in the relentless testing of his generalizations and a tireless search for evidence to weigh contested judgments. Because contending interpreters often claim to reveal prejudice and self-indulgent justification in the historical accounts of their adversaries, a serious historian must utilize the sharpest tools of criticism and self-criticism to cut through the tough tissues of historical argumentation. He may find kernels of truth beneath the protective layers of justification but he may also discover that such kernels are not enough—that a new quest for truth is necessary which must probe with new questions.

Reconstruction history offers a fascinating opportunity to search for critical truths about a complicated and significant event in our past: the attempt to reconstruct the political and social system of the defeated states of the Southern Confederacy—an area inhabited by more than a third of the total population of the United States. In the history of any nation, the record of such an attempt is equivalent to the richest archeological discovery in developing an explanation of the nature of a society and the possibilities for social change within its complex institutional framework. Although the Reconstruction record is one that reverberates out of the cabinet meetings of presidents, the halls of Congress, and the hearts and minds of congressional constituents, the South became the vital center of Reconstruction where political wills were put to the test and outcomes were determined. Hence the readings in this volume are so arranged as to focus on the Reconstruction process in the South.

We begin with a group of readings that deal with the purposes and policies of congressional Reconstruction. Before we turn to the South we need to examine such questions as: What kind of requirements were the radical Republicans in Congress trying to impose on the South? Which of their purposes were clearly defined and which were uncertain or ambiguous? How radical were the radical Republicans anyway? What can we say about their true motives? The first of the readings in this section is taken from a standard work written by J. G. Randall and David Donald which has had considerable influence on textbook versions of the character and purposes of the congressional Reconstruction measures. The second selection comes from a recent work by LaWanda and John H. Cox that focuses on the turning point in Congress that led to the adoption of a radical program. The third comes from Kenneth M. Stampp's reexamination of radical Reconstruction based on the recent writings of historical scholars.

Part II of this volume focuses on the political fabric of Reconstruction in the South with particular attention to those groups that were attempting to carry out the objectives of the radical program in the South. The selections in this group examine questions relating to the political forces that were identified with the Reconstruction process in the South. Who were the carpetbaggers and the scalawags and how shall we characterize their motives and political behavior? What was the political role of black freedmen and how much success were they able to achieve in the adoption of laws and programs that satisfied their needs? Did radical governments in the South attempt to go beyond the objectives of the congressional Reconstruction measures or did they merely follow the lead of radical Republicans in Washington? The first two selections by Richard Current and Jack B. Scroggs examine the behavior and accomplishments of carpetbagger politicians; the next two by David Donald and Allen W. Trelease explore the social backgrounds and electoral constituencies of Southern scalawags; the last two, by W. E. B. Du Bois and Vernon L. Wharton, focus on the political efforts of black freedmen in South Carolina and Mississippi.

Of course, one cannot understand the political dynamics of the Reconstruction process in the South without examining the forces of counter Reconstruction. The readings in Part III allow us to explore such questions as: Was lawless violence the main factor in the overthrow of Reconstruction in the South? Were there fundamental social and economic forces in the South that weakened the political will of carpetbag and scalawag leaders? Were there inherent weaknesses in the radical program anyway? The first selection in this group, written by John Hope Franklin, examines the use of organized violence and terror by the forces of counter Reconstruction. The selection by Horace Mann Bond raises some fascinating questions about the political pursuit of economic benefits by speculators and railroad promoters as a factor that undermined the idealistic purposes of Reconstruction.

The final group of readings contains some reflective judgments by professional historians about the meaning of Reconstruction and its relationship to the larger movement of American history. In a sense, all writings about the Reconstruction era or special aspects of it contain either explicit or implicit assumptions about the place of the Reconstruction experience in the grand scenario of American history. Hence the three selections in this group are offered as examples of how this has been done. The first selection in this group, written by C. Vann Woodward, investigates the ambiguities in radical policy as the source of ultimate failure. W. R. Brock attempts to explain the achievements, failures, and legacies of Reconstruction as outcomes that were controlled by the peculiar character of American ideas and institutions. The final selection by George M. Frederickson highlights the importance of deep-seated and enduring racial attitudes as a fundamental factor in the Reconstruction experience and its aftermath.

Perhaps there will be some who after reading this volume will feel that they have found a ready-made truth about the significance of the Reconstruction era. Others may be disheartened by evidences of sectional, racial, or ideological bias, whether explicit or implicit, in all of the selections. For them the temptation will be strong to take refuge in the belief that historians, when all is said and done, can only make personal statements about the past. But perhaps we can also use the Reconstruction experience to develop a sense of the past that recognizes the complexity and variety of human purposes and makes us more aware of the nature and difficulties of social change. The need for social change is strongly felt today; a rational use of history may teach us a wisdom that will help us fulfill that need.

I PURPOSES AND POLICIES OF CONGRESSIONAL RECONSTRUCTION

When historians speak of the Reconstruction of the South, they are usually referring to the measures that the congressional Republicans forced upon the defeated states of the Confederacy after the Civil War. Presidents Lincoln and Johnson had instituted moderate plans for the restoration of the Southern states to their proper constitutional status within the Union, but the majority of congressional Republicans by 1866 favored more drastic policies that would disenfranchise the Confederate political leadership and guarantee equal civil rights for black freedmen. These radical purposes produced a series of showdown battles between President Johnson and the Congress, climaxed by a nearly successful attempt to impeach the President. The following selections examine the questions relating to the political process that brought forth the key measures of congressional Reconstruction: Who were the radical Republicans? Why were they successful? What were their motives? What were the areas of agreement and disagreement among radical Republicans? How should we define radicalism?

J. G. Randall and David H. Donald
THE FABRIC OF RECONSTRUCTION LEGISLATION

For many years after its publication in 1937, J. G. Randall's The Civil War and Reconstruction *was recognized as the standard work on the Civil War era. After Randall's death, David Donald, also an authority on the Civil War and Reconstruction period, revised the book to take account of the tremendous outpouring of scholarly books and articles since 1937, particularly on the Reconstruction years. The following selection on the Reconstruction acts was left largely unchanged and reflects J. G. Randall's highly critical attitude toward the radical program of Reconstruction.*

"I was a Conservative in the last session of this Congress," Thaddeus Stevens announced in December, 1866, "but I mean to be a Radical henceforth."[1] Indeed, the Radicals were in control as the new session of Congress convened. The Democrats constituted "a hopeless, demoralized, and suspected minority,"[2] unable to do much more than denounce the Radical program. The conservative Republicans, never numbering more than a handful of congressmen, had been emphatically repudiated in the recent election. The large moderate majority of the Republican party found itself falling increasingly under Radical leadership. Able to thwart the more extreme Radical proposals, such as Stevens's plan to divide up Southern estates or Sumner's effort to abolish all segregation, they were, nevertheless, dragged along into adopting new and severe measures toward the South.

In viewing the evolution of the congressional plan of reconstruction it will be of advantage first to examine those measures designed to put Congress in control of governmental functions and to insure within Congress the ascendency of the Radical group, in other words to perfect the Radical machine. After elaborate debate the two houses resolved that no member from any of the insurrectionary states

Reprinted from J. G. Randall and David H. Donald, *The Civil War and Reconstruction* (Lexington, Mass.: D. C. Heath and Company, 1961), pp. 592–600. Used with permission.

[1] Oberholtzer, 1:422.
[2] Albert V. House, Jr., "Northern Congressional Democrats as Defenders of the South during Reconstruction," *J. S. H.* 6 (February 1940): 48.

FIGURE 1. Drawing of the scene outside the galleries of the House of Representatives during the passage of the Civil Rights bill. From *Harper's Weekly*, April 28, 1866, p. 269. (*Courtesy Boston Public Library, Periodical Department*)

should be admitted into either Senate or House until Congress should have declared such state entitled to representation. This made Congress the dominating agency in the process of restoration and opened the way for any conditions that the Radicals might wish to impose upon states seeking readmission. Control of the electoral college was taken in two laws: an act of February 8, 1865, which enumerated the eleven seceded states and excluded their electoral votes; and, for the election four years later, the Edmunds resolution of July 20, 1868, which excluded from the electoral college all states which should not have been recognized according to the congressional formula.[3] Congressional control of the army was attempted by the army appropriation act of March 2, 1867, which prescribed that all military orders emanating from the President or the secretary of war should be issued through the general of the army, whose headquarters were to be at Washington and who was not to be removed nor assigned to duty outside Washington without the approval of the Senate.[4] Contrary orders were declared void, and officers issuing or heeding them were made heavily punishable as guilty of misdemeanors. The act also declared the militia of the seceded states disbanded and forbade their organization or use except as authorized by Congress.

In declaring certain military orders of the President void, this law, in the opinion of competent authorities, infringed upon his constitutional power as commander-in-chief of the army, while it also involved a destruction of state militia functions. The significance of the law will be better appreciated when one recalls how far reconstruction was formulated along the lines of a military program. Grant as general of the army was counted upon to cooperate with the Radicals; and all the circumstances of the time show that the purpose of the act was to tie the President's hands by preventing him from removing the general or controlling the army through him.

By another law Congress seized control of its sessions. The first regular session of the Fortieth Congress, elected in 1866, would normally have begun in December, 1867. By act of January 22, 1867, however, an additional session of that and succeeding Congresses

3 *Cong. Globe,* 40th Cong., 2d sess. (July 20, 1868), 4236.
4 U.S., *Stat. at Large,* 14:486–487; Richardson, *Messages and Papers,* 6:472.

was provided, to begin on the 4th of March following the election.[5] Though the legality of this session was not successfully challenged, it was the opinion of Attorney General Stanbery that this first session of the Fortieth Congress was unconstitutional, since according to his view Congress had no authority to create an additional term, and the function of calling Congress into extra session belonged to the President. In addition to its other extraordinary measures Congress undertook control of the process of amending the Constitution. The method by which the Fourteenth Amendment was put through was not the untrammeled procedure indicated in the Constitution, but a special procedure in which the national legislature did more than merely "propose" an amendment as the Constitution contemplated.

Congress also brought the cabinet within its control by the tenure-of-office act, to be discussed later, and proceeded far in the control of the Supreme Court by so limiting its appellate jurisdiction as to avert a decision which might overrule the reconstruction acts. Finally, by the political use of the impeachment process the men on Capitol Hill narrowly missed seizing the presidency itself. As the successive features of the congressional program unfolded, there loomed the specter of congressional dictatorship; and conservatives feared some kind of revolution, with civil commotions more serious than those of the war through which the country had just passed.

Viewed from another angle, this matter of congressional control involved not merely laws but various types of political manipulation. If the Radicals were to carry out their program, it was essential that they have a two-thirds Radical majority (not merely a Republican majority) in both houses; and the story of the methods by which this majority was obtained would require considerable excursions into the field of partisan strategy. Radical managers took advantage of every opening to reshape the membership of the legislative chambers. Democratic congressmen elected in Kentucky were denied seats in 1867 on the ground that "loyal voters" had been "overawed," that the "elections were carried by . . . returned rebels," and that "several" of the representatives-elect from that state were "alleged" to be "disloyal." After refusal to permit these men to be sworn in, an investigation revealed that the charges were unsustained. By this

[5] U.S., *Stat. at Large,* 14:378.

method certain members were excluded while important reconstruction measures were passed, though they were later found to be entitled to their seats.[6] According to Thaddeus Stevens it was with the same motive that Daniel Voorhees, a Democrat from Indiana, was unseated[7] in the House of Representatives. The Senate unseated John P. Stockton of New Jersey ostensibly on the ground that the state legislature had chosen him by a plurality instead of a majority vote of the two houses; but the motive seems to have been the elimination of a member who did not support the Radical program. Where legislators could not be unseated or silenced in their opposition, they were marked for later vengeance. For supporting Johnson's policy Senator Cowan of Pennsylvania was punished by the Senate's refusal to confirm him when appointed minister to Austria. The New York *Tribune* referred to the rejection as a "hint to Mr. Johnson that the Senate does not intend to reward the men who abandoned their party in order to serve the President."[8]

When these measures and party devices had been completed, the Radicals were ready to impose their will upon the South and upon the country. The functioning of the legislative machine having been made effective, and preliminary measures having been passed in 1866, Congress at last proceeded to pass the main body of reconstruction legislation in 1867 and 1868.

The original reconstruction act was largely the work of John Sherman; for it was his substitute, not the earlier bill presented by Thaddeus Stevens, that was passed. Nonetheless the hand of Stevens was evident in the whole process. The law proceeded on the premise that no lawful governments existed in the seceded states and that they might be governed under the authority of Congress until restored by congressional decree. Temporary military rule and drastic reorganization of state governments on the basis of Negro suffrage were the main features of the bill. The ten states still deemed to be unrecon-

[6] *House Jour.*, July 3, 1867, p. 161; "Kentucky Elections . . . ," *House Misc. Doc. No. 47*, 40th Cong., 1st sess.; *Biog. Dir. of Amer. Cong.* (*House Doc. No. 783*, 69th Cong., 2d sess.), 295.
[7] Concerning the charge of political motives in unseating Voorhees, Stevens said: "I had been more earnest than usual . . ., inasmuch as at this moment every vote which was fairly ours should be considered." *Cong. Globe*, 39th Cong., 1st sess. (Feb. 23, 1866), 1003; C. G. Bowers, *The Tragic Era*, pp. 107–108.
[8] N. Y. *Semi-Weekly Tribune*, Mar. 15, 1867, p. 5.

structed were divided into five military districts and placed under Federal commanders who were clothed with functions superior to the state governments, being empowered to make arrests, conduct trials by military commissions, and direct the agencies and processes of civil government as well as of constitution making. Elections for state constitutional conventions were to be held in which persons of color were authorized to vote, while those disqualified under the proposed Fourteenth Amendment for supporting the Confederacy were excluded from voting. It was further prescribed that Negro suffrage and disqualification of ex-Confederate leaders must be permanently written into the newly formed state constitutions, which were to be ratified by a majority of qualified voters. When these steps had been taken in any state, when in addition its legislature had ratified the Fourteenth Amendment, and when that amendment had become a part of the Federal Constitution, the state might (if the Radicals so willed) "be entitled to representation in Congress."[9] Meanwhile existing civil governments in the Southern states were declared provisional only, being "subject in all respects to the paramount authority of the United States." Disqualified ex-Confederates were not to be permitted to hold office under these provisional, temporary governments.

In vetoing the bill President Johnson referred to the measure as one "without precedent and without authority, in palpable conflict with the plainest provisions of the Constitution, and utterly destructive to those great principles of liberty . . . for which our ancestors . . . have shed so much blood. . . ."[10] The bill was promptly passed over his veto, the roll call showing a vote of 135 to 48 in the House, and 38 to 10 in the Senate.[11]

The South had waited in anxious suspense while Congress dallied and debated; now at last when a reconstruction law had been passed after a delay of two years, its main effect was to plunge the Southern mind into a maze of uncertainty. Who in particular were disfranchised? Why was this disfranchisement extended to thousands who

[9] The act merely outlined a method. It left for the future the declaration whether that method had been complied with in particular states. For any state to be readmitted to the Union still required a special act of Congress as to that state. U.S., *Stat. at Large,* 14:428–429.

[10] Richardson, *Messages and Papers,* 6:500.

[11] *Cong. Globe,* 39th Cong., 2d sess., 1733, 1976.

had been Unionists following the close of the war? Were state governments in the South immediately to be annulled? How was a constitutional convention to be called? Would Congress later provide further details concerning these conventions? Did the Sherman bill embrace county officers (sheriffs, clerks, judges, etc.) in its disqualifying provisions, or only executive, legislative, and judicial officers of the state? How could competent men be obtained in the South for the new governments, with safe Southern men disfranchised and extremely few Southerners available who could take the prescribed oath? Must Southern governments be put into the hands of so-called Union men who were in fact disloyal and who had become "blatant Union men" from motives of gain and duplicity? Were Negroes eligible for office under the new bill? Would not those proscribed be finally pardoned? These were a few of the questions which the reconstruction act provoked.

Southerners had drunk the cup of surrender and had disbanded their armies. They had repudiated the Southern debt, had solemnly renounced secession, had accepted the antislavery amendment. This they thought would be the end. New governments, loyal to the United States, had been set up. The President had recognized them, and their representatives had made their appearance in Washington, to be denied recognition in Congress. The next phase was a long delay, with wrangling and voluminous debating. Then came the Fourteenth Amendment. Here the Southerners balked. Their legislatures refused ratification. But even if ratification had been given, what assurance did the South have that this would be a finality? The people regarded such men as Stevens and Wade as leaders at Washington; and these men had hinted of further conditions to be imposed. Now in March of 1867, when a supposedly comprehensive reconstruction bill was passed, Southern citizens were not only mystified as to its meaning, but were left in doubt as to whether, after all these new conditions had been fulfilled, they would then actually be readmitted to the Union.[12]

In addition to uncertainty as to ambiguities in the law, there was also evident in the South an attitude of indignation and defiance

[12] This summary of Southern questioning is based closely upon actual letters written to Senator John Sherman. Sherman MSS. (Libr. of Cong.), passim, especially nos. 27155, 27260, 27266.

which was in part a carry-over from wartime ardor, in part a distrust of Northern notions as to Negro rule, and in part a stout resentment against the proscription of Southern leaders. Thus with the passage of the reconstruction bill the Southern people did not know where they stood. There seemed a strong possibility that the Supreme Court would declare the law unconstitutional; but even without this added uncertainty the terms of the law itself seemed impossible to interpret in any manner conformable to Southern ideas of law and order. "After two years [wrote a Virginia editor], . . . we are just launched on the path of . . . reconstruction. Perhaps the bill means that the present government of Virginia is not even provisional—but void. Perhaps we shall not even have a 'provisional' government until there is an election under the . . . bill. If so, all the . . . legislation of the past six years are [sic] void; and we are . . . in perfect chaos."[13]

Of itself the reconstruction act accomplished nothing except to create puzzlement, confusion, and resentment in the South. Though declaring terms upon which new Southern governments were to be formed, the act was deficient in providing the initial impetus for launching such governments. The process of calling conventions according to the congressional model was left to the people. If, however, the people took no steps toward reorganization, they would remain under their existing state governments (formed on the Johnson model) subject to military rule. It soon became evident that the Southern whites elected to remain in this condition, where their state officials were in sympathy with dominant Southern aims, rather than wreck their existing governments, intrust governmental functions to the Negro, and proscribe those whom they regarded as typical Southerners and competent leaders. To quote a declaration by conservative whites in Arkansas, reconstruction by the congressional plan was "an impossibility." Any reconstruction such as contemplated by the Radicals would result "in the certain degradation, prostration and complete ruin of the State."[14]

To deal with this situation the Radicals in Congress resolved to set the wheels moving by their own outside impulse. For this purpose there was passed the supplemental reconstruction act of March 23,

---

[13] Charlottesville (Virginia) *Chronicle*, Feb. 26, 1867.
[14] Fleming, *Doc. Hist.*, 1:423–424.

1867. Under this law the Federal military commanders in the South were directed to take the initiative and to launch the necessary proceedings as to registration of voters, election of delegates, assembling of conventions, and adoption of state constitutions. President Johnson, of course, vetoed the bill, pointing out that governments existed in the South which had been made in the accustomed way and were conformable to the "acknowledged standards of loyalty and republicanism." He denounced the Federal imposition of universal Negro suffrage, which was a matter that belonged to the states; and he could not approve "this legislative machinery of martial law, military coercion, and political disfranchisement."[15]

The South, thus reduced to "conquered provinces," was organized into five military districts, each under the command of a major general. The assigning of generals to these commands belonged to the President; but Johnson's performance of this painful duty was hardly more than a matter of accepting the advice of the general-in-chief of the army. Schofield was appointed for the district comprising Virginia; Sickles for North and South Carolina; Pope for Georgia, Alabama, and Florida; Ord for Mississippi and Arkansas; Sheridan for Louisiana and Texas. There were numerous changes in these appointments: Stoneman, A. S. Webb, and Canby were the successors of Schofield; Meade followed Pope; and a series of generals succeeded to other commands.[16] Among the less objectionable to Southerners were Hancock and Meade; the more objectionable included Sheridan, Sickles, and Pope.

Perhaps the greatest disturbance appeared under Sheridan in Louisiana, where the suppression of civil government by military rule presented analogies to the wartime situation under Butler. Sheridan arbitrarily removed sundry officials, including a city judge, a city treasurer, the mayor of New Orleans, the attorney general of the state, and a board of levee commissioners who controlled the disbursement of $4 million. He also removed J. Madison Wells, governor of Louisiana, and appointed B. F. Flanders in his place. Further

---

[15] Richardson, *Messages and Papers*, 6:533. The veto was overridden the very day it was received (March 23, 1867). The vote in the House was 114 to 25 (25 not voting), in the Senate 40 to 7.
[16] *Ann. Cyc.*, 1867, 736; Fleming, *Sequel of Appomattox*, 140 n.

trouble arose in the matter of the registration of Negro voters and the denial of registration to whites. Finally such was the disorder and agitation under Sheridan that Johnson transferred him to another area and assigned the command over Louisiana and Texas to W. S. Hancock, whose administration proved less provocative.

Confronted with practical problems in the enforcement of the reconstruction acts, President Johnson sought advice from his attorney general, Henry Stanbery, who gave an opinion (June 20, 1867) that the military commanders were not authorized to promulgate codes in defiance of civil governments in the states, but were to cooperate with the existing governments, which, it will be remembered, had been set up under Johnson's plan. Stanbery's opinion was intended to offer guidance to the President in his difficult position; and the President through the adjutant general issued a series of instructions to the commanders in the South indicating the manner in which recent acts of Congress should be applied. At this point, however, the Radicals of Congress, seeing in the President's instructions an attempt to undo their work, arranged for a reassembling of Congress in July, at which time they passed a "third reconstruction act," calculated to interpret and make effective their preceding legislation.

This third reconstruction act resolved itself largely into a statement of the "true intent and meaning" of the preceding measures, thus piling up an accumulated mass of supplemental, explanatory, and interpretative legislation that only a Philadelphia lawyer could grasp. Congress now declared that existing state governments in the South were "not legal" and were fully subject to the military commanders and the paramount authority of Congress. The general of the army and the commanders of the military districts were directed to remove any state official who should "hinder, delay, prevent or obstruct the due and proper administration" of the reconstruction acts. Registration boards prescribed by the act of March 23 were empowered to deny registration on suspicion that oath-taking was not in good faith; and the provisions concerning the oath were given a stricter interpretation, so that participation in the "rebellion" could be established by parol evidence, without the requirement of record evidence. Registration officers were directed to revise registration lists in keeping with the new "interpretation," and the removal of such officers was authorized whenever "needful." To further emphasize the supremacy of the military power through Congress, it was provided that no military commander, nor any officer acting under him, should be bound "by the opinion of any civil officer of the United States." Finally there was added a curious clause which "enacted" that the reconstruction laws should "be construed liberally, to the end that all the intents thereof may be fully and perfectly carried out." This last clause was less a matter of legislation than a mandate as to the interpretation of legislation. Congress was introducing a distinction between the law and the "intent" of the law, and was appealing to executory officers to follow only a specified course in "construing" legislation whose purpose and meaning were continually undergoing restatement by Congress itself.

Three reconstruction acts had now been passed, two of them supplemental to the first. Some months elapsed; and it then became evident that the legislative machinery was not even yet accomplishing the purpose of the Radicals. As the law then stood (act of March 23, 1867, supplemental to the act of March 2, 1867) the adoption of a new constitution in a Southern state required a majority of all registered voters, not merely a majority of the votes cast. Seeing in this situation a chance to defeat the newly proposed Radical constitution in Alabama, framed by delegates said to represent merely the Negroes and nonresidents, a conference of conservative men, assembled at Montgomery, issued an appeal to the people of the state advising those opposed to the constitution to refrain from voting. Conservatives knew that the law was so framed against them that they could not defeat the constitution at the election; and by refraining from voting they hoped to accomplish more than by going to the Radical-controlled polls and trying to cast negative votes, because their known attitude would cause the whole vote to be lighter, and the Radicals, being under the necessity of changing their own law so as to permit the constitution to be adopted by a mere majority of the votes cast, would thus "exhibit . . . the fact that the constitution they impose is not the constitution of the people of Alabama, but . . . of a minority . . . , and that, a negro minority.[17] When the constitution

17 *Ann. Cyc.*, 1868, 15–16.

was voted on (February 4, 1868) it was defeated by reason of the fact that the affirmative vote of about 70,000 amounted to less than half the number of registered voters, which was about 167,000.

Because of this situation Congress now passed the "fourth reconstruction act," by which a majority of the votes actually cast was made sufficient to put a new constitution into force, no matter how small the minority taking part in the election. This meant that the cards were stacked in favor of the Radicals, whose intention to force their type of government upon the South was emphasized by another provision of law, which gave the franchise to any voter who had resided in the election district for ten days preceding the election, "upon presentation of his certificate of registration, his affidavit, or other satisfactory evidence," under regulations made by the district commander.[18] This fourth reconstruction act became law on March 11, 1868, without the President's signature, by the operation of the ten-days rule.

Thus by March of 1868 the Radical party had, three years after the close of the war, built up its structure of legislation and supplemental legislation. The reconstruction acts were now launched; minorities, though made up of outsiders and Negroes, were sufficient to establish new governments; district military commanders, with power to set up military commissions in the place of the civil courts, were in possession with "sufficient military force . . . to . . . enforce . . . authority";[19] opposition to the "directory" at Washington was ineffective; and the readiness to pile statute upon statute indicated a determination of the Radicals to permit no defeat of their purposes even by the provisions of their own laws.

[18] U.S., *Stat. at Large*, 15:41.
[19] Reconstruction act of March 2, 1867, sec. 2, U.S., *Stat. at Large*, 14:428.

LaWanda Cox and John H. Cox
CIVIL RIGHTS: THE ISSUE OF RECONSTRUCTION

Unlike Randall and other historians who emphasized vindictiveness and political expediency in their assessment of the radical program, LaWanda and John H. Cox argue that one must analyze principles as well as prejudices to fully understand the purposes and policies of the radical Republicans. The following selection examines the issue of Reconstruction as it was perceived by congressional Republicans in 1866.

. . . What had been taking place in the Republican party since the close of the civil conflict was a gradual metamorphosis, similar to the one that had taken place during the war. The war years transformed the Republicans, a political amalgam originally united on the principle of opposition to the extension of slavery, into a party committed to the destruction of slavery. This objective had been formally embodied in the party platform of 1864. The platform, however, had not included a plank supporting equal legal status for the freed slaves, despite the fact that such a plank was offered and considered. By the winter of 1865, Republicans generally had expanded their repudiation of slavery into a condemnation of legal discriminations which by then seemed to them the last vestiges of slavery. Important elements within the party held that the freedmen's rights must include an equality of suffrage, but on this more advanced position, Republicans were not yet agreed. They had, however, come to identify Republicanism with a defense of basic civil rights for the freed slave.[1] Sometimes this identification of Republicanism with the prin-

Reprinted by permission of The Macmillan Company from *Politics, Principle and Prejudice, 1865–1866* by John H. Cox and LaWanda Cox. Copyright © The Free Press of Glencoe, a Division of The Macmillan Company, 1963.

[1] Before the opening of Congress in December, 1865, Schuyler Colfax, Speaker of the House, made a speech which was widely regarded as a statement of majority Republican opinion. He abjured any inflexibility of policy, spoke warmly of what the President had already accomplished in securing commitments from the southern states, but made clear that some additional assurances were considered necessary. The first of these, and indeed the only one that was substantive, was that "the Declaration of Independence be recognized as the law of the land" by the protection of the freedmen in their rights of person and property including the right to testify. He made no mention of suffrage for the Negro nor of any punitive action against the South. For text of speech, see *New York Times,* Nov. 19, 1865.

ciple of equal status before the law was stated explicitly; sometimes
it was expressed through generalizations that invoked liberty, freedom, or humanity. A characteristic argument, advanced by one Republican paper, was that if the position on equal civil rights embodied
in Johnson's veto message were correct, then "all the principles of
democracy and freedom upon which our creed of Republicanism
rests are false and we must recant them."[2] When Republicans accused Johnson of treachery to the Republican party and Republican
principles, or with greater forbearance simply asked that he give
them some unmistakable evidence so that they might "continue to
confide in him as a *Republican*,"[3] they were identifying their party
with the principle of equality in legal status for all freedmen.

Thus what had once been an advanced, or "Radical," position
within Republican ranks, by 1866 had become accepted and moderate. To most opponents of equal civil status, however, the principle
still appeared "Radical." Herein lies one clue to the confusion in
the use of the term "Radical" which plagues any serious student of
the period. The term is inescapable; yet a man labeled a "Radical"
by one set of contemporaries or historians is often found designated
a "moderate" by another group of contemporaries or historians. All
would agree that Charles Sumner, Thaddeus Stevens, and Wendell
Phillips, extreme men though not of one mind, were the prototypes of
Radicalism. The term *radical*, however, has often been used to identify, and castigate, all Republican opponents of Andrew Johnson.
Many of these men were almost as critical of Sumner, Stevens, and
Phillips as were their Conservative adversaries. Few followed Stevens
in his demand for confiscation; most were ready to abandon or
drastically compromise Sumner's aim of Negro suffrage. Though they
wished to proceed with caution, there was no strong desire among
them for an indefinite postponement of restoration by reducing the
South to the status of "territories" or "conquered provinces." In
other words, many Radicals were moderate men. The Radical opponents of President Johnson were united in one demand—that of
national protection for the freedmen. On other issues of Reconstruction they held widely divergent views.

It has sometimes been assumed that a common economic attitude

[2] Clipping from a Buffalo paper, March 29, 1866, Scrapbook, Johnson MSS.
[3] Chicago *Evening Journal,* March 28, 1866, ibid.

united Radicals and marked them off from pro-Johnson men. This assumption is demonstrably false. Some were protariff men, some antitariff men; some advocated cheap money, some upheld a sound gold standard; some were spoilsmen, others were among the spoilsmen's bitterest critics.[4] In 1865 and 1866 substantial members of the business community were as often found in the ranks of the President's supporters as in those of the opposition.[5] John A. Dix, a key figure in the Johnson movement, was president of the Union Pacific. A twenty-thousand dollar reception and dinner at the famed Delmonico's, at the opening of Johnson's ill-fated Swing-around-the-Circle, was attended by many of the most powerful figures of New York business and finance.[6] As late as September, 1866, the *New York Times,* in an editorial entitled "Business and Politics—the Conservatism of Commerce"—spoke of the "great unanimity of the commercial and business classes in supporting the conservative policy of the Administration, and in opposing with their might the schemes of the Radical Destructives."[7]

Nor were the Radicals distinguishable from the general run of Union men, as is often claimed, by vindictiveness toward the South or clamor for the heads of "traitors." Indeed, New York's outstanding Radical leader, Horace Greeley, was a leading figure in the movement for amnesty and forgiveness. Henry Wilson, Radical senator

---

[4] See Stanley Coben, "Northeastern Business and Radical Reconstruction: A Reexamination," *Mississippi Valley Historical Review* 46 (June 1959): 67–90; Robert P. Sharkey, *Money, Class and Party: An Economic Study of Civil War and Reconstruction* (Baltimore, 1959); Irwin Unger, "Business Men and Specie Resumption," *Political Science Quarterly* 74 (March 1959): 46–70. Howard K. Beale's study made much of economic issues, but his findings showed that they had not been central to the political campaign of 1866. Johnson's failure to make them such, Beale considered "a fatal error in political judgment." *The Critical Year,* p. 299.

[5] Letters in the Johnson MSS indicate this support, see those of August Belmont, March 24, 1866, A. J. Drexel, May 3, 1866, Alexander T. Stewart, June 18, 1866; also reports of business support in the letters of W. G. Smith, March 2, 1866 (Buffalo), J. B. Hussey, March 3, 1866 (New York), W. J. Hilton, March 7, 1866 (Albany), R. B. Carnahan, March 16, 1866 (Pittsburgh), G. W. Morgan, July 14, 1866 (Ohio), D. S. Seymour, Nov. 8, 1866 (Troy).

[6] In the Tilden MSS there are printed letters outlining the arrangements, including a seating chart for the dinner, and itemizing the expenses with assessments. Tilden's share of the cost was $145.38. Smythe, Johnson's appointee as Collector of the Port, feared the plans for Johnson's New York visit would give the impression that "a *few* are to get hold of you" and advised the President to stop at the Fifth Avenue Hotel, rather than Delmonico's to "give '*the people'* " a better opportunity to see him. Smythe to Johnson, Aug. 25, 1866, Johnson MSS.

[7] *New York Times,* Sept. 2, 1866.

from Massachusetts, wrote to Johnson in support of a plea for the parole of Clement C. Clay of Alabama.[8] Even Thaddeus Stevens offered his services in the defense both of Clay and of Jefferson Davis.[9] The feeling against Southern leaders of the rebellion, which found expression both in a stubborn indignation at the prospect of their speedy return to the halls of Congress and in an emotional demand for Jefferson Davis' trial and conviction, cut across the division between pro-Johnson and anti-Johnson men. Thus in December, 1865, the House passed a resolution supporting the stringent Test Oath of July, 1862, as binding without exception upon all branches of government. Only one Republican registered opposition.[10] A few days earlier, without a single dissenting voice, the House had declared treason a crime that should be punished; thirty-four Democrats joined the Republicans in voting "yea."[11] In June, after the break with the President, a resolution calling for the trial of Jefferson Davis passed by a vote of 105 to 19, with no Republican voting against it. Six of the seven Conservatives who had broken with the majority of their party to support Johnson in the Civil Rights veto, registered their approval of this demand.[12]

The only common denominator that united the Radicals of 1866, and the only characteristic they shared which could logically justify the term *radical,* was their determination that the rebel South should not be reinstated into the Union until there were adequate guarantees that the slaves liberated by the nation should enjoy the rights of free men.[13] It is true that Johnson's opponents believed Congress should have some voice in Reconstruction and that they were profoundly

[8] Wilson to Johnson, March 3, 1866, Johnson MSS.
[9] McKitrick, *Andrew Johnson and Reconstruction*, p. 19, footnote 2.
[10] The roll came on a motion to table the resolution. McPherson, *Political Manual for 1866,* pp. 110–111.
[11] Ibid., p. 109.
[12] Ibid., p. 113; compare the vote p. 81.
[13] On the meaning of "Radical," compare McKitrick, *Andrew Johnson and Reconstruction,* pp. 53–67. The Chicago *Tribune,* the leading Radical newspaper, had some revealing comments. Before the Republican convention of 1860, it identified the "more radical" wing of the party as a body of men "somewhat in advance of the party's creed," zealous, honest and possibly impractical, who recognized that they had no power to interfere with slavery in the states but still hoped "that the election of a Republican President will in some way tend to the crippling of the institution they hate." In 1866, the *Tribune* defined as the vestige of slavery "all discrimination against freedmen." Until these be removed, it held that the South would not be at peace with itself or with the North. Chicago *Tribune,* Feb. 6, 1860, Feb. 16, 1860, and clipping on Freedmen's Bureau veto, Scrapbook, Johnson MSS.

disturbed by the prospect of a restored South, united with the Northern Democracy, immediately controlling the destinies of the nation. They were also extremely sensitive to any patronage moves that might seem to indicate Johnson's support of the Democracy or an intent to punish Republicans for failure to agree completely with the President's position. These attitudes, however, can hardly be termed radical; and they were not decisive factors with most of the men who broke with the President after the veto messages. Possibly, without the civil rights issue, one of these points of friction might have generated warfare and become the dividing line between Johnson's opponents and his supporters; but this is extremely doubtful. The testimony of such men as Samuel Bowles, Thurlow Weed, Jacob D. Cox, and John Cochrane must be given weight. They believed that the President could achieve his goal of speedy restoration and renewed fellowship between North and South if only he endorsed some effective national guarantee of the freedmen's civil rights as citizens.[14] One of the most distinguished students of congressional Reconstruction, thoroughly sympathetic to Johnson, concluded that the moderate leadership in Congress desired just three conditions and would have settled for two: a guarantee of "the negroes' civil rights" and recognition of "the prerogative of Congress."[15] Since executive action alone could not guarantee the South's permanent acquiescence in the freedmen's newly gained rights, such security could be had only by way of the second condition, acceptance of some congressional action in the matter. In other words, the two conditions were inseparable; Johnson's consent to the first would have automatically fulfilled the second. Had Johnson come to terms with the moderates on the civil rights issue, the truly radical men of the party would have been clearly distinguishable from Republicans generally; and the true "Radical" would have faced the choice of compromise or defeat. Instead, except for a handful of Conservatives who totally accepted Johnson's leadership, "Republican" tended to become synonymous with "Radical."

The Democracy had a major responsibility for the blurring of distinction between the terms *Radical* and *Republican*. Even before the vetoes, they had tended to stigmatize the entire Republican leader-

---

[14] See the quotations cited above, [original] footnotes 5, 6, 32, 43.
[15] Kendrick, *Journal of the Joint Committee on Reconstruction*, pp. 251–252.

ship in Congress as "Radical"; after the vetoes, they delighted in
maligning the Freedmen's Bureau Bill and the Civil Rights Act as
parts of a sinister Radical design to defeat Johnson's plan for speedy
restoration. This was good political strategy. Political expediency
and propaganda, however, are not a complete explanation. In the eyes
of Democrats, North and South, the claim of "equality," in any form,
for the newly freed Negro was indeed radical, an outrageous postwar
version of prewar Abolitionism. Both before and after the vetoes, one
finds expressions in the Democratic press and in private letters of the
period which indicate an unmistakable identification of "Radical"
with "Abolitionist." Thus, a Tennessee judge, complaining about the
interference of the military, started to write that this was "just what
the abominable Abolitionis [*sic*]" desired, then crossed out "Abolitionis" and substituted the word "Radicals."[16] It is true that Northern
Democratic spokesmen and responsible Southerners at times urged
upon the Southern states full equality in civil proceedings; but they
did so because this appeared to them not only an inescapable
concession to Republican opinion but a necessary condition for
Presidential support as well. Moreover, so long as exclusive state
authority were maintained, concessions made by state action before
restoration could be undone by state action after restoration.

There is a certain validity in the Democratic equation that denied
the historical differences between oldtime Abolitionists, postwar extremists, and those moderate Republicans of 1866 who upheld equal
civil rights for the Negro. Between pro-Johnson Conservatives and
anti-Johnson Radicals—whether the latter were moderate or extreme
—the dividing line was marked by a distinction in race attitude. Wide
differences existed on each side of the line, and there were those
who took their places in each camp for reasons primarily of political
expediency and advantage. Yet by 1866 all Radicals accepted, indeed
most held as an article of faith, a nationally enforceable equality of
civil status, even though their attitudes might differ in respect to
equality of suffrage and equality of social status for the Negro. The
position of Johnson supporters varied from extreme racism to an un-
comfortable accommodation to the probability that legal discrimina-

---

[16] T. Barry to Grider, March 8, 1866, Johnson MSS.

tion and inequitable treatment for the freed slave would follow upon an unrestrained local autonomy in race relations. The anti-Johnson side attracted men with a deep sense of concern and responsibility for the freed slave; the pro-Johnson ranks drew men who thought national responsibility had ended with the destruction of property rights in human beings. The latter preferred to base formal argument upon aversion to centralized government, a defense of states' rights, respect for the Constitution, and devotion to a reunited Union. But behind such arguments there most often lay some shade of that prejudice of race which still divides the nation.

The racist tendency among Northern Democrats hardly needs further demonstration. If evidence is desired, it can be found among the editorials with which the veto messages were greeted. Johnson does not believe, wrote one New England Democratic editor, "in compounding our race with niggers, gipsies and baboons, neither do we . . . [or] our whole Democratic people."[17] A Washington paper editorialized:[18]

> The negro is to have full and perfect equality with the white man. He is to mix up with the white gentlemen and ladies all over the land . . . at all public meetings and public places he is to be your equal and your associate. . . . How long will it be if Congress can do all this before it will say the negro shall vote, sit in the jury box, and intermarry with your families? Such are the questions put by the President.

The *Ohio Statesman* declared it was no crime for the President to "esteem his race as superior to an inferior race. In this hour of severe trial, when the President is endeavoring so to administer the government that the white man shall not be subordinated to the negro race, will not the white man stand by him."[19] The Radicals, commented a Pennsylvania paper with satisfaction, "now find that President Johnson regards this government as the White man's."[20] One set of huge headlines read:[21]

[17] *State and Union,* April 5, 1866, Scrapbook, ibid.
[18] *Constitutional Union,* March 28, 1866, ibid.
[19] Clipping on Civil Rights veto, ibid.
[20] Boylestown *Democrat,* Feb. 27, 1866, ibid.
[21] Wayne County [Ohio] *Democrat,* ibid.

ALL HAIL!
GRAND AND GLORIOUS!
GREAT VICTORY FOR THE WHITE MAN
REJOICE, WHITE MAN REJOICE!
THE HOUR OF YOUR DELIVERANCE HAS COME
SATAN IS BOUND
RADICALISM REBUKED
TAXPAYERS RELIEVED
PRESIDENT JOHNSON TURNS OUT TO BE
A FULL BLOODED WHITE MAN
HAS VETOED THE FREEDMEN'S BUREAU BILL
"THE NEGROES HAVE TO WORK"

The limitations of Andrew Johnson's own benevolence toward the freedmen have already been explored.[22] A word more should be added as to the overtones of race prejudice apparent in his veto message. These may have been unintended expressions of his own bias or, more probably, deliberate appeals to the race prejudice of others. The first veto offended much less overtly than the second, although it called forth at least once protest against its appeal to "a low prejudice against color."[23] The offending passage was the argument that Congress could hardly appropriate moneys for relief, lands, and schools for the freedmen when it had never considered itself authorized "to expend the public money for the rent or purchase of homes for the thousands, not to say millions of the white race who are honestly toiling from day to day for their subsistence." The Civil Rights veto claimed that "the distinction of race and color is, by the bill, made to operate in favor of the colored and against the white race." It also raised the emotion-laden subject of intermarriage between whites and blacks, although the matter had little relevance to the President's argument. And in a passage clearly not intended as a compliment, it equated "the entire race designated as blacks, people of color, negroes, mullattoes, and persons of African blood" with Chinese, Indians, and "the people called Gipsies."[24]

The racist attitudes of the Blairs and of James Gordon Bennett, men whose influence with Johnson was very considerable, have al-

[22] See above, Chapter 8.
[23] Portland *Press,* Scrapbook, Johnson MSS.
[24] For the texts of the messages we have used McPherson, *Political Manual for 1866.*

ready been sufficiently established.[25] The attitude of Conservative Republicans who stood with the President is less evident and requires examination.

Though not without criticism of the President, Gideon Welles agreed more completely with him than did any other member of the original Cabinet. Welles alone thoroughly approved of the Civil Rights veto. What he criticized in Johnson's conduct of affairs was *too little* of the very qualities most other critics have thought the Tennessean had in excess—inflexibility and boldness. The fact is that Welles at one end of the Republican spectrum was at least as dogmatic and extreme as was Charles Sumner at the other. An old Jacksonian Democrat, Welles's narrow views of national power and states' rights were unaffected by his adherence to the Republican party. Qualified only by fading personal loyalties and a stout defense of the war effort, his sympathies throughout the postwar period were with the Democrats. A sanctimonious curmudgeon, whom history has largely taken at his own self-evaluation, Welles had kind words for few men. Even so, the sustained animus and distortion that he directed against the Radicals in his famed diary are particularly malicious.

With a record of having broken with the Democratic party over slavery and of having ordered the wartime Navy to protect runaway slaves and to enlist Negroes, Welles's hostility toward the Radicals might be thought to have arisen entirely from his states'-rights views. This, however, was not the sole explanation. In the diary, Welles revealed a marked distaste for the "ingrained Abolitionism"[26] which he thought motivated Johnson's opponents. He was also frank in stating that he was "no advocate for social equality, nor do I labor for political or civil equality for the negro. I do not want him at my table, nor do I care to have him in the jury-box, or in the legislative hall, or on the bench."[27] The Washington correspondent of the Springfield *Republican,* while unconvinced by rumors that Welles had told his Democratic friends in Connecticut that he was opposed to Negro suffrage just before the state was to vote upon the question,

[25] See above, Chapter 3, footnotes 29, 30, 31; Chapter 5, footnotes 18, 21, 22, 25; Chapter 10, footnote 3.
[26] *Diary of Gideon Welles,* 2:369.
[27] Ibid., p. 374.

thought it quite likely that Welles, who "never was very radical on the slavery question . . . retains many of his prejudices against the colored people."[28] Welles agreed with Sumner that there was "a dreadful state of things South" and that "the colored people were suffering"; but his own concern was for the whites who had also passed through a terrible ordeal and had hardship enough without "any oppressive acts from abroad."[29] Sumner told Welles that he, New England's representative in the Cabinet, misrepresented New England sentiment;[30] in this judgment, Sumner was most certainly correct.

Senator Doolittle of Wisconsin, the strongest pro-Johnson Republican in Congress, was not without compassion for the Negro, but his view of future race relations precluded any possibility of equality. Before and during the civil conflict, Doolittle had been acutely aware of the race problem and the difficulty of its solution. In his opposition to the extension of slavery, a key consideration was the desire to save the western lands for white settlers. He had been willing that the North should join in paying the expense of colonizing Southern Negroes in Latin America, and he had developed a strong feeling of resentment against the Abolitionists.[31]

In the fall of 1865, Doolittle proposed as a solution of the Negro problem that a part of Texas, and perhaps of Florida as well, be ceded to the Federal Government for a segregated freedmen's territory. His object was to attract the entire Negro population of the South to these exclusively Negro territories by the offer of free homesteads. Only thus, in his view, could they "save themselves from being trodden under foot by the advancing tide of Caucasian emigration from Europe and from all the North."[32] Short of such a territorial haven, Doolittle apparently thought that the problem would be resolved only by the passing away of the Negro due to his excessively high death rate in freedom.[33] He believed that rather than the comprehensive freedom given by the Thirteenth Amendment, it would

---

[28] Springfield *Republican,* Sept. 30, 1865.
[29] *Diary of Gideon Welles,* 2:369.
[30] Ibid., p. 394.
[31] James L. Sellers, "James R. Doolittle," *Wisconsin Magazine of History* 17 (December 1933): 176; ibid. (March 1934): 287–288, 293, 302–303.
[32] Doolittle to Johnson, Sept. 9, 1865, Johnson MSS.
[33] J. C. G. Kennedy to Doolittle, March 9, 1866; notes for speech, March or April 1866, Doolittle MSS.

have been far better for the slaves had their emancipation been gradual, with those born after a certain date made free at twenty-one or even thirty years of age.[34] After the veto of the Civil Rights Bill, the Wisconsin legislature instructed Doolittle, who had not voted on its original passage, to support the measure. When he refused to do so, the legislature called for his resignation.[35]

The draft argument of Senator Edgar Cowan of Pennsylvania for Johnson's veto of the Freedmen's Bureau Bill is revealing. In it there is no kind word for the freedmen nor for the Bureau. Cowan viewed with distaste not only the military jurisdiction which the bill authorized but also the fact that it went "the whole length of putting the negroes upon the same footing precisely as the whites as to all *civil rights and immunities.*" He not only argued a want of power on the part of the Federal Government to purchase lands for the relief of destitute freedmen or to establish school buildings for their benefit, but added:[36]

> *The people were willing to emancipate the slave in order that he might have a chance to take care of himself—but they will be very unwilling to pay for his maintenance and support out of the public purse—and they say justly that if he is unable to cope with his neighbors, in the battle for life—he must be content with the fate which awaits him and not expect them to feed him at the nation's expense.*

After the first veto, it is clear that Cowan recognized that general opinion in the North was not altogether in accord with his own. He urged Johnson to veto the Civil Rights Bill, but warned that the President's public opposition to the measure should not include an attack upon its principle of equal status.[37]

Cowan had been one of the three Republican senators voting against the Civil Rights Bill on its passage in early February, before the first veto; the other thirty-three Republicans who voted supported the measure.[38] On the Freedmen's Bureau Bill a few days earlier he

[34] Doolittle to wife, Mary, Nov. 11, 1866, ibid.
[35] Sellers, "James R. Doolittle," *Wisconsin Magazine of History* 18 (September 1934): 26–27.
[36] Messages, Johnson MSS. See Cox, "Andrew Johnson and His Ghost Writers," p. 463.
[37] Cowan to Johnson, March 23, 1866, Johnson MSS.
[38] McPherson, *Political Manual for 1866,* p. 80.

had registered no vote, but in the course of discussion, when he had referred to himself as a friend of the Negro, Senator Henry Wilson had sharply attacked his record. "Why, Sir, there has hardly been a proposition before the Senate of the United States for the last five years leading to the emancipation of the negro and the protection of his rights that the Senator from Pennsylvania has not sturdily opposed. . . . He has made himself the champion of 'how not to do it.' "[39] A sympathetic student of Cowan's public career quotes Wilson's speech at length, and then comments, "These were strong words yet underneath them there was much truth."[40] The following May, Cowan was arguing that the men who were repudiating the Union-Republican platforms of Chicago (1860) and Baltimore (1864) were not those who stood by the President, but those "who go away after false lights, who wander in dangerous places, who cook up Freedmen's Bureau and civil rights bills."[41]

About James Dixon of Connecticut, the third of Johnson's Republican supporters in the Senate, we have little evidence. In October, 1865, he wrote the President that "the People desire justice to the Negro but they are tired of the perpetual reiteration of his claims upon their attention to the exclusion of all other interests. Moreover, as you will see by the recent vote of Connecticut on the question of extending suffrage to the colored population, there are grave doubts as to his fitness to govern the country, even *here*."[42] These words do not sound like those of a man with a deep concern for the Negro and his status. The same implication appears in an attack upon Senator Dixon by a fellow Connecticut Republican, who publicly accused him in 1863 of caring only for power. "I was forced to the conclusion that his [Dixon's] sympathies were not with his own section, but were with the Southern oligarchy. . . . That he hated republicanism for its humanity, and its self-sacrificing devotion to principle."[43]

The Thomas Ewings were among the most influential of Johnson's

---

[39] Quoted in B. J. Pershing, "Senator Edgar A. Cowan, 1861–1867," *Western Pennsylvania Historical Magazine* 4 (October 1921): 229–230.
[40] Ibid.
[41] *Speech of Hon. Edgar Cowan of Pennsylvania on Executive Appointments and Removals, Delivered in the Senate of the United States, May 9, 1866* (pamphlet, Washington, 1866), p. 13.
[42] Dixon to Johnson, Oct. 8, 1865, Johnson MSS.
[43] Mark Howard, *Despotic Doctrines Declared by the United States Senate Exposed; and Senator Dixon Unmasked* (pamphlet, Hartford, 1863), p. 8.

political counselors. Both father and son had a staunchly antislavery prewar record; yet the elder Ewing was known as a conservative Whig and Republican, not "as one of the 'earnest' or 'progressive' men of his time."[44] That the want of "earnestness" characterized his view of the Negro would seem evident from Ewing's notes for a public statement in 1867. In arguing against Negro suffrage in the South, he maintained that in the North "the popular mind cannot be excited to enthusiasm in favor of negro equality, social or political." Neither laborers, mechanics, nor professional men would admit a Negro man or woman on terms of equality to their parties, dinners, or dances, for the consequence would be mixed marriages. The feeling might be "vulgar prejudice, but if so, I am content to acknowledge myself therein essentially vulgar—I would be most unwilling to have a black daughter in law." According to Ewing, some Republicans thought that Providence would interfere and bring about Negro suffrage because it was founded on eternal justice, but God knew when he created man what was good for his creatures. "It is not probable that he will by a special miracle suddenly change his nature —his instincts, his prejudices and his passions, in order to adapt him to any man's or any party's purposes."[45]

Two intimate associates of Ewing's were brought into Johnson's Cabinet in 1866 on his recommendation, Henry Stanbery as Attorney General and Orville H. Browning as Secretary of the Interior. Though a Republican, Stanbery described himself to Democrats in 1868 as having been an "old guard" Whig who ceased to be one only when that party ceased to exist. Apparently he had not voted for Lincoln: "My last vote was given to that party [Whig] in the Presidential contest of 1860."[46] He was the author of those passages in Johnson's Civil Rights veto which appealed to race prejudice by interjecting the question of mixed marriages.[47] According to Gideon Welles, Stanbery told Cabinet members in 1867 that as a member of the Ohio legisla-

---

[44] From the Toledo *Commercial*, in Ellen Ewing Sherman, comp., *Memorial of Thomas Ewing of Ohio* (New York, 1873), p. 123.
[45] Ewing MSS.
[46] Speech in reply to a toast, published in *An Appeal to the Senate to Modify its Policy and Save from Africanization and Military Despotism the States of the South,* printed by order of the National Democratic Resident Committee (pamphlet, Washington, 1868).
[47] Messages, Johnson MSS. See Cox, "Andrew Johnson and His Ghost Writers," pp. 475, 477–479.

ture he had voted against Negro suffrage, and that he would do so
again were he in Ohio.[48] Before the Supreme Court in 1875, it was
Stanbery who argued the famous case of *U.S.* vs. *Reese,* thereby
helping to set aside the Civil Rights Enforcement Act of 1870.[49]

Stanbery's colleague in the Cabinet, Orville Browning, had been
an antislavery man, but one of the most conservative variety, an
outspoken opponent of Abolitionists.[50] During the war he deplored
Lincoln's action in issuing the Emancipation Proclamation.[51] The
Thirteenth Amendment, in Browning's opinion, merely gave the slaves
personal freedom and did not confer other rights "not necessary
incidents of personal liberty, and not necessary for its enjoyment";
and he was opposed to further legislation or constitutional amendment to secure additional liberties. "If the general government will
take its hands off, and let the thing alone, it will soon adjust itself
upon a better and more satisfactory basis for all parties, than it can
ever be forced to do by Federal interference."[52] Even after the ratification of the Fifteenth Amendment, Browning was numbered among
those who opposed suffrage and nonsegregation for the Negroes in
the conviction that, as an "inferior" race, their legal equality would
threaten Anglo-Saxon institutions.[53]

Alexander W. Randall, who came into the Cabinet along with
Stanbery and Browning, had been a vigorous war governor of Wisconsin, and then as Assistant Postmaster under Lincoln had assisted
effectively in mending the President's political fences in preparation
for his reelection in 1864.[54] Retaining that politically strategic post
under Johnson, Randall was soon recognized as an active political

[48] *Diary of Gideon Welles,* 3:4.

[49] Charles Warren, *The Supreme Court in United States History,* rev. ed., 3 vols.
(Boston, 1937), 2:603.

[50] J. G. Randall and David Donald, *The Civil War and Reconstruction* (Boston,
1961), p. 24. Maurice G. Baxter, *Orville H. Browning: Lincoln's Friend and Critic*
(Bloomington, Indiana, 1957), pp. 19–20, 67–69.

[51] For Browning's wartime position, see Baxter, *Orville H. Browning,* pp. 119–120,
141–143, 148.

[52] National Union Club Documents, *Speeches of Hon. Edgar Cowan, Hon. Jas. R.
Doolittle, Hon. Hugh McCulloch, Letter of Hon. O. H. Browning and an Address
by a Member of the Club; also the Condition of the South: A Report of Special
Commissioner B. F. Truman* (pamphlet, Washington, 1866), pp. 21–22; *Diary of
Gideon Welles,* 2:534, 638.

[53] Baxter, *Orville H. Browning,* pp. 228, 245–256.

[54] Joseph Schafer, "Alexander W. Randall," *Dictionary of American Biography,*
15:344–345.

lieutenant of the new President. In the Cabinet reorganization of 1866, he was raised to the rank of Postmaster General. While a young man in Wisconsin politics, Randall had helped prepare a proposal for Negro suffrage to be submitted for referendum in connection with the revision of the state constitution, an action which made him highly unpopular and kept him out of politics for some time.[55] Although associated with the Free Soil Democracy, he is said to have taken little part in its activities because of his opposition to the radical ideas of its leaders.[56] There is little evidence of his racial attitudes during the Johnson period. To judge from his position as reported by Gideon Welles, Randall was equivocal and politically minded rather than either prejudiced or deeply concerned in respect to matters touching equality for the freedmen.[57]

Hugh McCulloch, Secretary of the Treasury under both Lincoln and Johnson, believed firmly in the superior intelligence and energy of the white race.[58] He was reported to have said that "so far as the pretended equality of races was concerned," history showed that the Anglo-Saxon race in contact with an inferior one must "dominate or exterminate."[59] Like many another resident of Indiana, he was opposed to granting the vote to the Negroes even in the Northern states.[60] Charles Sumner, who found it difficult to condone the position of Seward and Welles on the question of Negro suffrage in the South, was inclined to more charity toward McCulloch as one "imbued with the pernicious folly of Indiana."[61] McCulloch was aware that Johnson's veto of the Civil Rights Bill, together with his February 22 speech, had "turned not only the Republican party but the general public sentiment of the northern states against him"; yet he had wanted the Administration forces to make an open attack upon the proposed Fourteenth Amendment.[62] In his reminiscences written more than two decades after the struggle between Johnson and

[55] Ibid.; H. A. Tenney and David Atwood, *Memorial Record of the Fathers of Wisconsin* (Madison, 1880), pp. 134–35.
[56] Clark S. Matteson, *The History of Wisconsin* (Milwaukee, 1892), p. 303.
[57] *Diary of Gideon Welles*, 2:534, 608–609, 617–618, 628; 3:64, 83.
[58] Hugh McCulloch, *Men and Measures of Half a Century: Sketches and Comment* (New York, 1889), p. 518.
[59] Mobile *Times*, Oct. 24, 1865, reprinted in New York *Herald*, Nov. 2, 1865.
[60] *Diary of Gideon Welles*, 3:4.
[61] Ibid., 2:394.
[62] McCulloch, *Men and Measures*, p. 381; *Diary of Gideon Welles*, 2:531, 534.

Congress, when the Reconstruction amendments were the law of
the land, McCulloch characterized the Negroes as "an alien race"
and held that the Federal Government should abstain "from all interference with local affairs" on their behalf. Once outside "interference" was discontinued and "colored people understand that the
government, by their emancipation, had done for them all it can do,
and that hereafter their welfare and elevation must depend upon
their own efforts, the great problem of what is to be the political
future of these states must be worked out by the joint action of the
two races."[63]

Lewis D. Campbell, perhaps Johnson's most active personal political emissary in the West, was a man who had only scorn for the
prewar Oberlin antislavery movement and its underground railroad
activities.[64] An ardent opponent of Negro suffrage in Ohio as well as
in the South, he held that in crushing secession, slavery had been
only an *incidental* casualty and that there was no basis for the idea
being promulgated by "wild one-idea fanatics" that the mission of
the Union party was "to advance the interests of the *black* man and
disregard those of the *white* man."[65] Campbell's perception was so
limited that when Sumner, during a private interview with the President at which Campbell was present, expressed concern for the
freedmen, the Ohioan saw in Sumner's attitude only the shedding of
"crocodile tears."[66]

The support given to the President by Seward and by Raymond is
of special interest. Neither man was a party to that prejudice of race
so common among adherents of Johnson's cause. Raymond broke
with the pro-Johnson movement during the campaign of 1866; Seward
remained loyal to the President until the bitter end. A definitive historical understanding and evaluation of Seward, if ever one can be
reached, must wait upon a comprehensive modern study of the man.
His prewar national repute was based upon his public identification
with the opposition to slavery as a moral wrong; he had rallied devotion to himself and to the Republican party by his appeal to "the
higher law" and the "irrepressible conflict." Whatever part the pull

63 McCulloch, *Men and Measures,* pp. 515–518.
64 Campbell to Johnson, Aug. 21, 1865, Johnson MSS.
65 Campbell to Johnson, Jan. 22, 1866, ibid.
66 Campbell to Johnson, May 1, 1866, ibid.

of oratory or of political ambition may have played in calling forth Seward's ringing phrases, there is no reason to think that they cloaked hypocrisy or an antislavery stand concerned only with the interest of white men. Seward's ardor may have weakened since the days when his words stirred the nation. There had been the cruel defeat of his presidential aspirations, due in considerable part to the very effectiveness of his phrases; there was the death of his wife, which severed a close personal tie between Seward and the moral intensity of antislavery sentiment.[67] The uncertainty of conjecture is compounded because in the postwar years, as we have noted,[68] Seward did not wish to reveal even in private his innermost convictions and intentions. Yet he retained more than compassion for the former slaves. He believed in their right to citizenship and equal status before the law—even equality of suffrage—though for the attainment of the latter, in his characteristically sanguine way, Seward would rely upon some vague development of the future rather than upon Federal authority.[69] It was Seward's adamant opposition that prevented an open attack upon the proposed Fourteenth Amendment, a position favored by the President, in issuing the call for the Philadelphia Convention to mobilize the pro-Johnson forces for the election battle of 1866.[70] After the Radical victory, the paper which Seward submitted as a basis for the President's message to Congress was conciliatory, leaving open

[67] The possible importance of the death of his wife was suggested to us by Professor Glyndon G. Van Deusen, who has a very special knowledge of the Seward MSS.
[68] See above, Chapter 2, footnote 28.
[69] *Diary of Gideon Welles*, 3:4.
[70] Ibid., 2:534–535, 608–610. In the Seward MSS are two documents, one of which suggests that between the overriding of the Civil Rights veto and the call for the Philadelphia Convention, Seward was trying to obtain a reasonable compromise on an amendment; the other indicates an unyielding position on the part of the President during the same period. The first is a copy of House Bill 543, for restoring the states lately in insurrection, submitted by Stevens for the Committee on Reconstruction April 30, 1866. In his own hand, Seward made changes and additions that would have softened the proposal but left intact the provisions for protecting civil rights. The second is a copy dated May 28, 1866, of the constitutional amendment suggested the previous January by the President that provided only for representation according to voters and direct taxation based on the value of property. On its reverse side is noted the following:
"No amendment to the Constitution, or laws passed by Congress, as conditions precedent to the admission by Congress of loyal Representatives.
Representation from the several States should be left where the Constitution now places it.
"No committals to any plan or proposition which may be made, while incomplete, and before thorough consideration by the President." Note particularly the first state-

an avenue for accommodation to congressional policy.[71] It was this draft message, its authorship unknown, which has been interpreted, erroneously, as evidence that Johnson in November, 1866, first decided not to oppose the Amendment further, then changed his mind, revived the quarrel with Congress and urged Southern states not to reconsider their refusal to ratify.[72] Not Johnson, but Seward, sought conciliation; and there is nothing to suggest a change of mind on the part of the Secretary of State.[73]

With these attitudes, why did Seward defer to Johnson? Why did he not like other moderates of similar sympathies break with the President? Why did he open himself to bitter repudiation by old friends and to political isolation, a fate which must at least have loomed as an ominous possibility by late spring of 1866?[74] Again, we cannot say with certainty; but a number of considerations come readily to mind. Seward believed that he had already made a major contribution to the cause of freedom by his part in the abolition of slavery and the treaty with Britain to suppress the slave traffic. With these great ends accomplished, and his always hopeful view of the future, perhaps he felt, as Weed had implied in explanation to an English friend's concern for the freedmen, that what "the Freedmen must suffer while the relationships arising between capital and labor are being adjusted" was a minor evil, to be borne with rather than publicly fought.[75] And the consequence of an open fight, the surrender of his post as Secretary of State without assurance of some

---

ment. It is in marked contrast to Seward's proposal on the April bill that when any state should ratify the amendment, its senators and representatives would be admitted (after taking the required oaths of office).

[71] Messages, Johnson MSS. See Cox, "Andrew Johnson and His Ghost Writers," p. 461.

[72] Beale, *The Critical Year,* pp. 400–402.

[73] Welles says that Seward's endorsement of the message in cabinet meeting was "formal not from the heart, but yet not against it." *Diary of Gideon Welles,* 2:628.

[74] Letters of criticism from old friends, some written in anger, more in sorrow, are preserved in the Seward MSS. See letters to Seward from J. Warren, Feb. 24, 1866, C. C. Royce, March 10, 1866, I. A. Gates, April 16, 1866, July 17, 1866, E. G. Cook, April 20, 1866, A. Conkling, May 4, 1866, L. M. Bond, May 24, 1866, R. Balcom, July 13, 1866, W. G. Bacon, July 16, 1866, D. C. Gamble, July 18, 1866, G. Hall, July 19, 1866, S. M. Hopkins, July 22, 1866, J. Henderson, July 27, 1866, C. L. Wood, July 29, 1866, and G. Dawson to F. W. Seward, July 14, 1866, July 18, 1866, Seward to Ryerson, April 30, 1866, Seward to Conkling, May 7, 1866, Seward to Balcom, July 14, 1866, Seward to Hopkins, July 25, 1866. The coldness of life-long friends broke Weed. Sarah Pellet to Seward, March 6, 1869, Seward MSS.

[75] A. F. Kinnaird to Weed, Dec. 30, 1865, Weed MSS.

other major position in national affairs, would have been a hard and selfless decision.

Since the days of battle for the Thirteenth Amendment, Seward had been committed to a reorganization of parties that would attract the support of Southerners and of Northern Democrats by a speedy and generous restoration of the secession states. He had undoubtedly been influential in directing Johnson toward that objective. Indeed, opinion in Congress in 1866 viewed him as the "head and front of the new party movement," though by the end of July he was thought to have given it up for "reconciliation between the President's particular friends and the body of the Union party."[76] And the President, while withholding full support for Seward's strategy as to both practical politics and basic policy, nevertheless deferred to him to an extent that would naturally have evoked Seward's loyalty and also his hope for a political victory that would renew his national influence and prestige. Then there was the Secretary's concern with the record and the achievement of his stewardship of foreign affairs. These were delicately balanced in 1865 and 1866, and he may well have felt that his departure from the Cabinet would lead to a dangerously adventuristic policy toward Mexico such as the Blairs had been urging. Or he may have been concerned lest any recognition

[76] Unidentified member of the House of Representatives, quoted in C. L. Wood to Seward, July 29, 1866, Seward MSS. For Seward's public position in May, see his Corning Hall, Auburn, speech, draft, and printed copy, ibid.

The failure of the Philadelphia Convention to organize a third party did not indicate that this goal was abandoned. One reason for postponement was the desire to win support from Republican ranks, which was essential to victory and also to the creation of a new party that would be more than a rejuvenation of the Democratic party under another label. Republicans were saying that no idea could be "more crazy than that of getting up a new Union party. There was nothing to be furnished from the Republican side but leaders, and the Democrats are not such d——d fools as to supply all the rank and file" without demanding leadership also. Unidentified member of the House of Representatives, quoted in C. L. Wood to Seward, July 29, 1866, ibid.

Raymond's curiously contradictory account of his interview with Johnson prior to the Philadelphia Convention is of interest in this connection. While Raymond opposed a third party and the President agreed that the convention should not attempt to organize one, Raymond yet reported his impression that the President was eager to gain a foothold in the South and to lay the foundation for a *"National"* party that would absorb the Democratic party of the North and West and all of the Union party except the Radicals. Raymond commented that this seemed to him a desirable object! "Extracts from the Journal of Henry J. Raymond (edited by his son), Fourth Paper: The Philadelphia Convention of 1866," *Scribner's ·Monthly* 20 (June 1880): 276–77; see also John A. Krout, "Henry J. Raymond on the Republican Caucuses of July, 1866," *American Historical Review* 33 (July 1928): 839.

on his part of basic disunity in the country weaken the nation's position abroad. In addition, Seward together with Stanton had become the symbol of Johnson's refusal to embrace the Democracy unconditionally.[77] To the Secretary, this role may have appeared not mere symbol but substance. What other man in the Cabinet could offset the full pressure of the Democracy? And if they were not kept at arm's length what might not be the consequences? The possible result was a matter of patronage and party power, but not that alone. There were extreme programs of action in the air, defiance of Congress with a denial of its legitimacy, recognition of a national legislature with Southern representatives seated by force if necessary. Contemporaries feared another civil war, more fratricidal than the first.[78] The possibility of such dire consequences may have stirred Seward's very real sense of devotion and responsibility to the nation.

Which considerations weighed with Seward, whether he viewed them as politician or statesman or something of both, we cannot know. But in his papers for 1868 there is an interesting passage, not revealing, but suggesting much. It appears in the draft of a response to an affectionate letter from a friend, a reply that was a far from modest affirmation of his historic role as "first secretary to the President." The passage reads: "The Government has been seriously endangered first by ambition on one side and the reckless passions on the other. I have been *felt* if not always *seen* in saving it from both. Only four months of trial remain, before the Government and the Constitution thus saved are in a constitutional way to be delivered into the keeping of a new administration when I shall be entitled to my discharge."[79]

Although Raymond voted to uphold Johnson's veto of the Civil Rights Bill, his entire course shows a consistent concern to protect the basic rights of the freedmen. In the summer and fall of 1865, the *New York Times* editorials made this objective abundantly clear and identified it with the President's policy. Raymond's paper even

[77] This fact is clearly evident from the correspondence in the Barlow MSS.
[78] Even so restrained a man as John Sherman wrote in early July, 1866: "I almost fear he [Johnson] contemplates civil war." J. Sherman to W. T. Sherman, July 8, 1866, *The Sherman Letters, Correspondence Between General and Senator Sherman from 1837–1891*, Rachel Sherman Thorndike, ed. (New York, 1894), p. 276.
[79] Italics added. Draft, Seward to Seymour, Oct. 14, 1868, Seward MSS.

found no difficulty in accepting the principle that color should not be a basis for exclusion from the voting franchise, although it did not favor the national government's forcing Negro suffrage upon the South.[80] It had hoped that the President might sign the Civil Rights Bill. The critical first section, with its "absolute equality of civil rights," was, according to the *Times,* "unquestionably just and right"; the objection was to the arbitrary enforcement provisions of the second section.[81] This position was very close to Senator Morgan's.[82]

Raymond was the Administration leader in the House, Chairman of the Union (Republican) National Executive Committee, and a close ally of Seward. These political commitments constituted a very formidable restraint upon his championship of equality for the freedmen. Yet in the House of Representatives, the *Times* editor voted "yea" on the roll call for the Fourteenth Amendment. The fact that no enabling legislation accompanied the passage of the Amendment, which would have made clear that its ratification was a condition for readmission of the rebellious states, helped Raymond reconcile his vote for the Amendment with his support of the President, who publicly opposed any prerequisite to the return of Southern representatives.[83] Raymond had considered the object of the Freedmen's Bureau Bill of "utmost importance" and explained that he had not supported the Civil Rights Bill because he, along with Bingham and others, thought that it was not warranted by the Constitution. He had introduced an alternate proposal to declare all persons born in the United States citizens, entitled to the privileges and immunities of citizenship. All the main principles of the Fourteenth Amendment he considered "eminently wise and proper."[84]

It was the desire to placate Raymond and to insure the support of the *Times* for the pro-Johnson movement which broke down the intent of Welles, Cowan, Doolittle, Browning, and McCulloch to in-

---

[80] See above, Chapter 4, footnote 49, and Chapter 8, footnotes 47 through 56.
[81] *New York Times,* March 26, 1866.
[82] See above, [original] footnotes 22 and 23.
[83] *New York Times,* July 30, 1866, June 15, 1866, and McKitrick *Andrew Johnson and Reconstruction,* p. 358.
[84] Raymond's letter to the committee requesting him to run again for Congress, Sept. 15, 1866, in Augustus Maverick, *Henry J. Raymond and the New York Press* (Hartford, 1870), pp. 175–184. See also Raymond's address of February, 1866, at Cooper Institute, in ibid., pp. 175–184.

clude an open attack upon the proposed Fourteenth Amendment in
their call for the Philadelphia Convention.[85] For that meeting, Raymond prepared an address which recognized the need for the enlargement of Federal powers in respect to the freedmen's rights,
and also the power of Congress and the states to make such amendments; but this part of his statement evoked sharp opposition and
was deleted.[86] The resolutions adopted by the convention stated that
it was the desire and purpose of the Southern states that all in-
habitants should receive "equal protection in every right of person
and property," but omitted any statement that might be interpreted
as acquiescence in Federal authority over civil rights unless by
amendment after the admission of the Southern states and with their
free consent.[87] This was the most that Raymond could achieve in his
effort to gain Southern agreement to the principle of "equal protection by law, and by equal access to courts of law, of all the citizens of
all the states, without distinction of race or color."[88] He himself was
ready to accept the provisions of the Fourteenth Amendment as
the platform of the party, and he felt that the President had "made
a great mistake in taking ground against those amendments."[89] Johnson's defeat in the fall elections of 1866 was interpreted by Raymond
as a popular decision in favor of the principles of the Amendment,
particularly "the absolute equality of civil rights to all the people of
the United States."[90]

Although Raymond's break with Johnson did not come over the
civil rights issue, his defection to the opposition was consonant with
his basic convictions in respect to equality of citizenship for the
Negro. Most other key Republican moderates who took their stand
against Johnson shared those convictions. Senator John Sherman

[85] *Diary of Gideon Welles,* 2:534, 618; 3:251.
[86] "Extracts from the Journal of Henry J. Raymond: The Philadelphia Convention,"
pp. 278–279; McKitrick, *Andrew Johnson and Reconstruction,* p. 411.
[87] Edward McPherson, *Handbook of Politics for 1868* (Washington, 1869), p. 241.
Raymond drafted the resolutions after hearing those proposed by William B. Reed
of Pennsylvania, Governor Sharkey of Mississippi, and Senator Cowan, all of which
he considered too prosouthern. "Extracts from the Journal of Henry J. Raymond: The
Philadelphia Convention," p. 278.
[88] Maverick, *Henry J. Raymond,* p. 189. See also Raymond's address to the convention in *The Proceedings of the National Union Convention Held at Philadelphia,
August 14, 1866* (pamphlet, n.p., n.d.), pp. 12–13.
[89] Raymond to R. Balcom, July 17, 1866, in Maverick, *Henry J. Raymond,* pp. 173–174.
[90] *New York Times,* Oct. 11, 1866, Nov. 12, 1866.

had long been troubled by the probability that freedmen would be oppressed if they had no share of political power. As for the Civil Rights Bill, he wrote, "I felt it so clearly right that I was prepared for the very general acquiescence in its provisions both North and South. To have refused the negroes the simplest rights granted to every other inhabitant, native or foreigner, would be outrageous."[91] The veto was a major factor in Sherman's repudiation of Johnson, whom he had hitherto defended. "The President's course on the Civil Rights Bill and constitutional amendment was so unwise that I could not for a moment allow anyone to suppose that I meant with him to join a coalition with the rebels and Copperheads."[92] Senators Lyman Trumbull of Illinois, James Grimes of Iowa, and William Fessenden of Maine were all men of moderation and principle, able to withstand terrific pressures, as their votes against Johnson's conviction on impeachment charges later made amply clear; their principles included a commitment to basic civil rights for the freedmen. All three wished to work with the President rather than against him, but, to use Welles's characterization of the latter two men, "their natural tendency would I knew incline them to the opposition. They are both intense on the negro."[93] The same might be said for other moderates, for Governor John Andrew of Massachusetts, for Henry Ward Beecher, for Samuel Bowles of the Springfield *Republican,* for John

[91] J. Sherman to W. T. Sherman, May 16, 1865, April 23, 1866, *The Sherman Letters,* pp. 251, 270; see also John Sherman, *Recollections of Forty Years in the House, Senate and Cabinet: an Autobiography,* 2 vols. (Chicago, 1895), 1:364, 366–367, 369.
[92] J. Sherman to W. T. Sherman, Oct. 26, 1866, *The Sherman Letters,* p. 278.
[93] *Diary of Gideon Welles,* 2:448. For Trumbull's repudiation of the President after the Civil Rights veto, see above, [original] footnote 24.

For Grimes, see William Salter, *The Life of James W. Grimes, Governor of Iowa, 1854–1858 and Senator of the United States, 1859–1869* (New York, 1876), pp. 75, 392; F. I. Herriott, "James W. Grimes versus the Southrons," *Annals of Iowa* 15 (July 1926): 325–327; Fred B. Lewellen, "Political Ideas of James W. Grimes," *Iowa Journal of History and Politics* 42 (1944): 383–395.

For Fessenden, see Francis Fessenden, *Life and Public Services of William Pitt Fessenden,* 2 vols. (Boston and New York, 1907), 1:283–287; 2:29–32, 34–35, 65–66, 314–315; and William A. Robinson, "William Pitt Fessenden," *Dictionary of American Biography,* 6:348–350.

For Trumbull, see Horace White, *The Life of Lyman Trumbull* (Boston, 1913), p. 277; also Arthur H. Robertson, *The Political Career of Lyman Trumbull* (M. A. Thesis, University of Chicago, 1910), pp. 37–39, 56, 59, 75. Robertson's study indicates that Trumbull's prewar view of the race problem included colonization and the conviction that Negroes could not be placed upon an equal social or political position with whites. However, by the winter of 1865–66, there can be no doubt of Trumbull's deep sense of national responsibility for the freedmen nor of his sincerity in fighting to secure for them equal rights, short of suffrage and officeholding.

Bingham of Ohio, for Henry Dawes of Massachusetts, for James Hawley of Connecticut, and for General O. O. Howard of the Freedmen's Bureau.

The case of the two influential Midwestern governors, Oliver P. Morton of Indiana and Jacob D. Cox of Ohio, is not so clear. Both were chief executives of a citizenry much given to discrimination against the Negro and closely divided between Republicans and Democrats. Although Cox had strong convictions in respect to the evil of slavery and took great satisfaction as a military officer in freeing refugee "contrabands," he disappointed antislavery men who had hoped that his early Oberlin training and his close relationship to Charles G. Finney would bring support for Negro suffrage. Such support Cox refused, and instead issued a public statement proposing separation of the races in the Southern states, with schools, homesteads, and full political privileges for the Negroes.[94] Later in advising Johnson to accept the Civil Rights Bill, Cox stressed political expediency; but he also assumed that the President as well as himself and "all true Union men" believed in the principle of equality before the law—that it was "right."[95] While still supporting Johnson, he accepted the Fourteenth Amendment, expressing privately his approval of all parts of the Amendment except the disqualifying clause of the third section.[96] In the campaign of 1867 to amend the Ohio Constitution, he argued for Negro suffrage since it had already been forced upon the South.[97]

Governor Morton was a political enemy of Radicals in Indiana; and his public opposition in September, 1865, to making Negro suffrage a condition for Southern restoration was widely publicized and enthusiastically received by pro-Johnson men. An examination of his speech discloses not an opposition to Negro suffrage as such

---

[94] George H. Porter, *Ohio Politics During the Civil War Period* (New York, 1911), pp. 210–213; Homer C. Hockett, "Jacob Dolson Cox," *Dictionary of American Biography*, 6:476–478; Jacob Dolson Cox, *Military Reminiscences of the Civil War*, 2 vols. (New York, 1900), 1:157–163; James Rees Ewing, *Public Services of Jacob Dolson Cox* (Ph.D. dissertation, Johns Hopkins University, 1902), pp. 8, 14–15; William C. Cochran, *General Jacob Dolson Cox: Early Life and Military Services* (pamphlet, Oberlin, Ohio, 1901), pp. 10–13.

[95] Cox to Johnson, March 22, 1866, Johnson MSS.

[96] Cox to Johnson, June 21, 1866, ibid.

[97] Ewing, *Public Services of Jacob Dolson Cox*, p. 15.

but the argument that Indiana was in no condition to urge voting privileges for Negroes in the South when the state itself discriminated so grossly against the "many very intelligent and well qualified" colored people within its own borders. Morton pointed out the restriction not only upon their political power but also upon their testimony in court, their access to public schools, and, if they had come into the state since 1850, their legal right to make valid contracts. He spoke highly of the fighting record of the Indiana colored regiment and pointed to the ironic fact that half the men who composed it could not legally come back into the state. The tone of the address was not one of defending discrimination but one of gently criticizing his fellow Hoosiers. As for Southern freedmen, Morton believed that they should have time to acquire property and obtain a little education, and then "at the end of 10, 15, or 20 years, let them come into the enjoyment of their political rights."[98] The governor was clearly in advance of state sentiment in advocating for Negroes the benefit of schooling and the right to testify in court. His sponsorship of the repeal of the state statute which excluded their testimony finally resulted in the elimination of that discrimination.[99] It was Morton who warned Johnson that a veto of the Civil Rights Bill would separate the President and the Union-Republican party, that if he did not sign the measure the two men could not again meet in political friendship.[100] Morton's decision to oppose Johnson was no doubt essentially a political one, but his attitude toward the Negro was not identical with that of the President.[101]

Behind conciliatory Republican leaders whose personal attitudes might in other circumstances have enabled them to accept a solution which would leave the future status of the freedmen in the hands of Southern whites, there was the pressure of mass Republican opinion. The overwhelming preponderance of Republican sentiment was behind a national guarantee for basic civil equality, short of suffrage,

[98] Printed in William Dudley Foulke, *Life of Oliver P. Morton*, 2 vols. (Indianapolis, 1899), 1:449.
[99] Ibid., pp. 434, 455; James, *Framing of the Fourteenth Amendment*, pp. 29, 200. See also Governor Morton's message of November, 1865, in W. H. Schlater (of the President's staff) to Johnson, Nov. 12, 1865, Johnson MSS.
[100] Foulke, *Life of Oliver P. Morton*, 1:466–467; McKitrick, *Andrew Johnson and Reconstruction*, pp. 309–310.
[101] Compare Beale, *The Critical Year*, pp. 106–107, 121–122, 178, 180, 184–186.

for the freedmen. This sentiment is unmistakable in newspaper editorials and private correspondence;[102] it was also reflected in the congressional vote on what was to become the Fourteenth Amendment. In the Senate, Republicans divided thirty-three to four in its favor. The "nays" were those of Senators Cowan, Doolittle, Norton of Minnesota and Van Winkle of West Virginia. Senator Dixon was absent and not voting. In the House, 138 Republican votes were cast for the Amendment; not a single Republican voted against it.[103] This vote was taken *before* Johnson made clear his political intentions by issuance of the call for the Philadelphia Convention.

After the Civil Rights veto, Republican opinion had crystallized in a determination to set further conditions before accepting Southern representatives back into the counsels of the nation, but not just any conditions.[104] The matters dealt with in sections two and three of the Fourteenth Amendment, namely the basis of future Southern representation, the granting of suffrage to the Negro, and the degree of proscription of Confederate leaders were negotiable; the question of equality before the law, federally enforceable, was no longer open to compromise. The issue of civil rights and national protection for the freedmen was not, as has sometimes been implied, the product of campaign propaganda and exaggeration, nor even of the shocking impact of the Memphis and New Orleans riots. The civil rights issue predated those developments.

Although in deference to Seward and Raymond the pro-Johnson leaders had attempted to evade discussion of the Fourteenth Amendment, it was generally recognized as being at stake in the ensuing campaign. After Radical victories in the states that voted in September and early October, pressure was put upon the President to accept the Amendment. As early as September 19, Bennett in the *Herald* foresaw defeat unless the President would "take up" the proposed Fourteenth Amendment and "push it through all the still excluded Southern States as rapidly as possible" with the kind of pressure he had used in behalf of the Thirteenth Amendment. Bennett at last deplored the condition he had done so much to provoke, "the widening of his [Johnson's] conflict with the radicals to a conflict

---

[102] See above, footnotes . . . 1–3.
[103] McPherson, *Handbook of Politics for 1868*, p. 102.
[104] Compare McKitrick, *Andrew Johnson and Reconstruction*, p. 443.

with Congress." He now viewed the Amendment as "not a radical measure, but a measure of the republican conservatives of Congress."[105] When Samuel S. Cox asked the President about the rumors that he would modify his opposition to the Amendment in keeping with "the poplar [sic] current," Johnson "got as ugly as the Devil. He was regularly mad. . . . There's no budge in him. Browning's letter is his view."[106]

S. L. M. Barlow's attitude toward the Amendment's role in campaign strategy is pertinent. He was much opposed to the President's yielding unless the Johnson forces should suffer defeat in New York. In that event, he thought the President might be "compelled to yield on the Constitutional amendment, but to yield to the pressure now, before our election, would destroy him & be in gross bad faith . . . as we are making a good fight & cannot now change our course."[107] If faced with defeat in November, however, Barlow thought Johnson could say to the South, "While I have not thought the ratification of the amendment necessary . . . the Northern people have decided otherwise—You must be represented. . . . Ratify the amendment therefore." Barlow explained that Johnson could "be supported in this, if necessary, *after* November, not only here but by the ablest presses of the South in New Orleans, Mobile, Charleston & Richmond —To change *now* would deprive him, practically of every paper and every voter—The Radicals would not be won back to him and he would lose the whole power of the democratic party."[108]

Browning's letter, to which Representative Cox referred, is additional proof of the importance of the Amendment as a campaign issue. It is also, and more importantly, added evidence that the opposition of the pro-Johnson forces to the Amendment was not merely limited to a distaste for section three, which denied Southern leaders state and national office. The heart of Browning's argument, approved by the President, was that section one, the civil rights guarantee, would restrict the states in functions properly their own. It would subject the "authority and control of the States over matters of purely domestic and local concern . . . to criticism, interpretation

[105] New York *Herald,* Sept. 19, 1866.
[106] Cox to Marble, Oct. 9, 1866, Marble MSS. See also Barlow to R. Taylor, Oct. 26, 1866, Barlow MSS.
[107] Barlow to R. Johnson, Oct. 24, 1866, Barlow MSS.
[108] Barlow to T. J. Barnett, Sept. 27, 1866, ibid.

and adjudication by the Federal tribunals, whose judgments and decrees will be supreme."[109]

Johnson's refusal, despite great pressure and much advice, to capitulate on the Fourteenth Amendment after his election defeat cannot be attributed alone to his stubborn nature. The explanation that he decided for conciliation, then reversed course on the basis of the Radicals' behavior, is exploded by the identification of the early conciliatory draft message as the work of Seward.[110] Another factor entered into policy considerations, the hope of ultimate victory and the tactical advantage to be gained by encouraging extreme action on the part of the opposition with a view to ultimate popular reaction against it. Doolittle wrote Browning on November 8: "The elections are over and we are beaten for the present. But our cause will live. If all the states not represented refuse to ratify the amendment . . . the extreme Rads will go . . . for reorganizing the southern states on negro suffrage. . . . That will present the issue squarely of forcing negro suffrage upon the South and upon that we can beat them at the next Presidential election."[111] A short time later, Weed was writing Seward that he had rebuffed Senator Morgan's suggestion of an organization in Congress against "extreme men." Weed explained, "I think that if the pressure should be withdrawn the Radicals would hang *themselves.*"[112] From Ohio the prediction reached the President that "If Congress resorts to rash and violent means to carry out the destructive purposes of the radicals, their own party will break to pieces."[113] From New York came more positive advice: "Are those proposed amendments to be adopted, changing the whole nature of our government. I trust not. I think a year or two of Radical-

---

[109] Browning to W. H. Benneson and H. V. Sullivan, Oct. 13, 1866, printed in *New York Times,* Oct. 24, 1866. See also the earlier public statement of Democratic and Conservative members of Congress to the effect that the "dignity and equality of the States" must be preserved, including "the exclusive right of each State to control its own domestic concerns"; published in the New York *Herald,* July 4, 1866.
[110] Professor Beale erroneously assumed that Seward's unidentified draft message had been prepared by Johnson and had reflected his views. *The Critical Year,* pp. 400–403.
[111] Doolittle to Browning, Nov. 8, 1866, Doolittle MSS; see also James, *Framing of the Fourteenth Amendment,* p. 178, and McKitrick, *Andrew Johnson and Reconstruction,* pp. 464–465, especially footnote 38.
[112] Weed to Seward, Nov. 24, 1866, Seward MSS. By the end of February, Weed was apprehensive of congressional reconstruction proposals and uncertain of the best presidential tactics; Weed to Seward, Feb. 21, 1867, ibid.
[113] P. W. Bartley to Johnson, Nov. 9, 1866, Johnson MSS.

ism more, will satisfy the country that the principles contained in that old instrument are too dear to us to be frittered away. . . . I believe that with you standing firmly on the ground you have assumed and each state organizing her conservative men on the Philadelphia platform, two years more will have seen the end of the Radical race."[114] Analysts of the 1866 election returns pointed out to the President that if the potential vote of the unrepresented South were added to the Conservative vote in the North, a large majority of the nation supported the President and opposed the Amendment, and that ultimately the President must triumph.[115]

Raymond's editorials in the *Times* had urged the President to accept the decision of the people in favor of the Amendment, and either to recommend its ratification by the Southern states or to stand aside while they made a settlement with Congress upon the basis of its principles. By the end of December, however, Raymond had come to the conclusion that Johnson's opposition to the Amendment was unyielding. The President, he explained, intended to hold to his earlier position in the conviction that his policy would ultimately prevail. Johnson believed that the Supreme Court would set aside any conditions Congress might impose upon the South or, failing such a resolution of the conflict, that the use of military power to enforce congressional policy would become so "expensive, odious and intolerable" that the voters would expel from power the party responsible for such a policy.[116]

The losses which the Radicals sustained in the state elections of 1867 seemed to justify the President's hope of victory and the strategy of no compromise. News of the defeat of the Radicals in Connecticut's April election of that year was received by Johnson as "the turn of the current" and by Welles as "the first loud knock, which admonishes the Radicals of their inevitable doom."[117] Welles believed that the returns from Pennsylvania and Ohio in October "indicates the total overthrow of the Radicals and the downfall of that party."[118] In November, 1867, Johnson celebrated the election results by a victory speech before a group of serenaders in which he held that

[114] S. Smith to Johnson, Nov. 10, 1866, ibid.
[115] T. S. Seybolt to Johnson, Nov. 8, 1866, F. A. Aiken to Johnson, Nov. 26, 1866, ibid.
[116] *New York Times,* Oct. 31, 1866, Nov. 3, 9, 12, 17, 19, 1866, Dec. 4, 27, 31, 1866.
[117] *Diary of Gideon Welles,* 3:78.
[118] Ibid., p. 232.

"the people have spoken in a manner not to be misunderstood."[119] The President's "stubbornness" of the previous November seemed to have prepared the way for success in the presidential election of 1868. The hope proved an illusion; but the hope was present, and died hard.[120]

In refusing to accept the equal rights provisions of the Civil Rights Act or of the Fourteenth Amendment, Johnson won lasting gratitude from white Southerners to whom the concept of equality between the races was anathema,[121] and this despite the ordeal of military government and immediate universal Negro suffrage which they in all likelihood would have been spared had Johnson's course been different. But with this decision, the President lost the confidence and respect of moderate Republicans. Lyman Trumbull and John Sherman both felt a sense of betrayal in Johnson's veto of the Civil Rights Bill. "Besides," confided Sherman to his brother, "he [Johnson] is insincere; he has deceived and misled his best friends."[122] The confidence in Johnson's assurances of justice for the freed people, which characterized Republican opinion, except that of extreme Radicals, in December, 1865, turned to distrust. No longer were misgivings directed toward Presidential policy alone; they came to embrace the President's intention and integrity, and corroded his public influence. "The truth is," Senator Fessenden wrote to Senator Morgan in mid-1867, "Mr. Johnson has continued to excite so much distrust that the public mind is easily played upon by those who are seeking only the accomplishment of their own purposes."[123] By standing adamant against a federally enforceable pledge of minimum civil

---

[119] *New York Times,* Nov. 14, 1867; McKitrick, *Andrew Johnson and Reconstruction,* p. 498.

[120] See above, Chapter 5, pp. 95–106.

[121] Of the 65 votes which Johnson obtained on the first ballot for the presidential nomination of the Democratic party in 1868, all but four were from southern delegates. Charles H. Coleman, *The Election of 1868: The Democratic Effort to Regain Control* (New York, 1933), pp. 164, 208.

[122] J. Sherman to W. T. Sherman, July 8, 1866, *The Sherman Letters,* p. 276. For Trumbull's reaction see *Cong. Globe,* 39th Cong., 1st sess., p. 1761 (April 4, 1866); and C. H. Ray to M. Blair, April 10, 1866, enclosure in Blair to Johnson, April 15, 1866, Johnson MSS. A digest and explanation of the bill, unsigned, but in Trumbull's handwriting, is in the Johnson MSS; see Cox, "Andrew Johnson and His Ghost Writers," p. 473.

[123] Fessenden to Morgan, June 26, 1867, Morgan MSS. The distrust, of course, involved party as well as principle. By mid-1866, it was widely believed that Johnson intended to bring the Democracy back into national power and ascendancy, and that he had deliberately sought to wreck the party that had elected him.

equality for the Negro as a prerequisite to restoration of the secession states, Johnson precipitated a great issue of moral principle central to the battle over Reconstruction; and he brought upon himself an unparalleled humiliation.

Kenneth M. Stampp
RADICAL RECONSTRUCTION

Kenneth M. Stampp is well known for his writings on slavery, the coming of the Civil War, and the Reconstruction years. His The Era of Reconstruction *was written to give wider currency to recent works of scholarship, particularly those that have questioned the "legend of Reconstruction" which portrays Reconstruction as a vicious and politically corrupt program that gave rise to Southern bitterness and set back progress for the black man by at least a century. In the following selection, Professor Stampp examines the radical program as it applied to the condition of the black freedmen.*

. . . Since the Negroes were crucial figures in radical reconstruction, it is essential to understand their condition at the time they gained their freedom. Most of them had by then lost all but a tiny fragment of their African culture. Though in slavery they had been denied full participation in the white man's culture, their ambition was to become an integral part of American society. They knew how to make a living as freemen, because they had experience as farmers, as skilled craftsmen, as domestic servants, or as unskilled urban laborers. What they still needed were economic opportunities, training in the management of their own affairs, and incentives for diligent toil.

Because the ante-bellum slave codes had prohibited teaching slaves to read or write, only a small minority of Negroes were literate. In this respect, as in most others, slavery had been a poor training school for the responsibilities of citizenship. It gave Negroes few opportunities to develop initiative or to think independently; it discouraged self-reliance; it put a premium on docility and subservience;

it indoctrinated Negroes with a sense of their own inferiority; and it instilled in many of them a fear of white men that they would only slowly overcome. A writer in *Harper's Weekly* reminded friends of the Negroes that the freedmen were but "the slaves of yesterday . . . with all the shiftless habits of slavery [to be] unlearned. . . . They come broken in spirit, and with the long, long habit of servility."

Yet there is little evidence that slavery had developed in many of its victims a fondness for bondage. Masters liked to think that their slaves were contented with their lot—and no doubt some of them found it not too painful to adapt to their condition. But the behavior of the slaves during the Civil War removed any doubt about whether the majority of them understood the meaning of freedom and were eager to enjoy its benefits. For as the federal armies advanced, the slaves fled from the plantations by the thousands, and the southern labor system collapsed. A Georgia planter spoke for many others when he complained bitterly about what he regarded as the "ingratitude evinced in the African character." "This war," he wrote, "has taught us the perfect impossibility of placing the least confidence in any Negro. In too numerous instances those we esteemed the most have been the first to desert us. . . . House servants . . . are often the first to have their minds polluted with evil thoughts."

In short, most Negroes, to the dismay of their former masters, joyfully accepted their freedom; and for a time many of them took special pleasure in making use of one of its chief prerogatives: the right to move from place to place without the consent of any white man. An agent of the Freedmen's Bureau gave several reasons for the restlessness of the Negroes immediately after emancipation: they wanted to see new things; they looked for relatives from whom they had been separated in slavery days; they went to the cities in search of work or to find schools for their children. "The shackles suddenly falling off," explained Carl Schurz, "it is by no means wonderful that their first impulse should be to have a holiday. Some felt inclined to use their freedom first in walking a little away from their plantations." Indeed, it was going to take a while for the Negroes to learn how to live as free men. As the *Nation* observed, "No great social revolution ever took place without causing great temporary loss and inconvenience." There was, after all, only one way that the Negroes could learn to live as free men, and that was for them to *start* living as free men—to make mistakes and profit from them.

This was precisely what the radicals proposed that the Negroes should do. The radicals, to reconstruct the South on a firm foundation, would throw out the Black Codes, which were hardly designed to prepare the Negroes for freedom anyway, give the Negroes civil rights and the ballot, and get white men accustomed to treating Negroes as equals, at least politically and legally. Aid to the freedmen was thus at the very heart of radical reconstruction; it was this aspect of the program, and little else, that justified designating as radicals the Republican leaders in Congress. Their attempt to give full citizenship to southern Negroes—in effect, to revolutionize the relations of the two races—was the great "leap in the dark" of the reconstruction era.

Some of the radicals believed that it would be essential to give the Negroes not only civil and political rights but some initial economic assistance as well. These four million people had emerged from bondage in complete destitution, without land, without shelter, without a legal claim even to the clothes on their backs. Neither Lincoln's Emancipation Proclamation nor the Thirteenth Amendment had required masters to make any settlement with their former slaves for past services, or provided for economic aid from the public treasury. In the words of Frederick Douglass, the freedmen "were sent away empty handed, without money, without friends, and without a foot of land to stand upon. Old and young, sick and well, they were turned loose to the open sky, naked to their enemies."

This condition of economic helplessness, some radicals thought, was what threatened to make Negro freedom purely nominal; it was this that enabled the white landholders, with the aid of the Black Codes, to reestablish bondage in another form. The congressional Committee on Reconstruction heard a great deal of convincing testimony about the use of southern vagrancy laws and various extralegal coercive devices to force Negroes back into agricultural labor under strict discipline. This testimony suggested that there was a close relationship between the securing of civil and political rights on the one hand and the establishment of economic independence on the other.

Near the end of the war, Edwin M. Stanton, Lincoln's Secretary of War, and General Sherman had a conference with twenty Negro leaders in Savannah. During the conference the question arose of how the freedmen could best be prepared to stand on their own feet.

The reply of the Negroes was: "The way we can best take care of ourselves is to have land, and . . . till it by our own labor." They were doubtless right, for in the agricultural society of the South white landholders had become so accustomed to exploiting Negro labor that nothing less than a sweeping program of land reform could have changed things very much. Land reform might have been accomplished by assisting the Negroes to take advantage of the Homestead Act as it was applied to the public lands of the South after the war; or by federal land purchases and resale to Negroes on long-term credits; or by the seizure of land from the former slaveholders.

Though all of these methods were considered, most of the drive for land reform centered on the third alternative, that is, confiscation. Those who favored confiscation justified it, first, as a penalty for treason and, second, as fair compensation to the Negroes for their many years of unrequited toil. This matter of land redistribution, whether achieved through confiscation or in some other way, was one of the most momentous questions the Republicans had to decide. They made their decision before the end of 1867, and it proved to be a crucial one in the development of their program.

The advocates of confiscation hoped to make use of the congressional act of 1862 which had subjected the property of those supporting the rebellion to seizure. But Lincoln, it should be remembered, had forced Congress to limit the time of the forfeitures to the lives of the guilty parties and to permit the return of confiscated lands to their heirs; moreover, he had made no serious attempt to enforce the act. In June 1866 the Johnson administration, holding that the act had been strictly a war measure, ended confiscations. However, the radicals who favored land reform refused to accept this ruling. Indeed, ever since 1862 they had been trying to strengthen the measure, especially to adopt an amendment preventing heirs from recovering forfeited lands.

In 1864, the American Freedmen's Inquiry Commission,[1] appointed by Secretary of War Stanton to visit the South, examine the condition of the Negroes, and make policy recommendations, concluded that without land reform a system of serfdom would develop. In the words of one of its members, "No such thing as a free, democratic society

---

[1] The commission consisted of three members: Robert Dale Owen, Samuel G. Howe, and James McKaye.

FIGURE 2. An 1868 cartoon by Currier and Ives: "Reconstruction or 'A White Man's Government.'" (*Historical Pictures Service, Chicago*)

can exist in any country where all lands are owned by one class of
men and cultivated by another." The commission recommended that
the Negroes be made "owners in fee of the farms or gardens they
occupy."

Early in 1865, General Sherman, faced with the problem of destitution among the masses of Negroes who had escaped from the
plantations, took the first step toward a wholesale redistribution of
land in one area of the Deep South. By his Special Field Order
Number 15, he set aside the South Carolina and Georgia sea islands
south of Charleston and the abandoned rice lands along the rivers
for a distance of thirty miles inland for the settlement of Negroes.
These lands were to be divided into farms of not more than forty
acres, and Negro families were to be given "possessory titles" to
them until Congress should decide upon their final disposition. General Rufus Saxton, a friend of the radicals with a genuine concern
for the welfare of the freedmen, was appointed Inspector of Settle-
ments and Plantations and placed in charge of the program. Saxton
colonized some 40,000 Negroes on the lands under his control, and
he presented evidence to the congressional Committee on Reconstruction that the program was a success. But President Johnson
saw to it that most of these lands were returned to their original
owners, and in January 1866 he removed Saxton.

A smaller but equally promising relocation experiment occurred in
Mississippi at a place called Davis Bend, about twenty-five miles
south of Vicksburg. Late in the war government officials seized a
large tract of land embracing six plantations, including those owned
by Jefferson Davis and his brother. Here, in 1864, about seventy-five
Negro farmers raised crops which enabled them to make profits
ranging as high as $1,000 after repaying credits advanced by the
government. The next year, most of this land was divided among
some 1,800 Negroes of all ages who organized themselves into
companies and partnerships of various kinds. After raising and
marketing their crops and paying all expenses, they finished the year
with a cash balance on hand of $159,200. Vernon L. Wharton believes
that this experiment suggests one of the tragic "might-have-beens"
of American history. "A wiser and more benevolent government,"
he writes, "might well have seen in Davis Bend the suggestion of a

long-time program for making the Negro a self-reliant, prosperous, and enterprising element of the population. . . . [Such a program] would certainly have greatly altered the future of the South, and it might have made her a much happier and more prosperous section."[2] Instead, President Johnson pardoned the owners of the Davis Bend plantations, and the land was returned to them.

The debate over land redistribution was resumed when Congress met in December 1865 and continued until early 1867 when that body finally passed a series of reconstruction measures. Sumner insisted that confiscation was a logical part of emancipation; the plantations, he said, "so many nurseries of the Rebellion, must be broken up and the freedmen must have the pieces." Stevens, the strongest advocate of confiscation, reminded his colleagues that "when that wise man the Emperor of Russia set free twenty-two million serfs, he compelled their masters to give them homesteads upon the very soil which they had tilled; . . . 'for,' said he, in noble words, 'they have earned this, they have worked upon the land for ages, and they are entitled to it.' " Stevens wondered whether America would do less for its emancipated slaves. "The whole fabric of southern society *must* be changed," he said, "and never can it be done if this opportunity is lost. How can republican institutions, free schools, free churches, free social inter-course exist in a mingled community of nabobs and serfs? . . . If the South is ever to be made a safe Republic let her lands be cultivated by the toil of the owners, or the free labor of intelligent citizens. This must be done even though it drive her nobility into exile."

In elaborating his confiscation plan, Stevens proposed to apply it to about 70,000 of the "chief rebels" who owned some 394 million acres of land. Thus confiscation would affect less than 5 percent of the South's white families. He would dispose of the land in this manner: give forty acres to every adult freedman and sell the rest to help pay the public debt, provide pensions for disabled veterans, and compensate loyal men for damage to property suffered during the war. To the objection that it would be inhuman to treat 70,000 southern landlords in this fashion, Stevens recalled Lincoln's pro-posal to remove the Negroes from the country. "Far easier and more

---

[2] Vernon Lane Wharton, *The Negro in Mississippi, 1865–1890* (Chapel Hill, 1947), pp. 38–41.

beneficial," he concluded, "to exile 70,000 proud, bloated, and defiant rebels than to expatriate 4,000,000 laborers, native to the soil and loyal to the government."

Another radical who favored confiscation was Representative George W. Julian of Indiana. Julian advocated confiscation because of a long and bitter opposition to monopolies of all kinds, including land monopolies. For the same reason he had opposed the granting of millions of acres of land from the public domain as subsidies to the railroads. In the South he hoped to create a society of independent landowning yeoman farmers, which brought him close to President Johnson as far as economic policy was concerned. The chief difference between them was that Julian desired to include Negroes in his program, for he denied their inferiority and demanded that they be given equal opportunities. To Julian the twin evils of the Old South had been slavery and the land monopoly of the planter class. Confiscation would destroy this monopoly, and the land could then be turned over to Negroes, poor whites, Union veterans, and immigrants. It must not be permitted to fall into the hands of northern capitalists, for Julian believed that this would simply create a new class of land monopolists whose dominion over the freedmen would be "more galling than slavery itself."

The congressional radicals won limited popular support for a program of confiscation. "Given two things," predicted the New York *Independent,* "the negro question solves itself—the easiest of all difficult problems: Land and the Ballot—land, that he may support his family; the ballot, that he may support the state. Grant these to the negro, and . . . he will trouble the nation no more." In defense of Stevens, *Harper's Weekly* declared that "every reflecting man" knew that without land the Negroes lacked "a vital element of substantial citizenship." However, judging from Stevens's mail, the most popular argument in favor of confiscation was that the proceeds from land sales could be used to reduce the public debt and thus to reduce taxes. Once convince the North "that all our taxes are to be removed," wrote A. G. Bemon, "and there will be but one solid vote for the [Republican] party."

But in the end, in spite of arguments such as these, the program of land reform was defeated. The moderate Republicans would not accept it, nor would some Congressmen who were normally counted as radicals. Not even the powers of Sumner and Stevens were great enough to force confiscation into the reconstruction acts of 1867. And this was a severe defeat for radicalism; or at least it defined some rather narrow boundaries within which the radicals could operate. It meant that their program would have only the most limited economic content; that the Negroes' civil and political rights would be in a precarious state for many years to come; and that radical influence in southern politics would probably collapse as soon as federal troops were removed. For the economic degradation of the Negroes strengthened the white man's belief in their innate inferiority, as well as the white man's conviction that for Negroes to possess substantial political power was unnatural, even absurd. The failure of land reform probably made inevitable the ultimate failure of the whole radical program—probably meant that, sooner or later, the southern white landholders and other propertied interests would regain control and reestablish the policies of the Johnson governments.

Why did confiscation—indeed, land reform of any kind—fail to pass Congress? In part it was due to the fact that many of the radicals did not understand the need to give Negro emancipation economic support. Most of them apparently believed that a series of constitutional amendments granting freedom, civil rights, and the ballot would be enough. They seemed to have little conception of what might be called the sociology of freedom, the ease with which mere laws can be flouted when they alone support an economically dependent class, especially a minority group against whom is directed an intense racial prejudice. Even William Lloyd Garrison, the most militant of the old abolitionist leaders, was ready to dissolve the American Anti-Slavery Society after the Thirteenth Amendment had been adopted. To Garrison legal emancipation and civil rights legislation were the primary goals, and the economic plight of the Negroes concerned him a good deal less.

Moreover, confiscation, or even the purchase of land for the Negroes, would have violated what most Republicans, radical or moderate, regarded as sound economic morality. Government paternalism of this sort would have a blighting influence on the initiative of those who received it. Since the Negro was free, his economic status must be determined by his own enterprise. "Now, we totally deny the assumption that the distribution of other people's land to the negroes

is necessary to complete the work of emancipation," declared the
Nation. Whether the ownership of land will prove a blessing or a
curse depends on how the holder has acquired it.

> *If he has inherited it from an honest father, as most of our farmers have,
> or has bought it with the proceeds of honest industry, it is pretty sure
> to prove a blessing. If he has got it by gambling, swindling, or plunder it
> will prove a curse. . . . A large fortune acquired by cheating, gambling, or
> robbery is almost sure . . . to kill the soul of him who makes it—to render
> all labor irksome to him, all gains slowly acquired seem not worth having,
> and patience and scrupulousness seem marks of imbecility.*

In addition, confiscation was an obvious attack on property rights
—so much so that it is really more surprising that some of these
middle-class radicals favored it, even when applied only to rebels,
than that most did not. "A division of rich men's lands amongst the
landless . . . would give a shock to our whole social and political
system from which it would hardly recover without the loss of liberty," warned the *Nation.* A proposal "in which provision is made for
the violation of a greater number of the principles of good government and for the opening of a deeper sink of corruption has never
been submitted to a legislative body."

Finally, many business friends of the Republicans saw the propertyless Negroes as a labor reservoir for northern industry, or for
southern industry or agriculture in which they might invest. Without
exception, Northerners who had purchased southern cotton lands
were opposed to confiscation. As a result, the land reformers were
outnumbered even in the ranks of the radicals. John Binny told
Stevens that the northern states "in monster public meetings would
lift their voice in thunder against it. . . . You would lose your majority
in Congress."

The Republicans did, however, make one less ambitious attempt
to give the freedman federal assistance. The disruption of the plantation system, caused by the war and the abolition of slavery, created
such widespread destitution among the Negroes that private benevolence was unable to cope with it. In March 1865 Congress created, as
an agency of the War Department, the Bureau of Refugees, Freedmen, and Abandoned Lands, commonly known as the Freedmen's
Bureau. It was to provide food, clothing, and medical care for both

white refugees and Negro freedmen; to settle them on abandoned or confiscated lands; and in general to help the freedmen in the period of transition from slavery to freedom—to get them back to work, to aid them in their dealings with the landholders, and to provide them with schools. But according to the original act, the bureau's work was to terminate within a year after the end of the war.

The congressional Committee on Reconstruction, however, collected much evidence indicating that the bureau needed not only to have its life extended but to be given additional power. The committee found that landholders were using the Black Codes to take advantage of the Negroes and were combining to keep down the wages of agricultural labor. Sometimes they bound Negroes to unfair labor contracts; sometimes they refused to pay them wages at all. The committee also found that Negroes were not always receiving fair trials in state and local courts, and that they were often maltreated by individual whites or by organized bands of "regulators." Therefore Congress, in February 1866, passed a new Freedmen's Bureau bill indefinitely extending the agency's life, increasing its power to supervise labor contracts, and authorizing it to establish special courts for Negroes when they were unable to get justice in the regular courts. In his veto message President Johnson argued that the bill was unnecessary and an unconstitutional violation of the rights of the states; but Congress eventually overrode the President's veto.

The bureau, though competently and conscientiously directed by General Oliver O. Howard, was highly unpopular with most white Southerners and has since been subjected to severe criticism. Its critics accused it of meddling in matters that were not properly within the jurisdiction of the federal government; of stirring up discontent among the Negroes and filling them with false hopes; of employing corrupt or incompetent administrators who wasted federal money; and of acting as a political agency for the Republican party. There was some truth in several of these charges. Some of the bureau agents did tell the Negroes that they were going to get land, not for the purpose of deceiving them but because the agents believed, or hoped, that Congress would actually give them land. Some of the agents were incompetent, some were corrupt, and some used the bureau's power to win Negro votes for the Republicans.

Such criticism, however, does not comprise a full appraisal of the bureau's work. Those who objected to it on the ground that the plight of the southern Negro was no concern of the federal government were, in effect, objecting to assistance of any kind; for Negro destitution was clearly a national problem which the individual southern states had neither the resources nor the desire to deal with. Actually, the most valid criticism that can be made of the Republican majority in Congress in this respect is that it failed to give the bureau sufficient power and funds to perform efficiently its manifold duties. As for the complaint that bureau agents stirred up discontent among the Negroes, the basis for it in most cases was that they encouraged Negroes to demand land, civil rights, and political enfranchisement. No doubt some agents did incite the freedmen in this fashion, and no doubt they distressed those who preferred to regulate race relations with some form of Black Code. White men who were accustomed to the humble, subservient Negro of slavery days were bound to find any change in his character unpleasant, any claim to equality almost intolerable. Insofar as the Freedmen's Bureau contributed to this result, it played a constructive role in the transformation of the Negro from slave to citizen.

There was, in fact, cause for criticizing numerous agents of the bureau for quite the opposite reason, that is, for showing no sympathy for, or interest in, the Negroes. Some agents allied themselves with the southern landowners and adopted their view that Negroes are by nature lazier and more shiftless than white men and need greater compulsion to make them work. Vernon L. Wharton's study of bureau activities in Mississippi shows that some agents cooperated with the planters to coerce Negroes, directly or indirectly, to remain on the land. One agent even whipped Negroes for their white employers when they were recalcitrant. In these and other cases, agents simply fell under the control of the white landholders among whom they lived and whose good opinion they sought to win. But in spite of cases such as these, the southern tradition holds that bureau agents were united in a determination to make life miserable for white men.

The tradition that the bureau was rife with corruption and incompetence is also an exaggeration. In 1866, President Johnson, seeking ammunition to use against the radicals, appointed a commission, consisting of General Joseph S. Fullerton and General James B. Steedman, to make a thorough investigation of the bureau's activities. The commission was as hostile to the bureau as Johnson himself. In North Carolina it uncovered a major scandal, but a scandal of little use to Johnson, for it involved the cheating and mistreating of Negroes, not whites. Elsewhere the commission turned up so little that would help the President that its tour of the southern states was cut short and finally abandoned. In the words of a recent scholar: "President Johnson . . . had gained from the Steedman-Fullerton investigation . . . little but laughter from the Radicals. . . . His best efforts to discredit the Freedman's Bureau had failed."[3]

A balanced evaluation of the Freedmen's Bureau, therefore, must stress its constructive achievements. First, while trying to make the Negroes self-supporting as soon as possible, the bureau provided emergency relief for those who were in desperate need. During its brief existence it issued more than fifteen million rations and gave medical care to a million people. Second, it spent more than $5 million for Negro schools, a pitifully inadequate sum but as much as Congress would grant. Usually the bureau furnished buildings and other physical facilities, while private benevolent societies provided teachers and books; together they established the first schools for Negroes in the southern states. Third, the bureau tried to prevent landowners from taking advantage of the Negroes. It set aside some of the provisions of the Black Codes, saw to it that Negroes were free to choose their employers, fixed the conditions of labor, and supervised the making and enforcement of labor contracts. Finally, the bureau tried to protect the Negroes' civil rights. Because of the legal discriminations of the Johnson governments, local administrators either established special freedmen's courts to handle their cases or sent observers into the regular courts to make sure that trials were conducted fairly. Though a system of special courts for Negroes was obviously undesirable as a permanent arrangement, there seemed at the time to be no other way in some localities to avoid flagrant injustice.

But in 1869, with its work scarcely begun, Congress provided for the termination of the bureau's activities, and soon after it ceased to

[3] George R. Bentley, *A History of the Freedmen's Bureau* (Philadelphia, 1955), p. 133.

exist. Even a Congress dominated by the radical-moderate coalition could support an experiment in social engineering for only a few short years, and it had to be justified on the grounds of an unprecedented emergency. Thus ended the one modest federal effort to deal directly with some of the social and economic problems confronting the postwar South.

The liquidation of the Freedmen's Bureau also meant that Congress had lost its most efficient agency to protect Negroes in the enjoyment of the civil and political rights they had recently been given. Congress had provided federal guarantees of civil rights to all persons, first by the Civil Rights Act passed over Johnson's veto in 1866, then by the Fourteenth Amendment ratified by the states in 1868. The Civil Rights Act clearly conferred citizenship on American Negroes: it declared that "all persons born in the United States and not subject to any foreign power, excluding Indians not taxed," are citizens of the United States. This act removed the doubts about the Negroes' status which had been raised before the war when the Supreme Court, in the *Dred Scott* case, held that Negroes were not citizens, and when the State Department sometimes refused to give Negroes passports. In addition, the Civil Rights Act provided that citizens "of every race and color" were to have equal rights in all states to make contracts, to sue, to testify in court, to purchase, hold, and dispose of real and personal property, and were to enjoy "full and equal benefit of all laws and proceedings for the security of person and property." Finally, all citizens were to be subjected "to like punishment, pains and penalties, and to none other." Violations of this law carried penalties of fine and imprisonment, and the Executive Department and federal courts were given ample powers to enforce it.

Fearing that the Supreme Court might rule against the constitutionality of the Civil Rights Act, the Joint Committee on Reconstruction, after much wrangling, incorporated its substance into the first section of the Fourteenth Amendment. This section, as revised in the Senate, was a compromise between radical and moderate Republicans—few were entirely satisfied with it, but all of them eventually gave it their support. First, it defined American citizenship: "All persons born or naturalized in the United States, and subject to the jurisdiction thereof, are citizens of the United States and of the State wherein they reside." Then, in terms that were both broad and vague, it prohibited the states from enacting laws "which shall abridge the privileges or immunities of citizens of the United States"; from depriving "any person of life, liberty, or property, without due process of law"; and (most important in recent years) from denying "to any person within its jurisdiction the equal protection of the laws."

For many years after reconstruction, as we know, the Fourteenth Amendment was almost a dead letter as far as the civil rights of Negroes were concerned; but the federal courts enforced it vigorously when any state tried to regulate railroads or other corporations. In law, corporations are "persons," and the courts repeatedly invalidated regulatory legislation as violations of the "due process" clause of this amendment. With this in mind, historians who stressed an economic interpretation of radical reconstruction insisted that the real, though secret, motive of the authors of the amendment was to protect corporations rather than Negroes. They based their case on the testimony of two members of the Joint Committee on Reconstruction who helped to frame the amendment. Representative John A. Bingham, who wrote the "due process" clause, claimed several years later that he had phrased it "word for word and syllable for syllable" to protect the rights of property. Still later, in 1882, Roscoe Conkling of New York, who was then representing a railroad corporation before the Supreme Court, declared:

> At the time the Fourteenth Amendment was ratified, individuals and joint stock companies were appealing for congressional and administrative protection against invidious and discriminating state and local taxes. . . . Those who devised the Fourteenth Amendment wrote in grave sincerity. They planted in the Constitution a monumental truth. . . . That truth is but the Golden Rule, so entrenched as to curb the many who would do to the few as they would not have the few do to them.

Of course, we cannot read the minds of those who framed the Fourteenth Amendment, but there is no contemporary evidence— nothing in the records of the Joint Committee or in the congressional debates—to indicate any thought at the time of giving protection to private corporations. Bingham's and Conkling's ex post facto arguments provide rather weak evidence; hence the case for an economic interpretation of Republican motivation must be regarded as unproved. There is, in fact, no reason to reject the explanation that Thad Stevens gave when the amendment was being discussed in Congress. Its purpose, he said, was "to correct the unjust legislation of the states [that is, the Black Codes], so . . . that the law which operates upon one man shall operate *equally* upon all. . . . Whatever law punishes a white man . . . shall punish the black man precisely in the same way and to the same degree. . . . Whatever law allows the white man to testify in court shall allow the man of color to do the same."

A far more significant question is how the framers of the Fourteenth Amendment defined civil rights and precisely which ones they intended to protect—a question that pro- and antisegregationists are still debating today. It is reasonably clear that they intended to prohibit the states from governing Negroes by special Black Codes, from making certain acts felonies for Negroes but not for whites, from providing more severe penalties for Negro felons than for white, and from excluding Negro testimony in cases involving whites. It is doubtful, however, that most of them regarded the exclusion of Negroes from jury service, or antimiscegenation laws, or the segregation of Negroes in public places as violations of civil rights. Few of the moderates would have thought so, and apparently not even all of the radicals did.

Actually, neither the radicals nor the Negroes of the reconstruction era considered social segregation to be the most urgent immediate issue. Though resenting it and occasionally speaking out against it, most Negro leaders acquiesced in segregation for the time being, in order to concentrate upon obtaining security of person, equality in the courts, and political rights. In the South the informal pattern of social segregation established for free Negroes in prewar years and enforced under the Johnson governments was challenged only sporadically. Nearly all of the schools subsidized by the Freedmen's Bureau were racially segregated. When Congress, in 1866, appropriated money for the schools of the District of Columbia, it again either approved of, or acquiesced in, a system of segregation. In fact, Senator Henry Wilson, a radical, admitted that a special system of Negro schools had been established and explained that the appropriation bill simply provided that "those in the colored schools will receive the same benefit that those receive who are in the white schools"—a fairly clear statement of the doctrine of "separate but equal." In short, most of the Congressmen who voted for the Fourteenth Amendment, and the states that ratified it, probably did not intend to outlaw state-enforced racial segregation. But the terms of the amendment, as we have seen, are broad and vague; and when the Supreme Court outgrew the sociology of the nineteenth century, it began to discover new meaning in the loose phrase "equal protection of the laws."

At least a few of the radicals, notably Senator Charles Sumner, believed from the start that they were proscribing segregation. Beginning with the reconstruction acts of 1867, Sumner tried, unsuccessfully, to require the southern states to establish "public schools open to all without distinction of race or color." For the next seven years, until his death in 1874, he urged his colleagues to subsidize biracial public schools, to desegregate the schools of the District of Columbia, and, above all, to adopt a Civil Rights Act that would outlaw all forms of racial segregation as violations of the Fourteenth Amendment. The debate on Sumner's numerous bills ran the gamut of arguments that have been heard ever since. The segregationists, North and South, denied that a separation of the races was a violation of civil rights, or that the Fourteenth Amendment was designed to interfere with matters that are purely social; and they warned that an attempt to integrate the public schools would simply destroy the system altogether. Sumner replied that segregated schools were "an ill disguised violation of the principle of equality," and that they injured the personalities of white children as well as Negro. "Pharisaism of race," he said, "becomes an element of character, when, like all other Pharisaisms it should be stamped out."

Sumner did not live to see a Civil Rights Act adopted, but the year after his death his long labors bore some fruit. In 1875, Congress passed an act whose preamble declared: "[It] is essential to just government [that] we recognize the equality of all men before the law, and . . . it is the duty of government in its dealings with the people to mete out equal and exact justice to all, of whatever nativity, race, color, or persuasion, religious or political." The act itself guaranteed to all persons, regardless of race or color, "the full and equal enjoyment of the accommodations . . . of inns, public conveyances on land or water, theatres, and other places of public amusement." It also prohibited the disqualification of citizens for jury service "on account of race, color, or previous condition of servitude." But there was not a word in the act about public schools—every effort to include them in its terms was defeated.

The Civil Rights Act of 1875 was significant nonetheless, because it was the first federal attempt to deal directly with social segregation and discrimination by the states or by private enterprises established to serve the public. "It is the completion of the promise of equal civil rights," said *Harper's Weekly*. "Honest legislation upon the subject will not at once remove all prejudice, but it will clear the way for its disappearance." In 1883, however, in a group of civil rights cases, the Supreme Court invalidated the act. It endorsed the position of the segregationists that the Fourteenth Amendment had not given Congress jurisdiction over the social relationships of the two races. There matters stood for the next seventy years.[4]

On the question of Negro suffrage, the Republicans eventually took a bolder and less ambiguous stand than they did on the question of segregation, but only after several years of hesitation and evasion. In the autumn of 1865 even Thad Stevens was noncommittal when he spoke to his constituents: "Whether those who have fought our battles should all be allowed to vote, or only those of a paler hue, I leave to be discussed in the future when Congress can take legitimate cognizance of it." But in most cases the radicals' early timidity resulted less from their own doubts than from their fear of public opinion in the North. Radicals were embarrassed by the fact that in most of the northern states the Negroes were then disenfranchised, and that in recent years the voters in several of them had rejected proposals to give Negroes the ballot.

As a result, few radicals made an explicit demand for Negro suffrage during the congressional elections of 1866, and the Fourteenth Amendment got at the matter only by indirection. The second section of the amendment simply provided that when a state denied adult male citizens the right to vote for reasons other than participation in rebellion or other crimes, such state was to have its representation in Congress reduced proportionately—a provision, incidentally, which in subsequent years was totally ignored. This

[4] The court did not invalidate that part of the act which prohibited the exclusion of Negroes from jury service.

weak and ineffective approach to Negro suffrage—the result of another compromise between radicals and moderates—caused Stevens privately to call the Fourteenth Amendment a "shilly-shally bungling thing," and Wendell Phillips to call it a "fatal and total surrender." "Of course, no man could afford to vote against the proposition," recalled George W. Julian, but it was "a wanton betrayal of justice and humanity. Congress, however, was unprepared for more thorough work. The conservative policy . . . was obliged, as usual, to feel its way cautiously, and wait on the logic of events; while the negro . . . was finally indebted for the franchise to the desperate madness of his enemies in rejecting the dishonorable proposition of his friends."

After their victory in the elections of 1866, the Republicans were, in the words of one of them, less "smitten by unnatural fear" and more inclined to recognize Negro suffrage as the "grand and all-comprehending" issue. Now they passed an act enfranchising the Negroes in the District of Columbia; and in their reconstruction measures of 1867, they required the southern states to write Negro suffrage into their constitutions. Finally, in 1869, after another relapse into timidity during the presidential election the previous year, the Republicans passed the Fifteenth Amendment, which unequivocally declared: "The right of the citizens of the United States to vote shall not be denied or abridged by the United States or by any State on account of race, color, or previous condition of servitude." The amendment was ratified by 1870; and thus, said the *Nation,* "the agitation against slavery has reached an appropriate and triumphant conclusion."

On reflection, however, the *Nation,* like many others, thought it would have been better to admit the Negroes to the franchise gradually, "and through an educational test." Some had suggested that Negro suffrage be postponed until 1876. Representative Julian presented the ablest defense of the almost immediate enfranchisement of the Negroes even though the great mass of them were illiterate. A literacy test, he argued, is "a singularly insufficient measure of fitness. Reading and writing are mechanical processes, and a man may be able to perform them without any worthiness of life or character. . . . If penmanship must be made the avenue to the ballot, I fear several honorable gentlemen on this floor will be disfranchised."

Julian observed that more than a half million illiterate white men were permitted to vote, and no one proposed to take the ballot away from them. He concluded: "By no means would I disparage education, and especially political training; but the ballot is itself a school-master. If you expect a man to use it well you must place it in his hands, and let him learn to cast it by trial. . . . If you wish to teach the ignorant man, black or white, how to vote, you must grant him the *right* to vote as the first step in his education."

When the Republicans turned from the Negroes to the white men of the South who had supported the rebellion, their reconstruction measures were remarkably lenient. The fourth section of the Four-teenth Amendment prohibited the southern states from paying any Confederate debt or any claim for emancipated slave property.[5] This amendment, in its third section, also withheld from the President the power to restore, by presidential pardon, political rights to Confederate leaders. As it was reported by the Joint Committee on Reconstruction, this section would have excluded those who had supported the Confederacy from voting in federal elections until July 4, 1870. "Here is the mildest of all punishments ever inflicted on traitors," said Stevens. "I would be glad to see it extended to 1876, and to include all State and municipal as well as national elections." Instead, the Senate softened it. In its final form it provided that persons who had held state or federal offices before the rebellion, and who had then supported the rebellion, were to be ineligible for public office until pardoned by a two-thirds vote of Congress. This disability applied to virtually the entire political leadership of the ante-bellum South; but for most of them it lasted only until 1872, when Congress passed a sweeping amnesty act. After that, all but a few of them were eligible once more to run for public office.

On March 2, 1867, the Republicans passed an act outlining their general plan of political reconstruction. Three subsequent acts, adopted on March 23 and July 19, 1867, and March 11, 1868, cleared up points left vague in the first act, provided machinery for the pro-gram's implementation, and established safeguards against presi-dential obstructionism. President Johnson, of course, vetoed these

---

[5] It also provided that the "validity of the public debt of the United States . . . shall not be questioned."

measures, but Congress passed them quickly and easily over his vetoes. Thus, two years after the end of the war, the process of reconstruction was begun anew. That Thad Stevens and the radicals now had their way may be attributed, first, to Johnson's recalcitrance to the very end; second, to the refusal of ten southern states to accept the terms of the Fourteenth Amendment; and, third, to the continued mistreatment of southern Negroes and Unionists.

These reconstruction acts were based on the assumption, as stated in the preamble of the first act, that "no legal State governments or adequate protection for life or property now exists in the rebel States." The purpose of the acts was to enforce "peace and good order . . . in said States until loyalty and republican State governments can be legally established." To this end, the Johnson governments were repudiated and the ten unreconstructed southern states divided into five military districts.[6] The district commanders were given broad powers to "protect all persons in their rights of person and property, to suppress insurrection, disorder, and violence, and to punish . . . all disturbers of the public peace." They could, when necessary, remove civil officeholders, make arrests, try civilians in military courts, and use federal troops to preserve order.

The district commanders were also given the responsibility of putting the new program of political reconstruction in motion. They were to enroll the qualified voters, including Negroes but excluding those barred from holding office by the Fourteenth Amendment, and to hold elections for delegates to state constitutional conventions. Each convention was to frame a new constitution providing for Negro suffrage; and when the constitution was ratified by popular vote, a governor and state legislature could be elected. The first legislature was to ratify the Fourteenth Amendment. Finally, after Congress had approved of the new state constitution and after the Fourteenth Amendment had become part of the federal Constitution, the state would be entitled to representation in Congress. Meanwhile, however, the civil government of the state was to be deemed "provisional only, and in all respects subject to the paramount authority of the United

---

[6] The first district consisted of Virginia; the second of the Carolinas; the third of Georgia, Alabama, and Florida; the fourth of Mississippi and Arkansas; the fifth of Louisiana and Texas.

States." When elections were held under such provisional government, those disqualified by the Fourteenth Amendment were not to be entitled to vote.

By 1868, six of the southern states had completed this reconstruction process and were readmitted. Four states—Virginia, Georgia, Mississippi, and Texas—delayed until after the Fourteenth Amendment had been ratified and the Fifteenth Amendment had been adopted by Congress. They were therefore required to ratify the Fifteenth Amendment as well. The Republican terms were then fully defined, and by 1870 political reconstruction had been completed in all of the southern states. . . .

II THE POLITICAL FABRIC OF SOUTHERN RECONSTRUCTION

Although a knowledge of the purposes and policies of the radical program in Congress is important, no one can fully understand the Reconstruction process without examining the political behavior of white and black men in the South who attempted to carry out the objectives of the congressional acts and constitutional amendments. To be sure, congressional radicals looked to the federal military commanders in the South to initiate the process of calling conventions and setting up new state governments. Likewise, the Freedmen's Bureau was expected to provide education, aid and protection to black freedmen as they moved into the new status of equal civil rights guaranteed to them by the radical program. More fundamental, however, for the long as well as the short run, was the effort by black and white groups in the South to organize the political coalitions that were needed to effectuate and sustain the political and social reconstruction of the South. Three groups were crucial in the interplay of political forces that were seeking to transform the South according to the objectives of the congressional radicals: carpet-baggers, scalawags, and black freedmen. The selections in this part of the book will help us to explore questions relating to the roles of these three groups in Southern Reconstruction: Who were the carpetbaggers and how shall we characterize their political behavior? Who were the scalawags and where should we locate them in the historical tendencies of Southern politics? How much political success were black freedmen able to achieve in officeholding and in the adoption of laws and programs that satisfied their needs as they perceived them?

Jack B. Scroggs
CARPETBAGGER CONSTITUTIONAL
REFORM IN THE SOUTH ATLANTIC STATES

Jack B. Scroggs has made a significant contribution to recent scholarship about the Reconstruction era by examining the political behavior of Southern Radicals and the complicated interplay between state Republican parties in the South and the congressional radicals. In the following article Professor Scroggs evaluates the role of carpetbagger political leaders in the constitutional reforms adopted by Reconstruction conventions in the South Atlantic states, 1867–1868.

The Reconstruction period brought to the South fundamental changes in state politics and in political theory, climaxing a strong ante-bellum movement in this direction. Among the many changes produced by the social-political revolution of the postwar era were lasting constitutional reforms of a progressive and democratic nature. Not least responsible for this development were the newly arrived Northerners —the carpetbaggers, who, along with the Southern scalawags, have long borne the major blame for all Reconstruction ills in the South. Accused by contemporaries of every conceivable crime, both political and civil, the term *carpetbagger* even among recent writers has carried with it the taint of ineptness, fraud, and corruption. This has tended to obscure the basic contributions made by the Northern immigrants who engaged in politics and to distort the role of the new Republican organizations in the South.

Only of local importance during the early stages of Reconstruction, these Northern "adventurers" achieved a commanding position in state politics with the advent of Radical control of the Reconstruction program early in 1867. The triumph of the Radicals in Congress brought about in the South a corresponding emergence of state Radicals, both white and Negro, and the Republican party developed as a formidable force in the new Southern political orientation. The strength of these new political organizations was clearly demon-

From Jack B. Scroggs, "Carpetbagger Constitutional Reform in the South Atlantic States, 1867–1868," *Journal of Southern History* 27 (November 1961): 475–493. Copyright 1961 by the Southern Historical Association. Reprinted by permission of the Managing Editor.

FIGURE 3. Thomas Nast cartoon—Vote for blacks, no vote for ex-Confederates. From *Harper's Weekly*, April 13, 1867, p. 240. (*Courtesy Boston Public Library, Periodical Department*)

strated in the results of the constitutional convention elections of 1867 in the five South Atlantic states—Virginia, North Carolina, South Carolina, Georgia, and Florida. The delegates to these conventions were largely representatives of the Negroes and lower-class whites, who, as it happens, composed the two segments of society most eager to secure constitutional reform. Although the carpetbaggers were never in a majority in these delegations, their influence on Southern politics reached its high point in the framing of the new constitutions.

The degree of carpetbagger leadership and influence in the constitutional conventions varied from state to state. In Virginia, North Carolina, and South Carolina, convention debates and proceedings were dominated by recently arrived Northerners.[1] The same was true

---

[1] Of the nineteen standing committees appointed to draw up the constitution of North Carolina, ten were headed by carpetbaggers, while in Virginia half of the standing committees were filled by Northerners. *Journal of the Constitutional*

of the Florida convention, but internal party schism brought ultimate defeat to the Radical Republican element there.[2] Georgia alone of the South Atlantic states was relatively free from carpetbagger influence in the formation of her new constitution.[3]

An appraisal of the motives of the carpetbagger leaders in the state conventions is difficult except in terms of the final products of their deliberations. Political and economic self-interest doubtless dictated the moves of many of the key Republican leaders, but in the drafting of new constitutions instances of attempts to limit the political freedom of any segment of the population were rare. Indeed, the primary aim of the carpetbagger group was the extension of political democracy, the assumption being that with complete political equality for all men Republican principles would prevail and the Southern Republican party would capture and retain control of the state governments. Demonstrating a lack of understanding of Southern society and politics, a great many of these leaders were struggling to impose constitutional changes on a reluctant South simply because they considered the changes long overdue.

Convention of the State of North-Carolina at its Session, 1868 (Raleigh, 1868), pp. 43–44; *Journal of the Constitutional Convention of the State of Virginia, Convened in the City of Richmond December 3, 1867* . . . (Richmond, 1867) pp. 28–29. See also *Proceedings of the Constitutional Convention of South Carolina, Held at Charleston, S. C., Beginning January 14th* . . . *1868* (Charleston, 1868), p. 37; and Raleigh *Daily Sentinel,* January 22–23, 1868.

[2] The regular Radical Republicans, under the leadership of Daniel Richards from Illinois, Liberty Billings from New Hampshire, William U. Saunders from Maryland and Jonathan C. Gibbs from Pennsylvania, reflected the opinion of the Republican National Committee, of which they were the agents in Florida. A more conservative group, led by Harrison Reed and Edward M. Randall, was closely tied with President Andrew Johnson. A third group, of less power and significance, was led by Thomas W. Osborn of Massachusetts. Ultimately, the more conservative Reed faction, in cooperation with Conservative leaders and the military, ousted the more numerous Radical group and seized complete control of the convention. L. D. Strickney to Elihu B. Washburne, May 21, 1868, and Daniel Richards to Washburne, February 2, 11, 12, 1868, in Elihu B. Washburne Papers (Division of Manuscripts, Library of Congress); William Watson Davis, *The Civil War and Reconstruction in Florida* (New York, 1913), pp. 470, 509–516; John Wallace, *Carpet Bag Rule in Florida; the Inside Workings of the Reconstruction of Civil Government in Florida After the Close of the Civil War* (Jacksonville, 1888), pp. 55, 64–68; "Report of the Secretary of War," *House Ex. Docs.,* 40th Cong., 3rd sess., vol. III, pt. 1 (Serial 1367), 77, 86–88.

[3] Clara Mildred Thompson, *Reconstruction in Georgia, Economic, Social, Political, 1865–1872* (New York, 1915), p. 193; Isaac Wheeler Avery, *The History of the State of Georgia from 1850 to 1881* . . . (New York, 1881), p. 377. Only two carpetbaggers received committee chairmanships in Georgia. *Journal of the Proceedings of the Constitutional Convention of the People of Georgia, Held in the City of Atlanta in the Months of December, 1867, and January, February and March, 1868* . . . (Augusta, 1868), pp. 40–41.

With control of three of the South Atlantic state conventions firmly lodged in the carpetbagger element, it was evident that fundamental changes would appear in the new constitutions of these states. Even in Florida and Georgia, where a certain amount of cooperation with native white Conservatives tended to alleviate the revolutionary nature of constitutional innovations, it was clear that a return to the *status quo ante-bellum* would not suffice. Unlike the conventions of 1865 which had primarily aimed at making only required amendments to old constitutions, the conventions of 1867–1868 were to embark on a program of basic constitutional reform.

Liberal constitutional provisions embodying the ideal of democratic equalitarianism which had developed during the past half century formed the framework of the new instruments of government. Many of these provisions were copied from constitutions of Northern states, and the carpetbaggers, as one would expect, were generally foremost in their advocacy. The states with the most able carpetbagger leadership emerged with the most democratic and progressive constitutions, and, as able Northern leadership decreased, the liberality of the documents tended to decrease proportionally. The Southern Republicans of course understood that democratizing of government would serve to strengthen the voting elements upon which they depended while at the same time weakening the former Democratic leaders who, standing to gain nothing from constitutional change, were on record as favoring no further change, and were declaring the whole process of Reconstruction an unconstitutional abridgement of the South's rights.[4]

When the constitutional conventions met in late 1867 and early 1868, they initially faced problems outside the realm of pure constitution-drafting. While the standing committees were preparing their reports, the convention sessions were taken up with the pressing matter of the people's destitute condition. The results of their deliberations were the passage of ordinances of relief, or stay laws, measures which the Radicals had freely promised in their campaign for

[4] See statement of Benjamin H. Hill in Americus, Ga., *Tri-Weekly Republican, July 13, 1867;* address of John Pool, of North Carolina, in Raleigh, N. C., *Tri-Weekly Standard*, April 9, 1868; Governor Charles J. Jenkins' letter to the people of Georgia in Americus *Tri-Weekly Republican,* April 16, 1867; Raleigh *Daily Sentinel,* October 16, 1867.

control of the conventions.[5] These ordinances intended to alleviate financial suffering were to remain in force only until adequate provisions could be inserted in the new constitutions.

The debate over a relief ordinance in the South Carolina convention disclosed a division in carpetbagger ranks in that state.[6] Carpetbaggers William J. Whipper and Niles G. Parker were the principal supporters of a temporary relief measure, basing their argument on the assumption that the legislation they favored would not only protect debtors but also those laborers who were dependent upon property owners for wages. In opposition, Negro carpetbaggers Richard H. Cain and Francis L. Cardozo maintained that by refraining from passing a relief act the convention would force the large plantation owners to sell their holdings and thereby permit the poor people of the state to purchase small farms. Whipper's answer to this was that "it would be perfect folly to entertain the opinion that in the present miserable destitution of the South the poor people will become the owners of the vast tracts of land if thrown into the market." He alleged that another consideration prompted the opponents of the ordinance when he joined native Negro R. C. De Large in asserting that a great part of the opposition was initiated by Northern and local investors who would be able to buy up the estates and become "large land monopolists." The dispute was resolved when General E. R. S. Canby issued a general relief order for the Carolinas, but the South Carolina convention carried relief further by declaring all contracts and liabilities for the purchase of slaves null and void.[7]

In North Carolina the question of relief initiated a vigorous debate over the constitutional status of the state itself, with the carpetbagger

[5] See circular in Americus *Tri-Weekly Republican,* September 21, 1867; Raleigh *Daily Standard,* March 6, 1868.
[6] South Carolina carpetbaggers were again split over the question of petitioning the national government for a million-dollar loan to purchase land for the freedmen. Despite carpetbagger C. P. Leslie's accusation that his fellow Radicals were acting solely from political considerations, knowing full well that Congress would not consider such a proposal, most of the carpetbaggers supported the petition, which was adopted by a large majority. *Proceedings of the Constitutional Convention of South Carolina, 1868,* pp. 196–197, 376–439.
[7] Ibid., pp. 104–125, 214–232. This provision was later declared unconstitutional as it impaired obligation of contracts. Francis Butler Simkins and Robert Hilliard Woody, *South Carolina During Reconstruction* (Chapel Hill, 1932), p. 100.

leaders displaying a considerable divergence of opinion. Albion W. Tourgée maintained the "old North Carolina was dead and buried in the tomb of the Confederacy." From a territorial status she must be brought back to statehood with adequate homestead provisions to protect the mass of people. Tourgée's constitutional position led naturally to his support of repudiation of the old state debt, but the convention refused to back him in this.[8]

In all of the South Atlantic states the conventions incorporated into the new constitutions permanent relief measures under the provisions protecting homesteads, which had the advantage of avoiding the odium attached to the term "stay laws." These liberal homestead provisions assured the citizen of retaining in his possession a minimum amount of property by exempting it from attachment for debts. Although an innovation in these states, homestead provisions provoked little opposition from any quarter, the only controversy developing over the amount of the exemption. The Radicals wished to make the exemption large enough to protect the small owners but not so large as to give protection to owners of large landholdings. North Carolina and South Carolina, following the leadership of the carpetbaggers, limited their homestead exemption to a moderate $1,500, while Florida provided for the exemption of $1,000 in personal property and one hundred and sixty acres in land, or one acre within the limits of an incorporated town.[9] Virginia gave a larger exemption, real and personal property to the value of $2,000;[10] and the Georgia convention under the sway of conservative business men and planters led by Joseph E. Brown and Rufus Bullock, gave the largest exemption, real and personal property to the value of $3,000. Other relief provisions were put into the new constitutions. In Georgia, for instance, a sweeping relief ordinance was included in the constitution over the protests of the Democrats who questioned its

---

[8] Raleigh *Daily Standard*, February 5, 1868; Raleigh *Daily Sentinel*, February 17–18, 1868; Wilmington, N. C., *Daily Journal*, February 18, 1868.

[9] Francis Newton Thorpe, ed., *The Federal and State Constitutions, Colonial Charters, and Other Organized Laws of the States, Territories, and Colonies Now or Heretofore Forming the United States of America*, 7 vols. (Washington, 1909), II, 717 (Fla., Art. X), 2818–19 (N. C., Art. X); *Proceedings of the Convention of South Carolina, 1868*, pp. 888–889.

[10] Thorpe, ed., *Federal and State Constitutions*, VII, 3896 (Va., Art. XI, Sec. 1).

constitutionality and charged that the forces of Brown and Bullock designed it as a snare to catch the ignorant debtor.[11]

In view of subsequent developments, of particular interest is the movement which developed in the conventions for specific provisions for the payment of the state debts and for limitation of state aid to companies and corporations. All of the conventions acknowledged responsibility for the old state debts, excepting war debts. Tourgée, the Ohio carpetbagger in North Carolina, opposed the payment of the state debt, arguing that since the war had left North Carolina in a territorial status, the old state debt had already ceased to exist, despite the demand of Northern speculators that it be paid. For his stand in favor of repudiation Tourgée was vigorously attacked by fellow Northerners in the convention, as well as by the Conservative press. With the entire carpetbagger element opposing him Tourgée lost his fight on the repudiation issue. He subsequently led in the movement for prompt payment of the state debt, and the convention passed an ordinance which provided for the payment of the interest due on state bonds and for the funding of the debt in new 6 percent state bonds.[12]

All five conventions set limitations upon the use of public credit. In South Carolina carpetbagger Niles G. Parker, chairman of the finance committee, presented a report which called for limiting the state debt to $500,000 and for prohibiting the legislature from extending the state credit to the aid of any private company. The North Carolina convention forbade the legislature to contract new debts except to supply a casual deficit or to suppress invasion or insurrection, unless the same bill included a tax to cover the deficit.

[11] Ibid., II, 836n–37n (Ga., Art. V, Sec. 17, Pt. 3, deleted by Congress), 838 (Ga., Art. VII, Sec. 1).
[12] Joseph C. Abbott, carpetbagger from New England, led the attack on Tourgée, declaring that his remarks were "infamous." Raleigh *Daily Sentinel*, January 23, February 15, 17–18, 1868; Raleigh *Daily Standard*, February 5, 1868; see also Wilmington *Daily Journal*, February 18, 1868. Subsequent investigations revealed that Tourgée was essentially right in his contention that bondholders were the driving force in the fight against repudiation. General Abbott, L. G. Estes, carpetbagger lobbyist Milton Littlefield, and G. Z. French, all carpetbagger opponents of Tourgée, were involved in heavy bond speculations with a New York group, and repudiation would have meant financial ruin to them. *Report of the Commission to Investigate Charges of Fraud and Corruption, Under Act of Assembly, Session 1871–1872* . . . (Raleigh, 1872), pp. 397–398, 522–524; *Journal of the Constitutional Convention of North Carolina, 1868*, pp. 308, 454–455.

Virginia went further in declaring the credit of the state would not "be granted to, or in aid of, any person, association, or corporation." Both the Georgia and Florida conventions provided that the state credit could be used in support only of internal improvements and in no other cases.[13]

The debates on the bills of rights in the conventions disclosed the determination of the carpetbaggers to incorporate in the new constitutions basic principles of equalitarianism despite the bitter opposition which greeted their attempts to eradicate the legal distinctions between the races. Only after a vicious parliamentary struggle did the carpetbaggers of North Carolina, in league with the Negro members, secure the adoption of a provision in the bill of rights stating that "all men are created equal." The South Carolina convention accepted an amendment offered by Negro carpetbagger B. F. Randolph which specifically forbade any distinction on account of race or color and provided that all citizens "enjoy all common, public, legal, and political privileges."[14] The Florida and Georgia constitutions contained no specific guarantee of equal civil and political rights.

All of the bills of rights reaffirmed the right to habeas corpus and provided that henceforth no one was to be imprisoned for debt except in cases of fraud; and in North Carolina Tourgée secured the adoption of a section stating that no man would be "compelled to pay costs or jail fees, or necessary witness fees of the defense, unless found guilty." The bills of rights in the Virginia, North Carolina, and South Carolina constitutions had sections designed to prevent in the future the imposition of property qualifications for voting or for holding office, and carpetbagger S. S. Ashley secured the adoption of a section guaranteeing all people in North Carolina the right to a public education. Finally, the bill of rights adopted in each of the

---

13 *Proceedings of the Constitutional Convention of South Carolina, 1868,* pp. 362–363; *Journal of the Constitutional Convention of North Carolina, 1868,* p. 304; Thorpe, ed., *Federal and State Constitutions,* II, 719 (Fla., Art. XIII, Secs. 7–8), 830 (Ga., Art. III, Sec. 5, No. 5, Sec. 6), V, 2814 (N. C., Art. V, Sec. 5), VII, 3895 (Va., Art. X, Sec. 12).
14 *Journal of the Constitutional Convention of North Carolina, 1868,* pp. 169–170; Raleigh *Daily Standard,* February 13, 1868; *Proceedings of the Constitutional Convention of South Carolina, 1868,* 353–56; Thorpe, ed., *Federal and State Constitutions,* VI, 3284 (S. C., Art. I, Sec. 39).

state conventions except in Georgia declared that all rights not delegated by the constitutions were reserved to the people.[15]

An important progressive measure sponsored by each convention was the establishment of a state controlled system of public education. It was generally conceded that improvements in public education were needed, but carpetbagger leaders were particularly active in fostering plans for raising the educational level of the South. Although there was no serious opposition in Virginia to a public school system, a bitter controversy developed over segregation of whites and blacks in a dual system. Extremists on both sides were silenced when the convention accepted a compromise offered by C. H. Porter from New York which evaded the issue by making no specific reference to either mixed or separate schools.[16] In North Carolina liberal provisions for public education were sponsored by Ashley, chairman of the committee on education. Tourgee gave him valuable aid, at one time unsuccessfully trying to amend the finance section so as to allocate to educational purposes all funds received from the poll tax. In North Carolina, as in Virginia, Conservatives attempted to insert provisions for the establishment of separate schools for the two races, but no stipulation was made in the section on segregation as adopted.[17] South Carolina carried the principle of equality even further by declaring that all public schools, colleges, and universities of the state would be open to all children and youths "without regard to race or color." Disagreement in South Carolina came over the issue of compulsory attendance in the public schools, with C. P. Leslie opposing the greater part of the carpetbagger leadership in their promotion of compulsory education. Leslie took the occasion to deliver a denunciation of the Massachusetts members of the con-

[15] Thorpe, ed., *Federal and State Constitutions,* II, 704–706 (Fla., Art. I, Secs. 1–2, 6, 16), 823 (Ga., Art. I, Secs. 13, 18), V, 2801–2803 (N. C., Art. I, Secs. 11, 16, 21–22, 27, 37), VI, 3283–85 (S. C., Art. I, Secs. 17, 20, 32, 41), VII, 3874–75 (Va., Art. I, Secs. 8, 10, 21); *Journal of the Constitutional Convention of North Carolina, 1868,* 214–15; Raleigh *Daily Sentinel,* January 22, February 17, 1868.

[16] Alrutheus A. Taylor, "The Negro in the Reconstruction of Virginia," *Journal of Negro History* 11 (April 1926): 481. Porter was a lawyer and later a member of Congress from Virginia. Lyon Gardiner Tyler, ed., *Encyclopedia of Virginia Biography, 5 vols.* (New York, 1915), III, 125.

[17] *Journal of the Constitutional Convention of North Carolina, 1868,* pp. 304–307, 342–343; Raleigh *Daily Sentinel,* March 5, 7, 1868; Thorpe, ed., *Federal and State Constitutions,* V, 2817–18 (N. C., Art. IX).

vention, but his fulminations failed to prevent the passage of the section requiring all children from six to sixteen to attend school for at
least twenty-four months.[18] Georgia and Florida followed the trend
and adopted provisions calling for the establishment of a system of
public schools and with no specific statement as to segregation of
the races.[19]

The conventions achieved other significant reforms. There was
a general revision of the state penal systems with a lowering of the
number of crimes punishable by death. Tourgée expressed the
attitude of the Northern immigrants on penal reform when he said,

> *Not only is punishment to satisfy justice but to reform the offender.
> That . . . is the key-note of civilization. Now as we are laying slavery and
> all its concomitants . . . a higher and nobler penal system should be
> devised.*

North Carolina, South Carolina, and Florida also made specific provisions for state penitentiaries.[20] The constitutions of Virginia, North
Carolina, and South Carolina included elaborate sections outlining
the form of a new county-township government, and in all of the
South Atlantic states except Florida provisions were made for the
popular election of county officers.[21] Local control of civil affairs

[18] Thorpe, ed., *Federal and State Constitutions*, VI, 3300 (S. C., Art. X). For the
debate on the issue see *Proceedings of the Constitutional Convention of South
Carolina, 1868*, pp. 685–709.
[19] *Journal of the Constitutional Convention of Georgia, 1868*, pp. 482–83; Thorpe,
ed., *Federal and State Constitutions*, II, 716 (Fla., Art. IX, Sec. 1), 838 (Ga., Art. VI).
Conservatives in Georgia attempted to preserve something of the stigma formerly
attached to "poor" schools in the South by adoption of a provision levying taxes for
"a general school fund for the indigent," but carpetbaggers secured the withdrawal
of the objectionable word "indigent." Augusta *Tri-Weekly Constitutionalist*, January
29, 1868.
[20] Raleigh *Daily Standard*, March 4, 1868; Thorpe, ed., *Federal and State Constitutions*, II, 718 (Fla., Art. XI, Sec. 2), V, 2820 (N. C., Art. XI). Despite their apparent
concern for penal reform, however, the new Radical state governments continued the
convict lease system which became notorious in the postwar South. Fletcher Melvin
Green, "Some Aspects of the Convict Lease System in the Southern States," in
Greene, ed., *Essays in Southern History . . .* (Chapel Hill, 1949), p. 116.
[21] The division of Virginia counties into townships was vigorously condemned by
Conservatives, who maintained that the new arrangement was cumbersome and
overly expensive. Hamilton James Eckenrode, *The Political History of Virginia During
the Reconstruction* (Baltimore, 1904), p. 102. In North Carolina this change resulted
in a transfer of power from the county courts to the voters. South Carolina pre-
viously had been divided into judicial districts rather than counties. Recent scholars

was avowedly designed to stimulate the interest of the masses of people in government. Tax reforms provided for by the new constitutions tended to shift the burden of taxation from individuals to the owners of property, and made taxes uniform throughout each state.[22] Property rights of women were extended by providing that property in the possession of a woman at the time of marriage or acquired by her thereafter was not liable in payment of the debts of her husband.

In all five states, the new constitutions altered to a greater or lesser degree the structure of the three traditional branches of state government. The executive branch underwent drastic changes in two of the states, while the remaining three states retained vestiges of ante-bellum centralization. In North Carolina the convention eliminated the old Executive Council, heretofore elected by the General Assembly, and over the protests of the Conservatives created four new elective positions: lieutenant governor, superintendent of public works, auditor, and superintendent of public instruction. The election of these officials, along with that of the secretary of state and attorney general, was placed in the hands of the voters. The tendency to make the officers of the executive department directly responsible to the people was evident in the constitution of South Carolina, but Georgia and Florida, under more Conservative influence, made all executive officers except the governor, and in the case of Florida, the lieutenant governor, either appointive by the governor or elective by the General Assembly. Virginia also reserved to the General Assembly the right to elect all executive officers except the governor and lieutenant governor. The period of required residence for election to the governorship was generally made low in order to assure the eligibility of the Northern newcomers, and each state abolished property requirements of candidates for the governorship. North Carolina Conservatives made determined efforts to retain a section requiring a freehold

conclude that reform of local government was the South Carolina convention's greatest permanent achievement. Simkins and Woody, *South Carolina During Reconstruction*, p. 101.

[22] There existed a belief among some Negroes and carpetbaggers that increased taxes on landed property would force the aristocratic landlords of the South to break up their holdings and sell small parcels to freedmen and poor whites. For an example of this attitude, see *Proceedings of the Constitutional Convention of South Carolina, 1868*, pp. 104–125.

to qualify for governor, but in vain. The Conservative press was loud in its condemnation of the changes in the executive branch:

> *The whole tenor of the report . . . [the Raleigh* Sentinel *declared], smacks of Yankee manipulations, and ignores the safe and staid temper of the Old North State, which has always eschewed inducements to experiment, at the sacrifice of her conservatism and well-earned integrity.*[23]

The judicial branch of the new state governments reflected the extent of the tide of democratic thought. In North Carolina Tourgée, unable to persuade the judiciary committee to approve his proposals to have the people elect the judges and to abolish the distinction between suits at law and suits in equity, carried his fight to the convention floor and secured the adoption of both proposals. The North Carolina convention appointed Tourgée, Victor C. Barringer, and W. B. Rodman as commissioners to prepare rules of judicial procedure and to codify the laws under the changes adopted by the convention. The *Sentinel* branded the popular election of judges as "the most dangerous stride towards mobocracy yet made by the destructives"; and North Carolina was, in fact, the only state in the South Atlantic area to take so democratic a stand. South Carolina provided that the General Assembly elect judges; and, although definite terms of office were fixed for each of the court judges, the carpetbagger leaders were not completely satisfied. D. H. Chamberlain declared that the "doctrine that the people are not to be trusted with the selection of those who are to administer justice to them, I believe to be wholly unfounded." Division among the carpetbagger leaders in South Carolina, however, prevented approval of popular election of judges even though one of their strongest leaders insisted in this connection that "the whole program of the age is in favor of removing power from the hands of the few, and bestowing it on the many."[24]

[23] Raleigh *Daily Sentinel,* January 29, 1868.
[24] *Journal of the Constitutional Convention of North Carolina, 1868,* pp. 180–186; Thorpe, ed., *Federal and State Constitutions,* V, 2812 (N. C., Art. IV, Sec. 26); Raleigh *Daily Sentinel,* February 12, 1868. Before the Civil War, Georgia and Virginia had provided for popular election of judges. Fletcher Melvin Green, *Constitutional Development in the South Atlantic States, 1776–1860 . . .* (Chapel Hill, 1930), pp. 240, 196. See also Thorpe, ed., *Federal and State Constitutions,* II, 802–804 (Ga., 1812 Amendment), VI, 3292–93 (S. C., Art. IV, Secs. 2, 13), VII, 3847 (Va., 1850, Art. VI, Secs. 6,

Virginia, like South Carolina, provided that the General Assembly elect her judges, but both Georgia and Florida eliminated any vestiges of local control of the judiciary by permitting the governor, with the consent of the senate, to appoint them. In fact the Georgia constitution, insofar as the judiciary was concerned, was less democratic than the constitution of 1865, which had provided for the election of supreme court judges by the General Assembly and lesser judicial officials by the voters. Carpetbagger A. L. Harris recognizing this retrogression protested against the enormous appointive power being concentrated in the chief executive.[25] North and South Carolina abolished county and district courts, and all five states fixed the tenure of office for judges at a specific number of years.

There were far-reaching reforms incorporated in the provisions of the new constitutions dealing with the legislative branches and with the suffrage. After replacing North Carolina's ancient title of House of Commons with the more common House of Representatives, the North Carolina convention abolished property qualifications for membership in either house.[26] The other four South Atlantic states continued to require no property qualifications for membership in either house. Virginia Radicals, however, inserted a section imposing the same disabilities for officeholding as were imposed by the Fourteenth Amendment,[27] and the native whites in the Georgia convention, when considering a section of the report of the committee on franchise providing that "all qualified electors" should be eligible to hold office, persuaded the Negroes that they were eligible for office without this clause, and that its inclusion would only serve to make it more difficult to secure ratification of the constitution. The political

10); *Proceedings of the Constitutional Convention of South Carolina, 1868,* pp. 601–602, 621.

[25] Thorpe, ed., *Federal and State Constitutions,* II, 712–714 (Fla., 1868, Art. VII, Secs. 3, 7, 9), 818–20, 835 (Ga., 1865, Art. VII, 1868, Art. V, Sec. 9), VII (Va., Art. VI, Secs. 5, 11, 13); Ethel Kime Ware, *A Constitutional History of Georgia* (New York, 1947), 123n; Thorpe, *Federal and State Constitutions,* II, 818–820; *Journal of the Constitutional Convention of Georgia, 1868,* p. 112.

[26] Thorpe, ed., *Federal and State Constitutions,* V, 2802, 2805 (N. C., Art. I, Sec. 22, Art. II, Secs. 9–10).

[27] Thorpe, ed., *Federal and State Constitutions,* VII, 3876–3877 (Va., Art. III, Secs. 6–7). Florida had never imposed a property qualification for such membership, and Virginia and Georgia had abolished property qualifications for legislators in the ante-bellum period. See Green, *Constitutional Development,* pp. 239, 294.

trick worked; by a vote of 126 to 12 the section was dropped, and the only specific guarantee of the right of the Negro to hold office in Georgia was lost.[28]

The liberalization of the qualifications for membership in the various general assemblies was effected with little difficulty, but on the long-standing question of the basis of apportionment the Conservatives waged a bitter battle. In North Carolina Conservative John W. Graham contended that unless the amount of taxes paid by a district were to be used in apportioning seats in the upper house in the time-honored manner, property would be left defenseless before the weight of sheer numbers. Carpetbagger John R. French gave voice to the more democratic view:

> *Our fathers wrought according to the light of their day, and have entered upon the reward of their honest toil. Another future opens before us. Not property, not a few families, however old, or however respectable, are to rule the North-Carolina of the hereafter—but the free and mighty people . . . these are to be her voters and her legislators.*[29]

The old rivalry between the Charleston area and the upcountry of South Carolina was revived in that state convention with the upcountry delegates expressing fear of continued lowcountry domination. In the three upper South Atlantic states the demands of the western areas were met by specific constitutional provisions of future apportionment of senators and representatives on the basis of population. Florida limited the number of representatives to four from any one county, and Georgia devised a complex system by which the state was divided into districts of three counties each for the purpose

[28] Augusta, Ga., *Tri-Weekly Constitutionalist*, February 16, 1868; Americus *Tri-Weekly Republican*, February 18, 1868; *Journal of the Constitutional Convention of Georgia, 1868*, pp. 148–150, 311–312. A competent historian of Reconstruction in Georgia gives former Governor Joseph E. Brown the credit for this political maneuver which allowed the Republicans to appeal to the whites of Cherokee Georgia by saying the Negro was given no right to hold office by the constitution and, on the other hand, to appeal to the masses of Negroes by saying they had that right as it was not specifically forbidden. Thompson, *Reconstruction in Georgia*, pp. 196–197.

[29] Raleigh *Daily Sentinel*, February 14, 1868; *Journal of the Constitutional Convention of North Carolina, 1868*, pp. 196–197. This longstanding argument over apportionment had been compromised in 1835 by making population the basis of representation in the lower house and taxation the basis in the upper house. *The Constitutions of the Several States of the Union . . .* (New York, 1854), pp. 260–261. For an account of this intrastate sectional controversy, see Green, *Constitutional Development*, pp. 228–229, 270–271.

of electing senators; and in the apportionment of representatives the six largest counties were allowed three each, the thirty-one next largest, two each, and the remaining ninety-five, one each.[30]

In the case of Florida the initial apportionment, and the limitation of representation from any one county to a maximum of four, meant that control would be assured for the whites, inasmuch as the Negroes were concentrated in the few populous counties. The Radicals tried to persuade Congress to disallow the second Florida constitution on the grounds that its legislature was unrepresentative, but their efforts were in vain.[31] Similarly, the Georgia constitution achieved white control of the legislature by its system of geographic apportionment.[32] Thus, the issue of representation was not entirely a continuation of the old struggle between democrats and aristocrats; Negro suffrage brought a new facet to the problem. As was true in Georgia and Florida, apportionment of seats in the legislature could be used as a means of maintaining white political supremacy.

The question of suffrage caused great apprehension among the Conservatives, and one reactionary organ predicted that once the Republicans decreed suffrage to be an "inherent right" there would remain "no security for the rights of property, and every man will hold whatever property he does hold at the mercy of the rabble."

[30] Thorpe, ed., *Federal and State Constitutions,* II, 726–27 (Fla., Art. XVII, Sec. 29), 827–28 (Ga., Art. III, Secs. 3–4), V, 2804–2805 (N. C., Art. II, Secs. 5–7), VI, 3285–86 (S. C., Art. II, Secs. 3–4, 6, 8), VII, 3880–83 (Va., Art. V, Secs. 2–3); *Proceedings of the Constitutional Convention of South Carolina, 1868,* pp. 527–37; Davis, *Civil War and Reconstruction in Florida,* pp. 511–12. For the Radical protest in Florida, see *House Misc. Docs.,* 40th Cong., 2d sess., vol. II (Serial 1350), no. 109. Only eight counties in Florida, heavily populated counties, had a Negro majority. White dominated counties with small populations were given representation out of all proportion to population figures. *A Compendium of the Ninth Census (June 1, 1870) Compiled Pursuant to a Concurrent Resolution of Congress* (Washington, 1872), pp. 32–33.

[31] *House Misc. Docs.,* 40th Cong., 2d sess., no. 109; Daniel Richards to Washburne, May 25, 1868, in Washburne Papers; Davis, *Civil War and Reconstruction in Florida,* pp. 511–512. Before the Civil War, the Florida constitution had been more democratic in respect to representation than the other South Atlantic states. The constitution of 1838 had provided for apportionment in both houses on the basis of federal enumeration. Thorpe, ed., *Federal and State Constitutions,* II, 676.

[32] Ibid., pp. 826–828. C. C. Richardson, a Georgia carpetbagger, severely condemned the apportionment devised by the convention as "the superstructure of an aristocracy . . . which has so riveted the shackles of legislation upon the mass of the people as to keep them bound in the almost hopeless chains of poverty, degradation, and ruin, and who now tenaciously cling to their Bourbon idea, and refuse to release their unscrupulous grasp upon the rights of the people." *Journal of the Constitutional Convention of Georgia, 1868,* p. 130.

But there was never any real doubt in any of the states about the inevitability of Negro voting, and Negro suffrage was generally accepted by Conservatives in all of the states except North Carolina as a necessity forced upon the states by an overbearing conqueror. In the Old North State young Plato Durham and William A. Graham resolutely opposed the universal manhood suffrage movement. Durham went so far as to press the issue by early presenting resolutions which stated that any attempt to abolish or abridge the natural distinction between the white and black race would be a crime against civilization and God. The resolutions were immediately tabled, but the able young Confederate veterans, who continued to harass the exponents of universal manhood suffrage for the remainder of the session, were able to define the position of the Conservatives in a minority report of the committee on suffrage. "We do not regard the right to vote as natural or inherent, but constitutional merely—to be regulated in such way as will best promote the welfare of the whole community." Durham and Graham condemned the whole scheme of universal manhood suffrage

> as intended to advance party purposes, in the expectation that the States of the South being Africanized and Radicalized may more than counterbalance the loss of electoral votes . . . in other sections of the Union.[33]

Attempts to limit Negro suffrage in this manner proved futile, and the sections of the new constitutions dealing with the franchise all embodied the principle of universal manhood suffrage. Radicals in the Virginia, North Carolina, and Georgia conventions sought to restrict the franchise of former rebels, but only Virginia placed restrictions on former Southern leaders, and this was done over the bitter opposition of some of the leading carpetbaggers and against the advice of General John M. Schofield.[34] Several of the South Carolina

[33] Salisbury *Old North State*, February 8, 1868; *Journal of the Constitutional Convention of North Carolina, 1868*, pp. 32-33, 233–238. The principle of Negro suffrage was the only issue involved; all of the South Atlantic states had adopted white manhood suffrage before the Civil War.

[34] J. E. Bryant, Georgia carpetbagger, advocated that those persons disqualified by the Fourteenth Amendment or by the Reconstruction Acts be disfranchised, with the added provision that these disabilities not extend beyond January 1, 1869, i.e., that they apply only for the first elections a provision already incorporated in the second Reconstruction Act. *Journal of the Constitutional Convention of Georgia, 1868,*

carpetbaggers favored the imposition of a poll tax as a requirement for voting in order to "instill into the minds and hearts of the people the sacredness of the ballot-box," and one South Carolina report on suffrage would have required after 1875 an ability to read and write as a requirement for voting. But the ideal of universal manhood suffrage exercised too great a hold on the minds of the delegates to allow any limitation on the right to vote.[35] With the exception of Virginia, all of the South Atlantic states extended the ballot to all males over twenty-one, born or naturalized in the United States, who had resided in their state for one year (six months in the case of Georgia); and all the constitutions except those of Georgia and Florida guaranteed qualified electors the right to hold a state office.[36]

Conservative delegates in the three conventions securely under carpetbagger domination were powerless to stop the changes instituted by the Northern "adventurers," but they persisted in offering amendments supporting the "white supremacy" position and used the debates on the convention floors to appeal to native whites and arouse their fear of Negro supremacy. William A. Graham, for instance, attempted to secure passage of an amendment to the section on militia providing that no white North Carolinian would have to serve with a Negro or ever obey an order from a Negro. Young Plato Durham was more extreme in his demands that no Negro or anyone with Negro blood ever be eligible for the office of governor, lieutenant governor, or any other executive office, and that intermarriage between the "Caucasian and African races" be prohibited.[37]

pp. 148–150. Virginia carpetbagger Edgar Allen warned the convention that it was being misled; and Negro carpetbag leader Thomas Bayne offered a resolution exempting all persons who were disfranchised from the payment of taxes. John C. Underwood also supported the move to give the franchise to all citizens of the state. Other Radicals, however, were conferring with congressional Republicans as to the advisability of further disfranchisement of rebels. Richmond *Whig,* April 18, 1868; Richard Lee Morton, *The Negro in Virginia Politics, 1865–1902* (1919), 58; *Journal of the Constitutional Convention of Virginia, 1868,* pp. 40, 90; J. W. D. Bland to Washburne, March 15, 1868, in Washburne Papers.

[35] *Proceedings of the Constitutional Convention of South Carolina, 1868,* pp. 724–726.
[36] North Carolina excepted from office those electors who denied the existence of God, those convicted of treason, felony, perjury, or an infamous crime (unless pardoned) or of corruption or malpractice in office. Thorpe, ed., *Federal and State Constitutions,* V, 2814–15 (N. C., 1868, Art. VI, Sec. 5).
[37] *Journal of the Constitutional Convention of North Carolina, 1868,* pp. 162–163, 175, 216; Raleigh *Daily Sentinel,* February 17, 1868. Although these amendments called forth the scorn of the Republicans, on the day before adjournment the convention accepted a Negro delegate's resolution declaring it to be the sense of the

As has been seen, in the two states of Georgia and Florida where carpetbagger influence proved less effective and native white Conservatives or groups cooperating with them controlled the conventions, the resulting constitutions were relatively conservative. The apportionment of seats in the legislature assured continued white domination of the General Assembly, and the broad appointive power of the governor and legislature in each state, even on the local level, made for centralization of power.[38] As long as the whites held the office of governor, they could effectively deprive the Negroes of any real share in state government. The constitutions of Georgia and Florida attest to the considerable confidence of the Conservatives in their ability to carry the forthcoming elections inasmuch as the technique could work in reverse if the Radicals captured control of the executive. The Florida constitution, even more clearly than that of Georgia, bears the stamp of Conservative influence. Some liberal constitutional reform was desired by Conservatives or Democrats in both states, but the Negro issue brought about a coalition of Conservative Republicans and former Democrats and Whigs dedicated to the maintenance of white supremacy at all costs.

Even so, constitutional changes adopted by the Reconstruction conventions of 1867–1868 made a sweeping extension of political democracy in the South Atlantic states. Except for the changed status of the Negro, the innovations represented reforms long sought and so designed to capture the support of a large number of Southern whites as well as the large new bloc of Negro voters. During the course of the ante-bellum period the poorer classes of Southern whites had successfully fought for an extension of the franchise to all white adult males and, with less success, for equal opportunities of officeholding. The imposition of Congressional Reconstruction extended the sphere of democracy still further by according the franchise, and generally the right to hold office, to all adult men, includ-

convention that intermarriage and illicit intercourse between the races should be discountenanced and that separate schools should be established for whites and Negroes. *Journal of the Constitutional Convention of North Carolina, 1868,* p. 473.
[38] *Journal of the Constitutional Convention of Georgia, 1868,* pp. 551, 554, 556; Thorpe, ed., *Federal and State Constitutions,* II, 712 (Fla., Art. VI, Secs. 17–19). The only county position made elective was that of constable. Ibid., p. 709 (Fla., Art. V, Sec. 26).

ing the Negro,[39] and by retaining and enlarging the principles of earlier bills of rights. The constitutional conventions of Virginia, North and South Carolina based apportionment of representation upon population for the first time, extended popular control of local government, and made most offices, both state and local, elective rather than appointive.

The carpetbagger who successfully championed political democracy revealed no such enthusiasm for extending economic democracy. The Northern settlers in the South, whose respect for property rights precluded an extensive program of debt repudiation or property confiscation, seemed to have been convinced that the same industry and commerce which had transformed the North would revolutionize the South. One carpetbagger expressed his confidence that "the plaster of profit laid upon the sores of war would work a miraculous cure."[40] Whenever Negro spokesmen did display a desire for radical economic measures, property-conscious Northerners and Southerners combined to block them.

The success of the Republicans in the South depended upon the adoption of major political changes, for without guarantees of continued political democracy the basis of Radical strength would be undermined; and Northern immigrants, the carpetbaggers, took the lead in providing for the South a democratic political structure. But time demonstrated that democratic institutions, too, were capable of manipulation.

[39] The Virginia provision limiting the vote was eliminated from the constitution in the ratification election which allowed a separate vote on this issue.
[40] Albion W. Tourgée, *An Appeal to Caesar* (New York, 1884), p. 58.

Richard N. Current
CARPETBAGGERS RECONSIDERED

Richard Current's writings on Lincoln and Northern and Southern politics during the Civil War era have greatly illumined our understanding of political behavior in a very complex period. His book on Three Carpetbag Governors *(1967) explored the differing situations confronted by leading carpetbag governors. In the following essay, Professor Current assesses a much broader sampling of carpetbag politicians in the South during the Reconstruction era.*

The story of the post-bellum South is often told as if it were a morality play or a television melodrama. The characters personify Good or Evil, and they are so clearly identified that there is no mistaking the "good guys" and the "bad guys." One of the villains, who deserves the boos and hisses he is sure to get, is the carpetbagger. As usually portrayed, this contemptible Yankee possesses as little honor or intelligence as he does property, and he possesses so little property that he can, quite literally, carry all of it with him in a carpetbag. He is attracted southward by the chance for power and plunder that he sees when the vote is given to Southern Negroes and taken from some of the Southern whites by the Reconstruction Acts of 1867. Going south in 1867 or after, he meddles in the politics of places where, as a mere roving adventurer, he has no true interest. For a time he and his kind run the Southern states. At last, when the drama ends, Good has triumphed over Evil, and the carpetbagger has got his come-uppance. But he leaves behind him a trail of corruption, misgovernment, and lastingly disturbed race relations.[1]

That picture may seem an exaggeration, a caricature. If so, it nevertheless has passed for a long time as a true, historical likeness, and it continues to pass as such. A standard dictionary defines *carpetbagger* as a term of contempt for Northern men who went south

From Richard N. Current, "Carpetbaggers Reconsidered," in *A Festschrift for Frederick B. Artz,* ed. D. H. Pinkney and Theodore Ropp. Reprinted by permission of the publisher. Copyright 1964, Duke University Press, Durham, North Carolina.

[1] This paper was presented, in an earlier form, at the annual dinner of the Mississippi Valley Historical Association in Chicago on December 28, 1959. Thanks are due to the Research Council of the University of North Carolina at Greensboro for a grant assisting part of the research on which the essay is based.

"to seek private gain under the often corrupt reconstruction governments."[2] Another dictionary, based on "historical principles," contains this definition: "One of the poor northern adventurers who,
carrying all their belongings in carpetbags, went south to profit from
the social and political upheaval after the Civil War."[3] A recent textbook refers to "the Radical carpetbaggers who had poured into the
defeated section after the passage of the First Reconstruction Act of
March, 1867."[4] The prevailing conception, then, is that these men
were late arrivals who waited till the Negro was given the suffrage
and who then went off with their carpetbags, cynically, to take advantage of the colored vote.

Even those who hold that view concede that "a few were men of
substance, bent on settling in the South,"[5] and that some of them took
up residence there before the passage of the Reconstruction Acts.
With respect to men of this kind, however, the question has been
raised whether they should be considered carpetbaggers at all. Many
of the Northerners active in Mississippi politics after 1867, the historian of Reconstruction in that state observes, had arrived as would-
be planters before 1867. "It is incorrect, therefore, to call them 'carpet
baggers,'" this historian remarks. "They did not go South to get
offices, for there were no offices for them to fill. The causes which
led them to settle there were purely economic, and not political."[6]

---

[2] *Webster's New International Dictionary of the English Language* (Springfield, Mass., 1934), p. 410.

[3] Mitford M. Mathews, ed., *A Dictionary of Americanisms on Historical Principles* (Chicago, 1951), p. 273.

[4] Richard Hofstadter, William Miller, and Daniel Aaron, *The United States: The History of a Republic* (Englewood Cliffs, N. J., 1957), p. 404. The use of the carpetbagger stereotype in recent historical writing could be illustrated at length. Nash K. Burger and John K. Bettersworth, *South of Appomattox* (New York, 1959), p. 124, speak of Congress having instituted "military reconstruction" in 1867 and go on to say: "It was now that the era of carpetbag and Negro rule flourished unabated in the South. When carpetbaggers arrived from the North to control the Negro. . . ." J. G. Randall, *The Civil War and Reconstruction* (Boston, 1937), p. 847, says the carpetbaggers went south to "make money and seize political power." The revised edition of this work, by Randall and David Donald (Boston, 1961), omits this passage but substi-
tutes no other definition or description of the carpetbaggers. In the preface to the best-selling novel by Harold Robbins, *The Carpetbaggers* (New York, 1961), there is an eloquent description, from the stereotyped view, of men who "came to plunder." The title is figurative, and the novel itself has nothing to do with Northerners in the postwar South.

[5] William A. Dunning, *Reconstruction Political and Economic, 1865–1877* (New York, 1907), p. 121.

[6] James W. Garner, *Reconstruction in Mississippi* (New York, 1901), p. 136. But Garner is inconsistent. See the next note.

Thus the brothers Albert T. and Charles Morgan, when they moved
from Wisconsin to Mississippi, "came not as carpetbaggers," for
they brought with them some $50,000, which they invested in planting
and lumbering enterprises (and lost).[7] And the much better-known
figure Albion W. Tourgée, who moved from Ohio to North Carolina,
was perhaps no carpetbagger, either, for he took with him $5,000
which he put into a nursery business (and also lost).[8]

Now, suppose it could be demonstrated that, among the Northern
politicians in the South during Reconstruction, men essentially like
the Morgans and Tourgée were not the few but the many, not exceptional but fairly typical. Suppose that the majority moved to the
South before 1867, before the establishment of the "corrupt reconstruction governments," and hence for reasons other than to seek
private gain or political power under such governments. One of two
conclusions must follow. Either we must say that true carpetbaggers
were much fewer and less significant than has been commonly supposed, or we must seek a new definition of the word.

In redefining it, we should consider the actual usage on the part of
Southerners during the Reconstruction period. We may learn something of its denotation as well as its connotation if we look at the way
they applied it to a specific person: the one-time Union army officer
Willard Warner, of Ohio and Alabama.

Warner might seem, at first glance, to exemplify the late-comer
rising immediately in Southern politics, for he completed his term in
the Ohio legislature and was elected to the United States Senate
from Alabama in the same year, 1868. But he was not really a new
arrival. He had visited Alabama and, with a partner, had leased a
plantation there in the fall of 1865. He bought land in the state the
next year, and he spent most of the spring and summer of 1866 and
most of the autumn and winter of 1867–1868 on his Alabama land.
He intended to make an economic career in the South (and indeed he
was eventually to do so).[9]

At first, Warner had no trouble with his Alabama neighbors. "A

---

[7] Frank E. Smith, *The Yazoo River* (New York, 1954), pp. 153, 156. Garner, forgetting
his own words of caution, refers on pp. 309–310 to "the well-known 'carpet-bagger,'
Colonel A. T. Morgan."
[8] Ethel S. Arnett, *Greensboro, North Carolina* (Chapel Hill, 1955), p. 400 n.
[9] Warner to John Sherman, April 15, June 21, 1866; Dec. 9, 19, 1867; Jan. 10, 1877,
John Sherman MSS, Library of Congress.

Northern man, who is not a fool, or foolish fanatic," he wrote from his plantation in the spring of 1866, "may live pleasantly in Alabama, without abating one jot of his self-respect, or independence."[10] At one time or another, as he was to testify later, the leading Democrats of the state, among them the ex-Confederate General James H. Clanton, came to him and said: "General, when we talk about carpet-baggers we want you to understand that we don't mean you; you have come here and invested what means you had in property here, and you have the same interest here that we have."[11]

The Alabamans changed their attitude toward Warner when he was elected to office with Negro support. Afterwards (1871) General Clanton himself explained:

> If a man should come here and invest $100,000, and in the next year should seek the highest offices, by appealing to the basest prejudices of an ignorant race, we would call him a political carpet-bagger. But if he followed his legitimate business, took his chances with the rest, behaved himself, and did not stir up strife, we would call him a gentleman. General Warner bought land; I fixed some titles for him, and I assured him that when men came there to take their chances with us for life, we would take them by the hand. But we found out his designs. Before his seat in Ohio got cold, he was running the negro machine among us to put himself in office.[12]

Another Alabama Democrat, from Huntsville, in the area where Warner had bought land, elaborated further upon the same theme in testifying before a congressional committee, as follows:

> Question: You have used the epithets "carpet-bagger" and "scalawag" repeatedly . . . give us an accurate definition. . . .
> Answer: Well, sir, the term carpet-bagger is not applied to northern men who come here to settle in the South, but a carpet-bagger is generally understood to be a man who comes here for office sake, of an ignorant or bad character, and who seeks to array the negroes against the whites; who is a kind of political dry-nurse for the negro population, in order to get office through them.

[10] Warner to Sherman, April 15, 1866.
[11] Testimony Taken by the Joint Select Committee to Enquire into the Condition of Affairs in the Late Insurrectionary States: Alabama (41st Congress, 2d session, House Report No. 22, part 8, Washington, 1872), 1:34.
[12] Ibid., p. 233.

Question: *Then it does not necessarily suppose that he should be a northern man?*

Answer: *Yes, sir; it does suppose that he is to be a northern man, but it does not apply to all northern men that come here.*

Question: *If he is an intelligent, educated man, and comes here for office, then he is not a carpet-bagger, I understand?*

Answer: *No, sir; we do not generally call them carpet-baggers.*

Question: *If he is a northern man possessed of good character and seeks office he is not a carpet-bagger?*

Answer: *Mr. Chairman, there are so few northern men who come here of intelligence and character, that join the republican party and look for office alone to the negroes, that we have never made a class for them. . . . They stand sui generis. . . . But the term "carpet-bagger" was applied to the office-seeker from the North who comes here seeking office by the negroes, by arraying their political passions and prejudices against the white people of the community.*

Question: *The man in addition to that, under your definition, must be an ignorant man and of bad character?*

Answer: *Yes, sir; he is generally of that description. We regard any man as a man of bad character who seeks to create hostility between the races. . . .*

Question: *Having given a definition of the carpet-bagger, you may now define scalawag.*

Answer: *A scalawag is his subservient tool and accomplice, who is a native of the country.*[13]

So far as these two Alabamans were concerned, it obviously made no difference whether a Northerner came before 1867 or after, whether he brought with him and invested thousands of dollars or was penniless, whether he was well educated or illiterate, or whether he was of good or bad character in the ordinary sense. He was, by definition, a carpetbagger and a man of ignorant and bad character if he, at any time, encouraged political activity on the part of the Negroes and thus arrayed the blacks against the whites, that is, the Republicans against the Democrats. He was not a carpetbagger if he steered entirely clear of politics or if he consistently talked and voted as a Democrat or Conservative.

This usage was not confined to Alabama; it prevailed throughout the South.[14] To speak of "economic carpetbaggers," as historians

[13] Testimony of William M. Lowe, ibid., pp. 887–88.
[14] In the text and footnotes of this paper more than seventy so-called carpetbaggers are mentioned by name. All are illustrations of this usage.

sometimes do, is therefore rather hard to justify on a historical basis. Politics—Republican politics—was the distinguishing mark of the man whom the Democrats and Conservatives after 1867 dubbed a carpetbagger, and they called him by that name whether or not he had gone south originally for economic rather than political reasons. To speak of "Negro carpetbaggers" is also something of an anachronism. Colored men from the North did go south and enter politics, of course, but in the Reconstruction lexicon (with its distinction among carpetbaggers, scalawags, and Negroes) they were put in a category of their own. Northern-born or Southern-born, the Negro was a Negro to the Southern Conservatives, and they did not ordinarily refer to him as a carpetbagger. From contemporary usage, then, we derive the following as a non-valuational definition: the men called carpetbaggers were *white Northerners who went south after the beginning of the Civil War and, sooner or later, became active in politics as Republicans*.

With this definition at hand, we can proceed to make at least a rudimentary survey of the so-called carpetbaggers as a group, in order to find out how well they fit the traditional concept with respect to their background. Let us consider first the state and local officeholders. There were hundreds of these people, and many of them left too few traces for us now to track them down. Studies have touched upon the subject in some of the states, and though fragmentary, these studies at least suggest that most of the men under consideration do not conform to the stereotype.

In Arkansas the carpetbag governor (1868–1872) Powell Clayton had owned and lived on a plantation since 1865. Many years later he was to gather data showing that the overwhelming majority of the so-called carpetbaggers, who were in office when he was, had arrived in Arkansas before 1867, and that the small minority who came as late as 1867 "did so when the Democrats were in full power, and before the officers to be elected or appointed, together with their salaries and emoluments, had been fixed by the [Reconstructed] State Constitution." Clayton adds:

> With a very few exceptions, the Northern men who settled in Arkansas came there with the Federal Army, and . . . were so much impressed with its genial climate and great natural resources as to cause them . . . to make it their future home. A number, like myself and my brother William,

> *had contracted matrimonial ties. Many of them had been away from home*
> *so long as practically to have lost their identity in the States [from which*
> *they had come]. . . . These were the reasons that influenced their settle-*
> *ment in Arkansas rather than the existence of any political expectations.*[15]

That, of course, is *ex parte* testimony, from one of the carpetbaggers
himself. Still, he supports his conclusion with ample and specific
evidence.

And, with respect to some of the other states, Southern historians
have tended toward similar conclusions. In Alabama, says one of
these historians, "Many of the carpet-bag politicians were northern
men who had failed at cotton planting."[16] In Florida, says another,
about a third of the forty-six delegates elected in 1867 to the state
constitutional convention were white Republicans from the North.
"Most of the Northerners had been in the state for a year or more
and were *bona fide* citizens of the commonwealth." " As a class," they
were "intellectually the best men among the delegates."[17] In Mississippi, says a third, "The genuine 'carpet baggers' who came after the
adoption of the reconstruction policy were comparatively few in number." The vast majority of the so-called carpetbaggers in Mississippi
were men who had arrived earlier as planters.[18]

Information is not available regarding all the carpetbag officeholders in all the reconstructed states. What is needed, then, is information about a representative sample of such officeholders. A
sample could be made of the carpetbag governors, of whom the
total was nine. Eight of the nine arrived in the South before 1867. Two
were officers of the Freedmen's Bureau, two were civilian officials of
the federal government, and four were private enterprisers—two of
them planters, one a lawyer, and the other a minister of the gospel.
The single late-comer, Adelbert Ames of Massachusetts and Missis-

[15] Powell Clayton, *The Aftermath of the Civil War in Arkansas* (New York, 1915),
pp. 298–306. These facts did not, and do not, exempt Clayton and his colleagues from
the "carpetbagger" epithet. Thus, for example, Thomas S. Staples, *Reconstruction
in Arkansas, 1862–1874* (New York, 1923), pp. 276–277, writes of Clayton: "Though
a carpetbagger, he claimed to be identified with local interests by virtue of the fact
that he had purchased a plantation in Jefferson County and had decided to become
a permanent resident of the state."
[16] Walter L. Fleming, *Civil War and Reconstruction in Alabama* (New York, 1905),
p. 718 n.
[17] William W. Davis, *The Civil War and Reconstruction in Florida* (New York, 1913),
pp. 476–477.
[18] Garner, *Reconstruction in Mississippi*, pp. 136, 414 n.

sippi, first appeared in Mississippi as a regular army officer and as a military governor, not as an adventurer in search of a political job.[19]

A larger sample consists of the entire body of white Northerners who during the Reconstruction period were elected as Republicans to represent Southern constituencies in either branch of Congress. Altogether, there were about 62 of these men, 17 in the Senate and 45 in the House of Representatives. It is impossible to be absolutely precise in listing these congressional carpetbaggers. There were a few borderline cases where, for example, a man was born in the South but raised or educated in the North, and it is hard to know whether he should be classified as a Northerner or not.

Of the 62 senators and congressmen, practically all were veterans of the Union army. That is not surprising, and it does not alter the accepted stereotype. More surprising, in view of the carpetbagger's reputation for "ignorant or bad character," is the fact that a large proportion were well-educated. About two-thirds of the group (43 of the 62) had studied law, medicine, or engineering enough to practice the profession, or had attended one or more years of college, or had been school teachers. Of the senators alone, approximately half were college graduates. Seemingly the academic and intellectual attain-

---

[19] R. K. Scott of South Carolina and M. L. Stearns of Florida were Freedmen's Bureau agents. Harrison Reed of Florida was a federal tax commissioner (1863) and a United States postal agent (1865). W. P. Kellogg of Louisiana was collector of the port of New Orleans. H. C. Warmoth of Louisiana was a lawyer, Joseph Brooks of Arkansas was a minister, and Powell Clayton of Arkansas and D. H. Chamberlain of South Carolina were planters.

Ames, a regular army officer, became provisional governor of Mississippi in 1868 and military commander of the district in 1869. He was elected United States Senator and served from 1870 to 1874; he was elected governor and served from 1874 to 1876. Though a late-comer to Mississippi, he at times considered establishing a permanent residence in the state. He wrote his wife, October 26, 1872: "I think I will get a house and home for us on the Gulf at Pass Christian or some other point near there. And for business we will go into raising oranges." On November 9, 1872, he bought a house for $6,100 in Natchez, a town that had appealed to his wife. The dangerous and disagreeable aspects of life for a Republican Northerner in Mississippi caused him to change his mind about living permanently there, even before he lost out in politics. See *Chronicles from the Nineteenth Century: Family Letters of Blanche Butler and Adelbert Ames,* compiled by Blanche Butler Ames and privately issued by Jessie Ames Marshall (Clinton, Mass., 1957), 1:403, 416.

Rufus B. Bullock, governor of Georgia from 1868 to 1871, has been called a carpetbagger but does not fit in the category as defined according to the most common contemporary usage. Though a white Republican Northerner, Bullock had settled in the South before the war and had served in the Confederate army. See C. Mildred Thompson, *Reconstruction in Georgia: Economic, Social, Political, 1865–1872* (New York, 1915), p. 217.

ments of the carpetbaggers in Congress were, on the whole, at least as high as those of the other members of Congress, whether from the North or from the South.

Still more significant is the fact that nearly five-sixths of the entire carpetbag group—50 of the 62—had arrived in the South before 1867, before the passage of the Reconstruction Acts, before the granting of political rights to the Negro. Of the 50 early arrivals, only 15 appeared on the Southern scene as Treasury Department employees, Freedman's Bureau officials, or members of the postwar occupation forces (and at least a few of these 15 soon left the government service and went into private enterprise). Thirty-five of the 50 were engaged in farming or business or the professions from the time of their arrival or soon after.

As for those other 12 of the 62—the 12 who did not begin to live in the South until 1867 or later—more than half (at least 7) took up some private occupation before getting public office. Their comparatively late arrival does not, in itself, signify that they moved south merely for "office sake."[20]

If, then, the 62 carpetbag congressmen and senators make up a representative sample, we must conclude that a majority of the carpetbaggers, taken as a whole, do not conform to the traditional view,

[20] Following is the list, by states, of the carpetbag congressmen and senators as defined and selected for this study (each senator is indicated by an asterisk): *Alabama*—A. E. Buck, C. W. Buckley, J. B. Callis, T. Haughey, F. W. Kellogg, B. W. Norris, G. E. Spencer*, W. Warner*. *Arkansas*—P. Clayton*, S. W. Dorsey*, J. Edwards, J. Hinds, A. McDonald, B. F. Rice*, L. H. Roots, W. W. Wilshire. *Florida*—H. Bisbee, S. B. Conover*, A. Gilbert*, C. M. Hamilton, T. W. Osburn*, W. J. Purman, A. S. Welch*. *Georgia*—J. W. Clift, C. H. Prince. *Louisiana*—C. B. Darrall, J. S. Harris*, W. P. Kellogg*, J. E. Leonard, J. McCleery, J. Mann, F. Morey, J. P. Newsham, L. A. Sheldon, G. A. Sheridan, G. L. Smith, J. H. Sypher, J. R. West*. *Mississippi* —A. Ames*, H. W. Barry, A. R. Howe, G. C. McKee, H. R. Pease*, L. W. Perce, G. W. Wells. *North Carolina*—J. C. Albott*, J. R. French, D. Heaton. *South Carolina*—C. W. Buttz, L. C. Carpenter, S. L. Hoge, J. J. Patterson*, F. A. Sawyer*, B. F. Whittemore. *Tennessee*—L. Barbour, W. F. Prosser. *Texas*—W. T. Clark. *Virginia*—R. S. Ayer, J. Jorgensen, J. H. Platt, C. H. Porter, W. H. H. Stowell.

There were also several Northerners elected as Democrats to represent Southern constituencies in Congress. These Democrats have not been included in the list. Information on the carpetbag congressmen and senators has been derived from the *Biographical Directory of the American Congress* (81st Congress, 2d session, House Document No. 607, Washington, 1950) and from standard biographical encyclopedias and other sources.

See also C. Mildred Thompson, "Carpet-baggers in the United States Senate," *Studies in Southern History and Politics, Inscribed to William Archibald Dunning* (New York, 1914), pp. 159–176. Miss Thompson does not undertake the same sort of analysis of backgrounds as is attempted here.

at least so far as their backgrounds are concerned. With comparatively few exceptions, the so-called carpetbaggers had moved south
for reasons other than a lust for offices newly made available by the
passage of the Reconstruction Acts. These men were, in fact, a part
of the multitude of Union officers and soldiers who, during or soon
after the war, chose to remain in or return to the land they had helped
to conquer.

To thousands of the young men in blue, at and after the war's end,
the South beckoned as a land of wondrous charm, a place of almost
magical opportunity. "Northern men are going to do well in every
part of the South. The Southern men are too indolent to work and
the Yankees are bound to win." So, for example, a cavalry sergeant
wrote from Texas to his sister back home in Ohio in 1866. "I have
some idea that I will not remain in Ohio long, and maybe I will locate
in the sunny South," he continued. "What think you of roses bloom-
ing in open air in November, and the gardens glorious with flowers."[21]

Here, in the South, was a new frontier, another and a better West.
Some men compared the two frontiers before choosing the Southern
one, as did the Morgan brothers, who first looked over Kansas and
then decided upon Mississippi. Albert T. Morgan afterwards wrote
that the former cry, "Go West, young man," had been changed to
"Go South, young man," and in 1865 the change was "already quite
apparent, in the purpose of those of the North who were seeking new
homes."[22] Many years later Albion W. Tourgée recalled the hopes
and dreams with which, in the fall of 1865, he had settled as a badly
wounded veteran in Greensboro, North Carolina:

*He expected the future to be as bright and busy within the conquered
territory as it had been along the ever-advancing frontier of the West. . . .
He expected the whole region to be transformed by the power of commerce, manufactures, and the incursion of Northern life, thought, capital,
industry, and enterprise. . . . Because he thought he bore a shattered life
he sought a milder clime. He took his young wife with him, and they*

[21] John A. Gillis (Victoria, Texas) to "Sister Hattie," Nov. 21, 1866, Sherman MSS.
There are, in the Sherman MSS, a number of other letters in which Northerners
described the attractions of the South. See, for example, the letters to Sherman
from W. P. Dumble (Nashville), June 23, 1865; J. Y. Cantwell (Decatur, Alabama),
Dec. 11, 1865, and Jan. 23, 1866; J. Davis, Jr. (Macon, Georgia), Jan. 31, 1866; and
John Friend (Fernandina, Florida), March 12, 1866.
[22] Albert T. Morgan, *Yazoo; or, On the Picket Line of Freedom in the South* (Washington, 1884), p. 25.

*builded their first home-nest almost before the smoke of battle dis-
appeared. . . . His first object was restored health; his next desire, to
share the general prosperity.*[23]

Once they had been released from the army, thousands of other
Union soldiers and officers returned to the South with similar dreams
of prosperity and a pleasant life. For the moment, land was cheap
and cotton dear. Labor was abundant, and the Negroes were expected to work more willingly for their liberators than for their late
masters. So the veterans turned south. At the end of 1865 a newsman
from the North learned that, in Alabama alone, there were already
five thousand of them "engaged in planting and trading." Even
more than the uplands of Alabama, Tennessee, and Georgia, the
Mississippi Valley was proving an "attraction to adventurous capital,"
this traveling reporter found. "Men from the Middle States and the
great West were everywhere, buying and leasing plantations, hiring
freedmen, and setting thousands of ploughs in motion."[24] No impe-
cunious wanderers were these, but bringers of "adventurous capital."
They paid cash for lands or leases, for wages, for supplies. At a time
when the South was languishing for money, these newcomers provided it, put it into circulation, and thus gave the economy a lift.[25]

Most of those who thus adventured with their capital were to lose
it. They failed for several reasons. At cotton planting the Yankees
were novices, unused to local conditions and deluded in their expectations of the Negro as a free worker, or so the Southerners
said.[26] Actually the Southerners as well as the Yankees ran into
economic difficulties during the first few years after the war. "Vari-

[23] Albion W. Tourgée, *An Appeal to Caesar* (New York, 1884), pp. 55–67. The conception of the carpetbagger as a frontiersman is borne out by David H. Overy, Jr.,
"The Wisconsin Carpetbagger: A Group Portrait," *Wisconsin Magazine of History*
44 (1960): 15–49. Overy writes, p. 15: "During the Civil War, Wisconsin soldiers on
duty in the South discovered a new frontier."
[24] John T. Trowbridge, *The South . . . A Journey through the Desolated States* (Hartford, 1866), pp. 380, 448.
[25] See, for example, Staples, *Reconstruction in Arkansas*, pp. 86–87. Staples says
that there was much suffering in Arkansas during the winter of 1865–1866 because
of the money scarcity. Money came "for the most part" from partnerships of Southern
merchants and planters with Northern capitalists. "New comers from the North
brought in more or less cash, which was thrown into immediate circulation through
the purchase of lands and initial supplies." Fleming, *Reconstruction in Alabama*,
pp. 717–718, says "Northern energy and capital flowed in" to that state in 1865 and
1866.
[26] Fleming, pp. 323–324.

ous causes have arisen to prostrate the people, leaving them nearly
ruined," a contemporary observed early in 1867, "among which I
may more especially mention the following, which could not have
been foreseen or provided against: The too great drouth at one
season, which destroyed and blasted their corn; too much rain at
another season, which injured their cotton; and then the army worm,
which came out of the ground in vast numbers, destroyed what was
left." There was, besides, the federal cotton tax, which both Northern
and Southern planters denounced as ruinous.[27]

Often, whether as planters or as businessmen, the Northerners
faced a special disadvantage—the hostility of the people around
them. "The rebels will not buy from a Galvanized Yankee, or Loyal
Unionist, nor from a Yankee either," a Unionist Virginian complained
late in 1865, "the result being that loyal or Northern merchants are
failing all over the South."[28] In many places the Yankees were boy-
cotted if they sympathized with or voted for Republicans. "Only one
hundred and one men were found base enough to vote for the Radical
ticket," a Memphis newspaper reported in April, 1866. "We have
held up the names of a portion of these men and written small pox
over their doors in order that our people might shun them."[29]

Discouraged and disillusioned after a year or two in their new
homes, large numbers of the Yankees abandoned them and returned
to the North. Others, of whom some were successful and some were
not, remained in the South. Of those who remained, many turned to
state and local politics as Republicans in 1867 or after. These com-
prised the majority of that class of men who eventually came to be
known as carpetbaggers.

Before 1867 the Northerners in the South possessed only limited
opportunities in politics. As Republicans, they could not hope to be
elected to office. As newcomers, they often found it difficult even
to vote, because of the residence requirements. The Georgia constitution, as remade after the war, extended the residence requirement

[27] James E. Yeatman (St. Louis) to John Sherman, Feb. 1, 1867, Sherman MSS.
Sherman received other letters from Northern planters in the South who protested
against the federal cotton tax. See, for example, R. N. Barr (Claiborne, Alabama) to
Sherman, July 19, 1867.
[28] Augustus Watson (Fredericksburg) to Thaddeus Stevens, Dec. 9, 1865, Stevens
MSS, Library of Congress.
[29] Memphis *Avalanche,* April 22, 1866, clipping enclosed in letter of William Wilder
to Stevens, Stevens MSS.

in that state from six months to two years. "Now it is generally admitted," a Northern settler in Georgia protested, "that this change . . . has been effected to prevent loyal men who were obliged to leave here during the war and those who have come here since the war from having any voice in choosing the officers of the State and representatives to Congress."[30] Of course, the newcomers could seek federal jobs, and many of them did so, but again they faced something of a handicap, for they understood that President Johnson preferred "Southern citizens" when "suitable persons" among them could be found.[31]

To the Northern settlers remaining in the South the congressional acts of 1867 suddenly brought political opportunity and also, as some of them saw it, political responsibility. Tourgée, for one, sought election to the new constitutional convention in North Carolina because, having failed in business and lost the savings he had brought, he needed the money he would be paid as a delegate. But he sought election also because he was concerned about Negro rights and wished to do what he could to protect them.[32] A more prosperous settler, a planter of Carroll Parish, Louisiana, who once had been an Ohio school superintendent, took an active interest in Southern politics for reasons that he explained, in April, 1867, to Senator John Sherman:

> On the closing of my services as a Soldier, I became a member of the firm of Lynch, Ruggles & Co., which was organized in Circleville, Ohio, for the purpose of buying lands in the South and planting. We have located at this point, which is 40 miles above Vicksburg, have purchased lands, have organized most efficient labor forces, & our investment now is on a scale which makes us on that account deeply interested in every effort made to bring peace to the South. . . .
> I . . . respectfully ask your advice as to the proper course to be pursued by Northern men in the South who sympathize with Congress in the present crisis. . . . I have never held a civil office and never intended to, if I can avoid it; but we have a large force at work, have their confidence,

---

[30] Frank S. Hesseltine (Savannah) to Stevens, April 26, 1866, Stevens MSS.
[31] W. B. Woods (Mobile) to John Sherman, Jan. 28, 1866, Sherman MSS. A. C. Bryant (Stevenson, Alabama), seeking Sherman's aid in obtaining a federal job, wrote, June 15, 1866: "It is hard for a Northern man to get a position here as the people feel naturally a strong prejudice against them & they are so poor themselves that they *go for everything in sight*."
[32] Roy F. Dibble, *Albion W. Tourgée* (New York, 1921), pp. 34–41.

and now as they are voters, they look to our advice, and I want to give it as wisely as possible. Other Northern men are similarly situated. . . .[33]

The position of some of these other Northern men was later recalled by C. M. Hamilton, a Pennsylvanian who had gone to Florida in 1864, as a Freedmen's Bureau agent, and had become after 1867 one of the most prominent carpetbaggers of that state. In 1871 he told a congressional committee investigating the Ku Klux Klan:

> *. . . when the reconstruction acts first passed Congress, the Yankees, as we are called, most of us soldiers who were in the South, rather stood back, did not really feel at that time that they [we] had any particular right to interfere in politics, or to take part in them. But the reconstruction laws were passed; reconstruction was necessary; . . . the democratic party of the South adopted the policy of masterly inactivity . . . ; there was a new element here that had been enfranchised who were without leaders. The northern men in the South, and there were but a handful of them in this State, who had been in the Army, took hold of this matter of reconstruction, and they have perfected it so far as it has been accomplished.*[34]

These Northerners, already in the South in 1867, felt they had a right and a duty to be where they were and to do what they did. They were Americans. They had fought a war to keep the nation one. South as well as North, it was *their* country. They had chosen to live in the Southern part of it. This was now their home, and they had a stake in its future as well as the future of the country as a whole. Their attitude should be quite understandable—as understandable as the feeling of the majority of Southern whites.

Naturally, the native Conservatives and Democrats resented the Northern Republicans and reviled them with such epithets as "aliens," "birds of passage," and "carpetbaggers." As applied to most of the men, however, these were not objective and descriptive terms. The Union veterans who settled in the South were impelled by a variety and a mixture of motives: restlessness, patriotic idealism, the desire to get ahead, and what not. But so were the pioneers at

[33] John Lynch to Sherman, April 20, 1867, Sherman MSS.
[34] *Testimony Taken by the Joint Select Committee to Enquire into the Condition of Affairs in the Late Insurrectionary States: Florida* (42d Congress, 2d Session, House Report No. 22, part 13, Washington, 1872), p. 289.

other times and places in the United States. So were the Southerners themselves who moved westward or northward during the Reconstruction period. At that time the newer states of the Southwest (such as Alabama, Mississippi, and especially Arkansas) were filled with fairly recent arrivals from the older states of the Southeast. And at that time there were more Southerners residing in the North than Northerners in the South.[35] The latter were no more "birds of passage" than the former. Perhaps the frontiersman has been too much idealized for his propensity to rove. Certainly the carpetbagger has been too much condemned for the mere act of moving from one part of the country to another.

Even if all this be conceded, there remain of course the other elements of the carpetbagger stereotype—the charges of misgovernment, corruption, and racial disturbance.

With regard to the charge of misgovernment and corruption, it is hard to generalize about the carpetbaggers as a class. Nevertheless, a few tentative observations may be made. First, the extent and duration of "carpetbag rule" has been exaggerated. In six of the eleven ex-Confederate states (Texas, Tennessee, Alabama, Georgia, Virginia, North Carolina) there was never a carpetbag governor; there was never a majority of carpetbaggers among the Republicans in or out of office; certainly there was never anything approaching carpetbagger domination of state politics. In all those states the Republicans held power only briefly if at all, and they held it, to the extent that they did so, by means of their strength among Negroes and scalawags. In the other five states (Arkansas, Mississippi, Louisiana, Florida, South Carolina) there were carpetbag governors part of the time, but even in these states the carpetbaggers could maintain themselves only with Negro and native white support. Second, the extent of illegal and illegitimate spending by the carpetbag governments has been exaggerated—if spending for schools, transportation, and other social and economic services be considered legitimate.[36] Third, the improper spending, the private use of public

---

[35] Tourgée, *An Appeal to Caesar,* pp. 150, 176–177. Tourgée's tables are taken from an article by E. W. Gilliam in the *Popular Science Monthly* for February, 1883. They include in "the South" all fifteen of the prewar slave states and also West Virginia.
[36] W. E. Burghardt Du Bois, "Reconstruction and Its Benefits," *American Historical Review* 15 (1910): 781–799.

funds, was by no means the work of carpetbaggers alone, nor were they the only beneficiaries: heavily involved also were native whites, including Conservatives and Democrats as well as scalawags.[37] Fourth, probably the great majority of the carpetbaggers were no more corrupt than the great majority of contemporary officeholders throughout the United States.[38]

Consider the carpetbag governors, who are generally mentioned as the most conspicuous examples of dishonesty. One of them, Joseph Brooks of Arkansas, did not succeed in exercising uncontested power, for either good or evil, and was soon ousted. Two of the governors, R. K. Scott of South Carolina and W. P. Kellogg of Louisiana, are rather difficult to defend. Four others—Powell Clayton of Arkansas, Harrison Reed and M. L. Stearns of Florida, and H. C. Warmoth of Louisiana—were loudly accused but never really proved guilty of misusing their offices for private profit.[39] Only one of the four, Warmoth, seems actually to have made much money while in Reconstruction politics, and he made a fortune. While governor, he admitted that there was "a frightful amount of corruption" in Louisiana. He explained, however, that the temptation came from the business interests who offered bribes, and he insisted that the Republicans, black as well as white, had resisted bribery as well as had the Democrats.[40] It might be more true to say that Louisiana corrupted Warmoth (if indeed he was corrupted) than to say that Warmoth corrupted Louisiana. The other two carpetbag governors,

[37] Jonathan Daniels, *Prince of Carpetbaggers* (Philadelphia, 1958), pp. 23, 289–299, and passim, eloquently shows the involvement of others besides the Northerner Milton S. Littlefield in the fraudulent financing of North Carolina railroads. With regard to Mississippi, Garner writes, p. 323: "The only large case of embezzlement among the state officers during the post-bellum period was that of the Democratic state treasurer in 1866."

[38] The period of Reconstruction in the South, it must be remembered, was the time of scandals in the Grant administration, in the Shepherd government of Washington, D. C., in the Tweed Ring in New York City, and in state and local government elsewhere.

[39] "It was never proved that he got any of the bonds," writes Dixon Y. Thomas with regard to the charge that Powell Clayton stole Arkansas railroad securities. *Dictionary of American Biography* (New York, 1928–1958), 4:187–188. "These charges were specific and definite enough, but the trial did not develop any substantial proof of the allegations," opines Davis with regard to embezzlement charges against Reed. *Reconstruction in Florida*, pp. 631–634.

[40] *New York Tribune*, March 14, 1872, clipping in the Warmoth MSS, Southern Historical Collection, University of North Carolina.

Adelbert Ames of Mississippi and D. H. Chamberlain of South Carolina, were economy-minded and strictly honest.[41]

There remains the charge that the carpetbaggers disturbed the
relations between the races in the South. Of course, the carpetbaggers did so. Their doing so was the basic cause of the animus against
them. This is the reason why the honest ones among them, the men
like Ames and Chamberlain and Warner, were as thoroughly hated
and as strongly opposed as were any of the Yankee scoundrels.
Most of the Southern whites opposed the granting of political rights
to the former slaves. The carpetbaggers encouraged the Negroes to
exercise such rights. Thus the carpetbaggers upset the pattern of
race relationships, the pattern of Negro passivity, which most white
Southerners considered ideal.

The party struggle in the postwar South amounted to something
more than ordinary politics. In some of its aspects it was equivalent
to a continuation, or a renewal, of the Civil War.

On the one hand, Southern Conservatives thought of themselves
as still fighting for home rule and white supremacy—in essence much
the same war aims as the Confederacy had pursued. Carpetbaggers,
on the other hand, saw their own basic objective as the reunification
of the country, which had been incompletely won at Appomattox,
and as the emancipation of the Negroes, who had been but partially
freed by the adoption of the Thirteenth Amendment.

On both sides the methods frequently were those of actual, though
irregular, warfare. The Ku Klux Klan, the White League, the Red
Shirts, and the various kinds of rifle companies were military or semi-
military organizations. So, too, were the state militias, the Union
Leagues and Loyal Leagues, and the other partisan institutions of
the carpetbaggers and their Negro allies. The carpetbaggers served,
so to speak, as officers of front-line troops, deep in enemy territory,

---

[41] Garner, *Reconstruction in Mississippi,* pp. 229–236, 297–305, 320–323, concedes
that, as governor, Ames made many good appointments and on the whole administered the state honestly and economically. Chamberlain was attorney-general of
South Carolina before becoming governor. A letter attributed to him and written
while he was attorney-general might be viewed as incriminating him in corruption.
However, a South Carolina Democrat has written: "No stolen money was ever
traced to him, and he positively denied any participation in the proceeds of public
rascality." As governor, he was not even accused of corruption or extravagance. See
Henry T. Thompson, *Ousting the Carpetbagger from South Carolina* (Columbia, S. C.,
1926), pp. 36, 92–93, 101–102, and passim.

"on the picket line of freedom in the South." The embattled Republicans undoubtedly suffered much heavier casualties than did their foes.

True, the Republicans had the advantage of support by the regular United States army, but often that support was more a potentiality than a fact, and at critical moments it failed to materialize. As for the warriors of white supremacy, they had the backing of Northern sympathizers in strength and numbers that would have gladdened the heart of Jefferson Davis in that earlier war time when he was angling for the aid of the Knights of the Golden Circle. The carpetbaggers were divided and weakened by the Republican party schism of 1872, by personal rivalries among themselves, and by jealousies between them and their Negro and scalawag associates. Finally, as some of the carpetbaggers saw it, they were stabbed in the back—abandoned by the government and the people at the North.[42]

The history of this losing campaign has been written almost exclusively from the Southern, or Democratic, or disillusioned Republican point of view: the story of the carpetbaggers has been told mainly by their enemies. Historical scholarship has given its sanction to the propaganda of the victorious side in the Reconstruction War. That propaganda, like most, has its elements of truth, and like most, its elements of distortion and downright falsehood. Not that the carpetbaggers were invariably the apostles of righteousness and truth. We would make little progress toward historical understanding if we merely took the same old morality play and switched the labels of Evil and Good. But surely the time has long since passed when we can, uncritically, accept the "carpetbagger" stereotype.

No doubt men can be found who fit it. No doubt there were political tramps who went south to make cynical use of the Negro vote and who contrived to win both office and illicit gain. But such men were few and comparatively unimportant. Far more numerous and more significant were those energetic and ambitious men who, with or without carpetbags, brought their savings or their borrowings to invest, who eventually got into politics for idealistic as well as selfish reasons, and who in office behaved no better and no worse than

---

[42] See, for example, Morgan, *Yazoo*, p. 487; Tourgée, *An Appeal to Caesar*, pp. 68–69; and Walter Allen, *Governor Chamberlain's Administration in South Carolina* (New York, 1888), pp. 507–520.

most of their contemporaries. Some of these men, like some others
of their time, proved corrupt. It would be interesting to know whether,
as peculators, the carpetbaggers took out more than a small fraction
of the money that, as speculators, they had brought in.

David H. Donald
THE SCALAWAG IN MISSISSIPPI RECONSTRUCTION

David Donald's numerous books and articles have established him as a fore-
most authority on the Civil War and Reconstruction era. He was one of the
first of recent scholars to perceive the necessity of reexamining the complex
pattern of internal politics in the South during the Reconstruction. The fol-
lowing article was a trail-blazing effort to reassess the social background
and the political role of the scalawags.

The scalawag is the forgotten man of Reconstruction history. In spite
of the excellent work of recent revisionists,[1] the old stereotypes as
to the political course of Reconstruction in the South have remained
largely undisturbed. On the one hand, it is said, were the Democrats,
the vast majority of the white population, battling valiantly for the
creed of the Old South, and on the other the Republicans, black in
morals as in skin. The Republican party, so the story goes, consisted
of the great body of uneducated Negroes, dominated by carpetbaggers from the North or—worst of all—by a few renegade Southerners[2] opprobriously termed scalawags. These were, it is usually

From David H. Donald, "The Scalawag in Mississippi Reconstruction," *Journal of*
Southern History 10 (November 1944): 477–460. Copyright 1944 by the Southern
Historical Association. Reprinted by permission of the Managing Editor.

[1] For an excellent summary of these new points of view, see Howard K. Beale, "On
Rewriting Reconstruction History," in *American Historical Review* [New York, 1895–],
45 (1940): 807–827.

[2] An illustration of this idea in college textbooks may be found in Samuel E. Morison
and Henry S. Commager, *Growth of the American Republic*, 2 vols. (New York, 1942),
2:46. For other secondary accounts conveying the same ideas, see James Ford
Rhodes, *History of the United States from the Compromise of 1850*, 7 vols. (New York,
1892–1906), 6:91; Walter L. Fleming, *The Sequel of Appomattox* (New Haven, 1919),

considered, the very lowest dregs of mankind; they were "southern white men . . . [who] sold themselves for office";[3] they were the veritable Esaus of the Caucasian race.[4]

A fresh study of the Reconstruction era in Mississippi, however, casts some doubt on the conventional interpretation of the scalawag's role in that troubled time. Republicans ruled Mississippi for five years after its readmission in 1870, and during this period one-third of the congressmen, one of the governors, two of the three supreme court justices, and about one-third of both houses of the state legislature were southern-born white Republicans.[5] Further analysis shows that almost every one of these officeholders had before the war been an old-line Whig and a bitter opponent of the Democrats.[6]

Surprisingly little attention has been paid to the postwar attitudes of southern Whig leaders. That party, after all, had been numerous. In 1852 its candidate in Mississippi had defeated no less a person than Jefferson Davis for the United States Senate. As Unionists the Whigs had cast a respectable vote for John Bell in 1860.[7] And, as late as 1863, they had secured a majority in the Mississippi legislature, selected a Whig for Confederate senator, and elected a former Whig as governor.[8] They were the wealthiest and best-educated element in the state.

It has generally been assumed that after the war southern Whigs immediately joined with the Democrats to combat carpetbag and Negro rule. Actually this was far from the case. Some few Whig leaders did from the beginning urge the disbanding of the old party

p. 153; E. Merton Coulter, *A Short History of Georgia* (Chapel Hill, 1933). p. 347; Claude G. Bowers, *The Tragic Era* (Cambridge, 1929), p. 199; and many others.

[3] *Senate Reports*, 44th Cong., 1st sess., No. 527 (2 vols.), 2:1071.

[4] John S. McNeilly, "War and Reconstruction in Mississippi, 1863–1890," in *Mississippi Historical Society Publications* (Oxford-Jackson, 1898–1925), Centenary Series, 2 (1918): 425–426.

[5] For example, of the 83 attending members of the state constitutional convention of 1868, 48 were southern-born white Republicans or "conservatives." James W. Garner, *Reconstruction in Mississippi* (New York, 1901), pp. 187–188. Of Mississippi's 22 representatives in Congress during the period, 8 were southern white Republicans. On the supreme court justices, see Dunbar Rowland, *Courts, Judges, and Lawyers of Mississippi, 1798–1935* (Jackson, 1935), pp. 97–99.

[6] This is certainly true of all the congressmen, of Governor James L. Alcorn, and of Chief Justice Ephraim G. Peyton. There is some uncertainty as to Justice Horatio F. Simrall's political affiliations before the war.

[7] Percy L. Rainwater, *Mississippi: Storm Center of Secession, 1856–1861* (Baton Rouge, 1938), pp. 18–19, 199.

[8] John K. Bettersworth, *Confederate Mississippi* (Baton Rouge, 1943), pp. 52–53.

in favor of such an alignment,[9] but their efforts came at a time when the Democratic party itself was virtually defunct, and when influential southern newspapers were urging a dissolution of that party.[10] But Whigs were not attracted by the Democratic policies or leadership anyway. "[W]ould it not be absurd," questioned one, "for Whigs to abandon their high conservative position, and aid in the reorganization of the Democratic party?"[11] Much of the prewar bitterness between parties still remained, and the editor of one of the best papers in the state asserted: "Men who think that 'the war' knocked all of the old Whig spirit out of the Whigs are just . . . fatally mistaken."[12]

Throughout the Reconstruction period, therefore, there were efforts to reorganize the party. Again and again Whig leaders called on the Democrats to abandon their party and join other moderates in battling both Radical Republicans and radical secessionists.[13] A general "Consultation" was held in 1870 so that Whig leaders over the state could agree on policies. The action of this group, termed by hostile Democrats "the grandest fizzle of the age,"[14] reflects the difficulties in the way of a third party in the South. Finding too much resentment connected with all the old party names, these men decided that a union of conservatives should be formed, "composed of Whigs, Democrats [and] Republicans,"[15] but as a commentator noted, the new party was to be "upon a Whig basis."[16] No very tangible results were to come from such efforts to revive the Whig party. The appeal was, after all, to a limited class of conservative planters and businessmen, and popular feeling was too strong for most Southerners to repudiate Democracy.

Many Whigs had realized these difficulties from the beginning and had joined the Republicans. Within two years after readmission to

[9] Raymond (Miss.) *Hinds County Gazette,* October 12, 26, 1870.
[10] Columbus *Index,* quoted in ibid., November 27, 1872. See the letter of Albert G. Brown in Raymond *Hinds County Gazette,* April 10, 1872, and James B. Ranck, *Albert Gallatin Brown: Radical Southern Nationalist* (New York, 1937), pp. 252 ff.
[11] Raymond *Hinds County Gazette,* October 19, 1870.
[12] Ibid., October 5, 1870. The editor was Major George W. Harper, who had been very prominent before the war as a Whig, and whose paper was now one of the most influential in the state.
[13] See, for example, the Boonville *Recorder,* quoted in Raymond *Hinds County Gazette,* October 5, 1870.
[14] Vicksburg *Herald,* quoted in Raymond *Hinds County Gazette,* December 7, 1870.
[15] Raymond *Hinds County Gazette,* November 30, 1870.
[16] Ibid., October 26, 1870.

the Union they were joined by most of their party. Although any statistics for this difficult period must be regarded skeptically, it has been estimated that from 25 to 30 percent of the Mississippi white voters had by 1873 joined the Republican party,[17] and nearly all of these were former Whigs.[18] Such action is not hard to understand. The Whigs were wealthy men—the large planters and the railroad and industrial promoters—who naturally turned to the party which in the state as in the nation was dominated by business interests.

A glance at the leadership of the scalawag element in Mississippi confirms these generalizations. Most important of all was James Lusk Alcorn, elected first governor of the reconstructed state in 1869 and later chosen United States senator. One of the wealthiest plantation owners in the rich Mississippi delta, a large slaveholder, and a Whig opposed to secession, he had reluctantly gone with his state in 1861 and had served briefly in the Confederate army. After the war he was one of the first to admit that secession had been wrong, indeed, treasonable.[19] Now a Republican leader, his program was basically a simple one: "I propose," he declared, "to vote with . . . [the Negro]; to discuss political affairs with him; to sit, if necessary, in political counsel with him."[20] By recognizing the legal equality of the Negroes, Alcorn hoped to gain their political support for his own policies.[21]

Alcorn's legislative program shows plainly the direction in which the Whig element hoped to lead the Republican party. First of all, the Negroes had to be conciliated by the adoption of civil rights measures.[22] On economic questions the governor naturally favored the

[17] John R. Lynch, *The Facts of Reconstruction* (New York, 1913), p. 106. Lynch, a Negro, was speaker of the state house of representatives. For another, similar estimate, see Vernon L. Wharton, "The Negro in Mississippi, 1865–1890" (Ph.D. dissertation, University of North Carolina, 1939), p. 285, who believes that the Republican party "included at times from fifteen to twenty thousand of the seventy to eighty thousand white votes."

[18] W. H. Braden, "Reconstruction in Lee County," in *Mississippi Historical Society Publications* 10 (1909): 139; *Senate Miscellaneous Documents,* 44th Cong., 2d sess., no. 45, p. 746.

[19] Garner, *Reconstruction in Mississippi,* p. 180. For a biographical sketch of Alcorn, see Dunbar Rowland, ed., *Encyclopedia of Mississippi History,* 2 vols. (Madison, Wis., 1907), 1:62–71.

[20] Wharton, "The Negro in Mississippi," p. 258.

[21] "His plan," a close personal friend testified, was "to unite the old whigs . . . and through them control the negro." Frank A. Montgomery, *Reminiscences of a Mississippian in Peace and War* (Cincinnati, 1901), p. 275.

[22] Garner, *Reconstruction in Mississippi,* pp. 285–286.

planter class, urging the rebuilding of levees, reduction of land taxes, leasing of convicts to secure a steady labor supply,[23] and state aid in the reconstruction of railroads.[24] The powers of the state government were to be expanded in order to exercise close control over county finances. It was, of course, a program of class legislation, but it was not corrupt. The administration was both intelligent and honest, and it has not been found that any of Alcorn's followers misused their state offices for personal profit.[25] There is much to be said for their program of guaranteeing civil rights, improving schools, and expanding the judiciary.

The Alcorn-Whig program was not to be carried through to completion. It met with difficulties on all sides. The Democrats, of course, objected violently, partly from politics, partly from principle. It was believed that the economic policies of the Alcorn administration tended to discriminate against the predominantly Democratic hill regions in favor of the Whiggish delta bottoms. The rallying point of the Democrats was opposition to Alcorn's plan of granting the Negro legal equality. A prominent Mississippi newspaper, doubtless voicing the sentiments of its readers, felt that "Nigger voting, holding office and sitting in the jury box are all wrong, and against the sentiment of the country."[26] For recognizing Negro rights Alcorn became known as "an open and avowed enemy of his race."[27] It was asserted that "the name of Benedict Arnold ought to occupy a more exalted and honorable . . . position in the annals of american history than that of J. L. Alcorn."[28] A Democrat had rather be called a horse thief than a scalawag.[29]

Carpetbaggers were also bitter against Alcorn and the southern Republicans. One Northerner declared that the governor was "an old whig and in some of his appointment he has put in his style of whig d——m rebels . . . and . . . he is fixing up a party of his own (whig)

[23] Wharton, "The Negro in Mississippi," pp. 435–452, gives a study of the convict-leasing arrangements.
[24] Garner, *Reconstruction in Mississippi*, pp. 288–289.
[25] Ibid., pp. 322–323. Professor Garner noted that "The only large case of embezzlement among the state officers during the post-bellum period was that of the Democratic state treasurer in 1866. The amount of the shortage was $61,962."
[26] Columbus *Democrat*, quoted in Wharton, "The Negro in Mississippi," p. 334.
[27] McNeilly, "War and Reconstruction in Mississippi," in loc. cit., p. 424.
[28] Eldridge McArthur to James L. Alcorn, April 21, 1871, James L. Alcorn MSS. (Mississippi Department of Archives and History, Jackson).
[29] Vicksburg *Herald*, quoted in Raymond *Hinds County Gazette*, May 8, 1872.

and using the negro for a blind."[30] The basic trouble was that, though he might advocate legal equality and civil rights as a measure of expediency, the southern planter could not bring himself to accede to the Negro's demand for social equality.[31] Many of the carpetbaggers had come to the South with preconceived and doctrinaire ideas concerning race relations in their adopted section and felt that the Negro's rights were not secure. More, perhaps, were disgruntled when well paid offices were filled by men of southern birth. These factors, intensified by Alcorn's known dislike of Northerners,[32] caused an early break between the Whig and the carpetbag factions of the Republican party. When the governor failed to call in federal troops after a minor disturbance in 1871, a Radical Republican charged that he was trying to gain "power and favor from the democracy at the price of . . . the blood of his friends."[33] After two years of rule by Alcorn, another was convinced that "old line whigs are worse men to-day than any whipped (in the war) Democrats."[34]

The Negroes, too, were dissatisfied with the Alcorn regime. Increasingly conscious of the importance of their votes, they demanded a share of the offices proportional to their numerical strength. The freedmen cared little about the Whigs' economic policies, but they distrusted their former owners and, prompted by the carpetbag leaders, were inclined to demand social and civil equality.[35]

The opposition of any one of these elements would have been formidable, and the chances for men of Alcorn's views to succeed were from the start very slight. But—contrary to the version of the Democratic state historians—these three groups worked closely together to bring about Alcorn's defeat. As early as 1871 the Democrats approached the carpetbag group for a political alliance.[36] This alignment was strikingly revealed the following year when Democrats and Radical Republicans joined forces to prevent a Whig paper from

---

[30] Beatty to Shill, June 21, 1870, Alcorn MSS. This is a copy, in which the given names and initials of both men have been omitted, and it has not been possible to identify them further.

[31] Wharton, "The Negro in Mississippi," p. 319.

[32] House Reports, 42d Cong., 2d sess., no. 22, p. 450. Note, however, that Alcorn himself was born in the North.

[33] Garner, Reconstruction in Mississippi, p. 291, note 4.

[34] Jackson Pilot, quoted in Raymond Hinds County Gazette, August 23, 1871.

[35] Garner, Reconstruction in Mississippi, p. 293.

[36] Senate Reports, 44th Cong., 1st sess., no. 527, 1:21.

securing the lucrative state printing contract.[37] Hoping to break the governor's control of the colored vote, the Democrats encouraged the political aspirations of the Negroes,[38] while carpetbaggers were more successful in organizing the blacks into Union Leagues.

The real test of the Whig program occurred in 1873, when Alcorn —who had resigned to take a seat in the United States Senate, leaving a faithful disciple in his place at Jackson—decided to run again for governor. His opponent for the Republican nomination was Adelbert Ames, a carpetbagger born in Maine and a son-in-law of Benjamin F. Butler of Massachusetts. Ames—variously characterized by the Democrats as "Addle-pate" Ames or "onion headed" Ames[39]— was a man of real ability and had a sincere belief in his duty to protect Negro rights, which he felt Alcorn was neglecting.[40] When the carpetbagger secured the Republican nomination, Alcorn bolted and formed a new party of his own, composed almost entirely of former Whigs.[41] Though this group had the nominal endorsement of the Democrats,[42] many Democratic leaders voted for the carpetbagger rather than for the delta planter.[43] Ames was elected by a huge majority.[44] While conservative papers blamed Alcorn's defeat on the indifference of the Democrats, it might also be attributed to the growing realization by the Negro of his political power.

This election of 1873 marked the end of a period. Former Whigs had joined and then dominated the Republican party in Mississippi. They had sponsored a legislative program that would attract to their party sound and conservative men regardless of former political affiliation. Now, repudiated by the Negro and carpetbag sections of the Republican party and rejected by the more fanatical element of the Democrats, they were thoroughly defeated. They had no choice but to make their way slowly and reluctantly over to the Democratic camp.

[37] Raymond *Hinds County Gazette,* February 7, 21, 28, April 24, May 1, 1872.
[38] Charles Nordhoff, *The Cotton States in the Spring and Summer of 1875* (New York, 1876), p. 76.
[39] Hazelhurst *Mississippi Democrat,* September 1, 1875.
[40] Garner, *Reconstruction in Mississippi,* p. 290.
[41] McNeilly, "War and Reconstruction in Mississippi," in loc. cit., pp. 462–463.
[42] Lynch, *The Facts of Reconstruction,* p. 76.
[43] McNeilly, "War and Reconstruction in Mississippi," in loc. cit., p. 466. Among these was a future governor of the state, John M. Stone.
[44] *Appleton's American Annual Cyclopedia* [New York, 1862–1903] 13 (1873): 515. Ames received 74,307 votets; Alcorn, 52,904.

The exciting next two years are the best known portion of the state's Reconstruction story. The account of the final restoration of "home rule" in Mississippi has been told many times by historians attracted by the drama of the carpetbag debacle. It was a time when party feelings ran high and when race relations were at a critical point. Old residents of the state still recall vividly the tension and excitement of these years. Mississippi was torn between two hostile political camps, and there was no longer a place for middle-of-the-road, Whig policies.

Beginning in 1874 the Democrats made definite plans to carry the elections of the following year, by persuasion if possible, by force if necessary. This is the entire content of the Mississippi Plan of 1875.[45] Objecting on many grounds to the corruption and excesses of the Radicals, they made the drawing of a color-line the central theme of their campaign—the universal opposition of all white men to any Negro participation in politics.[46] In order to secure the goal of white supremacy—meaning, of course, a Democratic victory—it was necessary first to rally all Democrats to the party standard, then to persuade the scalawags to vote on the color-line, to harry carpetbaggers out of the state, and to frighten the Negroes from the polls.

At the same time the Republican party was becoming a well-oiled political machine. Under the shrewd carpetbag leadership the Negroes were herded into the notorious Union Leagues and voted in droves as their leaders dictated. Both state and federal patronage were used to bolster a weakening regime. To an increasing extent the Republican party stressed the necessity for social and civil equality for its black members. And to an increasing extent southern-born white leaders were discarded for carpetbaggers or Negroes.

In this crisis Mississippi Whigs had to choose between open support of color-line policies and a program which they firmly believed would lead to racial amalgamation. While to some it was Hobson's choice, there could never have been any doubt as to the course the majority would eventually take. As men of wealth and property they were indignant over extravagances of the carpetbag government, which were reflected in high taxes; they disliked the Northerners as

---

[45] Frederic Bancroft, *A Sketch of the Negro in Politics* . . . (New York, 1885), p. 61.
[46] A good statement of the color-line creed can be found in *House Reports,* 43rd Cong., 2d sess., no. 263, p. iii.

aliens and resented their control over the Negroes; they were alarmed
by the facility with which federal troops could be called in whenever
the Republicans seemed about to lose an election. But it was the
Negro that was the deciding factor. For the southern planter who
had never been able to accept ideas of racial equality, the present
political power and organization of the colored vote, accompanied
by Radical proscription of conservative white leaders, made opposition to the Republicans inescapable.

Under these pressures the former Whigs gradually drifted into an
alliance with their Democratic foes of previous years. Even former
Governor Alcorn participated in color-line meetings in his county,
and he publicly declared that he was not and really never had been
a "negro Republican."[47] On the few recalcitrants tremendous social
and economic pressure was exerted. Democratic papers carried con-
spicuously the names of white Republicans who must no longer be
spoken to on the street and whose attentions must be scorned by
"every true woman."[48] The scalawag who persisted in his obduracy
was publicly labeled "a beast in man's clothing" or "a traitor to his
country."[49] Those who failed to renounce their Republican affiliations
faced ostracism.[50] "No white man," a former Republican wrote, "can
live in the South in the future and act with any other than the
Democratic party."[51]

Heartened by Whig support, the Democrats waged a lively campaign. There were political demonstrations in every town: parades
two miles long,[52] fireworks and Confederate cannon,[53] floats and
transparencies of spectacular size,[54] barbecues, picnics, and inter-
minable speeches.[55] Half the villages in the state claimed the local
rally as "The Grandest Affair of the Campaign."[56] The more martial

[47] Wharton, "The Negro in Mississippi," p. 333; Peter J. Hamilton, *Reconstruction*, volume 16 of *The History of North America*, edited by Guy Carleton Lee (Philadel-phia, 1905), p. 549.
[48] Canton *Mail*, quoted in Wharton, "The Negro in Mississippi," p. 336.
[49] *Senate Miscellaneous Documents*, 44th Cong., 2d sess., no. 54, p. 648.
[50] Nordhoff, *The Cotton States*, p. 81.
[51] Quoted in Lynch, *The Facts of Reconstruction*, p. 122.
[52] Susan Dabney Smedes, *A Southern Planter* (London, 1889), pp. 229–230.
[53] Garner, *Reconstruction in Mississippi*, p. 374, note 2.
[54] Hazelhurst *Mississippi Democrat*, October 13, 1875.
[55] Ernest F. Puckett, "Reconstruction in Monroe County," in *Mississippi Historical Society Publications* 11 (1910): 145–146.
[56] Hazelhurst *Mississippi Democrat*, October 13, 1875.

elements, donning the red-shirt badge of southern manhood, formed armed rifle companies and drilled and marched in public. These were no secret Ku Kluxers; they wanted the Negro and his friends to know that the entire white population of Mississippi was against continuance of Republican rule.[57]

Most of the color-liners were convinced that efforts to win the colored votes would fail, and it was felt that the best policy was to keep the Negroes from the polls. Republican meetings were disturbed by red-shirt horsemen who remarked loudly that "maybe they might kill a buck that day."[58] When Confederate cannon were fired in the immediate vicinity of Negro rallies, the terrified freedmen believed the war had begun again.[59] There were countless tales of torchlight processions, of disrupted Republican rallies, of nocturnal raids, of whippings, and worse.[60] Whenever the Negroes tried to retaliate, there occurred a race riot. At least a dozen of these conflicts happened during the campaign, and in every case the result was the same. Trained bands of white men were able to defeat the badly led Negroes; dozen of blacks were killed, few if any whites injured.[61]

Every race riot brought two results. The whites were more solidly united than ever. Whig and Democrat, secessionist and unionist, and even Confederate and Federal joined hands against what they regarded as aggression from the carpetbag-Negro combination. And on the other hand, the Republican party was completely demoralized. The Negroes were terrified;[62] President Grant refused to send additional troops;[63] and Governor Ames, to prevent a race war, virtually

[57] For a thorough discussion of the rifle clubs, see Ross H. Moore, "Economic and Social Conditions during Reconstruction in Mississippi" (Ph.D. dissertation, Duke University, 1938).
[58] *Senate Reports,* 44th Cong., 1st sess., no. 527, 1:757.
[59] Ibid., 1:88–90.
[60] Among many examples, the following articles in the *Mississippi Historical Society Publications* may be cited: John U. Kyle, "Reconstruction in Panola County," 13 (1913): 71; Fred M. Witty, "Reconstruction in Carroll and Montgomery Counties," 10 (1909): 127; and Julia C. Brown, "Reconstruction in Yalobusha and Grenada Counties," 12 (1912): 252.
[61] The following articles in the *Mississippi Historical Society Publications* contain important accounts of race riots: Fred Z. Browne, "Reconstruction in Oktibbeha County," 13 (1913): 289–291; Robert Bowman, "Reconstruction in Yazoo County," 7 (1903): 127–219; Charles H. Brough, "The Clinton Riot," 6 (1902): 53–63. See also, Wharton, "The Negro in Mississippi," p. 350 ff.
[62] See the letters from various Negro leaders to Governor Ames, in *Senate Reports,* 44th Cong., 1st sess., no. 527, II, Doc. Ev., 89 ff.
[63] The President was reported to have said that "the whole public are tired out with

surrendered to the Democratic leaders.[64] The Republican regime in Mississippi was doomed.

The important elections of 1875 were ominously quiet.[65] As one observer put it, the Negroes were afraid to make any trouble and the whites did not need to.[66] Election frauds, in spite of a number of hair-raising tales,[67] seem not to have been unusually large. The result was a sweeping Democratic success. Virtually all the counties now passed under the control of color-line administrations. The whites gained heavy majorities in both houses of the legislature and elected all but one of the congressmen, while in the only general race the Democratic candidate for state treasurer had a lead of over thirty thousand votes.[68]

The sequel of the election may be noted very briefly. The Republican governor, Ames, and the lieutenant governor were impeached when the new legislature met. The former, although there was no real case against him, resigned, and the latter was convicted.[69] By 1876 "home rule" was officially restored, and Mississippi has ever since been a Democratic state.

The combination of force and intimidation known as the Mississippi Plan received much attention in other southern states, where Democratic leaders imitated the Mississippi tactics.[70] Much of the political history of the South in the decades after 1875 was centered about the idea that white supremacy could be maintained only by preventing the Negro from voting. This point of view is closely connected with the customary explanation of the success of the Mississippi Plan. It has been held by every student of Reconstruction since William A. Dunning that white supremacy in the South was secured through the intimidation of the Negro. "The real Mississippi plan," it is contended,

these annual autumnal outbreaks in the South." *Appleton's American Annual Cyclopedia* 15 (1875): 516.
[64] Frank Johnston, "The Conference of October 15th, 1875, between General George and Governor Ames," in *Mississippi Historical Society Publications* 6 (1902): 65–77.
[65] Garner, *Reconstruction in Mississippi*, p. 392.
[66] *Senate Reports*, 44th Cong., 1st sess., no. 527, 2:1200.
[67] Ibid., 1:496; Bowman, "Reconstruction in Yazoo County," in loc. cit., p. 130; Braden, "Reconstruction in Lee County," in loc. cit., p. 143; Witty, "Reconstruction in Carroll and Montgomery Counties," in loc. cit., p. 128; and many others.
[68] *Appleton's American Annual Cyclopedia* 15 (1875): 517.
[69] Garner, *Reconstruction in Mississippi*, pp. 401–410.
[70] Alfred B. Williams, *Hampton and His Red Shirts* (Charleston, 1935), especially pp. 21–35.

"was to play upon the easy credulity of the negroes and inspire them with terror so that they would . . . stay away from the polls."[71]

This explanation seems to be an over-simplification of the problem. The difficulties of making an adequate study of a Reconstruction election in the South have seldom been realized. First of all, it is impossible to secure accurate statistics of population, since the 1870 census is almost worthless, even as an estimate. In most cases the number of potential and registered voters cannot be discovered. The disfranchised Confederate element is another unknown. It cannot be determined with any degree of accuracy what proportion of the vote each race cast, and it is even more impossible to ascertain how many Negroes were herded to the polls by Democratic landlords or by Republican politicians. Finally, the amount of actual election fraud, always considerable during the period, adds another indeterminable variable. The whole situation is one of the utmost complexity, and any sweeping generalizations must be received with caution.

But even in the face of these difficulties it can be determined that the conventional explanation of the success of the Mississippi Plan is not satisfactory. If the Negroes were kept from voting, there should have been fewer Republican ballots cast than in former years. This is not the case.[72] Actually the Republicans were nearly as strong as in previous elections, and if it is admitted that most whites had by 1875 left the Republican fold, the election returns show that in reality *more* Negroes voted than ever before.

It seems safe to conclude that in the Mississippi election of 1875 the Negroes as a general rule voted the Republican ticket. But there are exceptions even to this assertion. In certain counties anti-Ames Negro Republicans joined the Democrats to fight the administration's candidates, and "fusion" tickets were elected. In some five delta counties, moreover, the Democratic vote was so large as to justify the belief that wealthy landowners "voted" their colored tenants for the Democratic party.[73]

[71] Rhodes, *History of the United States,* 7:134. This is the view of all the general studies of the Reconstruction period, as well as of the more specialized studies, such as Garner, Moore, Wharton, and McNeilly, cited above.

[72] The total Republican vote was only about 3,000 less than it had been in 1873, the year of the Ames landslide. *Senate Reports,* 44th Cong., 1st sess., no. 527, II, Doc. Ev., 144–145.

[73] These were Grenada, Hinds, Holmes, Tallahatchie, and Warren counties, all of which are partly in the Delta, and in all of which the Negroes were a heavy majority

With the white population, the picture is somewhat clearer. To the old Democratic nucleus there were now added many recruits.[74] Southern white men who since the war had felt that the political situation was hopeless[75] now saw a chance for their principles to triumph and returned to support their party. But the greatest accession of Democratic strength came from the thousands of so-called scalawags—mostly former Whigs—who now denounced the Republican party and voted on the color-line.[76]

It appears, therefore, that a number of misconceptions concerning the course of Reconstruction need revision. The southern political scene in this postwar period was never simple. In Mississippi the importance of the former Whigs has generally been neglected. Toward the beginning of Reconstruction most of these joined the Republican party. Their moderate program of gradual adjustment to the realities of Reconstruction was defeated by a combination of extremists from all parties. By 1875 these Whigs, disgusted by Radical excesses and attracted by color-line principles, had gradually changed political allegiance and joined the Democratic party. Not until this shift was completed did the Democrats win an election. The triumph of the Democratic color-line policies, known as the Mississippi Plan of 1875, would seem to be due to the successful union of all southern whites into one party rather than to the intimidation of the Negro.

of the population. On "fusion," see John S. McNeilly, "Climax and Collapse of Reconstruction in Mississippi, 1874–1896," in *Mississippi Historical Society Publications* 12 (1912): 381 ff.

[74] In 1873 the Democratic candidate for state treasurer—also the Alcorn candidate—had received but 47,486 votes. In 1875 the color-line candidate obtained 98,715 votes. *Senate Reports,* 44th Cong., 1st sess., no. 527, II, Doc. Ev., 144–145.

[75] Edward Mayes, *The Life, Times, and Speeches of Lucius Q. C. Lamar* (Nashville, 1896), pp. 170–172.

[76] "The naked truth is, less than a baker's dozen of the [former] . . . Republican leaders . . . were supporters of Governor Ames in . . . 1875." Garner, *Reconstruction in Mississippi,* p. 398.

Allen W. Trelease
WHO WERE THE SCALAWAGS?

David Donald's investigation of the link between scalawaggery and old-line Whiggery in Mississippi led other historians to emphasize the persistence of Whiggery in Southern politics and the role of Southern Whigs in the eventual decision of the Hayes administration to withdraw the remainder of federal troops from the South in 1877. Using quantitative methods of analysis for Southern counties that contained the larger proportions of Republican voters, Allen Trelease raises some pertinent questions about interpretations that identify old-line Whigs with scalawags in the voting patterns of Mississippi and other Southern states during the Reconstruction years.

In the demonology of Reconstruction no reputation is blacker than that of the native white Republican. The illiterate and poverty-stricken Negro was often an object of compassion, and the carpetbagger could be partially excused as an outlander with no ties of kinship or sentiment in the land he plundered. But native white Republicans were traitors to race and section alike, and thus deserving of the deepest contempt. The term "scalawag," by which they were designated, is said to have come from Scalloway, "a district in the Shetland Islands where small, runty cattle and horses were bred." Later it became a synonym for scamp, loafer, or rascal, whence it found its way into the lexicon of Reconstruction politics. In this context some people would confine the term in all its impurity to actual officeholders or office seekers. The *Dictionary of Americanisms,* however, defines scalawag more broadly as "a Southerner who supported the Congressional plan of reconstruction."[1] It includes, therefore, white Republican voters, who are the real subject of this article.

Like so much of the conventional view of Reconstruction, the caricature of the scalawag as a traitor to race and section gained

From Allen W. Trelease, "Who Were the Scalawags?" *Journal of Southern History* 29 (November 1963): 445–468. Copyright 1963 by the Southern Historical Association. Reprinted by permission of the Managing Editor.

[1] John Hope Franklin, *Reconstruction After the Civil War* (Chicago, 1961), p. 98; E. Merton Coulter, *The South During Reconstruction* (Baton Rouge, 1947), p. 125; Mitford M. Mathews, ed., *A Dictionary of Americanisms,* 2 vols. (Chicago, 1951), 2:1,465.

more and more currency with the lapse of time, as the original receded from sight. What began as a political canard was carried over into canon within a generation by historians and the general public North and South, who came to accept the Democratic opposition's view of Reconstruction as historical truth. Many historians, like the Southern Conservatives of the period, made little or no effort to explain the alleged treason of the scalawags beyond assigning them such character deficiencies as disloyalty, cowardice, greed, or lust for power.[2] Others identified them with wartime Unionists who had opposed secession and cooperated unwillingly if at all with the Southern war effort.[3] Seldom until recently were the white Republicans credited with worthy motives, and then it was usually in the course of impugning their judgment. Rare indeed was the scholar who would agree with W. E. B. Du Bois's characterization of them as "that part of the white South who saw a vision of democracy across racial lines."[4] Commonly the only good word to be said of the whole lot was that a better element existed among them which went over to the Conservative camp at an early date.

Until the 1940s, white Republicans were usually identified with the lower or poorer elements of Southern society, if they were identified at all. An exception was Walter Lynwood Fleming, who referred to them in one of his later writings as possessing "whatever claims the [Southern Republican] party had to respectability, education, political experience, and property." By the same token, Fleming was one of the few until recently who paid any attention to their political antecedents, listing them as "former Whigs" as well as "former Unionists . . . Confederate deserters, and a few unscrupulous politicians."[5]

[2] Francis B. Simkins and Robert H. Woody, *South Carolina During Reconstruction* (Chapel Hill, 1932), p. 74; Ellis P. Oberholtzer, *A History of the United States Since the Civil War*, 5 vols. (New York, 1917–1937), 2:24; James G. Randall, *The Civil War and Reconstruction* (Boston, 1937), p. 847. For an example of contemporary invective, only slightly toned down by later historians, see Herbert Barnes, "The Scalawag," *Southern Magazine* 15 (September 1874): 302–307.

[3] William A. Dunning, *Reconstruction, Political and Economic, 1865–1877* (New York, 1907), p. 116; Walter Lynwood Fleming, *The Sequel of Appomattox* (New Haven, 1919), p. 222; William W. Davis, *The Civil War and Reconstruction in Florida* (New York, 1913), p. 483.

[4] James Ford Rhodes, *History of the United States from the Compromise of 1850*, 9 vols. (New York, 1893–1919), 6:91; W. E. Burghardt Du Bois, *Black Reconstruction* (New York, 1935), p. 350.

[5] Fleming, *Sequel of Appomattox*, p. 222. The near-contemporary estimates of North Carolina carpetbagger Albion Tourgée are interesting in this connection: "Those

Reconstruction historiography has itself been reconstructed since 1940. In the process the scalawag has been reclassified to a degree, if not fully rehabilitated. Much credit for this belongs to David Donald, whose 1944 article in this journal, "The Scalawag in Mississippi Reconstruction," represented one of the freshest breezes to sweep this landscape in many years. In Donald's view the Mississippi scalawags were predominantly "old-line" Whigs who had opposed the Democrats before the war, opposed secession at its commencement, and, whatever their attitude in wartime, were now eager to resume battle with the state-rights and (supposedly) egalitarian Democracy. As the cream of the old planter-business aristocracy, they accepted Negro suffrage in the hope of controlling the votes of their former slaves for their own purposes.[6] More recently, in his revision of James G. Randall's book, *The Civil War and Reconstruction,* Donald extends this interpretation to most of the South. The major exceptions, he says, were North Carolina and Alabama, where the scalawags were chiefly hill-country farmers who had opposed both the prewar plantation system and the war itself.[7]

By implication at least, Donald's interpretation gains support from the recent investigations by Thomas B. Alexander of "persistent Whiggery" in the postwar South. In the elections of 1865, held under Presidential auspices, former Whigs very nearly swept the field according to Alexander's findings. By 1869, he believes, the Southern Whigs fell into four groups. A small number of old "unconditional Unionists" were wholeheartedly in the Radical camp from the beginning of congressional Reconstruction. A larger number, answering Donald's description, were also in the Republican party, advocating universal suffrage and universal amnesty in the hope of leading the

Union men who really maintained their integrity and devotion to the Federal Union through the war, and embraced the republican view at its close, were . . . mostly of that class who are neither rich nor poor, who were land-owners, but not slaveowners." A few pages later, however, he categorized 24 percent of the white Republicans as illiterate and 55 or 60 percent as landless day laborers or sharecroppers. *A Fool's Errand . . .* [together with] *The Invisible Empire* (New York, 1880), pp. 132, 159.
6 David Donald, "The Scalawag in Mississippi Reconstruction," *Journal of Southern History* 10 (November 1944): 447–460. See also C. Vann Woodward, *Reunion and Reaction* (Boston, 1951), pp. 42–43; Bernard A. Weisberger, "The Dark and Bloody Ground of Reconstruction Historiography," *Journal of Southern History* 25 (November 1959): 431; T. Harry Williams, "An Analysis of Some Reconstruction Attitudes," ibid., 12 (November 1946): 475–476, 481.
7 *The Civil War and Reconstruction*, 2d ed. (Boston, 1961), pp. 627–628.

movement into more conservative channels. A third group, which Alexander believes to be the largest by 1869 or 1870 and destined to grow larger still after 1872, had affiliated with the Democrats or Conservatives in opposition to Radical Reconstruction. The fourth group, ever shrinking in size, consisted of die-hard Whigs who refused to join either existing party and worked for a rebirth of the old party of Henry Clay.[8]

Despite the appeal of Donald's ex-Whig interpretation, it has gained only partial acceptance. Speaking also of Mississippi, Vernon L. Wharton asserts that the white Republicans at first "were largely a poverty-stricken element who had been Unionists during the war." Then, more in keeping with Donald, he continues: "There was also an element of planters and businessmen which increased rapidly in numbers until 1874. Many of these men had been Whigs before the war. . . ." John Hope Franklin says in his recent survey of the period that the white Republicans were basically Unionists who had opposed secession and the war. Most of these people, he implies, were distinctly not of the planter class and had long resented its domination. He says nothing of prewar political affiliation.[9]

There is no agreement on the point of wartime Unionism either. Many of Donald's ex-Whig Republicans had been officers in the Confederate army, and E. Merton Coulter goes further yet in declaring that many prominent Southern Radicals had been outstanding secessionists. Coulter is more loath than the others to abandon the old Conservative fortifications; to him the scalawags were "those who had a grievance against the ante-bellum ruling class; who felt social inferiority; who disliked the rigors of war; who opposed conscription, impressment, and the suspension of the writ of habeas corpus during the war; in fact, almost 'every one that was in distress, and every one that was in debt, and every one that was discontented'. . . ."[10]

Until recently the only common ground among treatments of the scalawag was a common aversion to him, and now we have lost even that. Moreover, such characterizations as have been made were

[8] "Persistent Whiggery in the Confederate South, 1860–1877," *Journal of Southern History* 27 (August 1961): 311, 319–320.
[9] Vernon L. Wharton, *The Negro in Mississippi, 1865–1890* (Chapel Hill, 1947), p. 157; Franklin, *Reconstruction After the Civil War*, pp. 98–99.
[10] *South During Reconstruction*, p. 124.

frequently given in the process of moving on to other, more congenial topics. Apart from a few leaders like James L. Alcorn in Mississippi and Parson Brownlow in Tennessee, the native Republicans have received next to no attention. Thus despite their acknowledged importance in the Radical movement, they remain an unknown quantity.

A wider acquaintance can be gotten by several means. That which follows is primarily statistical. It attempts in the first place to isolate the bulk of the native white Republicans geographically through a comparison of election returns and census data for each Southern county for which election returns were available. Using this information, it tries next to supply a basis for closer study and surer generalization than has been possible heretofore concerning their economic and social conditions, their prior political affiliations, and their reasons for supporting the Radical party.

Several assumptions are made at the outset which, in the nature of things, will be more controversial than the arithmetic proceeding from them. The first is that Negroes during the period of Radical ascendancy cast their votes overwhelmingly for Republican candidates. Although there are exceptions, the assumption is borne out by an examination of election returns from the black belt counties and by a comparison of the Republican percentage of the vote with the percentage of Negroes in the population. (See Tables 1 and 2.) There are very few counties in which the proportion of Republican votes to the total number cast was significantly lower than the proportion of Negroes to the total population, and in some of these cases the result clearly was produced by Negro abstention, voluntary or enforced, rather than by their voting the Democratic ticket.

A second assumption hardly requires verification: despite the influential role of the Northern carpetbag element in shaping the course of Southern Reconstruction, the Northerners were so few in number in any locality that they cannot materially affect a statistical computation based on population and election totals.

The third assumption—the working principle on which this analysis mainly rests—follows from the first two: wherever the percentage of Republican votes significantly exceeds the percentage of Negro population, and where the total voter turnout in a fair election is near normal, we may expect to find native white Republicans.

Students of the period will recognize several methodological hurdles to be cleared in making a study of this nature. Many Reconstruction elections were carried or miscarried by fraud, violence, or intimidation; disfranchisement of ex-Confederates was a factor in some elections; and the census of 1870, which would normally be used in figuring the proportion of Negroes, was notoriously inaccurate in that respect. None of these obstacles can be evaded or explained away altogether; yet they are less critical on closer inspection than they at first appear.

It is true that most election returns of the time are not ideal bases for statistical analysis. In this study the Presidential election of 1872 was singled out for special attention, other contests being used only to ascertain the political complexion of each county during the period as a whole. For this latter purpose, from four to six (normally, five) elections were chosen in each of the ex-Confederate states, nearly all of them involving statewide contests for either the Presidency or high state office. They include the Presidential elections of 1868, 1872, and 1876, as well as intervening state contests, chiefly in 1870 and 1874. (For the states of Mississippi, Virginia, Texas, and Tennessee, the election of 1868 was not used; the first three had not yet been readmitted, and in Tennessee there was such wholesale proscription of ex-Confederates as to render the returns nearly valueless in determining actual opinion.)[11]

Of them all, the election of 1872 was the natural choice for a closer analysis in determining the location of white Republican voters. By comparison with the other Presidential elections of 1868 and 1876, it was conducted with relative fairness in nearly every state. Disfranchisement of ex-Confederates was largely over by that time and the wholesale proscription of Negroes was still in the future, except in Georgia.[12] In this election President Grant won a second

[11] Presidential election data are taken from W. Dean Burnham, *Presidential Ballots, 1836–1892* (Baltimore, 1955); returns from other elections are taken from *The Tribune Almanac and Political Register, 1870–1875* (New York, 1870–1875).
[12] The suffrage restrictions placed on ex-Confederates by the congressional Reconstruction acts were gradually superseded by state action as each state was readmitted to the Union. Disabilities contained in the Fourteenth Amendment applied to officeholding rather than voting, and nearly all of these were lifted by congressional action in 1872 and earlier. J. G. de Roulhac Hamilton, "The Removal of Legal and Political Disabilities, 1868–1898," *South Atlantic Quarterly* 2 (October 1903): 346–358, and 3 (January 1904): 39–51. The radical state constitutions of 1868, as

term by defeating the Democratic-Liberal Republican coalition headed by Horace Greeley. Although Greeley, the old abolitionist crusader, failed perceptibly to warm the hearts of Southern Conservatives, this contest had the advantage of presenting to all Southern voters the Reconstruction policies of the Grant administration in about as clear-cut a fashion as any policy is apt to be presented in an American election. It fell during the period of Radical ascendancy in most states and found two-party politics in as active and healthy a condition as the South has known them since before the Civil War. The Liberal Republican movement had comparatively little impact in the South, where 1872 constituted the high watermark of postwar Republicanism.

Population figures for 1872 normally would have been drawn from the preceding census, then only two years old. But in view of the inadequacy of the 1870 census, especially in its underenumeration of Southern Negroes,[13] that of 1880 was chosen as being more accurate on the whole.[14] The difference in time was not so critical as it might appear on the surface, since census data were used primarily to determine the proportion of Negroes rather than total population.

finally adopted, provided for universal manhood suffrage in Virginia, North Carolina, Georgia, Florida, and Mississippi. In 1870 this was secured in Louisiana by constitutional amendment and in Tennessee by the adoption of a new constitution. Disfranchisement in South Carolina and Texas was very slight to begin with, and apparently was negligible by 1872. In Alabama the originally heavy disqualifications were lifted in part by legislative action in 1868; Fleming says that "several thousand" were still disfranchised after 1870, but this did not prevent the state from showing a voter turnout of 65 percent in 1872, the largest in the South. Only Arkansas, therefore, applied significant restrictions upon white voters by 1872, the number of persons affected being very hard to estimate. See William A. Dunning, *Essays on the Civil War and Reconstruction* (New York, 1931), pp. 196–198; Coulter, *South During Reconstruction*, pp. 136, 349; Charles W. Ramsdell, *Reconstruction in Texas* (New York, 1910), pp. 252–255; William A. Russ, Jr., "Disfranchisement in Louisiana (1862–1870)," *Louisiana Historical Quarterly* 18 (July 1935): 579–580, and "Radical Disfranchisement in South Carolina (1867–1868)," *Susquehanna University Studies* 1 (1939): 155; Walter Lynwood Fleming, *Civil War and Reconstruction in Alabama* (New York, 1905), pp. 749, 752.

Louisiana is of comparatively little significance in the present study. Frauds were so extensive there in 1872 that it is impossible to know the true vote in many parishes; for this reason only those parish totals are included on which the two parties agreed—a minority of the whole. For the election of 1872 in Georgia, see note 18 below.

[13] Francis A. Walker, "Statistics of the Colored Race in the United States," American Statistical Association, *Publications* 2 (1890): 95–99, 106.

[14] *Tenth Census,* Vol. I, *Statistics of the Population of the United States . . .* (Washington, 1883).

There is no evidence to suggest that this ratio changed significantly in many places between 1872 and 1880.[15]

Changes in county boundaries occurring between 1872 and 1880 create another complication, but only in Texas was the number of changes significant. In most cases they had little effect on the proportion of Negro population in the counties so altered, if we are to judge by similar changes between 1880 and 1890. Such counties, therefore, were not omitted from the computation.

The natural first step in determining political patterns and isolating the white Republicans is to look at the electoral majority of each county in the light of its racial composition. When all Southern counties making returns in 1872 are arranged according to their proportion of Negro population, with black belt counties like Issaquena in Mississippi and Beaufort in South Carolina at the top and white counties like those of the Appalachian highlands at the bottom, several predictable but nonetheless striking facts emerge. The predominantly Negro counties were overwhelmingly Republican in 1872 and most of them remained in that column through 1876. By the same token, the white counties tended to vote Democratic during these same years, although there were frequent exceptions. In 1872 all the 27 counties where Negroes constituted 80 percent or more of the population were Republican; those 70–79 percent Negro were Republican by 44 to 4; the proportion falls gradually through those counties having 20–29 percent of their population Negro, only 17 percent of which voted Republican; then the proportion voting Republican rises to 26 percent in each of the last two classes. This last phenomenon, in counties where less than a fifth of the population was Negro, can be explained only by the presence of substantial numbers of white Republicans.

The same pattern holds true of these counties in a majority of the elections chosen between 1868 and 1876. In these elections the

---

[15] The appropriate data are not readily available prior to 1880, but in only 28 of the 950-odd counties in the ex-Confederate states did the proportion of Negroes to total population vary by 10 percent or more in 1880 from the figures for 1890. In only five counties was the variance more than 15 percent. U. S. Bureau of the Census, *Negro Population, 1790–1915* (Washington, 1918), pp. 776–797. Even in Texas, despite a rapid increase in total population during this period, the proportion of Negroes county by county remained nearly the same.

number of counties in the Republican column is somewhat less in each Negro population class, but the two sets of figures, if reduced to lines on a graph, run nearly parallel. The greatest spread—that is, the greatest Republican attrition for the period as a whole, compared with the high of 1872—appears in those counties having between 30 percent and 59 percent Negroes. Here, presumably, Negro disfranchisement was most feasible and most effective by 1876 in creating Democratic majorities, and here, too, a relatively slight shift in white sentiment could more easily transform Democratic minorities into majorities. Although these figures, for both 1872 and the other election years, do not indicate the numbers of individual voters involved, they suggest that the freedmen were overwhelmingly Republican in sentiment, that most whites voted Democratic, and that the white Republican minority was largely concentrated in counties with the smallest Negro populations. Further evidence on these points can be gotten by comparing the Republican and Negro percentages in 1872 in each county.

A standard criticism of the American electoral process is that so few eligible voters bother to participate. The situation was generally worse a century ago. Across the country only half of the adult males (according to the 1880 census) cast votes for President in 1872, but unlike today the South exactly equaled the national average. Alabama led the former Confederacy with a turnout of 65 percent, while Arkansas and Georgia brought up the rear with 43 percent.[16] The South's relatively favorable position was owing in large measure to an active two-party system and Negro suffrage.[17]

[16] Texas registered only 30 percent, but its large population increase in this period makes the 1880 totals there too high to be applied meaningfully in 1872. As noted above, Arkansas had disfranchised certain classes of ex-Confederates, which may help to account for her poor showing, but a large population growth is probably at least as responsible. Georgia is accounted for, at least in part, by Negro disfranchisement.

[17] In fact, the voter turnout corresponded significantly to the proportion of Negro population, ranging from 65 percent in the black belts down to 32 percent where Negroes were less than a tenth of the whole. Viewed from another perspective, voter participation exceeded the sectional average in those counties where the percentage of Republican votes to the total number cast roughly equaled the proportion of Negro population—where, in other words, there was apparently a fairly clear division between Negro Republicans and white Democrats. The average turnout fell where the Republican percentage was materially less than that of Negroes, indicating that freedmen were being disfranchised. And in those counties presumably containing

In so far as white Democrats failed to vote, their action would raise artificially the percentage of Republican voters in a given county. And since the computations which follow are based on a comparison of the Republican percentages with Negro population ratios, it could lead to an exaggeration of white Republican strength. Nonvoting among Negroes would of course create the opposite effect. For this reason abstention involving one race more than the other is a matter of some concern. The available figures on turnout of eligible voters between 1868 and 1880 would indicate that abstention was a recognizable factor in 1872 in South Carolina, North Carolina, and Georgia. In all three states fewer persons voted than in 1868, and the number of voters rose sharply again in 1876. White persons were primarily involved in the Carolinas; only in Georgia is there evidence of non-voting on a large scale among Negroes.[18]

With so many pitfalls and incalculables, it is wise to concede a wide margin for error and look for white Republicans in quantity only in those counties where the Republican percentage exceeded the percentage of Negroes by at least twenty. (Tables 1 and 2 both show horizontally the relationship between these two proportions, giving the number of counties in each category. Table 1 is arranged vertically by states, and Table 2 according to density of Negro population.) In about half of the Southern counties for which we have 1872 election results (411 out of 843), these two percentages were within ten points of one another. Probably these figures are more than coincidental, and represent a substantial division between white Democrats and Negro Republicans. These counties were to be found in every region of the South, in areas that were preponderantly white as well as in the black belts. As a matter of fact, about two-thirds of the black belt counties fell in this category, as did a majority of all counties which were more than 40 percent Negro in composition.

most of the white Republicans—where the Republican percentage was materially greater than the Negro—voter participation was higher, but still below the sectional average. This last group of counties was predominantly white in population, and corresponded in this regard to the white counties as a whole.
[18] The historians of Reconstruction in North and South Carolina mention apathy among Democrats in both states in 1872. Simkins and Woody, *South Carolina During Reconstruction,* pp. 467–468; J. G. de Roulhac Hamilton, *Reconstruction in North Carolina* (New York, 1914), pp. 591–592. Negro disfranchisement in Georgia in 1872 is referred to in C. Mildred Thompson, *Reconstruction in Georgia* (New York, 1915), p. 275, and Jack B. Scroggs, "Southern Reconstruction: A Radical View," *Journal of Southern History* 24 (November 1958): 424–425.

TABLE 1

Republican percentage of vote in Southern counties in 1872 compared with percentage of Negroes in the population—by states (figures in line with states represent number of counties)

	Exceeds Negro percentage by:						Diff. less than 5%	Less than Negro percentage by:						Totals
	50 or more	40–49	30–39	20–29	10–19	5–9		5–9	10–19	20–29	30–39	40–49	50 or more	
Ala.	1	3	3	6	7	7	22	6	6	3	1			65
Ark.	9	4	4	9	11	8	9	4	1	1				60
Fla.			2	2	7	5	13	6	2		1			38
Ga.	4	4	4	5	12	12	35	9	16	19	6	5	5	136
La.*						4	7	1	1	1				14
Miss.				1	13	12	38	3	4					71
N. C.	5	11	10	20	19	14	12	1						92
S. C.			3	6	16	4	2	1						32
Tenn.	20	12	7	8	12	9	16	5	2					91
Tex.	6	3	6	7	34	25	46	5	2			1		135
Va.**		2	2	9	25	17	45	8		1				109
Totals:	45	39	41	73	156	117	245	49	34	25	8	6	5	843

354   411   78

* Incomplete

** Includes independent cities which voted separately

TABLE 2

Republican percentage of vote in Southern counties in 1872 compared with percentage of Negroes in the population—by density of Negro population (figures in line with percentage represent number of counties)

% Negro 1880	Exceeds Negro percentage by:						Diff. less than 5%	Less than Negro percentage by:						Totals
	50 or more	40–49	30–39	20–29	10–19	5–9		5–9	10–19	20–29	30–39	40–49	50 or more	
90+							2							2
80–89						8	8	1	1	2			2	20
70–79			1		1	7	26	2	4	5			3	47
60–69			1	2	14	12	32	8	7	4	1	3		87
50–59			1	3	12	14	54	12	6	5	3	3		110
40–49			2	4	18	20	36	5	3	2	1			93
30–39			7	14	31	20	25	9	4	3	3			111
20–29	2	3	11	13	31	13	20	9	6	4				108
10–19	12	15	9	13	21	16	16	1	3					108
5–9	16	9	9	16	16	4	7	2						79
0–4	15	12		8	12	3	19							78
Totals:	45	39	41	73	156	117	245	49	34	25	8	6	5	843

(Sub‑totals shown by brackets: 354 · 411 · 78)

Below that point, the smaller the proportion of Negroes, the more likelihood there was of finding white Republicans.

In less than 10 percent of the counties (78, of which two-thirds were in Georgia) the Republican percentage was materially below that of Negroes, indicating that substantial numbers of freedmen either voted Democratic or did not vote at all. That the latter was common is shown by a relatively low voter turnout in these counties, especially in those where the Republican and Negro proportional differences were greatest. Columbia County, Georgia, for example, with a population 71 percent Negro, cast but 6 percent of its vote for Grant and only 14 percent of its adult males voted at all. Counties with a similar population distribution in other states commonly showed a voter turnout of 65 percent and a Republican majority of about 70 percent.

In the remaining counties (354 out of 843, or 42 percent of the whole) the Republican percentage exceeded that of Negroes by at least ten. It is here that we must look for the great majority of white Republicans. In almost half (156) of these counties the Republican percentage was larger by only 10 to 19 points; in the rest it ranged up to a differential of more than 50. The presence of white Republicans by no means insured Republican victories in these counties; in fact a slight majority (179 to 173) went Democratic in 1872 and even more voted that way in a majority of other elections of the time. (See Table 3.) In most of those which went Republican, Negro voters contributed significantly to the victory and often the Negro Republicans outnumbered the white. As a general rule, however, most of the white Republican votes were cast in counties where the Negro population was slight. More than nine-tenths of the counties in which white Republicanism is identifiable had white majorities, and over half were at least 80 percent white in composition. (See the left-hand columns of Table 2.) In only 45, or about 5 percent of all Southern counties, did the Republican percentage outweigh the proportion of Negroes by 50 or more, indicating an absolute majority of white Republicans among the electorate.[19]

[19] These counties, by states, are as follows: *Alabama:* Winston; *Arkansas:* Crawford, Franklin, Newton, Perry, Pike, Pope, Sarber (now Logan), Sebastian, Searcy; *Georgia:* Charlton, Fannin, Gilmer, Pickens; *North Carolina:* Ashe, Cherokee, Mitchell, Polk, Wilkes; *Tennessee:* Anderson, Blount, Campbell, Carter, Claiborne, Cocke, Cumberland, Fentress, Hancock, James (now part of Hamilton), Jefferson, Johnson, Loudon,

Geographically, the counties containing the largest proportions of white Republicans are chiefly concentrated in the mountain regions of East Tennessee, western North Carolina, and northwest Arkansas. (See Map.) Those with smaller proportions are scattered more widely, with every state except Louisiana represented by at least nine counties in which the Republican percentage outweighed that of Negroes by 10–29 points. Texas and, deceptively, South Carolina are the only states besides the three mentioned above in which the statewide differential was more than ten.[20] In Texas the greatest number of white Republicans was found along the Rio Grande River and in the central part of the state. Both areas were more or less frontier regions, the former containing a large Mexican and the latter a large German element in its population. Elsewhere hilly, remote, and less prosperous areas were most prominent, such as the northern parts of Alabama and Georgia.[21] Fully half of Arkansas is represented, nearly all of it lying above a diagonal line drawn between the northeast and southwest corners of the state. By contrast, the areas most noticeable by their lack of white Republicans are east Texas, Louisiana (in so far as we have reliable election records), the bulk of Mississippi, Florida, Georgia, and Virginia, and the southern half of Alabama.

In no state, taken as a whole, were white Republicans even close to a majority of all white voters in 1872. Any estimate of their total numbers is hazardous in the extreme because it must rest on so many variables. In terms of votes cast, however, a figure in the neighborhood of 150,000 might be near the mark. Almost half of this number were found in the two states of Tennessee and North Carolina,

Marion, Morgan, Roane, Scott, Sevier, Union, Washington; *Texas:* Kendall, Kinney, Medina, Presidio, Starr, Zapata.

[20] Louisiana, for the reason given above, is represented very incompletely in all calculations. As suggested earlier, South Carolina probably appears here primarily as a result of white abstention from voting. There were very few white Republicans in the state, according to the witnesses before the congressional Ku Klux committee who were asked about this subject; here too most of them were apparently concentrated in the up-country, in such counties as Spartanburg and York. See *Testimony Taken by the Joint Select Committee to Inquire into the Condition of Affairs in the Late Insurrectionary States,* Senate Reports, 42d Cong., 2d sess., no. 41: *South Carolina,* 5, 56, 196, 208, 247, 738. North Carolina, where abstention was also a factor, would almost certainly have appeared in the list anyway.

[21] The presence of Republicanism in north Georgia is substantiated in Judson C. Ward, "The Republican Party in Bourbon Georgia, 1872–1890," *Journal of Southern History* 9 (May 1943): 197–198.

TABLE 3
Political Behavior, 1836–1876, of Counties Containing White Republicans

Rep. vote % in 1872 exceeds Negro pop. % by:	Total Counties	1836–1852* (Majority of Pres. elections)		1860				1872		1868–1876 (Majority of Pres. elections)	
		Whig	Dem.	Democrat (Breckinridge)	Democrat (Douglas)	Const. Union (Bell)	Union Majority**	Rep.	Dem.	Rep.	Dem.
50 or more	45	15	16	20	0	16	18	45	0	33	10
40–49	39	12	16	21	0	14	18	28	10	12	27
30–39	41	10	16	22	0	10	14	15	26	3	37
20–29	73	18	33	35	1	22	24	29	44	10	61
10–19	156	22	85	98	2	26	35	56	99	33	120
Totals:	354	77	166	196	3	88	109	173	179	91	255

* Omits South Carolina
** Combined popular majority for Bell and Douglas

where they may have constituted a third of all white voters. Arkansas, Texas, and Virginia, in that order, accounted for most of the remainder. Throughout the South, white Republicans cast perhaps 10 percent of all the votes recorded in 1872, about 20 percent of those cast by white men, and about 20 percent of those cast by Republicans.[22]

Few as they were, these voters provided the margin of victory in many counties. The election of 1872 found 384 Southern counties in the Republican column, compared with only 248 during a majority of the elections sampled from 1868 through 1876. Most of the Republican attrition in these other contests occurred in predominantly white counties or those of nearly equal racial distribution, rather than in the black belts. While 173 counties with appreciable numbers of white Republicans cast Republican majorities in 1872, only 71 did so in 1876 and only 91 in a majority of the sampled elections. (See Table 3.) On the other hand, counties in which Negroes formed 70 percent or more of the population (and in which, accordingly, there were few white Republicans) showed little change in voting behavior: these counties went Republican in 1872 by a margin of 71 to 4 and remained in that column during most of the sampled elections by a margin of 66 to 7.[23] Although Negro disfranchisement was a factor by 1876 in creating some of these shifts, the white Republican minority

[22] These are very rough guesses, subject to considerable modification. However, they are so much at variance with the estimate made (many years later) by John R. Lynch, the Mississippi Negro congressman, which both Donald and Wharton have cited approvingly, that the disagreement should be noted. After 1872, Lynch wrote, accessions of white aristocrats to the Republican party provided the Negro with a more congenial leadership than theretofore, and by 1875 about 25–30 percent of the Southern whites were affiliated with it. These, he said, were "among the best and most substantial men of that section." *The Facts of Reconstruction* (New York, 1913), p. 106. Actually, as Donald and others have pointed out, most of the aristocrats who became Republicans had done so before 1872. By that year the flow was out of, rather than into, the party because of their inability to control it or to compete with the carpetbaggers for Negro support. By 1875 Radicalism was a lost cause in all but four Southern states, due to white defection and the suppression of Negroes. See Donald, "The Scalawag in Mississippi Reconstruction," pp. 449–450, 453–460; Alexander, "Persistent Whiggery in the Confederate South," pp. 319–323; and Wharton, *The Negro in Mississippi*, p. 157. Wharton's estimate of 15,000–20,000 white Republicans in Mississippi (ibid.) also seems much too high, the figure likely being nearer 7,000. Fleming is probably closer to the mark, if a bit too conservative, in his estimate of 4,000–5,000 in Alabama. *Civil War and Reconstruction in Alabama*, pp. 735, 771.

[23] In every election several counties are excluded from the computation because

White Republican Voters, 1872

Republican Vote % exceeds Negro Population % by:

▨ 50% or more   ▦ 40-49   ▦ 30-39   ▨ 20-29   ▨ 10-19

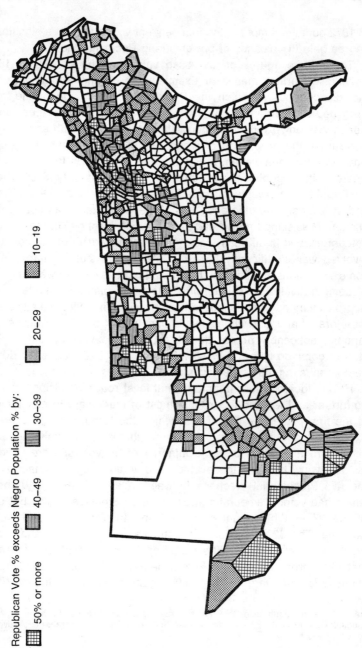

Adapted from Allen W. Trelease, "Who Were the Scalawags," *Journal of Southern History* 29 (November 1963):459.

of 1872 contained most of the independent voters who to a significant degree held the balance of power during Reconstruction.

Through its figures on assessed valuation, the census of 1880 provides a further means of examining the white Republicans. In the 125 counties in which the Republican percentage of the vote exceeded the percentage of Negroes by 30 or more, the per capita wealth was only $106, compared with $145 for the South as a whole. The larger the proportion of white Republicans, in fact, the lower was the per capita wealth. It amounted to only $90 in those counties where white Republicans were presumably in a majority, $104 where the Republican percentage exceeded that of Negroes by 40–49 points, and $122 where the difference was 30–39. Nine states (all but Louisiana and Mississippi) possessed counties in at least one of these three categories, and in all but Texas the per capita wealth of the counties involved was significantly less than that of the state at large. With some exceptions, the chief of them being in Texas, these were regions of comparatively low soil fertility where the plantation system and Negro slavery had not penetrated extensively. The evidence suggests, therefore, that most white Republican voters of 1872 were small farmers, noticeably poorer than the Southern average, and having little in common with the ex-slaveholders who had frequently dominated affairs in their respective states.

Having located these people with at least rough precision, we can go further and test the theory that most of them were former Whigs. In the first place, the counties in which the Republican percentage exceeded that of Negroes by 40 or more (that is, where white Republicans were a majority or large minority of all voters) were divided almost evenly between those which had voted Whig in a majority of the five Presidential elections between 1836 and 1852, and those which had voted Democratic. (See Table 3.) Significantly, all but one of the 27 ex-Whig counties were found in Tennessee and North Carolina. The 32 ex-Democratic counties, on the other hand, were scattered in seven states. Where the Republican percentage exceeded that of Negroes by only 10 to 39, the proportion of ex-Democratic counties is much larger (134 to 50); again, most (35) of the ex-Whig

their returns are doubtful or they are reported as equally divided; furthermore, new counties were formed from time to time, so that numerical totals rarely match over a period of years.

counties were in Tennessee and North Carolina, with Virginia contributing 11 of the remaining 15.[24]

If we reverse our viewpoint and examine the postwar affiliation of all ante-bellum Whig counties, we must note first that about half of these had Negro majorities. The black belt counties were largely Whig in their prewar affiliation and, as we have seen, the white minority which cast these votes before 1861 was almost solidly Democratic during Reconstruction. That these counties voted Republican overwhelmingly after the war was owing almost exclusively to the newly enfranchised black majority. In the ex-Whig counties where whites predominated slightly less than half (53 out of 117) voted Republican in 1872 and less than a quarter (26) did so in most of the sampled Reconstruction elections. Again Tennessee, North Carolina, and, to a lesser extent, Virginia, were conspicuous variants. They accounted for 50 of the 53 white ex-Whig counties voting Republican in 1872, and 24 of the 26 voting that way in a majority of the sampled contests between 1868 and 1876. (Even in these three states almost as many of the white ex-Whig counties voted Democratic as Republican in 1872, and a large majority did so in most of the sampled elections.) Only in these three states, apparently, was there much ground for identifying postwar Republicans with prewar Whigs, and even there the correspondence was by no means complete.

One may still object, perhaps, that elsewhere white Republicans constituted a Whig minority before the war, too few in number to carry their counties in most of the elections between 1836 and 1852, and thus not shown in the preceding calculations. This objection is not sustained by an examination of the formerly Democratic counties outside of these three states, where white Republicans in 1872 were a majority or near-majority of all voters. There were 29 such counties, located in Alabama, Arkansas, Georgia, and Texas, nearly all of them less than 10 percent Negro in composition. In these counties the Republican voters of 1872 so far outnumbered the highest total of prewar non-Democratic voters—those who cast Constitutional Union party ballots in 1860—that almost half of them had to have switched from the Democratic party. This proportion may well have been much greater. Moreover the Republican gain was not owing significantly

[24] South Carolina is omitted because her Presidential electors were not chosen by popular vote until after the war.

to population growth, for except in Texas the total vote in these counties was smaller in 1872 than in 1860.[25]

In general, therefore, a sound basis for identifying prewar Whigs with postwar Republicans exists only in Tennessee, North Carolina, and to some extent in Virginia. Elsewhere the converse was often true: most of the white Republicans of 1872 seem to have been Jacksonian Democrats before the war. Furthermore, the Whig areas of white population which went Republican during Reconstruction were the habitat of the Appalachian highlander. The planter-businessman aristocracy to which Professor Donald and others have referred seems in general to have found the postwar Democratic or Conservative camp more congenial.[26] Doubtless the minority of this group who did join the Radicals carried more weight in terms of leadership and prestige than their numbers alone would indicate, but they were hardly more typical of the white Republicans as a whole than of their own class.

Unionism before and during the war is more difficult to trace through election returns. To a degree, support of John C. Breckinridge in 1860 implied sympathy for a stronger assertion of Southern claims against the North, while Stephen A. Douglas and John Bell were more definitely Unionist candidates. Lincoln of course drew almost no votes from the states that were shortly to form the Confederacy. Of the counties with a significant number of white Republicans in 1872, 196 had cast a plurality of their votes for Breckinridge, 88 voted for Bell and the Constitutional Union ticket, and only 3 went for Douglas. (See Table 3.[27]) Bell and Douglas together received a majority of the votes cast in 109 of these counties, slightly more than a third of the total. Even among the top few counties where white Republicans were most numerous in 1872, less than half had cast "Unionist" (Bell plus Douglas) majorities in 1860. The states of North Carolina and Tennessee again contribute—as they did in the

---

[25] In these counties the Republican vote of 1872 exceeded the Constitutional Union vote of 1860 by 87 percent. This figure, broken down by states, is as follows: Alabama (4 counties) 222 percent; Arkansas (12 counties) 58 percent; Georgia (8 counties) 107 percent; and Texas (5 counties) 151 percent.

[26] According to these findings, very few white Republicans were to be found in Mississippi, the state Donald was concerned with. It is possible, therefore, that the Whig planter element in the party loomed comparatively larger there than in most states.

[27] South Carolina is again omitted, as her Presidential electors in 1860 were chosen by the legislature.

analysis of formerly Whig areas—a larger percentage of the "Unionist" counties where white Republicans were later prominent. As a matter of fact, support for the Whig party between 1836 and 1852 so nearly coincided with support for Bell in 1860 that (even after Douglas's votes were added to Bell's) both of these bear the same relationship to postwar Republicanism. Support for Bell and Breckinridge, at least, seems to have reflected political habit as much as Unionist or secessionist feeling in 1860. A majority of Whig voters probably supported Bell in 1860 and became Democrats or Conservatives during Radical Reconstruction.

A better index to Unionist sentiment lies in the attitudes reflected during the secession movement in the several states, and in evidences of wartime disaffection. Here the correlation with postwar Republicanism seems a good deal clearer.[28] It is well established that, while Unionism was to be found in all parts of the South in 1860 and afterward, the areas of greatest concentration were the mountain regions of East Tennessee, western North Carolina and Virginia, and adjacent portions of other states, as well as northern Alabama, northwest Arkansas, and parts of west and north Texas.[29] These, as we have seen, are almost precisely the areas where white Republican votes were most numerous in 1872. A great many Unionists (including many in the regions mentioned) never affiliated with the Republican party and some Republicans had been Confederate sympathizers, active as well as passive, during the war. But the correspondence between the two is closer than that between Whiggery and Republicanism—so close as to be more than coincidental.[30]

[28] The several state campaigns fought over the issue of secession or of calling a secession convention do not lend themselves readily to the kind of analysis attempted above. No single yardstick can be held up to all of these contests; the demarcation between Unionists and secessionists was not always clear, and conditions and attitudes varied greatly from state to state as well as from one month to the next during the secession crisis.

[29] Georgia L. Tatum, *Disloyalty in the Confederacy* (Chapel Hill, 1934), esp. pp. 4–13; Ella Lonn, *Desertion During the Civil War* (New York, 1928), esp. frontispiece map; Ralph A. Wooster, *The Secession Conventions of the South* (Princeton, 1962), esp. pp. 262–66; Allan Nevins, *The Emergence of Lincoln*, 2 vols. (New York, 1950), 2: 322–324, 423, 428; Clement Eaton, *A History of the Southern Confederacy* (New York, 1961), pp. 19–42, 266; E. Merton Coulter, *The Confederate States of America, 1861–1865* (Baton Rouge, 1950), pp. 84–85.

[30] An examination of Southern Republican newspapers and political speeches reveals far more appeals to men of Unionist leanings during and prior to the war, than to former Whigs as such. Southern Republicans also commonly regarded Andrew Jackson as one of their forebears because of his opposition to nullification in 1832.

It is worthwhile, therefore, to attempt a reconstruction of the relationships which existed between these three elements of Whiggery, Unionism, and Republicanism. The Southern Whigs were not a class party, associated everywhere and exclusively with a single economic interest. In most states, however, they appear to have been strongest among the large planters and among those professional and mercantile groups closely allied with or dependent upon the planters. Except for East Tennessee and adjacent parts of North Carolina and Virginia, they were weaker in the "white belts" of small farms and few slaves.[31]

Unionists in 1860–1861 fell into two main categories. The first of these was composed of large planters and their allies, though by no means all or even necessarily a majority of them, and the second consisted of persons near the opposite end of the spectrum— yeoman farmers in the more isolated parts of the South where slavery had penetrated comparatively little. Of the two groups, the former had been primarily Whig in politics and was decidedly the more lukewarm in opposing the tide of secession. True conservatives, they abhorred disunionist extremism; but they also had a vested interest in the status quo and the South's peculiar institution. Their Unionism was often conditional, therefore, taking the form of cooperationism in preference to immediate and separate state action in withdrawing from the Union. But once the die was cast, they either threw in their lot with the Confederacy (frequently rising to positions of military or political prominence), or retired to the sidelines for the duration.

The second group, more often Democrats than Whigs except in parts of the Appalachian highlands, was more uncompromising. Its members were either openly or covertly disloyal to the Confederacy, and some even served in the Union army; among these people especially the wartime peace societies flourished. Their militant hostility to the dominant order in the South was born of economic and social conditions, which in turn sprang from their geographic environment. Lacking slaves, they had no vested interest in protecting or perpetuating that institution, and in fact were often hostile to it. The threats

---

[31] Cf. Arthur C. Cole, *The Whig Party in the South* (Washington, 1913); Charles Grier Sellers, Jr., "Who Were the Southern Whigs?" *American Historical Review* 59 (January 1954): 335–346; Grady McWhiney, "Were the Whigs a Class Party in Alabama?" *Journal of Southern History* 23 (November 1957): 510–522.

to white supremacy or the "Southern way of life" posed by abolitionists and free soilers were often no more immediate to them than to farmers of Pennsylvania or Illinois. Their opposition to the dominant planter class in their respective states was of long standing; by 1860 it was a customary and primary political motivation, regardless of the local vagaries of party affiliation. Occasionally ethnic factors entered the picture too, as among the Texas Germans, who tended to be antislavery in outlook.[32]

Under Presidential Reconstruction, as Professor Alexander has shown, the first group of Unionists came fully into its own. Political leaders who had been least conspicuous in the secession movement —and most of these were ex-Whigs—tended to dominate the scene in most states in 1865 and 1866.[33] Only in Tennessee did the mountain Unionists (also Whigs primarily) sufficiently coincide with this group, or were they sufficiently numerous, to take over themselves the process of Reconstruction. Elsewhere they were a relatively small minority which supported the Johnson governments without exercising much control over them.

With the passage of the Reconstruction acts in 1867 and 1868, the political scene changed abruptly in every state but Tennessee. The

[32] The literature on Southern Unionism is large and, in conformity with the conclusions reached here, it helps to compensate for the dearth of writings on the scalawag. For the matters discussed here see, in addition to the works already cited, Thomas B. Alexander, "President Whiggery in Alabama and the Lower South, 1860–1867," *Alabama Review* 12 (January 1959): 37–40; Clarence P. Denman, *The Secession Movement in Alabama* (Montgomery, Ala., 1933), 117–119; Hugh C. Bailey, "Disaffection in the Alabama Hill Country, 1861," *Civil War History* 4 (June 1958): 183–193, and "Disloyalty in Early Confederate Alabama," *Journal of Southern History* 23 (November 1957): 522–528; Ted R. Worley, "The Arkansas Peace Society of 1861: A Study in Mountain Unionism," ibid., 24 (November 1958): 454–455; Jack B. Scroggs, "Arkansas in the Secession Crisis," *Arkansas Historical Quarterly* 12 (Autumn 1953): 190–191, 196–197, 221; J. Carlyle Sitterson, *The Secession Movement in North Carolina* (Chapel Hill, 1939), pp. 10–20, 104–106, 158 ff., 216–225; Lillian A. Kibler, "Unionist Sentiment in South Carolina in 1860," *Journal of Southern History* 4 (August 1938): 355, 359, 361; J. Reuben Sheeler, "The Development of Unionism in East Tennessee," *Journal of Negro History* 29 (April 1944): 195–196, 202; Ella Lonn, *Foreigners in the Confederacy* (Chapel Hill, 1940), esp. pp. 46–52; Claude Elliott, "Union Sentiment in Texas, 1861–1865," *Southwestern Historical Quarterly* 50 (April 1947): 449–477; Charles W. Ramsdell, "The Frontier and Secession," in *Studies in Southern History and Politics Inscribed to William Archibald Dunning* . . . (New York, 1914), pp. 63–79; Henry T. Shanks, *The Secession Movement in Virginia, 1847–1861* (Richmond, 1934), pp. 113–115, 137, 156–160; Shanks, "Disloyalty to the Confederacy in Southwestern Virginia, 1861–1865," *North Carolina Historical Review* 21 (April 1944): 118–135.

[33] Alexander, "Persistent Whiggery in the Confederate South," pp. 311–313.

old Whig planters, lawyers, and merchants presently in control were as shocked at the implications of Radical Republicanism as most Democrats and secessionists. Although some of them, like Alcorn in Mississippi and Lewis E. Parsons in Alabama, decided to go along with the new dispensation in the hope of controlling or at least tempering it, a larger number were actively or passively hostile from the outset. Those who joined the Republican party were disillusioned on discovering that they could not control the movement in the interests of conservatism; moreover they were reviled by their fellows as traitors to their caste and class, and they soon began dropping out. Such men certainly fall in the category of native white Republicans— or scalawags, if we must use the term—but they provided only part of the leadership before 1872 or thereabouts and almost none of the votes.

The great majority of native white Republicans, as the statistical analysis above shows, came within the second category, the hill-country farmers. Merely to establish their identity as a group and point out their dissimilarities from the surrounding white majority is to leave a great deal unsaid. It must suffice as a basis of generalization, however, until fuller studies are made, indicating in some detail where they stood on the issues of the day, both local and general, and why. For many of these people, though by no means all, affiliation with the Radicals was a natural resumption of their earlier political outlook.

While opposing many interests of the planter class, the Republican party was identified with policies which had been almost uniquely popular in the mountain areas before the war. These included political and social reform of an egalitarian cast, together with such governmental aids to economic development as the protective tariff and subsidies for railway construction. They held a natural appeal for people living in areas of relatively unprofitable agriculture but blessed with abundant supplies of power, labor, and mineral resources. In some mountain districts the local Whig party was most closely identified with these demands before the war, and in other areas it had been the Democrats. But probably no party in the nineteenth century, locally as well as nationally, was as closely associated with all of them as the Republican party in the years immediately following the Civil War. Many of the mountaineers therefore gravitated to the Republican party during Reconstruction, where they remain in large measure today. Their radicalism was a factor in temporary fusions with the Populist party and other insurgent groups after Reconstruction, and is still recognizable in recent years.[34]

The spectacular events taking place between 1860 and 1877 make it easy to overlook the substantial element of continuity which underlay them. Even during Radical Reconstruction, party allegiance was in some measure dependent upon local issues, habits, and loyalties as opposed to the greater questions of state and national concern. This was especially true, in all likelihood, of the more remote districts where the Negro and slavery were less critical issues. Thus despite the overall appeal of the Radical program in these regions, there is no more reason to believe that all mountain Republicans consistently favored all Republican policies (where these were consistent) than that all white Democrats consistently opposed them.[35]

The question of racial equality is a case in point. Anti-Negro prejudice had infected nearly all Southern whites (and most Northerners, too) regardless of party, class, or geographic location.[36] In most areas there were enough freedmen to constitute at least the illusion of a threat to white supremacy; thus few whites joined the Republican party to begin with and many of those who did dropped out early. Personal conviction united with social pressure—often

[34] See Sitterson, *Secession Movement in North Carolina*, pp. 17–18; V. O. Key, Jr., *Southern Politics in State and Nation* (New York, 1949), pp. 280–285; and C. Vann Woodward, *Origins of the New South, 1877–1913* (Baton Rouge, 1951), pp. 99–106, 275–277. Many of the views expressed here concerning the relationships of Whiggery and Republicanism are substantiated in the case of Tennessee in Milton Henry, "What Became of the Tennessee Whigs?" *Tennessee Historical Quarterly* 11 (March 1952): 57–62. He holds that the wealthier ex-Whig counties tended to become Democratic during Reconstruction while the poorer ones (most of them being in East Tennessee) became Republican.

[35] There is a good discussion of this question in Thomas B. Alexander, "Whiggery and Reconstruction in Tennessee," *Journal of Southern History* 16 (August 1950): 291–305. See also three articles by Verton M. Queener: "East Tennessee Sentiment and the Secession Movement, November, 1860–June, 1861," East Tennessee Historical Society, *Publications* 20 (1948): 59–83; "The Origin of the Republican Party in East Tennessee," ibid., 13 (1941): 66–90; and "A Decade of East Tennessee Republicanism, 1867–1876," ibid., 14 (1942): 59–86. Although there are no comparable studies of the white Republican movement in other states, it is likely that the others conformed to the same general pattern discernible in Tennessee.

[36] For racial attitudes in the hill country, see Alexander, "Whiggery and Reconstruction in Tennessee," p. 299; Queener, "East Tennessee Sentiment and the Secession Movement," pp. 66–68, and "Decade of East Tennessee Republicanism," pp. 59–86; Sitterson, *Secession Movement in North Carolina*, pp. 104–106; Fleming, *Civil War and Reconstruction in Alabama*, pp. 771–773, 779–780.

expressed physically—to keep a large majority in the party of conservatism and white supremacy. But if this preoccupation was indeed the "central theme of Southern history," it confirms once more the highlanders' isolation from the main stream of Southern life. For they almost alone enjoyed the luxury of ignoring it without undue pain. Among them as among Northerners, traditional loyalties and antipathies within the white community, as well as issues normally unrelated to the race question, had freer rein. There was comparatively little distinction locally between the top and bottom rails of society, and Radical policies did little or nothing to disturb unpleasantly the customary ways of life. These small farmers were free, therefore, to join (or not to join) the anti-planter, Radical, Union party with less reference either to the albatross of Negro equality or to other major issues of Reconstruction policy.[37]

If secession and the "solid South" of later days were sectional responses to purely sectional conditions, it may be said that Southern white Republicanism (like mountain Unionism) was in part an even more provincial response to yet more local issues. Although a working political democracy may have come closer to realization in parts of the hill country than elsewhere in the South, Du Bois's "vision of democracy across racial lines" was—alas—too utopian.

[37] As a group of north Georgia Democrats put it in 1868, "This is the 'Missionary ground,' politically speaking, of the State. The people of this section, being free from the burden of the negro, are divided." J. W. Avery et al. to Alexander H. Stephens, September 28, 1868, in Stephens Papers (Emory University, Atlanta). In time, however, and particularly after Reconstruction, when the hope of winning elections at the state level gave way to patronage mongering, the Republican party in several states split into "lily white" and "black and tan" factions. See Key, *Southern Politics,* pp. 286–291; Woodward, *Origins of the New South,* pp. 276–277, 461–465; and Ward, "The Republican Party in Bourbon Georgia," pp. 207–209.

W. E. Burghardt Du Bois
THE BLACK PROLETARIAT IN SOUTH CAROLINA

Central in the thinking of many radical Republican leaders was the role of black freedmen in the Southern Reconstruction. They looked upon the blacks as the foundation blocks of their effort to replace a social system that had been based on slavery with a new social order based on equal rights. But very little attention was paid by historians to the role of black freedmen in the Reconstruction process until W. E. B. Du Bois wrote his classic study of "Black Reconstruction" in 1935. The following selection from that work describes the problems of black freedmen and the efforts of their spokesmen and leaders to shape the process of Reconstruction in South Carolina.

A great political scientist in one of the oldest and largest of American universities wrote and taught thousands of youths and readers that

> *There is no question, now, that Congress did a monstrous thing, and committed a great political error, if not a sin, in the creation of this new electorate. It was a great wrong to civilization to put the white race of the South under the domination of the Negro race. The claim that there is nothing in the color of the skin from the point of view of political ethics is a great sophism. A black skin means membership in a race of men which has never of itself succeeded in subjecting passion to reason; has never, therefore, created any civilization of any kind.*[1]

Here is the crux of all national discussion and study of Reconstruction. The problem is incontinently put beyond investigation and historic proof by the dictum of Judge Taney, Andrew Johnson, John Burgess and their confreres, that Negroes are not men and cannot be regarded and treated as such.

The student who would test this dictum by facts is faced by this set barrier. The whole history of Reconstruction has with few exceptions been written by passionate believers in the inferiority of the

From W. E. B. Du Bois, *Black Reconstruction in America, 1860–1880* (New York: Harcourt, Brace and Co., 1935), pp. 381–383, 384–390, 392–400, 402–412. Reprinted by permission of Mrs. Shirley Graham Du Bois, owner of copyright.

[1] John W. Burgess, *Reconstruction and the Constitution*, p. 133.

Negro. The whole body of facts concerning what the Negro actually said and did, how he worked, what he wanted, for whom he voted, is masked in such a cloud of charges, exaggeration and biased testimony, that most students have given up all attempt at new material or new evaluation of the old, and simply repeated perfunctorily all the current legends of black buffoons in legislature, golden spittoons for fieldhands, bribery and extravagance on an unheard-of scale, and the collapse of civilization until an outraged nation rose in wrath and ended the ridiculous travesty.

And yet there are certain quite well-known facts that are irreconcilable with this theory of history. Civilization did not collapse in the South in 1868–1876. The charge of industrial anarchy is faced by the fact that the cotton crop had recovered by 1870, five years after the war, and by 1876 the agricultural and even commercial and industrial rebirth of the South was in sight. The public debt was large; but measured in depreciated currency and estimated with regard to war losses, and the enlarged functions of a new society, it was not excessive. The legislation of this period was not bad, as is proven by the fact that it was retained for long periods after 1876, and much of it still stands.

One must admit that generalizations of this sort are liable to wide error, but surely they can justifiably be balanced against the extreme charges of a history written for purposes of propaganda. And above all, no history is accurate and no "political science" scientific that starts with the gratuitous assumption that the Negro race has been proven incapable of modern civilization. Such a dogma is simply the modern and American residue of a universal belief that most men are sub-normal and that civilization is the gift of the Chosen Few.

Since the beginning of time, most thinkers have believed that the vast majority of human beings are incorrigibly stupid and evil. The proportion of thinkers who believed this has naturally changed with historical evolution. In earliest times all men but the Chosen Few were impossible. Before the middle class of France revolted, only the Aristocracy of birth and knowledge could know and do. After the American experiment a considerable number of thinkers conceived that possibly most men had capabilities, except, of course, Negroes. Possibly never in human history before or since have so many men believed in the manhood of so many men as after the Battle of Port Hudson, when Negroes fought for Freedom.

All men know that by sheer weight of physical force, the mass of men must in the last resort become the arbiters of human action. But reason, skill, wealth, machines and power may for long periods enable the few to control the many. But to what end? The current theory of democracy is that dictatorship is a stopgap pending the work of universal education, equitable income, and strong character. But always the temptation is to use the stopgap for narrower ends, because intelligence, thrift and goodness seem so impossibly distant for most men. We rule by junta; we turn Fascist, because we do not believe in men; yet the basis of fact in this disbelief is incredibly narrow. We know perfectly well that most human beings have never had a decent human chance to be full men. Most of us may be convinced that even with opportunity the number of utter human failures would be vast; and yet remember that this assumption kept the ancestors of present white America long in slavery and degradation.

It is then one's moral duty to see that every human being, to the extent of his capacity, escapes ignorance, poverty and crime. With this high ideal held unswervingly in view, monarchy, oligarchy, dictatorships may rule; but the end will be the rule of All, if mayhap All or Most qualify. The only unforgivable sin is dictatorship for the benefit of Fools, Voluptuaries, gilded Satraps, Prostitutes and Idiots. The rule of the famished, unlettered, stinking mob is better than this and the only inevitable, logical and justifiable return. To escape from ultimate democracy is as impossible as it is for ignorant poverty and crime to rule forever.

The opportunity to study a great human experiment was present in Reconstruction, and its careful scientific investigation would have thrown a world of light on human development and democratic government. The material today, however, is unfortunately difficult to find. Little effort has been made to preserve the records of Negro effort and speeches, actions, work and wages, homes and families. Nearly all this has gone down beneath a mass of ridicule and caricature, deliberate omission and misstatement. No institution of learning has made any effort to explore or probe Reconstruction from the point of view of the laborer and most men have written to explain and excuse the former slaveholder, the planter, the landholder, and the capitalist. The loss today is irreparable, and this present study limps and gropes in darkness, lacking most essentials to a complete picture; and yet the writer is convinced that this is the story of a normal working-class movement, successful to an unusual degree, despite all disappointment and failure.

South Carolina has always been pointed to as the typical Reconstruction state. It had, in 1860, 412,320 Negroes and 291,300 whites. Even at the beginning of the nineteenth century, the 200,000 whites were matched by 150,000 Negroes, and the influx from the Border and the direct African slave trade brought a mass of black slaves to support the new Cotton Kingdom. There had always been small numbers of free Negroes, a little over 3,000 at the beginning of the century, and nearly 10,000 in 1860.

It was estimated by the census that land values declined 60 percent between 1860–1867, and that all farm property, between 1860–1870, decreased from $169,738,630 to $47,628,175. In May, 1865, a meeting was held in Charleston, and a committee was sent to talk with President Johnson. He asked them to submit a list of names from which he might select a Provisional Governor, and he finally selected Benjamin F. Perry. This was, on the whole, an unfortunate selection. Perry was a devoted follower of Johnson, and believed that Johnson had the power and backing to put his policies through. He immediately succeeded in having all Negro troops withdrawn, and he was certain that the North was with him and Johnson in standing for a purely white man's government.

The Johnson convention met and took some advance steps. By a small majority, they did away with property qualifications for members of the legislature, but refused to count Negroes as basis of apportionment. This was a blow at the former slaveholders, and a step toward democracy so far as the whites were concerned, but it was coupled with absolute refusal to recognize the Negroes. Perry insisted on letting property retain its right of representation in the legislature, despite the opposition of President Johnson.

The convention wanted to abolish slavery only on condition that Negroes be confined to manual labor, and that slave owners be compensated. They were given to understand, however, that Johnson would not accept this, and they finally declared that since the slaves had been emancipated by the United States, slavery should not be reestablished. In the elections for this convention, there was little interest. Only about one-third of the normal vote was cast on the coast, and inland, there were, in many cases, no elections at all.

In the election which followed again only 19,000 votes were cast. Ex-Governor Orr received a small majority, and would have been beaten by Wade Hampton, if Hampton had not refused the use of his name. Orr was a man of striking personality, and had once been Speaker of the United States House of Representatives.

The legislature which met after this election passed one of the most vicious of the Black Codes. It provided for corporal punishment, vagrancy and apprenticeship laws, openly made the Negro an inferior caste, and provided special laws for his governing.

> *Neither humanity nor expediency demanded such sharp distinctions between the races in imposing punishments. The restriction of Negro testimony to cases in which the race was involved was not common sense. The free admission of such testimony in all cases would not have involved the surrender of power by the whites since they were to be the judges and jury. The occupational restrictions, instead of tending to restore order, created the impression that the dominant race desired to exclude the blacks from useful employment. It was impractical for a poverty-stricken commonwealth to have projected such elaborate schemes of judicial and military reorganization.*[2]

There was increased difficulty in the economic situation. The war had ended late in the spring of 1865, so that the crops of that year were short, and there were crop failures for the next two years. All this complicated matters. In addition to this, the spendid start which the Negroes had on the lands of Port Royal, and on the Sea islands, was interrupted. Johnson's proclamation and orders of 1865 provided for the early restoration of all property except property in slaves and such of the Port Royal lands as had been sold for taxes. The landlords hurried to get their pardons and to take back their lands. The Negroes resisted sometimes with physical force. When some of the landlords visited Edisto Island, the Negroes told them:

> *You had better go back to Charleston, and go to work there, and if you can do nothing else, you can pick oysters and earn your living.*

[2] Simkins and Woody, *South Carolina During Reconstruction*, pp. 51–52.

But these white men were not used to earning their own living. They were used to having Negroes do that for them, and now they had the Federal Government back of their claims. General Howard came down to facilitate the transfer and explain the condition to the Negroes. Still the black folk were dissatisfied. They drew up a petition to President Johnson, asking for at least an acre and a half of land. The planters became overbearing and the Negroes angry. Saxton, who had placed them on the land, was dismissed, and Howard deprived of his power. So that finally, by Federal force, Negroes were compelled to leave most of the lands and to make contracts as common laborers. The third Freedmen's Bureau Bill gave this the force of law. Thousands of Negroes migrated to Florida during 1866–1867, because of the land difficulties, the labor contracts, and the crop failures. Two thousand five hundred migrated to Liberia.

Landholders used force, fraud and boycott against farm labor. It was declared in 1868 that in South Carolina:

> The whites do not think it wrong to shoot, stab or knock down Negroes on slight provocation. It is actually thought a great point among certain classes to be able to boast that one has killed or beaten a Negro.[3]

The following resolutions were passed at public meetings of planters in South Carolina:

> Resolved, That if inconsistent with views of the authorities to remove the military, we express the opinion that the plan of the military to compel the freedman to contract with his former owner, when desired by the latter, is wise, prudent, and absolutely necessary.
> Resolved, That we, the planters of the district, pledge ourselves not to contract with any freedmen unless he can produce a certificate of regular discharge from his former owner.
> Resolved, That under no circumstances whatsoever will we rent land to any freedmen, nor will we permit them to live on our premises as employees.[4]

In the Abbeville district of South Carolina it was said:

> Here a planter worked nearly one hundred (100) hands near Cokes-

[3] Ibid., p. 326.
[4] *Congressional Globe,* 39th Congress, 1st session, part I, p. 93.

> burg, ten (10) of them on the South Carolina railroad for six (6) months
> (the planter receiving their wages), and the remainder on his plantation,
> raising a crop of corn, wheat, rice, cotton, etc. After the crop was har-
> vested the laborers were brought to Charleston, where, being destitute,
> they had to be rationed by the government. After their arrival in this city
> the planter distributed fifty dollars ($50) among them. The largest amount
> any one received was one dollar and twenty-five cents ($1.25) and from
> that down to fifty cents (50¢), some receiving nothing. One peck of dry
> corn a week was the only ration furnished the farm hands.[5]

Meantime, the growth of sentiment in favor of Negro suffrage was
quickened because of the action of South Carolina and other states.
Chief Justice Chase visited the state and spoke to the Negroes. He
said, "I believe there is not a member of the Government who would
not be pleased to see universal suffrage."

The Negroes were already bestirring themselves. In May, 1864, at
Port Royal, they held a meeting which elected delegates to the National Union Convention, which was to be held in Baltimore in June.
In November, 1865, the colored people met at Zion Church, Charleston, and protested against the work of the convention and of the
legislature. The legislature refused to receive this petition, and determined to ignore the matter of Negro suffrage entirely. Orr attended
the National Union Convention in Philadelphia in 1866, and advised
the legislature to reject the Fourteenth Amendment. This the legislature did with only one negative vote in both Houses.

The military commanders, under the Reconstruction legislation, did
much to abolish discrimination. One captain of a vessel was fined
who refused to allow a colored woman to ride as a first-class
passenger, and General Canby, a Kentuckian, whom Johnson appointed in March, 1867, ordered that Negroes serve on juries. This
led to excitement and protests.

Northern capitalists began to appear in the state. They were, at
first, welcomed:

> Men of capital are coming from the North by every steamer in view of
> investing in cotton and rice. We are glad to see such a lively trade in
> South Carolina; it benefits everyone.

[5] Report of the Joint Committee on Reconstruction, 1866, part II (Abbeville District),
p. 225.

Later, and especially when they began to take part in politics, they were loaded with every accusation. Some of them were army officers; others, employees of the Freedmen's Bureau; some were farmers, and some religious and educational leaders. The Negroes, naturally, turned to them for leadership and received it. They helped organize the Negroes in Union Leagues in order to teach them citizenship and united action. Northern visitors continued to come. Senator Henry Wilson of Massachusetts spoke at Charleston:

> After four bloody years, Liberty triumphed and slavery has died to rise no more. . . . The creed of equal rights, equal privileges and equal immunities for all men in America is hereafter to be the practical policy of the Republic. . . . Never vote unless you vote for the country which made you free. Register your names. Vote for a united country. Vote for the old flag. Vote for a change in the constitution of the state that your liberties may be consummated.

Under the Reconstruction law of 1867, 46,882 whites and 80,550 blacks voted; the planter class refrained from participation in hope that the scheme would fail:

	Whites	Blacks	Total
Total Registration	46,882	80,550	127,432
"For the Convention"	2,350	66,418	68,768
"Against a Convention"	2,278		2,278
Not Voting	42,354	14,132	56,486
Majority "For a Convention"			66,490

In ten of the thirty-one counties there were white majorities, and in the remaining twenty-one counties, black majorities.

Party conventions began to meet. The first one was that of the Union Republican Party, which met in Charleston with nine county representatives. It adjourned to Columbia, where nineteen counties were represented. It was attended by colored and white men, including some Southern men like Thomas J. Robertson, a wealthy native.

The reaction among the whites led to three parties. Governor Orr and his party accepted the Reconstruction acts, and planned to work with the Negroes. Wade Hampton proposed to accept the acts, but only with the idea of finally dominating the Negro vote and having

Negroes follow the lead of their former masters. Hampton owned large plantations in South Carolina and Mississippi.

The New York *Herald* summarized his views as follows: "He appeals to the blacks, lately his slaves, as his political superiors, to try the political experiment of harmonizing with their late white masters before going into the political service of strangers. . . . The broad fact that the two races in the South must henceforth harmonize on a political basis to avoid a bloody conflict is the ground covered by Wade Hampton."

A third party was led by former Governor Perry and Thomas W. Woodward.

> "Strange to say," wrote Perry, "there are many persons in the Southern States whose high sense of honor would not let them adopt the Fourteenth Amendment, who are now urging the people to swallow voluntarily the Military Bill, regardless of honor, principle, or consistency." If the state were forced to acquiesce in the tyranny of Congress, he added, "she need not embrace the hideous thing. . . . If we are to wear manacles, let them be put on by our tyrants, not ourselves." He argued the folly of attempting to control the Negro vote. "General Hampton and his friends," he asserted, "had just as well try to control a herd of wild buffaloes as the Negro vote." Woodward was violent in denouncing the compromisers. "Why, oh, why, my Southern nigger worshippers," he cried, "will you grope your way through this worse than Egyptian darkness? Why not cease this crawling on your bellies and assume the upright form of men? . . . Stop, I pray you, your efforts at harmony, your advice about conventions, your pusillanimous insinuations about confiscations, etc., or you will goad these people by flattery to destruction, before they have a chance to pick out the cotton crop."[6]

Perry proposed to appeal to the courts, and advised the whites to register and vote against the constitutional convention. The convention of whites was held a week before the constitutional convention, with twenty-one of the thirty-one districts represented. This convention made cooperation on the part of Negroes of any intelligence utterly impossible. It declared:

"The fact is patent to all . . . that the Negro is utterly unfitted to exercise the highest function of a citizen. . . . We protest against this subversion of the social order, whereby an ignorant and depraved

[6] Simkins and Woody, *South Carolina During Reconstruction,* pp. 85–87.

race is placed in power and influence above the virtuous, the educated, and the refined." The nation was informed that the white
people of South Carolina "would never acquiesce in Negro Equality
or supremacy." The president of the convention complained that the
declarations were filled with adjectives and epithets, which put a
weapon in the hands of the enemies of the movement.

The state convention, when it met, had Negro members for the first
time in the history of the state. Seventy-six of the one hundred and
twenty-four delegates were colored. As in Mississippi and elsewhere,
a number of the planter class had early contemplated an effort to control the Negro vote, and thus quickly to get rid of military rule. On
the other hand, the Negroes, because of the educated free Negro
element, some considerable talent among the slaves, and the influx
of Negroes from the North, showed unusual foresight and modesty.
The convention was earnest, and on the whole, well-conducted. Of
the seventy-six colored men, it is said, fifty-seven had been slaves.

"The native whites felt," said the correspondent of the *New York
Times,* "that the destinies of the state were safer in the hands of the
unlettered Ethiopians than in those of the whites of the body." "Beyond all question," was the effusive comment of the Charleston *Daily
News,* "the best men in the convention are the colored members.
Considering the influences under which they were called together,
and their imperfect acquaintance with parliamentary law, they have
displayed, for the most part, remarkable moderation and dignity. . . .
They have assembled neither to pull wires like some, nor to make
money like others; but to legislate for the welfare of the race to
which they belong."

There were twenty-seven Southern white members of the convention, some of them honest and earnest, and some of them with ques-
tionable antecedents. One of them had made up a purse to buy a cane
for Brooks, after he had assaulted Sumner; another had assisted in
hauling down the Union flag from Fort Sumter; a third had been a
slave trader. Among the Northerners were colored and white men of
education and character, as well as some adventurers.

To the chagrin of many white onlookers, the convention was not a
disorderly group; "the delegates did not create 'the Negro bedlam'
which tradition has associated with them. President Mackey said that
he had 'no unpleasant reminiscences of those acrimonious bickerings

which, in all deliberative assemblies, are often incidental to the excitement of debate and the attrition of antagonistic minds.' "[7] There was no tendency to insult the white South, and even deference was paid to the defeated Confederate soldiers.

This was in striking contrast to the wild and unscrupulous attacks made by the press upon this convention. Some called the experiment "the maddest, most unscrupulous, and infamous revolution in history," and said that it was snatching power from the hands of the race that settled the country and transferring it to its former slaves, an "ignorant and feeble race."

The representative of one paper was expelled from the floor for sneering at the "ringed, striped, and streaked convention." Other papers received all possible courtesies.

The real basis of opposition to the new regime was economic. Nothing showed this clearer than one fact, and that is that the chief and repeated accusation against the convention and succeeding legislatures was that they were composed of poor men, white and black. The white 47 delegates were said to have paid altogether $761 in annual taxes, of which one conservative paid $508. The total taxes paid by the 74 Negroes were $117, of which a Charleston Negro paid $85. Twenty-three of the whites and fifty-nine of the colored paid no taxes whatever. . . .[8]

When the convention opened, ex-Governor Orr was invited to address them. In his speech he stressed the fact that the freedmen needed education, and that they did not represent the intelligence nor wealth of the state, and he recommended limited suffrage, a homestead law and education.

The plight of debtors after the losses and changes of war brought much debate in the constitutional convention. A white delegate advocated a three months' moratorium on debt collections, and a colored member supported the proposal. But Cardozo, a colored man, and later the Treasurer of the State, said:

> I am opposed to the passage of this resolution. The convention should be certain of the constitutionality of their acts. The law of the United States does not allow a state to pass a law impairing the obligations of

[7] Ibid., p. 105.
[8] *Ku Klux Conspiracy, South Carolina,* part 2, pp. 1238–1250.

contracts. This, I think, is therefore a proper subject for the judiciary. I am heartily in favor of relief, but I wish the convention to have nothing to do with the matter.

R. G. DeLarge, a colored delegate, afterward Land Commissioner, said:

It has been said in opposition to this measure, that the proposed legislation was for a certain class; however, no gentlemen can rise and argue that the proposed measure is for the benefit of any specific class. I hold in my hands letters from almost every section of the state addressed to members of the convention, crying out for relief. These letters depict in strong language the impoverished condition of the people, and demand that something should be done to relieve them. I deny in toto that this is a piece of class legislation, and I believe nothing but the zeal of the member who spoke yesterday induced them to speak of it as such. It is simply a request to General Canby to relieve the necessities of a large part of the people of the state. Some members have gone farther, and said it was a shame to keep the freedmen from becoming purchasers and owners of land. . . .

It has been argued that the execution of the laws compelling the sale of the lands will benefit the poor man by affording him an opportunity to get possession of the lands. That argument, I am confident, cannot be sustained. If they are sold, they will be sold at public sale, and sold in immense tracts, just as they are at present. They will pass into the hands of the merciless speculators, who will never allow the poor man to get an inch without first drawing his life's blood in payment. The poor freedmen are the poorest of poor and unprepared to purchase lands. The poor whites are not in condition to purchase lands. The facts are, the poor class are clamoring, and their voices have been voiced far beyond the limits of South Carolina, away to the seat of the government, appealing for assistance and relief from actual starvation.

The problem of the land came in for early consideration. The landless, it was felt, should be aided in the acquirement of property and the landed aristocracy discriminated against. It was proposed that Congress be petitioned to lend the state one million dollars to be used in the purchase of land for the colored people; that the legislature be required to appoint a land commission; and that homesteads up to a certain value be exempt from the levy of processes.

One must view this action in light of what had taken place with regard to land in South Carolina. When Northern forces captured

Port Royal in November, 1861, the Federal authorities took over 195 plantations and employed over 10,000 former slaves in raising cotton. Early in 1862, they imported labor superintendents from the North, and organized the enterprise. In July, 1862, Congress laid a direct tax on the land of the states in rebellion. When the absentee landholders of Port Royal failed to pay, their plantations were sold at public auction to satisfy a part of the debt of $363,570 which had been imposed upon South Carolina. Considerable other property, which was regarded as abandoned, was seized in Charleston. The lands that were auctioned off were bought largely by Northerners, although a few Negroes who had got hold of a little money from their labor bought certain plantations.

On January 16, 1868, General Sherman issued his celebrated Field Order, Number 15. All the Sea Islands, from Charleston to Port Royal, and adjoining lands to the distance of thirty miles inland, were set aside for the use of the Negroes who had followed his army. General Saxton executed this order, and divided 485,000 acres of land among 40,000 Negroes. They were given, however, only possessory titles, and in the end, the government broke its implied promise and drove them off the land.

In the convention, the whole matter of land for the landless came up for considerable debate. Cardozo said that he did not believe in the confiscation of property, but since slavery was gone, the plantation system must go with it. Whipper, another colored man, was more inclined to protect the interests of the planters, and reminded the members that they were representatives of all classes in the community and not simply of a particular class.

This debate on the economic situation was prolonged. All contracts and liabilities for the purchase of slaves, where the money had not yet been paid, were annulled. J. J. Wright, colored, and later a state supreme court judge, said of this measure:

> I know it is said by our opponents that we are an unlawful assembly, and that we are an unconstitutional body. I know we are here under the laws of Congress, lawfully called together for the discharge of certain duties, and the repudiation of debts contracted for slaves. . . .
> It is the duty of the convention to do what? It is our duty to destroy all elements of the institution of slavery. If we do not, we recognize the right of property in man.

A homestead law to the value of $1,000 on real estate and $500 in personal property was passed. Rainey declared that Congress would probably never pass an act confiscating the land, but the other colored members, including Ransier, wanted to petition Congress for a loan of a million dollars to purchase land.

A colored delegate said on this matter:

> *My colleague presented a petition asking the Congress of the United States to appropriate one million dollars for a specific purpose—to purchase homesteads for the people of South Carolina; not the colored people, as the gentleman from Barnwell has attempted to prove, but to all, irrespective of color. He has also attempted to prove that the money cannot be obtained, but has failed to carry conviction to the minds of any of the members. There is plenty of land in the state that can be purchased for two dollars an acre, and one million will buy us five hundred thousand acres; cut this into small farms of twenty acres and we have twenty-five thousand farms. Averaging seven persons to a family that twenty acres can sustain, and we have one hundred and seventy-five thousand persons, men, women and children, who for a million dollars will be furnished means of support; that is, one-fourth of the entire people of the state.*

Mr. R. C. DeLarge, colored, continued on the same subject:

> *There are over one thousand freedmen in this state who, within the last year, purchased lands from the native whites on the same terms. We propose that the government should aid us in the purchase of more lands, to be divided into small tracts and given on the above-mentioned credit to homeless families to cultivate for their support. It is well-known that in every district the freedmen are roaming from one side to the other, not because they expect to get land, but because the large landholders are not able to employ them, and will not sell their lands unless the freedmen have the cash to pay for them. These are facts that cannot be contradicted by the gentleman from Barnwell. I know one large landholder in Colleton District who had twenty-one freedmen working for him upon his plantation the entire year. He raised a good crop but the laborers have not succeeded in getting any reimbursement for their labor. They are now roaming to Charleston and back, trying to get remuneration for their services. We propose to give them lands, and to place them in a position by which they will be enabled to sustain themselves.*
>
> *In doing this, we will add to the depleted treasury of the state, and the large plantation system of the country will be broken up. The large plantation will be divided into small farms, giving support to more people and yielding more taxes to the state. It will bring out the whole resources*

of the state. I desire it to be distinctly understood that I do not advocate this measure simply for the benefit of my own race.

After much discussion by various white members on the same subject, Mr. F. L. Cardozo, colored, voiced the thought of colored men who demanded that the government furnish land for the freedmen:

> *The poor freedmen were induced, by many Congressmen even, to expect confiscation. They held out the hope of confiscation. General Sherman did confiscate; gave the lands to the freedmen; and if it were not for President Johnson, they would have them now. The hopes of the freedmen have not been realized, and I do not think that asking for a loan of one million, to be paid by a mortgage upon the land, will be half as bad as has been supposed. I have been told by the Assistant Commissioner that he has been doing on a private scale what this petition proposes. I say every opportunity of helping the colored people should be seized upon. We should certainly vote for some measure of relief for the colored men, as we have to the white men who mortgaged their property to perpetuate slavery, and whom they have liberated from their bonds.*

Mr. W. J. Whipper, colored, was more conservative, and only wanted protection from immediate monopoly:

> *The present owners will be compelled before long to sell portions of their land, and sell them to freedmen or whoever can pay for them. But if sold now, they will be sold in large bodies, or large tracts, so that nobody but a capitalist will be able to buy.*

This demand for land was characterized as demagoguery by the property-holders, but land was, as many speakers suggested, the economic means of raising the level of the electorate. A petition was passed by a great majority, asking Congress to appropriate funds for buying land. But Senator Wilson replied that this was impractical, and the convention, thereupon, created a state commission for buying lands and selling them to the freedmen.

The convention attacked race discrimination squarely. A colored man, Dr. B. F. Randolph, offered the following amendment: "Distinction on account of race or color in any case whatever shall be prohibited, and all classes of citizens, irrespective of race and color, shall enjoy all common, equal, and political privileges." He said:

> It is, doubtless, the impression of the members of the convention that the Bill of Rights as it stands secures perfect political and legal equality to all the people of South Carolina. It is a fact, however, that nowhere is it laid down in the instrument, emphatically and definitely, that all the people of the state, irrespective of race and color, shall enjoy equal privileges. Our forefathers were no doubt anti-slavery men, and they intended that slavery should die out. Consequently, the word color is not to be found in the Constitution or Declaration of Independence. On the contrary, it stated "all men are created free and equal." In our Bill of Rights, I want to settle the question forever by making the meaning so plain that a wayfaring man, though a fool, cannot misunderstand it. The majority of the people of South Carolina, who are rapidly becoming property-holders, are colored citizens—the descendants of the African race—who have been ground down by three hundred years of degradation, and now that the opportunity is afforded, let them be protected by their political rights. The words proposed as an amendment were not calculated to create distinction, but to destroy distinction, and since the Bill of Rights did not declare equality, irrespective of race or color, it was important that they should be inserted.

Thus, discriminations of race and color were abolished by the constitution, and practical application was attempted in the case of the public schools, and the militia.

The convention framed the most liberal provisions for the right of suffrage that any of the Southern constitutions provided. They did not attempt, as in Virginia, Alabama, and Mississippi, to restrict the voting of whites further than was provided by the Reconstruction acts. Indeed, Whipper, a colored delegate, wished to petition Congress to remove all political disabilities from the white citizens. In this Cardozo and Nash agreed, and the motion was passed.

Of course, they made no distinction in race and color. The rights of women were enlarged. The property of married women could not be sold for their husbands' debts, and for the first time in its history, the state was given a divorce law.

Education was discussed at length, and a free common school system voted for.

"It is sufficient to say here that for the first time the fundamental law of the state carried the obligation of universal education and demanded the creation of a school system like that of Northern states."[9]

9 Simkins and Woody, *South Carolina During Reconstruction*, p. 100.

Nothing that the convention did aroused more opposition among property-holding whites. In the first place, as a white woman told a Northern teacher:

> *I do assure you that you might as well try to teach your horse or mule to read as to teach these niggers.*[10]

In the second place, the whites calculated that the school system would cost $900,000 a year, and that the new taxation would fall upon them.

In the debate on the school system, there was not a moment's hesitation, but there was considerable difference of opinion as to whether education should be made compulsory or not.

R. C. DeLarge, colored, said in the debate, "The schools may be open to all, but to declare that parents shall send their children to them whether they are willing or not is, in my judgment, going a step beyond the bounds of prudence. Is there any logic or reason in inserting in the constitution a provision which cannot be enforced?"

Mr. A. J. Ransier, colored, said, "I am sorry to differ with my colleague from Charleston on this question. I contend that in proportion to the education of the people so is their progress in civilization. Believing this, I believe that the committee has properly provided for the compulsory education of all children in this state between the ages named in the section."

Mr. J. A. Chesnut, colored, spoke on separation in schools:

> *Has not this convention the right to establish a free school system for the poorer classes? Then if there be a hostile disposition among the whites, an unwillingness to send their children to school, the fault is their own, not ours. Look at the idle youth around us. Is the sight not enough to invigorate every man with a desire to do something to remove this vast weight of ignorance that presses the masses down? I have no desire to curtail the privileges of freedmen, but when we look at the opportunities neglected, even by the whites of South Carolina, I must confess that I am more than ever disposed to compel parents, especially of my own race, to send their children to school. If the whites object to it, let it be so.*

Mr. F. L. Cardozo said,

[10] Ibid., p. 424.

It was argued by some yesterday with some considerable weight that we should do everything in our power to incorporate in the constitution all possible measures that will conciliate those opposed to us. No one would go further in conciliating others than I would. But we should be careful of what we do to conciliate.

In the first place, there is an element that is opposed to us no matter what we do, which will never be conciliated. It is not that they are opposed so much to the constitution we may frame, but they are opposed to us sitting in the convention. Their objection is of such a radical and fundamental nature, that any attempt to frame a constitution to please them would be abortive.

In the next place, there are those who are doubtful; and gentlemen here say if we frame a constitution to suit these parties, they will come over to our side. They are only waiting to see whether or not it will be successful.

Then there is the third class who honestly question our capacity to frame a constitution. I respect that class, and believe if we do justice to them, laying our corner-stone on a sure foundation of republican government and liberal principles, the intelligence of that class will be conciliated, and they are worthy of conciliation.

Before I proceed to discuss the question, I want to divest it of all false issue of the imaginary consequences that some gentlemen have illogically thought will result from the adoption of this section with the word "compulsory." They affirm that it compels the attendance of both white and colored children in the same schools. There is nothing of the kind in the section. It simply says that all the children shall be educated; but how, it is left with the parents to decide. It is left to the parent to say whether the child should be sent to a public or private school. There can be separate schools for white and colored. It is left so that if any colored child wishes to go to a white school, it shall have the privilege of doing so. I have no doubt, in most localities colored people will prefer separate schools, particularly until some of the present prejudice against their race is removed.

The committee proposed that persons coming of age after 1875 must be able to read and write before voting, but Cardozo opposed it because he said it would take more than ten years and a great deal of money to complete the system, and he wanted to extend the time to 1890. Three other colored members spoke against any qualification, and it was, therefore, stricken out.

To bridge over the interval before the state school system could be installed, Mr. B. F. Randolph, colored, presented the following petition, which was referred to the Committee on Miscellaneous Provisions of the Constitution: "We, the undersigned, people of South

Carolina, in convention assembled, do hereby recommend that the Bureau of Refugees, Freedmen and Abandoned Lands be continued until the restoration of civil authority; that then a Bureau of Education be established, in order that an efficient system of schools be established."

"Perhaps the convention's achievement of greatest permanent importance was the reform of local and judicial administration."[11]

Judicial circuits were to be called counties, and some new counties were arranged. A Court of Probate was established in each county, and justices of the peace were given wider jurisdiction. Judges were to be elected, instead of appointed, and in spite of much criticism, the new system worked well. From 1870 to 1877 the Supreme Court was composed of a Negro, a native Southerner, and a Northerner. Its administration was fair and its decisions just. Most of the circuit judges were native whites and honest men. Mixed juries were the rule, and no fault was found with them. They did not hesitate to convict colored prisoners. The trial judges came in for the greatest criticism. Among them were numbers of ignorant and unqualified persons, and there was a good deal of misappropriation of fees and costs. On the other hand, it was difficult to get proper trial judges, because so many qualified whites refused to serve.

Wright, the Negro who was on the Supreme Court, was the first colored man admitted to the bar in Pennsylvania. He had been connected with the Freedmen's Bureau; then became a member of the constitutional convention, and a state senator. He was elected to the bench in February, 1870, to fill out an unexpired term, and was reelected in December, 1870, for the full term. He resigned under Hampton in August, 1877.

Although he lisped, Wright was a good speaker, decidedly intelligent, and generally said to be the best fitted colored man in the state for the position.

Some reforms were made in the county government. Most of the officers were to be elected by popular vote, and boards of commissioners were appointed for the highways, and for collection and disbursement of taxes.

Some of the delegates wanted to legislate concerning wages,

11 Ibid., p. 101.

which caused great indignation among the planters. It was suggested, for instance, that planters be required to pay back wages from the time of the issue of the Emancipation Proclamation, and that the division of one-half of the crop for tenant farmers be made compulsory. Such legislation was inherently just and reasonable but fifty years too early for public opinion in any modern country.

Among other things, the constitution abolished imprisonment for debt, and dueling, and did away with property qualifications, for voting or holding office. The colored members, despite their inexperience, gave evidence, here and there, of care and thrift. For instance, when the question of the pay of members of the convention came up, a discussion arose. Mr. L. S. Langley moved that the pay per diem of $12 in bills receivable be laid on the table. J. J. Wright moved that $10 be inserted. N. G. Parker, white, moved to fix the pay at $11. C. P. Leslie, colored, demurred:

> *I desire to say a word before that resolution be passed, and be put right on record. I am perfectly willing to receive $3 per day in greenbacks for my services. I think that sum all they are worth, and further, if I got any more, it would be so much more than I have been in the habit of receiving, I might possibly go on a spree and lose the whole of it. Now I ask any of the delegates in this body if they were called upon to pay a similar body of men out of their pockets, how much they would be willing to pay each member. I will stake my existence on it they would not pay more than $1.50 per day to each member. I want to be recorded as always being opposed to a high tariff, but not against any reasonable compensation. But this eight or nine dollars a day, when we consider all the surroundings and conditions of the people, looks too much like a fraud.*

The new constitution for South Carolina was adopted by the Convention in April, 1868. It was eventually adopted by the people— 70,000 voting for it, 27,000 against it, and 35,000 abstaining.

The constitution was written in good English and was an excellent document, "embodying some of the best legal principles of the age. In letter it was as good as any other constitution the state has ever had, or as most American states had at that time. This assertion is supported by the practical endorsement which a subsequent generation of South Carolinians gave it; the conservative whites were content to live under it for eighteen years after they recovered control of the state government, and when in 1895 they met to make a new constitution, the document they produced had many of the features of the constitution of 1868.". . .[12]

The first governor, under the new regime, was Robert K. Scott, born in Pennsylvania, a colonel of Union troops during the war, and assistant commissioner of the Freedmen's Bureau. Scott faced great difficulties, and is generally conceded to have been a well-meaning man. A well-born native Southern white was Franklin J. Moses, Jr. His father had been a prominent South Carolinian senator before the war, and was respected by all people. Moses married the daughter of a distinguished Southerner; was private secretary to one of the former Governors, and became a lawyer and an editor in favor of Johnson's Reconstruction. When the Reconstruction acts were passed he went over to the side of the carpetbaggers and Negroes; he took a prominent part in the constitutional convention, and afterward became Speaker of the House, and in 1872, Governor. He was denounced as unscrupulous and dishonest, and extravagant in his manner of living.

The colored leaders formed a very interesting group. Francis L. Cardozo was free-born of Negro, Jewish and Indian descent. He was educated at the University of Glasgow, and in London, and went to New Haven, where he served as a Presbyterian minister. After the war, he came to Charleston and was Principal of Avery Institute. He was secretary of state during 1868–1872, and treasurer of the state during 1872–1876. He was a handsome, well-groomed man, with cultivated manners, and honest in official life. He was accused in several instances, but no dishonest act was ever proven against him.

Joseph H. Rainey was the first Negro to represent South Carolina in the House of Representatives. Robert Brown Elliott, born in Massachusetts, was educated at Eton College, in England. He was a first-rate lawyer; served in the legislature, and was twice elected to Congress. He had a commanding presence, and a fine gift of oratory. Richard A. Cain was a leader, and afterward bishop in the A.M.E. Church. His paper, *The Missionary Record,* was the most influential Negro paper in South Carolina. He served in the Senate and two terms in Congress. Robert C. DeLarge was a tailor from Charleston,

[12] Ibid., pp. 93–94.

and had been an agent in the Freedmen's Bureau. He served in the legislature, and while his education was limited, he had large influence. Beverly Nash had been a slave before the war, and afterward a waiter. When grown he learned to read and write, and became an earnest and hard-working leader.

Alonzo J. Ransier was elected lieutenant-governor in 1870. He was a free Negro, and became a member of the constitutional convention of the legislature, and auditor of Charleston County. In 1872, he went to Congress. He made a good presiding officer of the state senate, being dignified and alert. Richard H. Gleaves was lieutenant-governor in 1872–1876. He was from Pennsylvania, and had acted as probate judge. He was intelligent and knew parliamentary law. Samuel J. Lee was a Negro Speaker of the House, in 1872–1874. He was born in the state, worked as a farmer and laborer in lumber mills, and was self-educated. He was polished and a good lawyer. Stephen A. Swailes, a colored man of Pennsylvania, was a Union soldier, and school teacher. He became a senator, and was known for his integrity and ability as a speaker. Robert Smalls was the one who stole the Confederate ship *Planter* and delivered it to the Union authorities. He was self-educated and popular. He was a member of Congress until after Reconstruction. These men were all poor and doubtless some of them accepted bribes and shared in graft. But very few of them were thoroughly venal or purchasable against their convictions. When it came to personal favors or sharing in gifts and gains which followed legislation of which they honestly approved, some of them were certainly approachable.

Negroes were conspicuous members of the legislatures. "There was a large proportion of former slaves, and at first perhaps two-thirds of them could not write, but by 1871, most of them had learned at least to read and write. Many of them were speakers of force and eloquence, while others were silent or crude. In the Senate, it was said that some of the colored members spoke exceedingly well, with great ease and grace of manners. Others were awkward and coarse."[13]

One observer recorded that "The President of the Senate and the Speaker of the House, both colored, were elegant and accomplished

[13] Ibid., pp. 128–129.

men, highly educated, who would have creditably presided over any commonwealth's legislative assembly."

"The majority of the voters of the state were Negroes, and in every session but one that race had a majority in the legislature. They outnumbered, and in many cases outshone, their carpetbag and scalawag contemporaries."[14]

In the first legislature there were 127 members, of whom 87 were colored, and 40 white. According to the available figures, the composition of Reconstruction legislatures in South Carolina seems to have been as follows:[15]

TABLE 1

	Senate		House		Total		
	Negroes	Whites	Negroes	Whites	Negroes	Whites	Total
1868–1869	10	21	78	46	88	67	155
1870–1871	10	20	75	49	85	69	154
1872–1873	16	17	80	42	96	59	155
1874–1875	16	17	61	63	77	80	157
1876–1878	4	14	58	64	62	78	130

It will be seen from these figures that the white members of the legislature, from their control of the Senate, were always able to block Negro legislators; and that Negro control of the legislature was only possible because most of the white Senators voted with the Negroes. In the legislature of 1874, the whites had a majority in both Houses. It can hardly be said, therefore, that the Negroes of South Carolina had absolute control of the state at any time.

The economic status of the legislature of 1870–1871 is shown by their given occupations: 10 lawyers, 31 farmers, 9 physicians, 17 clergymen, 12 teachers, 16 planters, 13 merchants, 3 merchant tailors, 3 clerks, 2 masons, 8 builders, 1 engineer, 1 marble dealer, 8 carpenters, 2 hotel keepers, 1 druggist, 1 bookkeeper, 1 wheelwright, 4 coachmakers, 1 tanner, 2 mechanics, 1 chemist, 1 auditor, 1 hatter, 1 blacksmith, 1 tailor.

[14] Ibid., p. 128.
[15] These figures are from Taylor, Simkins and Woody, and Work's compilation in the *Journal of Negro History*, 5:63. Simkins and Woody's figures have many inaccuracies and the figures of Taylor and Work are incomplete. Compare also Reynolds, *Reconstruction in South Carolina*.

The state sent seven Negroes to Congress; made two of them lieutenant-governors; and for four years, two of them were speakers of the House. One was secretary of state and treasurer of the state. Another was adjutant and inspector general. These men were of various colors and mixtures of blood, and there was a good deal of difference of opinion, as to whether the mulattoes or the full-blooded blacks were superior. But one observer asserted that "the colored men generally were superior in decency and ability to the majority of the native white Radical legislators."[16] And another said that "the quadroons and octoroons of the Senate are infinitely superior in personal appearance to their white Yankee and native compeers."[17]

Most of these men had been slaves, although a few of them were well-educated. They had ability, and in some cases, more than ordinary ability. But above all, they were in the midst of a mighty social and economic change, and were swayed by the social and political revolution around them. "The bottom rail was on the top," and the former ruling oligarchy was now displaced by those who represented neither the wealth nor the traditions of the state.

The bitterness of this campaign against the Reconstruction governments was almost inconceivable.

> One unfamiliar with the situation would think the editors and their correspondents had gone crazy with anger or were obsessed with some fearful mania, so great was the ridicule, contempt, and obloquy showered upon the representatives of the state. With the deepest scorn for a scalawag, with all the Southern hatred for an adventuring Yankee, and with either sympathy or shame for the ignorant, misled Negro, the press, the aristocracy, the poor whites, the up-country, the low-country—all with one voice protested against the "unlawful assembly" in Columbia maintained in power, they said, by the Federal bayonet. The Fairfield *Herald* battled "against the hell-born policy which has trampled the fairest and noblest States of our great sisterhood beneath the unholy hoofs of African savages and shoulder-strapped brigands—the policy which has given up millions of our free-born, high-souled brethren and sisters, countrymen and countrywomen of Washington, Rutledge, Marion, and Lee, to the rule of gibbering, louse-eaten, devil-worshiping barbarians, from the jungles

[16] *News,* March 17, 1870, in Simkins and Woody, *South Carolina During Reconstruction,* p. 130.
[17] *News,* March 10, 1871, in Simkins and Woody, *South Carolina During Reconstruction,* p. 130.

of Dahomey, and peripatetic buccaneers from Cape Cod, Memphremagog, Hell, and Boston.[18]

A new system of taxation came in with the Reconstruction government. It provided for a uniform rate of assessment on all property at its full value. This was a departure from the system previous to the war, which put a low valuation on land and slaves and heavy taxation on merchants, professions and banking. The merchant before the war paid five or six times as great a rate of taxation as the planter. In 1859, the total tax value of lands in the state was $10,257,000, while lots and buildings in Charleston were valued at $22,274,000. The tax on all the land of the state averaged less than five cents an acre in 1860. When the new system came in, it was difficult to find persons to administer it and every landholder objected to it.

The new system met all sorts of opposition from unsympathetic administrators and the newspapers of the state. Governor Scott expected $300 million worth of property as a basis of taxation, but less than $115 million were returned. This the Board of Equalization raised to $180 million. As the assessments decreased, the rate of taxation increased. The total assessment in 1869 was $181 million, and in 1877, under Hampton, $101 million. As the average rate of taxes rose, the propertyholders said that the Negro government wanted to raise taxes so as to confiscate the land.

The new government could not collect the tax levied. It met an organized and bitter boycott of property. In 1868, $175,688 of assessed tax was uncollected; in 1869, $248,165, and in 1870, $524,026—a total of nearly a million dollars in three years. Part of this delinquency was due to real poverty; but part was due to deliberate obstruction on the part of propertyholders. Taxation had to be increased to cover delinquency and to meet new expenses. In 1860, taxation on a half billion of property was $1,280,383; in 1870, $2,767,675 was assessed on $183 million. The increase of taxation was partly accounted for by gradually increased expenditures for education, construction, and charitable institutions.

At the same time, the inflation of the currency makes comparison with conditions previous to the war difficult. More money was cer-

---

[18] Simkins and Woody, *South Carolina During Reconstruction*, pp. 121–122.

tainly raised by the state during Reconstruction. But, on the other hand, a much larger proportion of the expenditures was designed to aid the laboring poor, and did aid them largely. Indeed, it might have changed the whole economic position of the proletariat if it had been efficiently and honestly expended.

In the legislature in 1868, the free common school system was organized temporarily, and permanently in 1870. Relief was extended to various classes of citizens, especially poor laborers. In 1868 and 1869, an act was passed providing for a land commissioner, who was to act under a board. Land was to be purchased in various parts of the state, and was to be sold in plots of not less than twenty-five and not more than one hundred acres to actual settlers. Two hundred thousand dollars' worth of bonds were provided to finance this proposal, and later this was increased to $500,000. The land commissioner was to hold office at the pleasure of an Advisory Board, consisting of chief state officers.

One of the chief sources of corruption in nearly all the reconstructed states was railroad building. And the reasons for this are easily misconceived because of the changed economic status of railroads today. It must be remembered that at the beginning throughout the country and the world, the railroad was a public highway, and for this reason a public enterprise toward whose building and maintenance the public rightly contributed. It was only after the railroad was built and established by public funds, that private interests monopolized it and sequestered its income to make individual millionaires.

In the South, the railroads had lagged. The planters would not submit to public taxation, and they would not divert funds from their private luxury consumption, in order to furnish capital. South Carolina was particularly a case in point. Charleston, by all rules of commerce, should have been one of the great ports of the United States. It was a gateway to the West; it should have at least connected its own uplands with the coast, and it might have tapped the West through Cincinnati, and the great cotton belt through the Southern South. But efforts toward this end before the war had but small success.

It was perfectly natural that the first thought of those who were reconstructing the state should turn toward railroad building as a means of economic rehabilitation. The usual method was the old one of loaning credit of the state. It meant, not that the state invested money, but simply that the state permitted the issue of bonds and guaranteed the payment of interest and principal. On a sound economic proposition, conducted by honest men, this was simply a way of securing private capital for a semi-private enterprise, which would greatly increase the prosperity of the state.

Railway mileage in South Carolina had increased from 289 to 973, between 1850–1860. By 1865, there were 1,007 miles. Then construction practically stopped, and effort was turned toward rebuilding the railroads and giving them new equipment.

The difficulty was that a flock of cormorants whose business was cheating and manipulation in the issue and sale of bonds and other certificates of enterprise, moved first West and then South, and took charge of railroad promotion. They were largely Northern financiers, in some cases already discredited in the centers of finance and driven out of the overworked investment fields North and West. They came South with an address and a technique which only trained, experienced, and honest administrators could have withstood. They flaunted the chances of quick and easy money before the faces of ruined planters, small Northern investors, and the few Negroes who had some little capital. The result was widespread graft, debt and corruption in South Carolina and North Carolina, in Florida and Georgia, in Louisiana, and in other states.

There was, however, in the reorganization, for instance, of the Greenville and Columbia Railroad, nothing worse than the ordinary stock-jobbing enterprise common all over the nation; and prominent Southerners, like ex-Governor Orr and J. P. Reed, were concerned in it. Instead of concentrating efforts on the rebuilding of the railroad and its equipment, most of the time and energy was spent in seeking to market stock in New York. This failed and the road was bankrupt by the end of the Reconstruction era, just as it was at the beginning.

In the same way, the Blue Ridge road, backed not only by carpetbaggers but by leading white Southerners, was prostrate after the war and sued for state aid. The legislature authorized aid in 1868, but the contract for rebuilding demanded much more money than the bonds provided for. Eventually the road was sold to a private company composed as usual not only of carpetbaggers but of planters. Matters were so manipulated that a state contingent liability of $4 million of bonds was transmuted into an actual state indebtedness of $1,800,000. Again little was done actually to restore the road, and the company went into bankruptcy.

Thus in most cases, bankrupt corporations bequeathed to the Reconstruction regime by ante-bellum organizers, came before the Legislature to secure capital for rebuilding, and then fell into the hands of speculators who tried to make money out of the stock, rather than out of the rebuilding of the road; and these speculators were largely men trained in shady finance in Wall Street, and helped by much of the best element of the Southerners in South Carolina, as well as by the new carpetbag capitalists.

This was a difficult situation, calling for blame and criticism, but to place the blame of it mainly upon the Negro voter and the Negro laborer is a fantastic distortion of the truth. The money misused went primarily to Northern promoters and Southern white administrators. And while, of course, a poverty-stricken electorate was gripped and bribed by such organized thieves, the remedy for this was not the disfranchisement of labor but its education, and such an increased share of the product of industry as to make life livable, without theft or sale of soul.

The appropriations to meet the new expenses had to grow. The fact is that South Carolina had been a state absolutely dominated by landed property. It is said that the ante-bellum state was ruled by 180 great landlords. They had made the functions of the state just as few as possible, and did by private law and on private plantations most of the things which in other states were carried on by the local and state governments. The economic revolution, therefore, which universal suffrage envisaged for this state, was perhaps greater than in any other Southern state. It was for this reason that the right of the masses to vote was so bitterly assailed, and expenditures for the new functions of the state denounced as waste and extravagance.

The result of all this had to be increased taxation. The rate of taxation in 1868–1872 was 9 mills; in 1872–1876 over 11 mills. Yet this was excessive only by comparison with the past and because of recent severe losses. In Northern states, like Illinois, Massachusetts, New York and Pennsylvania, the average was 21½ mills on the dollar.

The grip of poverty was on the South and poverty always is felt most poignantly by those to whom poverty has been unknown. The planters, used to ease and a certain degree of luxury, were the ones that felt the new poverty as a terrible, heaven-shattering thing. They looked upon any action as justifiable if it restored to them the income which they had lost.

On the other hand, both the poor whites and the Negroes were not only poverty-stricken, but, for that reason, peculiarly susceptible to petty graft and bribery. Economically, they had always been stripped bare; a little cash was a curiosity, and a few dollars a fortune. The sale of their votes and political influence was therefore, from the first, simply a matter of their knowledge and conception of what the vote was for and what it could procure. With experience, their conception of its value rose until some of them conceived the idea of making the ballot a power by which they could change their social and economic status, and live like human beings. But before most of them rose to this conception, there were thousands to whom their vote and petty office-holding were simply a means of adding to their small incomes. And when one considers that this was a day when the line between using political power for personal advantage and using it for social uplift was dim and difficult to follow throughout the whole nation, the wonder is that the labor vote of South Carolina so easily ranged itself behind the new school system, the orphanages, the land distribution, and the movements toward reform in public efficiency.

The ascendancy of property over labor and the suffrage was in this day openly maintained by bribery, and if this had been uncommon in the prewar South, it was simply because universal suffrage had not been established and capital ruled by social sanction rather than by money. In the new situation, property began systematically to attack labor in two ways: First, it deliberately encouraged extravagance, graft and bribery, so as to hasten the downfall of the labor regime. And secondly, it utterly upset the credit of the state, so as to prevent the new state from importing capital.

The failure of taxation to raise the required revenue compelled the state to borrow, and here it fell into the hands of Northern money sharks and Southern repudiators. The state debt October 1, 1867, was $8,378,255. The Constitutional Convention of 1868 repudiated $3,000,000 of this as a Confederate debt, and made the total debt $5,407,306. From this beginning, the state debt increased to $10,665,

908 in 1871, while committees claimed that there was evidence of total liabilities outstanding to the amount of 15 or even 30 millions.

> *The exact amount of the debt was not known; the figures from the reports of the treasurer, comptroller-general, and financial agent did not agree; and it was claimed by the opposition press and even by some of the state officials that there were large issues of fraudulent bonds on the market, and that certain of the state officials had profited thereby.*
>
> *While the Conservative press continually reviled the Radical government, on no topic was it so prolific or bitter as that of finances and taxation.*[19]

The total debt, bonded and contingent, seems to have been:

1860	$12,027,090
1865	15,892,946
1868	14,896,040
1871	22,480,914

In this case, the total indebtedness in 1871 is not clear. The Governor's report makes it a little less than twelve million, but the investigation committee insists that because the state government had printed and issued certain bonds, the amount of which was not definitely known, it was possible that the state might eventually be liable for thirty million dollars.

This did not mean, as many assume, that the state officials received or squandered any such sums. The methods by which small amounts of actual cash received became a paper debt of huge amounts is explained in the Governor's special message of January 9, 1865.

> *In the fall of 1868, I visited New York City for the purpose of borrowing money on the credit of the state on coupon bonds, under the provisions of the acts of August 26, 1868. I had the assistance of Mr. H. H. Kimpton, United States Senator F. A. Sawyer, and Mr. George S. Cameron. I called at several of the most prominent banking houses to effect the negotiation of the required loan, and they refused to advance any money upon our state securities, for those securities had been already branded with the threat of a speedy repudiation by the political opponents of the administra-*

[19] Ibid., pp. 154–155.

tion, who have ever since howled the same cry against the state credit.
As the persons who made this threat controlled the press of the state,
they were enabled to impress capitalists abroad with the false idea of
a speedy reaction that would soon place them again in authority.

As the capitalists well knew that these persons when in power in 1862
did repudiate their debts due Northern creditors, their distrust of our
bonds was very natural and apparently well-founded. It soon became
evident to every man familiar with our financial standing in New York that
to negotiate the loan authorized, the question was not what we would
take for the bonds, but what we could get for them. After much effort,
and the most judicious management, I succeeded in borrowing money,
through Mr. Cameron, at the rate of four dollars in bonds for one dollar
in currency, the bonds being rated at 75 percent below their par value,
or at 25 cents on the dollar. This loan, however, was only effected at the
extravagant rate of 1½ percent per month, or 18 percent a year—a rate
only demanded on the most doubtful paper, to cover what is deemed a
great risk—for the money loaned.

Subsequent loans were effected at a higher valuation of the bonds,
but at the rates of interest varying from 15 to 20 percent, in addition to
commissions necessarily to be paid the financial agent. If, then, $3.2
million in money has cost the state $9,514,000 in bonds, it does not,
therefore, follow that the financial board has criminally conspired against
the credit of the state, and still less, that any one member of the board
can justly be held up to public execration or stigmatized by an accusation
of "high crimes and misdemeanors" for the assumed results of its action.
It is proper that I should add that the armed violence which has prevailed
in this state for the past three years has had upon our bonds the same
effect as actual war in lessening their purchasing-value, as money is
dearer in war than in peace. Ku-Kluxism made capitalists shrink from
touching the bonds of this state, as a man would shrink from touching a
pestilential body.[20]

If there were outstanding in 1874 twenty or even thirty millions of
evidences of debt, it is unlikely that this represented more than ten
millions in actual cash delivered, and all monies collected and paid
beyond that were not the stealing necessarily of South Carolinians,
white or black, but the financial graft of Wall Street and its agents,
made possible by the slander and reaction of the planters.

The rise of a group of a people is not a simultaneous shift of the
whole mass; it is a continuous differentiation of individuals with inner
strife and differences of opinion, so that individuals, groups and

[20] 42nd Congress, 2nd session, House Reports, II, no. 22, part I, p. 120.

classes begin to appear seeking higher levels, groping for better
ways, uniting with other like-minded bodies and movements. Every
indication of this was present among Negroes during Reconstruction times. There was not a single reform movement, a single step
toward protest, a single experiment for betterment in which Negroes
were not found in varying numbers. The protest against corruption
and inefficiency in South Carolina had in every case Negro adherents
and in many cases Negro leaders.

The responsibility of Negroes for the government of South Carolina
in Reconstruction was necessarily limited. They helped choose the
elected officials and furnished a large number of the members of the
legislature. But most of the administrative power was in the hands of
the whites, and these were either Northerners, who had come South
as officers or officials or to invest money, or native Southerners, both
aristocrats and poor whites, who had undertaken to guide the Negro
vote.

Vernon Lane Wharton
THE NEGRO IN MISSISSIPPI POLITICS

*A dozen years after Du Bois' pioneering book, Vernon Lane Wharton
published a scholarly study of the black freedmen in Mississippi in the
decades after the Civil War. The following selection contains his analysis of
black participation in politics and officeholding during the Reconstruction
years.*

Negro Officials in County and Municipal Governments

By a provision of the new constitution of the state, the terms of all
local officials expired with the readmission of Mississippi to the
Union. Appointments to local offices were then to be made by the
Governor with the advice and consent of the senate. Thus there

Vernon Lane Wharton, *The Negro in Mississippi, 1865–1890,* University of North
Carolina Studies in History and Political Science (Chapel Hill: University of North
Carolina Press, 1947), pp. 167–180. Used by permission.

were no municipal or county elections in the state until the fall of
1871. The Governor, J. L. Alcorn, as an old and relatively conservative citizen of the state, made appointments that at least were up to
the usual standard for such officials. In some cases, the entire county
lists were made up of Democrats or old Whigs.[1] Alcorn's selections
for the judiciary were made up almost entirely of leading members of
the state bar.[2] Altogether, the total of his appointments included 247
Republicans, 217 Democrats, and seventy-two members of other opposition groups.[3] So far as possible, Alcorn avoided the appointment
of Negroes.[4] It appears that no member of that race except Robert
H. Wood of Natchez was made mayor of any town.[5] With the possible
exception of Coffeeville and Greenville, no town had a Negro majority
on its board of aldermen.

Even after the election of 1871, a Negro majority in a municipal
government seems to have been unknown.[6] The city of Jackson, with
a powerful Republican machine that maintained its control for thirteen years after the overthrow of the party in the state, only once had
more than one Negro on its city council of six members. The one exception followed the election of 1874, when two Negroes became
aldermen.[7] In Natchez, where the Negroes held an enormous majority, they placed only three members on a council of seven.[8] Efforts of
the Negro majority to gain control of the board in Vicksburg in 1874
lost the support of the white members of their party, and with it the
election.[9]

The chief complaint against the participation of the freedmen in
the government of the towns grew out of their appointment as police-
men. The presence of such officials helped to bring on the Meridian

---

[1] Fred M. Witty, "Reconstruction in Carroll and Montgomery Counties, *P.M.H.S.* 10:
120.
[2] Mississippi *Weekly Pilot,* October 1, 1870; Hinds County *Gazette,* October 5,
November 2, 1870; J. S. McNeily, "War and Reconstruction in Mississippi,"
P.M.H.S.C.S. 2:393.
[3] Hinds County *Gazette,* September 6, 1871.
[4] Jackson *Clarion-Ledger,* November 27, 1890.
[5] Hiram Revels' statement in his "Autobiography" that John R. Lynch served as
mayor of Natchez seems to be an error.
[6] John R. Lynch, *The Facts of Reconstruction,* p. 92.
[7] Goodspeed Publishing Company, *Biographical and Historical Memoirs of Mississippi,* 2:174.
[8] Edward King, *The Great South,* p. 293; Natchez *Tri-Weekly Democrat and Courier,*
August 13, 1873.
[9] J. W. Garner, *Reconstruction in Mississippi,* pp. 329–330.

riot in 1871,[10] and furnished the central theme of the attack on the Republican government in Jackson.[11] The general attitude of the whites, as expressed by Ethelbert Barksdale, was that "negroes ought not to be put in a position to discharge constabulary functions which it is proper for white men to exercise." Law enforcement implied domination, and as Barksdale said, the white race was "not in the habit of being dominated by the colored race."[12]

In general the few towns which had Republican governments as late as 1874 overthrew them before the state government fell in the fall of 1875. The Democrats took Vicksburg in August, 1874, and Columbus in December. Yazoo City was captured in April, 1875, and Okolona in August. The methods generally used in this process, combining persuasion, intimidation, economic pressure, and violence, were similar to those used later in the state campaign. For towns which had Negro majorities, the legislature assured the continuation of Democratic control by excluding from the corporate limits large portions of the Negro residential sections.[13] The one important exception to the overthrow of Republican municipal governments in the years 1874 and 1875 was the city of Jackson, where a peculiar situation and a large number of white votes maintained that party in power until 1888.

Very little information is available as to the participation of the Negroes in the various county governments. More than half of the counties held white majorities, and most of these naturally eliminated in the elections of 1871 the few Negro officials appointed by Alcorn in 1870. In the elections of 1873, the Democrats carried thirty-nine of the seventy-four counties, and in 1875 sixty-two of the seventy-four. Of course, in several of the predominantly white counties, black beats at times elected one or two supervisors or justices of the peace. Yalobusha, Scott, and Lawrence counties, as examples, generally had one Negro supervisor on the board of five.[14] Such Ne-

[10] *Report on the Condition of Affairs in the Late Insurrectionary States,* "Mississippi," 1:479.
[11] Jackson *Clarion-Ledger,* December 26, 1889.
[12] *Senate Miscellaneous Documents,* no. 166, 50th Congress, 1st session, p. 276.
[13] J. C. Brown, "Reconstruction in Yalobusha and Grenada Counties," *P.M.H.S.* 12:217, 269; Lee Richardson and Thomas D. Godman, *In and Around Vicksburg,* p. 97.
[14] J. C. Brown, op. cit., 13:270; Forrest Cooper, "Reconstruction in Scott County,"

groes were almost entirely without influence, and generally found it to their advantage to be "very quiet, good negroes," to use the description given of those in Lawrence.[15]

Even in the minority of the counties which had Negro and Republican majorities the freedmen seldom obtained many of the offices. By 1873, however, they became assertive enough to take control of a number of counties in which the white population was small. In Marshall County, for example, three of the five supervisors were Negroes who could barely read and write.[16] The three on the board in Yazoo County, the three in Warren, four of the five in Madison, and all five in Issaquena were described as "illiterate."[17] In these counties, there were also varying numbers of Negro justices of the peace, few of whom were capable of carrying out properly even the simple duties of their office. There were also a small number of Negro chancery and circuit clerks varying in ability from an "illiterate" in Yazoo to the highly cultured L. J. Winston, who remained as circuit clerk in Adams County, under white Democratic control, until his appointment as collector of the port of Vicksburg in 1897. According to John R. Lynch, "Out of seventy-two counties in the State at that time, electing on an average twenty-eight officers to a county, it is safe to assert that not over five out of one hundred of such officers were colored men."[18] This statement seems to be approximately correct.

The most important office in the counties, both in responsibilities and in financial returns, was that of sheriff. According to Lynch, not more than twelve Negroes in Mississippi ever held this office.[19] Available material supplies the names Blanche K. Bruce of Bolivar, J. J. Evans of De Soto, John Brown of Coahoma, Winslow of Washington, Sumner of Holmes, Merrimon Howard of Jefferson, Peter

P.M.H.S. 13:164; Hattie Magee, "Reconstruction in Lawrence and Jeff Davis Counties," *P.M.H.S.* 11:175.
[15] H. Magee, op. cit., 11:175.
[16] J. W. Garner, op. cit., p. 309.
[17] *Senate Reports,* no. 527, 44th Congress, 1st session, pp. 1704, 876, 616; J. W. Garner, op. cit., p. 310. Illiteracy was fairly common among the officials of the hill counties before the war. E. C. Coleman, "Reconstruction in Attala County," *P.M.H.S.* 10:149–150.
[18] John R. Lynch, op. cit., p. 93.
[19] Ibid., p. 17.

Crosby of Warren, William McCary and Robert H. Wood of Adams,
W. H. Harney of Hinds, Scott of Issaquena, and Joe Spencer Watkins
of Monroe. In regard to Sumner and Watkins, there is almost no
information. Of Blanche K. Bruce, it is sufficient to say that his
handling of the office of sheriff fully merited the confidence of the
white planters who supplied his bond of $120,000. The offices of
Evans and Winslow seem to have been managed very largely by the
whites who supplied their bonds.[20] Charges of embezzlement against
Evans,[21] an ex-slave who was described as a good, sound Negro,
seem to have been entirely unjustified.[22] Scott, judged by his testimony before the Boutwell Committee, was a man of intelligence and
ability who, although he was elected by the votes of the Negroes,
was completely under the control of white Democrats. Almost exactly
the same description applies to Merrimon Howard of Jefferson, although he at times showed a bit more independence than Scott.[23]
John Brown, run out of Coahoma County after a "race riot" during
the campaign of 1875, six years later was declared to have em-
bezzled a large sum for which his sureties were liable.[24] Peter Crosby,
whose violent expulsion by white leaguers led to the Vicksburg riots
of 1874, was a member of the infamous ring of that city. Yet, strangely
enough, subsequent examination of his accounts disclosed them to
be entirely in order.[25] Nordhoff's statement that he was illiterate is
incorrect.[26] W. H. Harney of Hinds County was a Canadian Negro of
some education and ability. He was popular with whites and blacks
alike until the development of the bitter campaign of 1875. Charges
that he was from twelve to twenty-one thousand dollars short in his
accounts occupied the courts for five years. Newspaper reports of
the settlement are confusing and contradictory.[27] William McCary and

[20] Irby C. Nichols, "Reconstruction in De Soto County," *P.M.H.S.,* 11:307; *Senate Reports,* no. 527, 44th Congress, 1st session, p. 1446.
[21] J. W. Garner, op. cit., p. 306.
[22] I. C. Nichols, op. cit., p. 307.
[23] *Senate Miscellaneous Documents,* no. 45, 44th Congress, 2d session, pp. 156–157.
[24] Jackson *Weekly Clarion,* July 21, 1881.
[25] Charles Nordhoff, *The Cotton States,* p. 79.
[26] *Senate Reports,* no. 527, 44th Congress, 1st session, "Documentary Evidence," p. 85.
[27] Hinds County *Gazette,* December 29, February 24, 1875, April 5, 1876, July 31, 1878, July 14, 1880, August 3, 1881; Jackson *Weekly Clarion,* July 14, 1881.

Robert Wood were intelligent members of families who had been free and respected residents of Natchez for several generations.[28] Their conduct seems to have given general satisfaction.

In regard to the quality and activity of county governments between 1870 and 1875, a few generalizations may be drawn. As compared with the period before the war, this was one of greatly increased activity. Bridges, roads, and public buildings destroyed or allowed to go to pieces during the war had to be reconstructed. In addition, the greatly increased business of country stores, the rapid growth of small towns, and expanded social and political activities called for the building of new roads. Under the new system of public education, there were schools to be built and a great number of teachers to be employed. The admission of the freedmen to the courts more than doubled their business. Then too, there was a great burst of enthusiasm for the building of railroads. County after county and town after town made contributions for this purpose after overwhelmingly favorable votes by whites and blacks, and Democrats and Republicans alike. All of this implied an enormous increase in county expenditures, and a proportional increase in taxation. Furthermore, the burden of this increase fell directly on the owners of real estate. The large revenue from the head-tax on slaves was no longer available, and the Republican party, made up largely of propertyless Negroes and of business and professional men, quickly lightened the heavy levies that formerly had been made on artisans, professional men, and commercial enterprisers.

Interestingly enough, there seems to be no correlation at all between the rate of taxation and the political or racial character of the counties. In 1874, at the height of Negro-Republican control, the average rate for the thirty-nine Democratic counties was $12\frac{7}{13}$ mills. That for the thirty-four Republican counties was $13\frac{7}{17}$—a difference of less than one mill. The county tax in the Democratic units ranged from 6.2 mills in Pontotoc to 20.3 in Chickasaw. In the Republican counties, the range was from 5.3 in De Soto to 23.2 in Colfax. Negro influence was probably greatest in Madison, Issaquena, Amite,

[28] Natchez *Daily Courier*, November 8, 1866; John R. Lynch, *Some Historical Errors of James Ford Rhodes*, pp. 17–18.

Washington, Warren, Yazoo, Wilkinson, and Hinds. As compared with a state average of 13, the rates in these counties were, respectively, 11, 16, 11, 13.5, 14, 10, 19, and 11.4 mills.[29] Warrants in counties with heavy Negro populations were running at from forty to seventy-five cents on the dollar.[30] On the other hand, those in Lee County, where no Negro or Republican of any kind ever held office, fell to thirty cents.[31] The conclusion must be drawn that everywhere in the state a large part of the increase in expenditures was unavoidable. Then too, the wave of extravagance which was sweeping the nation did not fail to touch Mississippi. To a certain extent, the situation probably reflects the new feeling of self-importance and the new influence that had come to the poor whites.

The question of how much fraud existed in the various counties is difficult to answer. Charges, in general terms, were frequently made in the Democratic press. The leading Republican paper assembled the available evidence, and attempted to show that a great deal more dishonesty had been uncovered in Democratic than in Republican counties.[32] With the exception of J. H. Jones, who charges graft in Wilkinson,[33] it is the general conclusion of the few students who have investigated individual counties that while there was some extravagance, there is no evidence of open fraud.[34] Their conclusions are hard to reconcile with the many charges which were prevalent at the time.

There can be little doubt that there was a rotten situation in Vicksburg, a city which seldom knew an honest government before the war, and has almost never had one since. City expenditures were enormous. Most of them went for improvement of streets and wharves, and other projects which were really necessary for a town that was rapidly becoming a city, but if half of the charges of extravagance and graft were true, the city was getting little for its money. In this exploitation, Democrats and Republicans shared alike. It is

[29] Mississippi *Weekly Pilot,* January 1, 23, 1875; J. W. Garner, op. cit., p. 313.
[30] Vicksburg *Times and Republican,* February 2, 1873.
[31] W. H. Braden, "Reconstruction in Lee County," *P.M.H.S.* 10:136.
[32] Mississippi *Weekly Pilot,* October 23, 1875.
[33] J. H. Jones, "Reconstruction in Wilkinson County," *P.M.H.S.* 8:164.
[34] F. M. Witty, op. cit., 10:119, 120, 122; E. C. Coleman, op. cit., 10:150, 155, 156, 161; W. H. Braden, op. cit., 136; R. Watkins, op. cit., 12:183, 208; H. Magee, op. cit., 11:181.

also true that the enormous grants to railroads met almost no opposition at the polls.[35] It is therefore difficult to say just how much of the extravagance and corruption was real, or how much of it should be charged to Negroes and white Republicans.

The Vicksburg ring also controlled the government of Warren County, and there can be little doubt, in spite of the curious fact that Sheriff Crosby's accounts were found to be in order, that several of the county officials, Negroes and whites, were engaged in extensive embezzlement through such methods as the forgery of warrants.[36] Unfortunately, it must be recorded that the thrifty black and white taxpayers who joined the violent white "Modocs" in overthrowing the Republican city government in 1874, and the county government in the following year, saw control pass into the hands of the least desirable element of the whites. The result was that conditions in city and county became worse rather than better.[37]

In conclusion it may be stated that although Negroes formed a majority of the population in thirty counties in Mississippi, they almost never took advantage of their opportunity to place any large number of their race in local offices. Of those who did hold offices, the twelve sheriffs were moderately satisfactory; most of them were at least capable of exercising the functions of their office. No Negro in the state ever held any higher judicial office than that of justice of the peace, and those who held that office seem generally to have been incompetent. Among the small number of chancery and circuit clerks there was a wide range of ability; most of them were not suitable men for their positions. Negroes who gained election to the boards of supervisors of the various counties, even in those cases where they formed a majority, generally were dominated by white Republicans, either natives or Northerners. Although many of the Negro supervisors were ignorant and incompetent, little difference can be discovered in the administration of their counties and that of counties under Democratic control.

[35] C. Nordhoff, op. cit., p. 76; Hinds County *Gazette,* July 31, 1872.
[36] J. W. Garner, op. cit., p. 293; Mississippi *Weekly Pilot,* March 6, 1875.
[37] C. Nordhoff, op. cit., pp. 76, 81–82; *Hinds County Gazette,* April 21, 1875; Mississippi *Weekly Pilot,* August 21, 1875; Vicksburg *Herald,* August 17, 1875; Hinds County *Gazette,* June 19, 1878, February 3, 1883.

Negroes and State Government

The first legislature under the new constitution assembled in Jackson in January, 1870. Of the 107 men in the house of representatives, twenty-five were Democrats and eighty-two were Republicans. The number of Negro representatives, originally thirty-one, was immediately reduced to thirty by the death of C. A. Yancey of Panola County. Thus, in a state which held a large Negro majority, members of that race made up less than two-sevenths of the total membership of the house, and less than three-eighths of the Republican majority. Their representation in the senate was even smaller. In the total membership of thirty-three, and in a Republican group of twenty-eight, only five were Negroes.[38]

Of the thirty Negroes in the house, eight had served in the constitutional convention. A dozen or more of the group, either by education or unusual native ability, were entirely capable of meeting their obligations as legislators. Among these were H. P. Jacobs, Henry Mayson, J. F. Boulden, M. T. Newsome, Merrimon Howard, John R. Lynch, J. Aaron Moore, H. M. Foley, J. J. Spelman, and J. H. Piles. All of these men made distinguished records in fields other than politics. Almost as capable were Albert Johnson, Nathan McNeese, A. K. Davis, Doctor Stites, Emanuel Handy, Richard Griggs, and W. H. Foote. The other fourteen members were inclined to be self-effacing, and took little part in the formation of policy.

Of the five members of the senate, three, Charles Caldwell, Hiram Revels, and T. W. Stringer, have already been discussed. Robert Gleed, of Columbus, was a man of fair education, good character, and some financial ability, although he had been a slave until the close of the war.[39] An excellent speaker, he was employed by the Democratic administration after the overthrow of the Republican regime to lecture to the Negroes of the state on educational and agricultural matters. The fifth senator, William Gray of Greenville, was a young Baptist preacher of some education and much natural cleverness. A leader in the demands for civil rights for Negroes, he

---

[38] J. S. McNeily, "War and Reconstruction in Mississippi," *P.M.H.S.C.S.* 2:381; John R. Lynch, *The Facts of Reconstruction,* pp. 44–45.
[39] J. W. Garner Papers, Mississippi State Archives, Alexander Warner to J. W. Garner, May 4, 1900; J. W. Garner, op. cit., p. 295; *Senate Reports,* no. 527, 44th Congress, 1st session, p. 795.

was lacking in tact, and was probably at times guilty of double-dealing both in politics and in religious affairs.

The election of a new house of representatives in 1871, for the term of 1872 and 1873, brought a heavy reduction of the Republican majority. Of the 115 members, the Republicans claimed sixty-six. Actually, however, several of the white members of their group, calling themselves independents, generally voted with the Democrats and against the administration. Negro membership rose to thirty-eight, but R. R. Applewhite of Copiah was completely under Democratic control, and later announced himself a member of that party. The Negroes now had a theoretical control of the Republican caucus in the lower house, but actually any attempt to press their advantage was generally blocked by the desertion of a number of their white colleagues. It was only after Alcorn urged it as a political necessity that John R. Lynch received enough white Republican votes to gain the speakership.

It may therefore be said that during the first four years of Republican control the dominant group in both houses of the legislature was a combination of native and Northern white Republicans, who were influenced by the desires of their Negro constituents, but were also attentive to the large white element in their party, an element whose numbers they earnestly desired to increase. Their leader until late in 1871 was Governor Alcorn, an old Whig with Hamiltonian sentiments and a dream of bringing into the Republican party of the state men in the Democratic and Conservative groups who shared his beliefs. When Alcorn resigned in November, 1871, to take his place in the United States Senate, he was succeeded by R. C. Powers, a man of the same sentiments.[40] Both of these men wished to carry out a program which they considered to be for the best interests of whites and blacks alike. Both of them, like many of the White Republicans in the legislature, avoided social contacts with the Negroes as much as possible, and were absolutely opposed to any real control of their party by the Negroes.

In this situation, the Negro minority in the legislature generally followed the lead of the white Republicans, with whom, in matters of routine legislation, they were usually naturally in accord. In such

---

[40] J. W. Garner, op. cit., p. 281; Dunbar Rowland, *History of Mississippi,* 2:176; J. S. McNeily, op. cit., 2:426.

routine business, the more able Negroes, including Stringer, Boulden, Jacobs, Spelman, and Lynch, were about as prominent as any of the white leaders. In fact, when the proportion of their numbers is kept in mind, a survey of the *Journals* reveals little difference between the whites and Negroes in attendance, in service on committees, or in activity on the floor. Negro members almost never suggested legislation to obtain special privileges for their race. The more able Negroes either recognized the weakness of their position or had no desire to gain undue advantage. The few who would have gone further received no encouragement or support.

In his inaugural address, in January, 1870, Governor Alcorn outlined clearly the two basic problems faced by the Republicans. "The obligations resting on us under the new order of things," he said, "extend very greatly the breadth of duty of the State Government. The 'patriarchal' groupings of our society in the days of slavery, confined the work of our political organizations, to a very great extent, to the heads of what we called 'families.' " Under the new regime every individual had become a distinct entity. In addition to the great increase in the number of individuals concerned, a large increase in the *amount* of government was contemplated. The costs of the new administration must be much greater than those of the old. He would therefore urge the legislature to take advantage of every opportunity for economy. In regard to the state's new citizens, he said: "In the face of memories that might have separated them from me as the wronged from the wronger, they have offered me their confidence. . . . In response to that touching reliance, the most profound anxiety with which I enter my office . . . is that of making the colored man the equal, before the law, of any other man. . . ."[41] Thus, in the beginning, Alcorn presented the problems that doomed the Republican regime. There were many whites who were alienated by the extension of the powers of the state, and even more by the increase in costs and taxes. A larger group, including, to a certain extent, Alcorn himself, absolutely refused to accept the implications of Negro equality before the law. Such revolutions, unless maintained by overwhelming force, cannot be accomplished in a decade.

With a treasury balance of about fifty dollars in cash and five

---

[41] Mississippi *House Journal*, 1870, pp. 56–57.

hundred dollars in negotiable paper, the Republicans entered upon
the program that was to reconstruct the state. During the next four
years, they set up, organized, and maintained at state expense a bi-
racial system of common school education which, although it did not
approach the national average in facilities or expense, was an
amazing advance beyond anything the state had known before. They
gave state support to normal schools at Holly Springs and Tougaloo,
and established Alcorn as a Negro counterpart to the state university.
They completely reorganized, coordinated, and centralized the state
judiciary, and gave to it a new code of laws. Old public buildings
were renovated and enlarged and new ones were constructed. State
hospitals were set up and supported at Natchez and Vicksburg, and
the facilities of the state asylums for the blind, deaf and dumb, and
insane were greatly expanded. All racial discrimination was eliminated from the laws of the state. Finally, after much disagreement,
the legislature granted to the Negroes in 1873 a civil rights bill, which
in theory guaranteed to them equal access to all places of public
entertainment.

Although much of this legislation was expensive, and almost all
of it was controversial, a partial acceptance of the program and a loss
of faith in the Democratic party produced a sweeping victory in 1872,
and the election of Republicans to five of the six congressional seats.
By the summer of 1873, the Republican party had reached the height
of its power in the state. In this very strength, however, there was a
great weakness. The breakdown of Democratic opposition, in the
state as in the nation, opened the way for a struggle among the dis-
cordant elements in the dominant party. Between 1867 and 1872, it
had appeared that this struggle, when it came, would involve a choice
by the Negroes between Northern and native whites as their leaders.[42]
In spite of efforts of the Democrats to aggravate differences on this
basis, it had greatly declined in importance by 1873. The great line
of division had come to be the question of the extent to which
Negroes were to be allowed to hold offices and to dominate the
councils of the party.

This became apparent in the state and county conventions in the
summer of 1873. The Negroes, after six years of domination of the

[42] Hinds County *Gazette,* November 1, 1867, July 5, August 9, 30, 1871.

party by whites, now declared that they must have a larger share of the offices. Although, in general, their demands were not yet proportional to their party membership, the Negroes overestimated their ability to supply suitable candidates. This became evident when, after Bruce's refusal to accept the lieutenant-governorship, that office went to the weak A. K. Davis. Matters became worse when the Vicksburg ring, threatening violence and secession, secured the post of superintendent of education for Cardozo. This left James Hill, candidate for the office of secretary of state, as the only really acceptable candidate offered by the Negroes for the three state positions which they demanded. Similar weaknesses were to be found in many of the men whom they chose for places in the legislature and in the county governments. The most important point at issue, however, was the fact that it was now clear that actual domination of the party by the mass of its Negro membership would probably come in the near future. By thousands of white members of the party, and by a majority of its white leaders, such a development could not be accepted.

J. L. Alcorn, already repudiated by the Negroes, undertook to lead the opposition, and announced his candidacy for the governorship in opposition to Adelbert Ames. With him went most of the Republican leaders who were native whites, and a number of those from the North. To this group, calling itself the "Republican Party of Mississippi," the Democrat-Conservative organization immediately threw its support.[43]

In an election in which the color line was rather sharply drawn, Ames defeated Alcorn by a vote of 69,870 to 50,490. Seventy-seven of the 115 members of the lower house were Republicans of either the Alcorn or the Ames faction. Fifty-five were Negroes, but one or two of these were Democrats. In a senate of thirty-seven members, twenty-five were Republicans, including nine Negroes. All of the seven state officers were regular Ames Republicans, and three of them, the lieutenant-governor, the secretary of state, and the superintendent of education, were Negroes. Furthermore, a Negro from Warren County, I. D. Shadd, soon became the none-too-competent speaker of the house.

In his inaugural address, Governor Ames made a good impression.

---

[43] *Appleton's Cyclopedia,* 1873, p. 514.

After pledging himself to work for economy and reform, he turned to the race problem, analyzed the causes of conflict, and called for tolerance and a mutual recognition of rights and interests.[44] Thus, as Alcorn had done four years before, Ames recognized the two great problems which neither of them could solve. The elevation of the Negro involved a rapid expansion of state services which were inconsistent with the old ideas of economy. The readjustment of the relationship between the races was a matter beyond the power of the governor or the legislature.

The heavy increase in the number of Negroes in the government of the state did not greatly decrease its efficiency or change its character. The secretary of state was both competent and honest, and the superintendent of education at least was competent. The Negro legislators, as a group, were fairly capable of handling their duties, and probably represented their race more worthily than did the Negroes in any other Southern legislature. Visiting the state in 1874, Edward King wrote:

> . . . [Negroes] lounge everywhere, and there are large numbers of smartly dressed mulattoes, or sometimes full blacks, who flit here and there with the conscious air which distinguishes the freedman. I wish here to avow, however, that those of the negroes in office, with whom I came in contact in Mississippi, impressed me much more powerfully as worthy, intelligent, and likely to progress, than many whom I saw elsewhere in the South. There are some who are exceedingly capable, and none of those immediately attached to the government at Jackson are incapable. In the Legislature there are now and then negroes who are ignorant; but of late both branches have been freer of this curse than have those of Louisiana or South Carolina.
>
> A visit to the Capitol showed me that the negroes, who form considerably more than half the population of Mississippi, had certainly secured a fair share of the offices. Colored men act as officials or assistants in the offices of the Auditor, the Secretary of State, the Public Library, the Commissioner of Emigration [sic], and the Superintendent of Public Instruction. The Secretary of State [James Hill], who has some negro blood in his veins, is the natural son of a well-known Mississippian of the old regime, formerly engaged in the politics of his State; and the Speaker of the House of Representatives at the last session was a black man. The blacks who went and came from the Governor's office seemed very

[44] Mississippi *Senate Journal*, 1874, pp. 24–25.

intelligent, and some of them entered into general conversation in an interesting manner.[45]

In spite of Ames' evidently sincere interest in economy, he and his legislature found it very difficult to make any substantial reduction in the expenses of the state government. Under the Republican administration, expenses had grown to what the Democrats declared were fantastic proportions. As a matter of fact, when the abnormal years of the war are omitted, the figures of the state auditors do give the impression that the Republican administrations were extravagant [see Table 1].

Thus the average yearly cost of the state government under the six years of Republican control was $1,431,205.35, or almost twice the normal expenditure of the years immediately preceding the war. Even more spectacular, however, had been the increase in taxation of real estate. For many years, real property had been practically exempt from taxation in Mississippi. In 1869, the last year of Democratic control, the rate on this class of property was only one mill, or a tax of only twenty dollars a year on a plantation assessed by its owner at twenty thousand dollars and worth perhaps fifty thousand. The great sources of revenue were a tax of a dollar a bale on cotton, and privilege and license taxes which seem to have been inordinately high. The Republican regime reversed this system; after abolishing the tax on cotton and almost entirely eliminating the privilege taxes, the Republicans placed almost the entire burden of the support of the state on real and personal property. The result was a rate that rose from five mills in 1871 to fourteen in 1874. However pleasing such a system might be to the advocate of the single tax, there can be no doubt that it brought wrath to the landowners in a period of agricultural depression.

So strong had the protest of the landowners become by the spring of 1875 that the legislature could no longer afford to overlook it. Governor Ames insisted that changes were necessary, and the representatives undertook the problem. The reductions for which they provided, like those made later by the Democrats, were more apparent than real. For a centralized government in a state of more than a million people, it was a simple fact that a cost of $1.4 million

[45] Edward King, *The Great South*, pp. 314–315.

TABLE 1

Year	Democratic Administrations
1856 through 1860—average	$ 767,438.78
1865	1,410,250.13
1866	1,860,809.89
1867	625,817.80
1868	525,678.80
1869	463,219.71
1876	518,709.03
1877	697,018.86
1878	707,022.46
1879	553,326.81
1880	803,191.31

Year	Republican Administrations
1870	$1,061,249.90
1871	1,729,046.34
1872	1,596,828.64
1873	1,450,632.80
1874	1,319,281.60
1875	1,430,192.83

per year was not extravagant [see Table 1]. To meet the situation, the legislature put back on the counties the cost of jury, witness, and inquest fees that had been assumed by the state. Thus, at one blow, an item of two hundred thousand dollars a year was chopped from the cost of the government of the state, but it was added to that of the counties. In addition, the legislature presented to the people a constitutional amendment to provide for a great reduction in the number of the circuit judges. It also reduced printing costs by cutting down the number of the legislative journals, and by eliminating the publication of departmental reports. Then, against the opposition of about half of the Negro members, it reduced the salaries of the governor and other state officials, and provided for biennial rather than annual sessions of the legislature. Appropriations to the state universities were reduced, and scholarships were abolished. Another amendment to the constitution provided for the distribution of income from state lands, fines, and liquor licenses rather than their incorporation in the

permanent school endowment fund. The ratification of this amendment was to allow a heavy reduction in the state school tax. Finally,
turning to the system of taxation, the legislature reduced the *ad
valorem* levy to nine and one-fourth mills, placed a tax on railroads,
and made a partial return to the use of privilege taxes.[46] Ironically
enough, the effect of most of these reforms could not become apparent until the following year, at which time their benefits were
easily claimed by the triumphant Democrats. Their adoption went
almost unnoticed in the midst of the tumultuous movement toward
the revolution of 1875.

Unlike the Republican administrations in most of the other Southern states, those in Mississippi financed their enterprises almost
entirely through taxation. When the party assumed control in January,
1871, the state had an empty treasury and a debt of $1,178,175.33.[47]
When the Democrats returned to power in January, 1876, they found
$524,388.68 in the treasury and a debt of $3,341,162.89.[48] With the
deduction in each case of permanent funds which the state owed to
itself, and consideration of the treasury balance, the payable debt
in 1876, as in 1871, was approximately half a million dollars, a negligible amount.

Furthermore, the Republican state regime left a remarkable record
of honesty. The conclusion of J. W. Garner seems to be approximately
correct:

> So far as the conduct of state officials who were entrusted with the
> custody of public funds is concerned, it may be said that there were no
> great embezzlements or other cases of misappropriation during the period
> of Republican rule. . . . The treasurer of the Natchez hospital seems to
> have been the only defaulting state official during the administration of
> Governor Ames. He was a carpetbagger, and the amount of the shortage
> was $7,251.81. The colored state librarian during Alcorn's administra-
> tion was charged with stealing books from the library. The only large case
> of embezzlement during the post-bellum period was that of the Demo-
> cratic treasurer in 1866. The amount of the shortage was $61,962.[49]

It may be added that the next embezzlement of any importance was

---

[46] Mississippi *Session Laws,* 1875.
[47] Mississippi *Senate Journal,* 1872, *Appendix,* p. 125.
[48] Mississippi Auditor of Public Accounts, *Report,* 1876.
[49] J. W. Garner, op. cit., pp. 322–323.

that of the Democratic "redemption" treasurer who was elected in 1875. His shortage was $315,612.19.[50]

Altogether, as governments go, that supplied by the Negro and white Republicans in Mississippi between 1870 and 1876 was not a bad government. Never, in state, counties, or towns, did the Negroes hold office in proportion to their numbers, although their demands in this direction were undeniably increasing. The Negroes who held county offices were often ignorant, but under the control of white Democrats or Republicans they supplied a form of government which differed little from that in counties where they held no offices. The three who represented the state in the national Congress were above reproach. Those in the legislature sought no special advantages for their race, and in one of their very first acts they petitioned Congress to remove all political disabilities from the whites. With their white Republican colleagues, they gave to the state a government of greatly expanded functions at a cost that was low in comparison with that of almost any other state. The legislature of 1875 reduced that cost to some extent, and opened the way for further reductions by the passage of constitutional amendments. It also removed some of the apparent injustices in the system of taxation. But one situation it did not alter. The Republican party had come to be branded as a party of Negroes, and it was apparent that the Negroes were more and more determined to assert their right to control that party. It is also true that many of the Negroes, probably a majority, favored a further expansion of the functions of the state, entirely at the expense, according to the whites, of white tax-payers. The way was open for the formation of a "white-line" party.

[50] Hinds County *Gazette,* March 22, 1890; J. Dunbar Rowland, *History of Mississippi,* 2:242–245; J. D. Rowland, *Encyclopedia of Mississippi History,* 2:743–744.

III COUNTER RECONSTRUCTION

The political roles of the carpetbaggers, scalawags, and black freedmen were significant factors in the politics of Southern Reconstruction, but the political power of the former Confederates and their supporters—the majority of Southern whites—became an unrestrainable counterforce, particularly after 1868. The resistance of Southern whites to Reconstruction took many forms: political mobilization of "conservatives" or Democrats in states with white majorities, social and economic retaliation against whites who collaborated with radical Republican governments, terrorization of black freedmen by conspiratorial armed bands of whites like the Ku Klux Klan who committed innumerable atrocities all over the South. By 1876, all of the former Confederate states had come under the control of "conservative" or "redeemer" governments, with only South Carolina, Florida and Louisiana remaining in the control of radical Republicans. The rapid collapse of radical Republican governments in the South in the 1870s has led historians to raise significant questions about the methods and objectives of the Reconstruction process in the South. The selections in this part of the book explore some of these questions: Was lawless violence the main factor in the overthrow of Reconstruction? Were there fundamental social and economic forces at work in the nation as well as in the South that weakened the humanitarian objectives of the radical Republicans?

John Hope Franklin
COUNTER RECONSTRUCTION

John Hope Franklin is well known for his writings on black history in the pre-Civil War and post-Civil War periods. The following selection from his work on Reconstruction surveys the lawlessness that characterized much of Southern white resistance and assesses its importance in overthrowing the radical Reconstruction governments in the South.

The reaction of the former Confederates and their supporters to the taking over of the reconstruction program by Congress could hardly have been unanticipated. When abolitionists had called for an end to slavery in the ante-bellum period, Southerners had said that the North was making war on their institutions and their way of life. Whenever there had been slave revolts or rumors of them, planters, and even most non-slaveholders, were thrown into a frenzy of preparation for the great upheaval that they seemed to think was inevitable. "We must prepare for any eventuality," they were accustomed to saying; and whether the dangers of which they spoke were real or fancied, they had no intention of being caught short. All too frequently, long before the Civil War came, these fears had erupted with a violence that to some observers made the South appear a dark and bloody land.

Even when the former Confederates were rather firmly in control of Southern state and local governments in the early postwar years, violence was an important part of the pattern of life. In 1866 the head of the Freedmen's Bureau in Georgia complained that numerous bands of ruffians were committing "the most fiendish and diabolical outrages" on the freedmen. The former slaves themselves made many representations to Congress and the President that they were in constant danger of physical harm at the hands of the former Confederates. Northern teachers of freedmen frequently saw their efforts literally turn to ashes as local white opponents set fire to the Negro schools; and the reports of the Bureau contain many instances of bodily harm inflicted upon Northern teachers by those in the South who were unalterably opposed to the education of the former slaves. If violence was an integral part of the old order and even of the new order controlled by former Confederates, it was only natural that it would be a prime factor in any move to oppose the still newer order administered by those whom the former Confederates regarded as natural enemies.

The targets of attack now were, of course, the Union League, the Heroes of America in North Carolina, the Lincoln Brotherhood, a Radical group that flourished in Florida, and other similar organizations. The work of the League was especially reprehensible to the former Confederates. In addition to teaching Negroes what their political rights were and instructing them in the mysteries of voting, the League also fired the self-respect of the former slaves by telling them that they were the social equals of whites. To many who had supported the Lost Cause this was worse than the burning of Atlanta and Sherman's path of devastation from that city to the sea. Another target was the several state militias, which, in addition to being charged with the responsibility of keeping the hated Radical governments in power, frequently boasted of having Negro contingents to participate in the discharge of this responsibility. If Radical governments were to be placed in power by "Negro votes" and were to be kept there by "Negro militias," they invited opposition by every means, including violence, at the disposal of the former Confederates.

The young Tennesseans who organized late in 1865 the frolicking secret lodge that was to be known as the order of the Ku Klux Klan, or the Invisible Empire, could hardly have been unaware of what they were doing. Even if they were bored and impatient with life, as has been claimed in their defense, this was nothing new for young bloods in the village of Pulaski, Tennessee. Nor were wanton attacks on helpless Negroes new. If the young men were looking for fun, they did not have to go beyond the nearest Negro settlement, and furthermore they would be performing a service to the white community if they whipped Negroes to keep them in line. Long before Negroes became a political factor and while the governments of the Southern states were still in the hands of the former Confederates, the Klan organization was being perfected and was spreading to many parts of the South. It described itself as an institution of "chivalry, humanity, mercy, and patriotism." Within a matter of months it had selected its name, adopted its ritual, and had begun to terrorize the Negroes of the area. Soon there were other chapters (dens) with officers bearing such ominous titles as dragons, hydras, titans, furies, and night-hawks.

In the spring of 1867 delegates from several states met in convention at Nashville, placed General Nathan B. Forrest at the head of the organization as the Grand Wizard, and sent its members back to their respective homes fired with a determination to nullify the program of congressional reconstruction that was just getting under way. No longer was it sufficient to frighten or terrorize Negroes by ghoulish dress, weird rituals, and night rides. By social and business ostracism of the white Radicals, by intimidation and any effective means of violence conceivable against Negroes, by the purchase of votes of any sellers, and by glorifying the white race and especially white womanhood, the Klan grimly moved to wreck each and every phase of Radical Reconstruction.

While the Klan made rapid strides in Tennessee, North Carolina, and Alabama, other similar groups were springing up elsewhere. In Louisiana it was the Knights of the White Camellia. In Texas it was the Knights of the Rising Sun. In Mississippi it was the White Line, and on and on throughout the former Confederate states. Scores of other counter reconstruction organizations flourished in various parts of the South. Among them were the Constitutional Union Guards, the Pale Faces, the White Brotherhood, the White League, the Council of Safety, and the '76 Association. As the months and years went by, more such organizations came into existence. Old or new, large or small, they had one aim in common: the maintenance and, later, the reestablishment of white supremacy in the South. They had one means in common: any and every kind of intimidation and violence against the Negro and his supporters. Even if they were, in some instances, autonomous and even amorphous, these groups were at least held together loosely by the ideals, aims, and methods which they shared with the Invisible Empire.

It would be a historical fallacy to assert that the Ku Klux Klan and its compatriots were organized to combat the Union League and to overthrow Radical Reconstruction. They came on the scene much too early to support such a view and they were, indeed, too much a reflection of the general character of Southern life to require the unique conditions of Radical Reconstruction to spawn them. Radical Reconstruction was, however, a powerful stimulus for such endeavors, and the struggle against it gave the Klan respectability and a dignity that it had not anticipated. The lawlessness of the Jayhawkers and Bushwhackers of 1865 became the holy crusade of the Klansmen of 1868. Within a matter of months it was being claimed that the "instinct of self-protection" prompted the organization of the Klan. "It was necessary," one of them argued, "in order to protect our families from outrage and to preserve our own lives, to have something that we could regard as a brotherhood—a combination of the best men in the country, to act purely in self-defense, to repel the attack in case we should be attacked by these people."

The real stimulus, then, to the growth and expansion of Klan activities was not the attacks on innocent white families by Negroes and others but the apparent determination on the part of Negroes and their Radical friends to assume and wield political power. For the former Confederates this was indeed an attack as real as any they could imagine. The oath of the Klansmen to aid those fellow members in distress and "pecuniary embarrassment" was liberally construed, while their promise to protect female friends and widows of Confederate veterans drew into the fold many who would not have been attracted for other reasons. They proceeded on the basis of that ancient principle that the best defense was a well-planned offense. At times wearing hoods and robes, at other times without disguise, they rode over the land at night "terrifying, whipping, or murdering whites and Negroes who, for one reason or another, were to them undesirable." Negro offenses ranged from insolence to voting and holding office. White offenses ranged from participating in Radical governments to associating with Negroes on a basis of equality.

Acting "purely in self-defense" assumed curious forms. It involved the murder of respectable Negroes by roving gangs of terrorists, the murder of Negro renters of land, the looting of stores whose owners were sometimes killed, and the murder of peaceable white citizens. On one occasion in Mississippi a member of a local gang, "Heggie's Scouts," claimed that his group killed 116 Negroes and threw their bodies into the Tallahatchie River. It was reported that in North Carolina the Klan was responsible for 260 outrages, including 7 murders and the whipping of 72 whites and 141 Negroes. In one county in South Carolina 6 men were murdered and more than 300 were whipped during the first six months of 1870. Meanwhile, the personal indignities inflicted upon individual whites and Negroes were so varied and so numerous as to defy classification or enumeration. There were the public whippings, the maimings, the mutilations, and other almost inconceivable forms of intimidation.

If the doctrine of political and social equality of whites and Negroes was to be spread by the Union League, then the League was an enemy of the South and deserved any obloquy and violence that could be directed against it. League officials, Negro and white, were bitterly assailed, their property frequently destroyed, and themselves whipped and sometimes murdered. League members were warned to stay away from the polls on election day if they and their families wanted to remain alive. One newspaper editor, calling for the organization of a chapter of the Klan in every community, declared in 1868 that this was the most effective way for the men of the South "through whose veins the unalloyed Caucasian blood courses" to crush, "with one mighty blow, the preposterous wicked dogma of Negro equality." He left little to the imagination when he exclaimed, "If to every tree in our forest-like streets were attached a rope; and to the ends of each rope a Northern and Southern Radical, gathered from the Loyal League assembled in our courthouse, then might we once more live in peace and harmony." In this spirit the Klan undertook to destroy the main political arm of Radical Reconstruction in the South.

Since the Freedmen's Bureau had been an important factor in the establishment of congressional reconstruction and since it had assisted the Union League in the "political education" of the Freedmen, it was viewed by the Klan as another special enemy. Encouraged by President Johnson's opposition to the Bureau and by the widespread opposition among former Confederates to the Bureau since its inception, the Klan proceeded to drive the Bureau out of the political picture altogether. The attack on Bureau officials was systematic and effective. Sometimes they were simply warned to leave town, sometimes they were flogged. An agent of the Bureau in Tennessee slept for months with a revolver under his pillow, "a double-barreled shot gun, heavily charged at one hand and a hatchet at the other, with an inclination to sell the little piece of mortality with which I am entrusted as dearly as possible." Even after the Bureau

FIGURE 4. "If He Is a Union Man or a Freedman: Verdict—'Hang the D--- Yankee and Nigger.' " From *Harper's Weekly*, March 23, 1867, p. 185. (*Courtesy Boston Public Library, Periodical Department*)

had been officially disbanded, former employees were marked objects of the wrath of the Klansmen.

Perhaps nothing aroused the hatred of Klansmen as much as the so-called Negro militia units. Conservatives called the units a "dangerous offensive design" to spy on those opposing Radical Reconstruction. Those in the state legislatures sought to block appropriations for the militia and, failing in this, to enjoin the expenditure of the funds that had been appropriated. The opposition moved steadily toward outright violence. The names of Negro militia leaders were recorded in "Dead Books," while in some communities coffins "were paraded through the streets marked with the names of prominent Radicals and labeled with such inscriptions as 'Dead, damned and delivered.'" Negro militiamen were attacked individually and stripped of their weapons, including pocket knives. When they learned through spies of the shipment of arms into the state for the use of the militia, the enemies of Radical Reconstruction would intercept the shipment and either appropriate it for their own use or destroy it altogether.

Personal violence against militiamen, white or Negro, was the favorite weapon of the Klansmen. In South Carolina, Joseph Crews, a white organizer of the Negro militia, carried on a running fight with his bitter enemies for several years. Finally, in 1875, he was ambushed and killed by a shotgun blast. Frequent raids on the homes of militiamen resulted in property being taken, mutilated, or burned. In Marion, Arkansas, a Negro militia captain was murdered on the streets "in broad daylight." After discharging both loads of a double-barreled shotgun into his body, the assailant fired five revolver shots into him and then rode away unmolested. In Mississippi the well-known Negro state senator, Charles Caldwell, had commanded a company of Negro troops that had been ordered to maintain the peace in Clinton. For this deed, Caldwell was lured into a cellar, shot many times there, and then carried into the streets where his body was "grotesquely turned completely over by the impact of innumerable shots fired at close range." Murders, lynchings, drownings were the hazards facing Negro and white militiamen who undertook to support congressional reconstruction in the South.

The more "respectable" members of Southern communities, repelled by these excesses, argued that the terrorist organizations had been taken over by the low, irresponsible elements of the population. They were composed of "drunken and lawless vagabonds" declared one disgusted South Carolinian. They were "ignorant and without education to the last degree" asserted the Democratic minority of a congressional investigating committee. The Klan fell into the hands of "cut-throats and riffraff, for private gain and vengeance," one historian has recently claimed.

It is difficult to understand how the flower of Southern manhood could have surrendered the leadership of the Klan to so irresponsible an element of the community. Klan leaders in Alabama were Generals James H. Clanton, erstwhile Whig lawyer, and John T. Morgan, a future United States senator. Mississippi's leading Klansman was General Albert Pike, poet, journalist, and explorer. In North Carolina leaders were Zebulon Vance, former governor, and William L. Saunders, Confederate colonel and editor of the state's colonial records; and in Georgia, General John B. Gordon, wealthy insurance executive. The Grand Wizard was General Nathaniel Bedford Forrest, the strong man of Fort Pillow. When Forrest denounced lawlessness employed by "bogus" Klans in 1869, the "respectable" element supported his position. He dissociated himself and his outfit from those who were seizing the opportunity to satisfy private vengeance and to disarm harmless Negroes who had no thought of "insurrectionary movements." The distinction was not nearly so clear as Forrest attempted to make it. He would have been hard put to distinguish between the "lawful" violence of the Klan and the "unlawful" violence of the disreputable element. The assassination of an Alabama judge by the Klan should be no different in the eyes of the law from the murder of Negro would-be voters by hoodlums. In the final analysis, the "respectable" organization remains a prime instigator of the use of violence as a counter-reconstruction measure.

Congressional reconstruction would have no chance of success unless it could put down the lawlessness that was rapidly destroying every semblance of political and economic stability in the South. If they were ever to take a stand and fight for their survival, the state governments realized that the time was now at hand. Governor William G. Brownlow of Tennessee, among the most vigorous defenders of Radical Reconstruction, was outraged that the violent counter-reconstruction movement should have had its formal inception in his state. These "rebellious elements," he declared, were composed of ex-rebel soldiers and their sympathizers, who were "plotting and planning mischief in every respect." The legislature of 1868 complied with his request to enact a law "to preserve the public peace." These and similar measures in other states came to be known as the "Ku Klux laws." Any person belonging to secret organizations engaged in night prowling "to the disturbance of the peace" or sheltering members of such organizations was to be punished by a fine of not less than $500 and imprisonment for a term of not less than five years and was to be "rendered infamous." Informers were to receive one-half the fines if citizens and three-fourths if public officers. There were other provisions, including the assessment ranging from $500 to $5,000 for the state school fund on a county permitting a Klansman to reside within its borders and civil damages ranging from $10,000 to $20,000 in favor of the victim of Klan violence.

Other states followed Tennessee's lead, and within two years there was a network of Ku Klux laws extending across the South designed to combat the counter-reconstruction efforts. In the same year Alabama enacted a similar law and added that "the fact of a man's hiding his face and wearing a costume was *prima facie* evidence of guilt." In the following year Arkansas and North Carolina passed Ku Klux laws, with Mississippi and South Carolina following in 1870 and 1871, respectively. Governors sought to speed the process of destroying the Klan by declaring martial law, appointing special constables, and offering rewards for the apprehension of the night riders. On the whole, the laws were ineffective and their enforcement was generally impossible. As the authorities realized this, they became more desperate. Few means were left to bolster governments that were sagging badly under the weight of counter-reconstruction.

One possibility was military power. In Tennessee full control over the state militia was placed in the governor's hands, and Brownlow did not hesitate to use it. Late in 1868 Governor Powell Clayton declared martial law in thirteen Arkansas counties and sent militiamen into the disturbed areas to maintain the peace. In the summer of 1870 Governor William W. Holden of North Carolina ordered a Union veteran, Colonel George Kirk, to raise troops and put down threatened insurrections in several Piedmont counties. Scores of Ku Klux suspects were hanged for alleged outrages. These and similar measures merely stiffened the resistance of the enemies of reconstruction and strengthened the conviction that the Klan was fully justified. Reports of the number and conduct of Negro troops on a scene of trouble were frequently exaggerated, and even when that was not the case their use was universally condemned by the former Confederates. Unable to predict what dire consequences might flow from the wielding of military power by Negroes and their friends, the Conservatives began to assert that life for them was becoming "unendurable."

As the whites lashed back at the Ku Klux laws and resisted their enforcement with all the resources they could muster, the supporters of reconstruction began desperately to turn to the federal government for support. From the beginning of congressional reconstruction the new governments had kept the authorities in Washington informed of developments. The Northern press followed every incident with lively interest and gave full play to the stream of Ku Klux atrocity stories coming out of the South. At least a portion of the North was becoming aroused. The Republican party in the South was rapidly disintegrating, violence was threatening Northern investments there, and the war and the reconstruction amendments to the Constitution were being nullified by the Klan and its confederates. The Klan was a "hell-born cabal," declared John W. Forney of Philadelphia. It was "another secession snake," the editor of the New York *Tribune* shouted with characteristic directness. Sooner or later, for one reason or another, the federal government would have to take official cognizance of counter reconstruction in the South.

Perhaps no one took very seriously the order of the Grand Wizard in the spring of 1869 that the Invisible Empire was to dissolve, bury or burn its regalia, and destroy its ritual and records. Certainly, the anti-Klan laws enacted by the states did little to discourage the Klan or coerce its dissolution. Nor could the irresponsible violence of the so-called lower elements have filled the Klan with sufficient disgust to cause it to want to dissociate itself from the more extreme counter-reconstruction measures. In the midst of growing criticism and public outrage against the Klan, the dissolution order of the Grand Wizard appears to have been more of a tactical move than an honest effort to reduce the violence associated with the name of the Klan. Such an order, the leaders hoped, would mean that the Klan could no longer be held responsible for hundreds of crimes described in issue after issue of Northern newspapers. And if the work of the Klan was to be effective, whether performed by the white-robed "better elements" or by others, there was no need to invite the criticism of and, perhaps, punishment by those who possessed the means of vengeance. The path to survival and success was underground, and most of those committed to the Klan's objectives followed that path.

The order of dissolution did not, however, divert attention from the Klan. Leaders in Congress became convinced that some measure of federal support was necessary if the reconstructed states were to survive. The enactment of appropriate legislation would provide the ground on which the "Republican party must stand in carrying into effect the Reconstruction," declared Senator John Pool of North Carolina. Without it the "whole fabric of Reconstruction, with all the principles connected with it, amounts to nothing at all, and in the end it will topple and fall." Congress, busily engaged in admitting the last of the Confederate states, soon diverted some of its attention to the defense of the new governments and enacted measures to enforce the reconstruction amendments. At the end of May, 1870, a law was passed designed to protect Negroes exercising the franchise. Persons hindering, obstructing, or controlling qualified electors in their effort to vote were to be fined and imprisoned. The Klan or others in disguise who interfered with anyone in the enjoyment of his constitutional rights were to be found guilty of committing a felony. Federal district and circuit courts were to have jurisdiction, and federal marshals and other officers were to enforce the law.

The first federal intervention was, on the whole, ineffective. Operating underground, the Klan was able to continue its work by threat and by violence. When charges were brought against alleged offenders, witnesses were usually afraid to testify. When they did testify, juries declined to convict. Through the summer and fall conditions in the former Confederate states deteriorated steadily. The Klan was openly active in the Alabama election of August, 1870. Its members paraded in full regalia, despite the Alabama law, the new federal statute, *and* the Grand Wizard's dissolution order of the previous spring. In Mississippi the Klan took on new life in 1870 in

GRANT 1870

order to oppose the establishment of schools for Negroes and to resist the new taxes that it regarded as unreasonable. In North Carolina Governor Holden carried on a running fight with the Klan, and when it appeared that he was not strong enough to cope with the organization, he wired President Grant for support. Holden did not receive any reinforcements and consequently was unable to perpetuate his regime. But he had given the President some indication of the difficulties the reconstruction governments were experiencing, and the President would not forget what he had learned.

In a special message to Congress on December 5, 1870, President Grant declared that "the free exercise of franchise has by violence and intimidation been denied to citizens in several of the states lately in rebellion." On the basis of the information that had come to him regarding conditions in the South, the Senate established a committee of seven to inquire into those conditions. The committee not only examined the voluminous reports turned over to it by the President but called before it a large number of witnesses from North Carolina—federal and state officials, Klan leaders, and private citizens, white and Negro. The five Republican leaders concluded that the state of North Carolina had insufficient force to cope with the Klan. It was indulging in "a carnival of murders, intimidation, and violence of all kinds." The two Democrats on the committee dissented, declaring that the claim of anarchy in North Carolina was "absurdly untrue."

As a result of the majority report Congress was in a mood to strengthen its legislation of the previous year. On February 28, 1871, it amended the Enforcement Act of May 31, 1870. Supervisors of elections were to be appointed by federal courts, and interference with the discharge of their duties was to be a federal offense, punishable by fine and imprisonment. Federal courts were given jurisdiction over the election supervisors and their work.

Before this law could be tested, a new session of Congress had convened, and the sentiment was strongly favorable to a much more vigorous effort to sustain the new governments in the South. A fresh flood of reports of outrages had come to the attention of the President, and he was ready to take the initiative. Numerous altercations and riots in South Carolina were especially disturbing. They confirmed his growing conviction that life and property were insecure and that the carrying of the mails and the collection of revenue were being endangered. In a special message to Congress he indicated that the power of the states to deal with the problem was inadequate and that he was not certain his own powers were sufficient for such emergencies. Therefore, he recommended legislation to facilitate his enforcement of the law. He then issued a proclamation condemning the lawless elements in South Carolina and ordering them to disperse within twenty days.

Almost immediately Congress responded by drawing up a bill, known as the Third Enforcement Act, which became law on April 20, 1871. Opposition to the bill was bitter, and debate was acrimonious. Not only did Democrats oppose it but several important Republicans spoke out with deep feeling. James A. Garfield in the House called the measure "extreme," while Carl Schurz in the Senate said that the bill gave the President power that he, Schurz, was unwilling to confide in any living man. The majority of members of both houses had been persuaded that the President was justifiably alarmed, and they gave him what he asked for.

The new law, known as the Ku Klux Act, declared that the activity of unlawful combinations constituted a "rebellion against the government of the United States." In areas where such combinations were at work the President could suspend the privilege of the writ of habeas corpus and proclaim martial law. Persons having knowledge of conspiracies could be held responsible for injuries done if they made no effort to prevent the conspirators from carrying out their designs. The President then issued a proclamation calling public attention to the new legislation. He warned that while he would be reluctant to exercise the powers granted him, he would use them "whenever and wherever it shall be necessary to do so." It was not until October 17 that he suspended the writ in nine South Carolina counties that had been especially chaotic and violent during the summer of 1871.

In South Carolina and in other states where the President directed his attention federal troops were used to make arrests and to enforce the law. At the trials in Greenville and Columbia many were found guilty and given fines and prison terms. In Mississippi there were trials under the new law as early as June, 1871, but no convictions. In North Carolina there were hundreds of arrests. Some of the accused confessed their guilt and were released upon providing information that implicated others. By the time the law expired in 1872 there had been hundreds of arrests and some convictions. But the South had not succumbed to federal force. "Short memories," "illness of the defendants," and other reliable alibis frequently destroyed the government's cases. The general attitude of witnesses, the accused, and the public was that the interference by the government was unwarranted and that their previous and current actions were fully justified.

Meanwhile, Congress had injected itself into the reconstruction picture in still another way. At the time the Ku Klux Act was under consideration Congress passed a resolution establishing a joint committee of twenty-one members to "inquire into the condition of the late insurrectionary states." There were five Republicans and two Democrats from the Senate and eight Republicans and six Democrats from the House. Senator John Scott of Pennsylvania was designated chairman. Among the more prominent members from the Senate were Zachariah Chandler of Michigan, Francis P. Blair of Missouri, and New York-born Benjamin F. Rice of Arkansas. From the House, the better-known members were Benjamin F. Butler of Massachusetts, Samuel S. Cox of Ohio, and William E. Lansing of New York. Six committee members were from former Confederate states, while Missouri, Delaware, and Kentucky each had one member. On April 20, 1871, the day on which President Grant signed the Ku Klux Act, the joint committee was organized for work. Like its predecessors this committee strengthened vastly the investigative role of Congress. A subcommittee of eight was to hold hearings in Washington, and three subcommittees were to hold hearings in various parts of the South. By the middle of February, 1872, the committee had completed its work and was ready to make its report.

Persons from every segment of the population appeared before the committee. Governors, senators and representatives, state legislators, mayors, and sheriffs; United States Army officers, ex-Confederate generals and other veterans; planters, lawyers, doctors, editors, merchants and artisans; teachers and clergymen; and Negroes "by the score." Wade Hampton and Governor James L. Orr of South Carolina appeared. Former governor Joseph Brown of Georgia, Governor Robert Lindsay of Alabama, and Nathaniel B. Forrest, widely recognized as the Grand Wizard of the Invisible Empire, all gave testimony.

Suspected members of the Klan and former Confederates in general gave little helpful information. Witnesses usually denied membership in the Klan or any knowledge of its activities. Even when they admitted membership in some organization, they could not remember who asked them to join or who were members. General James H. Clanton of Alabama said that he did not think there had ever been an organization known as the Ku Klux Klan in his state. The testimony of General Forrest and others similarly situated was no more helpful. Indeed, when pressed by members of the committee, some of them became voluble, loosing a flood of invectives and profanities against Negroes and the committee.

Negro witnesses were "more co-operative." Some of them "made good witnesses and told graphic and convincing stories which had the ring of truth," a historian of the Klan has declared. One of them told how he was whipped because he had not lifted his hat when he met a white man on the road. Another related how a Negro was killed by a mob after an altercation with a white man. A Negro woman told how the Klan dragged her husband from their home and lynched him, presumably because he was politically active. Many told of threats and intimidation directed at those Negroes who wielded some political influence or who merely voted. Thus, the Negroes and their friends emphasized the lawless, political character of the Klan, while the former Confederates feigned ignorance of it or claimed that it confined its role to that of peacemaking and law enforcement.

The division within the committee was not unlike the division among the witnesses. The Democratic members criticized the committee for confining its work to six states—North and South Carolina, Georgia, Mississippi, Alabama, and Florida. They argued that the committee's work and its report had been politically inspired, that any violence in the South had been provoked by the corruption of the Republican party and the irresponsible rule of the new governments. The Republicans, who wrote the majority report, recommended continuing protective measures by enforcement of federal laws. This should be maintained until there was "no further doubt of the actual suppression and disarming of . . . [the] widespread and dangerous conspiracy" that it had discovered. The committee urged the North to be patient while the strong feeling engendered by the war gradually subsided. Meanwhile, the South's "reluctant obedience" to federal authority was hoped for, but "less than obedience" the government would not accept.

The report of the joint committee, covering thirteen large volumes, was one of the most extensive that a congressional committee had ever made. Almost as much was gained from what the report did not say as from what it did say. The bellicosity of some of the former Confederate witnesses and the artful evasiveness of some of the others clearly indicated that many Southerners had no intention of accommodating themselves to federal control or congressional reconstruction. The earlier decision of the Klan to go underground paid off handsomely, for the members could now say they knew of no organization whose purpose was to resist the law. Even without the committee's saying so, it was clear that counter-reconstruction had been so successful that the new governments in the South could not stand without the most vigorous and direct support of the federal government. And if any of the Republican members had looked to the South for strong party support in the election of 1872, they must have been depressed by what they saw. The reconstruction governments were showing signs of collapse, and the party in power was collapsing even more rapidly.

Counter reconstruction was everywhere an overwhelming success. In the face of violence the Fourteenth and Fifteenth Amendments provided no protection for the Negro citizen and his friends. The federal enforcement laws of 1870 and 1871 proved wholly inadequate, especially when enforcement was left to the meager forces that remained in the South at the time of their enactment. Negroes could hardly be expected to continue to vote when it cost them not only their jobs but their lives. In one state after another, the Negro electorate declined steadily as the full force of the Klan came forward to supervise the elections that federal troops failed to supervise. Towns, counties, and states went Democratic. Overthrow of existing governments became systematic and inevitable. As early as April, 1868, the Democratic convention of South Carolina had said to the Negroes of the state, "It is impossible that your present power can endure, whether you use it for good or ill." Within two years this

MISSISSIPPI KU-KLUX IN THE DISGUISES IN WHICH THEY WERE CAPTURED.
[FROM A PHOTOGRAPH.]

FIGURE 5. Captured Mississippi Ku Klux Klansmen. From *Harper's Weekly*,
October 19, 1872, p. 805. (*Courtesy Boston Public Library, Periodical Department*)

promise was well on its way to fulfillment in South Carolina and
elsewhere.

While the success of counter reconstruction through violence was
itself a kind of vindication of violence, it is now clear that reconstruction could have been overthrown even without the use of violence.
Except for the exasperation of Grant in 1870 and the Enforcement
Acts of 1870 and 1871, the federal government was, more and more,
leaving the South to its own devices. Even more important was the

enormous prestige that the former Confederates enjoyed. In time they were able to assume leadership in their communities without firing a shot or hanging a single Negro. What they lacked in political strength they made up in economic power. By discharging or threatening to discharge Negro employees who persisted in participating in politics, they could reduce the Negro electorate to a minimum. By refusing to pay taxes to support the expanded and inflated functions of the new governments, they could destroy Radical Reconstruction in a season. But the former Confederates relied on no one method. By political pressure, economic sanctions, *and* violence they brought Radical Reconstruction crashing down almost before it began.

Horace Mann Bond
SOCIAL AND ECONOMIC FORCES IN ALABAMA RECONSTRUCTION

As early as 1938, Horace Mann Bond raised some significant questions about the Reconstruction process in an article which was published in The Journal of Negro History. *The following selection from that long and carefully detailed article asks us to look behind the usual historical scenario composed of carpetbaggers, scalawags, black freedmen, and white "redeemers" to basic social and economic forces that were to shape the future of Southern life.*

The story of Reconstruction in Alabama, more than a twice-told tale, has become a commonly accepted pattern for the historical description of the South. In the definitive work of Walter Lynwood Fleming,[1] the central figures and facts are set forth with a conviction, and

Reprinted by permission of the author and publisher, from Horace Mann Bond, "Social and Economic Forces in Alabama Reconstruction," *Journal of Negro History* 23 (July 1938): 290, 310, 313–326, 330–348. Copyright © 1938 by The Association for the Study of Negro Life and History, Inc.

[1] *Civil War and Reconstruction in Alabama* (New York: The Columbia University Press; Macmillan, 1905).

documentation, that for thirty years has closed the subject to further investigation.

The central figures in this stereotype are the shiftless, poor white scalawags; the greedy carpetbaggers; the ignorant, deluded, sometimes vicious Negroes; and the noble, courageous and chivalrous Southrons who fought and won the battle for White Supremacy. The accepted facts are: the imposition of a corrupt carpetbagger-Negro regime on a proud State; the accumulation of a debt of $25,503,593;[2] the final victory of Honesty; and the shouldering of this immense debt by a war-ridden, despoiled people who toiled for generations under the incubus of fearful interest payments.

We enjoy, today, an advantage in perspective over Fleming, who was himself the son of a planter partially ruined by the War, and whose thesis, in some degree, was the expression of a class-attitude affected by the events of the Civil War and Reconstruction, thinking in terms of ethical evaluations, and seeking, as even historians will, to fix blame. It is pertinent to remember that Fleming wrote, and published, less than thirty years after the occurrence of the events he described.

There is precedent for linking the long-favored figures of the Reconstruction history to the less romantic forces by which ". . . the planting class was being trampled in the dust—stripped of its wealth and political power—(while)—the capitalist class was marching onward in seven league boots."[3] With an eye to what happened in Alabama, Russ says that the process of disfranchisement in the South "played an important part in producing modern Industrial America," through keeping the "ex-leaders of the South" out of Congress until it was too late to change the new industrial order which had become firmly entrenched in the interim.[4] Whether these grand motives affected policy in Alabama, so far as internal politics was concerned, may be doubted.

What is doubtless is the value of the point of view for interpreting

---

[2] In *Black Reconstruction* (New York: Harcourt, Brace and Co., 1935), W. E. B. Du Bois hints at a reexamination of the nature of the Alabama debt. However, he gives Fleming's figure as *bona-fide* for 1874, and makes no later correction of this as a final figure or the Alabama debt.

[3] Charles A. and Mary Beard, *The Rise of American Civilization*, 2:105.

[4] William A. Russ, Jr., "Registration and Disfranchisement under Radical Reconstruction," *The Mississippi Valley Historical Review* 12:2, p. 180.

the record of Reconstruction in Alabama, for Alabama was more likely to witness the working of unsuspected economic forces than any other Southern state. Its natural resources were unique in the South; and, in an age when Coal was power, and Iron the other necessity for industry, it was already known that the Northern hill-country of Alabama had both in unexampled proximity. The bankers in Philadelphia and New York, and even in London, and Paris, had known this for almost two decades. The only thing lacking was transportation.

We propose to examine here the thesis, that the most important elements involved in the Reconstruction of Alabama were the economic factors incident to the State itself and to the times. . . .

Capital in Alabama—Railroads, Coal, and Iron

In 1850 the "Little Giant," Stephen A. Douglas, visited Alabama, spending most of the time in Mobile. The result of his visit was eminently successful; the Alabama Congressional delegation, which in 1848 had been unanimously opposed to the Railroad Bill of that year as introduced by Douglas, in 1850 furnished the small majority by which it became law.[5] One reason for the change was that the 1850 bill made possible, with later enactments, a grant of 3,077,373 acres to various Alabama roads, in a compromise addition to the terms of the 1848 bill which specified a grant to the Illinois Central. The Alabama roads thus favored were the Mobile and Ohio, planned to make a juncture with the Illinois Central at Cairo; the Selma, Rome, and Dalton; the Alabama and Chattanooga; the South and North Alabama; and the Mobile and Girard.[6]

In 1852 a young man named Jabez Lamar Monroe Curry "traversed the counties of Talladega, Calhoun, and Randolph, making speeches, and obtaining rights of way and subscriptions" for the Alabama and Tennessee River Railroad Company, in which his father was a prominent stockholder.[7] In 1853 this young man was elected to the State

---

[5] William Elejius Martin, *Internal Improvements in Alabama*, Johns Hopkins Studies in Historical and Political Science (Baltimore: Johns Hopkins Press, 1902), pp. 66–67.

[6] William Elejius Martin, *Internal Improvements in Alabama*, p. 68.

[7] E. A. Alderman and A. C. Gordon, *J. L. M. Curry, A Biography* (New York: Macmillan Co., 1911), p. 105. This road later merged with the Selma, Rome, and Dalton.

Legislature from Talladega County, and was immediately appointed Chairman of the Committee on Internal Improvements.[8] He held membership also on the Committee on Education. Curry sponsored legislation to give state aid to railroads from his Committee on Internal Improvements.[9] Two measures which had more relationship than one might imagine were also sponsored by Curry; one became the basis for the foundation of the first public school system in Alabama, and the second authorized the appointment of a State Geologist whose duty it was to survey "the mineral resources, their location, and the best means for their development" in the interests of the State of Alabama.[10]

A fellow member of the legislature of 1853–1854 was one Luke Pryor, who had been elected from Madison County. He was "pledged to the work of securing authority to subscribe two hundred thousand dollars to the capital stock of the Tennessee and Alabama Central Railroad, at Nashville and Decatur, and secured the bill raising that tax, enacted over the veto of Governor Winston."[11] Curry's biographers give him the same credit; "his influence in the legislature, *or other undisclosed causes,* served to pass the State aid bills over the Governor's veto."[12]

The power behind Luke Pryor was James W. Sloss, described by Armes as Pryor's "side partner in railroad and commercial ventures."[13] Sloss's name is unheralded and unsung in the more romantic annals of Alabama Reconstruction, and yet his influence, on close inspection, will be found connected with every important industrial and commercial enterprise in the State during the latter half of the nineteenth century. Like Curry's father,[14] Sloss had accumulated capital for investment in railroads, not from planting, but from storekeeping.[15] If the ventures of men like Sloss were less spectacular than those of the great planters of the Black Belt, and of his own Tennessee Valley; and if they are less known to history, it is because this was the Southern version of the new class of capitalists and

---

[8] Ibid., p. 105.
[9] Ibid., p. 106.
[10] Ibid., p. 107.
[11] Owens, *Biography of Alabama,* 4:1396.
[12] Alderman and Gordon, op. cit., p. 106.
[13] Armes, *The Story of Coal and Iron,* p. 107.
[14] Alderman and Gordon, op. cit., pp. 40–42, 108.
[15] Owens, *Biography of Alabama,* 4:1572–1753.

industrialists, manipulating great affairs of State in the obscurity of public inattention while public officials basked in the outward gaze of the multitude.

In 1855 Sloss was president of the Tennessee and Alabama Central Railroad, and it was for this line that Luke Pryor "was sent to the State Legislature."[16] Meanwhile, some five hundred miles to the North of Sloss's smaller principality, James Guthrie, President of the Louisville and Nashville Railroad, "was establishing that road as the political control of the State" of Kentucky.[17] The L. & N. early had visions of extending its empire to the South,[18] and James Sloss's enterprise in Alabama stretched northward toward Nashville, in the same direction which expansion for the L. & N. would, of necessity, involve. It was, perhaps, no accident that James Guthrie, President of the L. & N., in 1860, came into bitter conflict with the supporters of the "Little Giant" at the Charleston Convention.[19] In 1860 the candidate for a presidential nomination was still the former protagonist of the Illinois Central and the Mobile and Ohio Railroads. Could the feud, even thus early, have involved the ultimate goal of tapping Alabama's mineral wealth?

The Civil War left Alabama's railroads in poor condition; rolling stock, tracks, bridges, and other equipment were indiscriminately destroyed by contending armies in the ebb and flow of the tide of battle. Such disaster, however, does not seem to have overcome the fortunes of the north Alabama capitalists and politicians who were the associates of James Sloss. Robert Patton, a member of the Sloss north Alabama coterie, had a brother-in-law, J. J. Griers, who was in constant communication with General Grant during the War.[20] Patton was later Provisional Governor under the short-lived Johnson regime, and during his tenure of office worked in close cooperation with the Sloss interests.[21] George Houston, who became Luke Pryor's law

[16] Armes, op. cit., p. 107.
[17] George F. Milton, *The Eve of Conflict* (Cambridge: The Riverside Press, Houghton, Mifflin and Co., 1935), p. 403.
[18] Ellis Merton Coulter, *The Cincinnati Southern Railroad and the Struggle for Southern Commerce, 1865–1872.* Reprinted from *A History of Kentucky* (Chicago: American Historical Society, 1922), p. 7.
[19] Milton, op. cit., p. 374.
[20] *O.R.R.* Ser. I. Vol. XLIX, Pt. 1, pp. 590, 718; Pt. II, p. 560; Fleming, *Civil War and Reconstruction*, p. 146.
[21] The Patton Government began the convict lease system in 1866 with a lease to James W. Sloss and others. (*First Biennial Report of the Inspectors of Convicts*, con-

partner in 1866,[22] had a most uncertain record of loyalty to the Confederacy.[23] Samuel Noble, later associated with Sloss in developing the mineral resources of north Alabama, and an ally of William "Pig-Iron" Kelley,[24] traded through the lines with the connivance of Confederate and Federal officials.[25]

The Louisville and Nashville Railroad also emerged from the war with enhanced prospects. As the direct carrier between North and South of the immense Federal business, the line had extraordinary profits during the War,[26] and its "wonderful prosperity" then attained continued until 1870.[27] By the end of the War Sloss's railroad interests were already inextricably bound up with the L. & N. In 1865 three small roads in north Alabama, including the Tennessee and Alabama, combined under Sloss's leadership.[28] In 1866 Albert Fink, General Superintendent of the L. & N., spoke in his Report to the Directors as though the Sloss roads were already a part of the L. & N. system, as, indeed, they probably were.

> . . . Decatur and Montgomery Railroad. *This road, when completed, will, by connecting Decatur with Montgomery, Alabama, form a most important link, in the through line from Louisville, to Montgomery, Mobile and Pensacola, and open to the enterprise of Louisville the rich country tributary to the above cities.*[29]

By 1867 the L.&N. had come to terms with the Mobile and Ohio,

taining reprints of special message by Rufus W. Cobb, Governor, dated November 27, 1882. Montgomery: Barrett & Co., 1886.) Patton served as Vice-President of the Alabama and Chattanooga Railroad in 1869–1870 while this road was still partially under the control of the Sloss interests (*Poor's Manual, 1869–1870*, p. 420). The Tennessee and Alabama Central, a Sloss affiliate, held a mortgage on the Alabama and Chattanooga during this period. (Armes, *The Story of Coal and Iron*, p. 216.)
[22] Owens, *Biography of Alabama*, 4:1396.
[23] Fleming, *Civil War and Reconstruction*, pp. 190–195.
[24] "Pig-Iron" Kelley's first visit to Alabama in 1867 was to view the mineral resources of North Alabama and to make speeches for Republican Reconstruction. In Mobile one of his speeches to Negroes precipitated a race riot. In 1885 he revisited the State and published a brief book, *The Old South and the New* (New York: G. P. Putnam's Sons, 1888) giving his impressions. Kelley was financially interested in Samuel Noble's iron works at Anniston. His second impressions were bucolically peaceful. He was an adherent of Booker T. Washington and favored the industrial education of Negroes.
[25] Fleming, op. cit., p. 194.
[26] *Affairs of Southern Railroads*, p. 622.
[27] Coulter, *The Cincinnati Southern*, p. 11.
[28] *Affairs of Southern Railroads*, p. 697.
[29] Ibid.

negotiating a ten-year lease of the property.[30] But at Nashville the L.&N. found a strong competitor for the Alabama mineral regions' trade, in the Nashville and Chattanooga.[31] The struggle between the competing interests may be simplified as follows: Should the L.&N. affiliates, by way of the Nashville and Decatur (later the North and South Railroad) have access to Alabama's coal and iron, or should the Nashville and Chattanooga, and its controlling capitalists, win the field through extending a line from Chattanooga to the southwestward along the Tennessee River Valley?

Railroads and Reconstruction: First Phase

Officially, in the public eye and that of later historians, the actors in this dramatic struggle were, respectively, Republicans and Democrats, fighting for the slogan of "White Supremacy," on the one hand, or "Equal Rights" on the other. Not apparent on the political stage, but working powerfully behind the scenes, were such men as James Guthrie, Albert Fink, and James Sloss of the L.&N.; and V. K. Stevenson, the principal apparent owner of the Nashville and Chattanooga.[32] These men in turn had their masters. A local, but not altogether a minor capitalist, was Josiah Morris, a Montgomery banker, who is listed as a large stockholder and a director of all the Sloss railroad affiliates.[33]

V. K. Stevenson is said to have been supported by "Boston Financiers," made visible in the person of Russell Sage.[34] The L.&N. was financed largely by local Louisville capital, with frequent and sizable contributions from the municipality itself. The name of August Belmont—and this suggests, not only the activity of the Chairman of the National Democratic Party, but also of the omnipresent and

[30] Coulter, *The Cincinnati Southern*, p. 8; *Poor's Manual, 1870–1871*, p. 267.
[31] *Affairs of Southern Railroads*, p. 623.
[32] Armes, op. cit., p. 243.
[33] Morris died March 18, 1891, at Montgomery. The following newspaper account appeared at that time in the *Birmingham Age-Herald:* "He was the richest man in Alabama. . . . He held 660 shares of the 2,000 of the Elyton Land Company, which in 1874 sold for $17 a share. At his death they were valued at $4,000 a share. He got many shares as the result of a loan to Colonel F. M. Gilmer, who deposited the stock as collateral, and could not repay the loan. He was a private banker. He was a calm, and unemotional old man. He was in no sense a developer, as the term is nowadays used. He did not build towns, or railroads, nor factories; but his millions strengthened the confidence of the public."
[34] Armes, op. cit., p. 243.

almost omnipotent Rothschilds, of whom he was the American agent,[35]—was also linked to the financing of the L.&N., especially in enterprises connected with the opening of Alabama coal fields.[36]

Sam Tate, a prominent figure in Tennessee railroad building and politics, was also a factor in Alabama.[37] Tate was the builder and president of the Memphis and Charleston, a road traversing North Alabama from the Mississippi line, on the west, running just south of the Tennessee River to Decatur, where a bridge had been built, and terminating at Stevenson, with a connecting line from that point to Chattanooga.[38] Like Albert Fink, of the L.&N., Tate had the same vision of the possibilities of exploiting Alabama's mineral resources:

> Decatur to Montgomery *is another important connection, feeding your entire line with an abundance of iron and coal, with seventy-five miles of your line from which tonnage for local consumption would alone be profitable, to say nothing of the immense amount of western produce you would carry over your lines to feed the thousands of operatives that will be employed in developing the vast resources of mineral wealth in the mountains south of Decatur. Your fostering aid and care should be extended to this road, too, as early as practicable, as it will be one of its most productive arteries.*[39]

Indeed, at this time (1866) a close cooperation was in effect between the L.&N., represented by Fink, and the Memphis and Charleston, as represented by Tate. Fink rebuilt the bridge for the Memphis and Charleston at Decatur which had been destroyed during the War.[40] Tate got the contract for building the road he and Fink had proposed.[41]

By act of February 19, 1867, the General Assembly of Alabama embarked on the adventure of giving the State endorsement to railroad bonds of certain extant companies,[42] in the amount of $12,000

[35] Herbert L. Casson, *The Romance of Steel* (New York: A. S. Barnes and Co., 1907), p. 301.
[36] Ibid.
[37] James Phelan, *History of Tennessee, the Making of a State* (Boston and New York: Houghton Mifflin Co., 1889), pp. 284–290.
[38] *Affairs of Southern Railroads*, p. 723.
[39] Ibid.
[40] Ibid., p. 722.
[41] Armes, op. cit., pp. 246–247.
[42] George E. Houston, "Message of the Governor, including Report of the Commissioners on the Public Debt," *Journal of the House of Representatives*, 1875–1876 (W. W. Screws and Co., 1876), p. 209.

a mile. This legislation was enacted in the face of impending congressional reconstruction. This was the Provisional Assembly, with Governor Robert Patton, North Alabamian, and associate of Sloss, in control; and the endorsements included only those roads which were controlled by the coterie associated with Sloss. The South and North, the Montgomery and Eufaula, the Montgomery and Mobile, the Northeast and the Southwest, and the Wills Valley Roads were the beneficiaries.[43] An examination of the directorates of these railroads will show the presence of Sloss, of Pryor, of Houston, of Morris; i.e., the leading politico-capitalists who figured in the Democratic (Conservative) Party during Reconstruction.[44]

When a Republican General Assembly was convened on July 13, 1868—the work of railroad endorsement had been done hurriedly in the waning days of the Provisional Assembly, when pending bills in Congress assured Republican control by the next year—a brief period ensued during which strange industrial and capitalistic bedfellows made political peace for mutual profit.

The Wills Valley and the Northeast and Northwest roads were combined and incorporated as the Alabama and Chattanooga. The formal date of the merger was October 6, 1868.[45] In a series of acts of the General Assembly during the session of 1868–1869, the State endorsement for railroad bonds was increased from $12,000 to $16,000 a mile.[46] The increased endorsement was not a "Republican" grab; for a brief period Sloss enjoyed a paramount interest in the South and North, and the Alabama and Chattanooga, which became the particular beneficiaries of the raised endorsement. Robert Patton, his associate in politics and business, and formerly Governor under the Provisional Government, became a Vice President of the new Alabama and Chattanooga road, whose bonds he had aided in endorsing shortly before as Governor.[47] John T. Milner, Engineer of

[43] Fleming, op. cit., p. 591.
[44] See *Affairs of Southern Railroads,* and *Poor's Manual* for the years indicated, for lists of directors and officials.
[45] *Poor's Manual, 1868–1869,* pp. 419–421.
[46] *Ku Klux Conspiracy, Alabama Testimony,* pp. 193–199, 359–361, 1056, 1058, 1411, 1417–1418.
[47] *Poor's Manual, 1870–1871,* p. 104. In 1866 Patton, as provisional Governor, began the Alabama convict lease system in a contract signed with a Mr. Smith and a Mr. McMillan. Subsequently, it was shown that these men were "dummies" for a group which included James W. Sloss and Sam Tate. The convicts were used first for rail-

the South and North, and John C. Stanton, who held a like responsibility with the Alabama and Chattanooga joined in bribing members
of the Assembly. A history of industrialization in Alabama, bearing
the official approval of the Birmingham Chamber of Commerce, has
this account of the manner in which the finances of the South and
North were rescued under Republican rule.

> *Mr. John T. Milner, Engineer of the Road, said that John Whiting, a
> Montgomery cotton factor, President of the South and North Railroad,
> told him "he spurned the idea of getting among these Yankees at all,
> much less of paying them for their votes," but he said that "I might do so
> if I felt like it. So I went."*[48]

Milner's ventures were financed principally by Josiah Morris, the
Montgomery banker. Stanton was the field agent of Russell Sage.
The South and North, as an extension of the main line of the Louisville and Nashville, through 1868–1869 apparently had a working
agreement with the Alabama and Chattanooga, through which the
two lines were to be connected at a strategic point in the mineral
region where a great industrial city would be built. The legislators
were generous both with the South and North, planned to run from
Montgomery to Decatur and there to connect with the L.&N., and
with the Alabama and Chattanooga, which was planned to run from
Chattanooga across the state to Meridian, and from there, eventually,
to New Orleans. In 1868 the South and North received the 2 and 3
percent funds as a loan from the State.[49] By February 5, 1870, the
Alabama and Chattanooga was loaned $2 million by the State.[50]

A recounting of the liabilities assumed for these two railroad

road construction, and the highly lucrative, however iniquitous, system of lease to
coal mines and foundries followed shortly thereafter. (*First Biennial Report of the
Inspectors of Convicts to the Governor, from October 1, 1884–October 1, 1886*,
p. 352. Montgomery: Barrett & Co., 1886.) Incidentally, it is interesting to note that
a Captain John H. Bankhead was one of the first official figures in the new convict
system. So much is made in the current press of the aristocratic antecedents of the
Bankhead family (great planters, hundreds of slaves, etc., etc.) that it would probably be indelicate to expand here the speculation that at least a considerable
portion of the Bankhead fortune was founded on the beginning of the convict lease
system in Alabama, *after the Civil War;* and that the political as well as economic
great-god-father of the present Senator and Congressman was none other than
unsung James W. Sloss of North Alabama.

[48] Armes, op. cit., p. 216.
[49] Martin, *Internal Improvements in Alabama*, p. 71.
[50] Fleming, op. cit., p. 593.

systems shows that between 1867 and 1871—under, first, a Provisional, "Conservative" government, and, later, under a "Radical" Republican government—the State incurred what have been called *debts* of approximately $17 million in endorsements and loans. Of this amount L.&.N. affiliates (the South and North, the Montgomery and Eufaula, etc.) accounted for $7 million; while obligations assumed for the Alabama and Chattanooga, and railroads represented in this merger, equalled approximately $10 million.[51] Since the Alabama "debt" at the end of Reconstruction has been estimated at a maximum of $30 million, and $9 million represented ante-Reconstruction obligations, it is obvious how largely the manipulations of these two railroad systems alone entered into the final financial picture of the period.[52]

The apparent cooperation of the two groups of capitalists—the L.&.N. group, on the one hand, and the Alabama and Chattanooga (Russell Sage) on the other—came to an end in November 1870. The Democratic candidate for Governor, Lindsay, was elected over his Republican opponent, with a Democratic lower House and a Republican hold-over Senate. An agreement had been reached between the sponsors of the lines financed by the Louisville and Nashville, and the Alabama and Chattanooga, to locate the crossing of the railroads at a certain site in Jefferson county. The Stanton brothers, of the Alabama and Chattanooga (agents for Russell Sage) had taken options on the land surrounding the proposed crossing.[53] A group of Alabama capitalists, including Josiah Morris, W. S. Mudd, F. M. Gilmer, James W. Sloss, and others, took options on a new site, and, unknown to the Stantons, changed the route of the South and North so that it intersected with the Alabama and Chattanooga through the area which they controlled.[54]

The triumph of the local capitalists threatened to be of but brief duration. V. K. Stevenson and Russell Sage had acquired a majority of the $2,200,000 worth of bonds issued by the state in endorsing the

---

[51] George S. Houston, "Message of the Governor," *House Journal, 1875–1876,* pp. 187–217.
[52] *Poor's Manual for 1878–1879*, p. 993.
[53] Armes, op. cit., pp. 243–245.
[54] Ibid. This was the nucleus of the Elyton Land Company, which, with the development of Birmingham, made such immense fortunes for those who were able to maintain their stock.

building of the South and North.[55] They now (1871) threatened to foreclose on their mortgage, demanding as an alternative that the South and North, already constructed from Montgomery to the Alabama and Chattanooga crossing, be turned over to the latter railroad for operation.[56]

In this crisis Albert Fink, said already to have had an agreement with James Sloss, "and at all times a helper and cooperator, along with Luke Pryor[57] and George Houston,[58] of the South and North," met the backers of the L.&N. at a hastily convened conference in Louisville.[59] Perhaps ratifying a convention already in force, the L.&N. agreed to take open and complete control of the South and North, averted Russell Sage's threatened foreclosure, and dated the agreement as of May 19, 1871.[60]

The point of these inter-industrial feuds to our discussion is that they dominated every political maneuver that took place in the State during these troublous times. The Democratic and Republican Parties in Alabama, viewed from this angle, seem to have been only the obverse aspects of the L.&N. Railroad on the one hand, and the Alabama and Chattanooga Railroad on the other. The political tactics developed during this struggle was strikingly similar to contemporary developments in other states.

In Kentucky and Tennessee the L.&N. was said to "hide behind the City of Louisville" in its classic feud with Cincinnati. Promoters in the latter city proposed to build a road from Cincinnati to Chattanooga which would become the natural competitor of the L.&N.[61] Unable to obtain capital elsewhere, the promoters managed to get a grant of $10 million from the City of Cincinnati itself.[62] The L.&N. "ably supported Louisville in this fight," against the threatened competition from the sister city on the Ohio.[63] When proposed legislative aid to the Cincinnati-sponsored road was pending in the Ken-

[55] Armes, op. cit., p. 243.
[56] Ibid.
[57] Later United States Senator from Alabama.
[58] As the "Bald Eagle of the Mountains," Houston won the battle for "White Supremacy," in 1875, became Governor, and later United States Senator.
[59] Armes, op. cit., p. 245.
[60] Ibid.
[61] Coulter, *The Cincinnati Southern*, p. 28.
[62] Coulter, op. cit., pp. 32–34.
[63] Ibid., p. 44.

tucky legislature, ". . . it was claimed by the friends of the bill that this gigantic corporation (i.e., the L.&N.) was the main source of opposition, trying to hide behind the City (Louisville)."[64] The L.&N. adopted as its principal tactical weapon in Kentucky, identification with the political, social and ideological pattern of the stricken South. "Isaac Caldwell, who was one of Louisville's stanchest defenders, accused Cincinnati of helping to vote Negro suffrage upon Kentucky, and then immediately coming and asking a special favor for doing so."[65] Louisville (i.e., the L.&N.) hired merchants ". . . to go South and appeal to the disloyalty of their political record to seduce custom, and when they find that the South demands a better market than she affords, it again appeals to the more sectional feeling at home to prevent the South from getting to that market."[66] If there is any truth in this partisan accusation, it is the suggestion that capital —as represented by the L.&N.—preceded the politicians in appealing to racial and sectional interests. The fact that the L.&N. in Alabama was closely identified with local capitalists, while the Alabama and Chattanooga had such men as the "Stantons of Boston" in the chief place of prominence in operations there, is an important key to politics in the State during the crucial years of Reconstruction.

Industrial Conflict and Debt, 1871–1876

With this background, both political and industrial conflict in Alabama during the latter stages of Reconstruction becomes understandable. Reference has been made above to the close cooperation existing between the officials of the affiliated lines of the L.&N. in Alabama, and the Democratic administration elected in the fall of 1870. According to the terms of state endorsements, the State was liable for interest payments in the event of defaults by the roads. The Alabama and Chattanooga defaulted payment of interest due immediately after the new Democratic administration went into office, as of January 1, 1871.[67] Governor Lindsay did not take over the road at that time, stating that to do so would acknowledge the validity of the grants to the Road, which his faction rejected as the corrupt malpractice of the

---

[64] Ibid.
[65] Ibid., p. 15.
[66] Ibid.
[67] *Journal of the House, 1870–1871*, p. 82.

prior Republican administration. When the railroad made its second default in June, 1871 (two weeks after the Louisville and Nashville had contracted to take over the South and North), Lindsay had different advice from his supporters; and he seized the road for the State, and appointed Colonel Gindrat and James H. Clanton as receivers.[68] Clanton was, at the time, Chairman of the Democratic State Executive Committee.[69] He was also a director of the Montgomery and Eufaula Road, soon to become officially an affiliate of the L.&N. system.[70] Among his fellow directors were Josiah Morris, of Montgomery, and Bolling Hall,[71] politician, director of the South and North, and one of the founders of the Elyton Land Company.

Clanton is frequently quoted in Fleming's work on Reconstruction as a paragon of pure political motive.[72] The Montgomery and Eufaula Railroad, with the Alabama and Chattanooga, was a beneficiary of the extensive endorsements and State loans negotiated during the prior period.[73] In 1871 Clanton was killed in a brawl in Knoxville by one Nelson, who was employed by the Stanton, or Alabama and Chattanooga interests.[74] There is a certain irony in Fleming's eulogy of Clanton: "He was killed in Knoxville by a hireling of one of the railroad companies which had looted the state treasury and which he was fighting."[75]

The Alabama and Chattanooga dragged through a long period of litigation during the next few years. From July, 1871, to October, 1872, it was operated by the State.[76] The interest on the A.&C. bonds alone amounted to $500,000 a year.[77]

In 1872 David P. Lewis, Republican, was elected Governor of Alabama. Lewis immediately took steps to relieve the State of the dev-

---

[68] William H. Moore, *Report of the Commissioner to investigate and audit claims against the State of Alabama, on account of the Alabama and Chattanooga Railroad* (Montgomery: Arthur Bingham, State Printer, 1873), pp. 3–4. In the meantime, it will be remembered that the L.&N. had openly agreed to take over complete control of the South and North. See p. 325, above.
[69] *Ku Klux Conspiracy, Alabama Testimony*, p. 226.
[70] *Poor's Manual, 1868*, p. 251.
[71] Owens, op. cit., 3:726.
[72] Fleming, op. cit., pp. 508, 512, 625, 630, 638.
[73] Houston, "Message of the Governor," *House Journal, 1875–1876*, pp. 187–217.
[74] William Garrett, *Reminiscences of Public Men in Alabama for Thirty Years* (Atlanta: Plantation Publishing Company's Press, 1872), pp. 632–645.
[75] Fleming, op. cit., p. 508.
[76] Moore, op. cit., p. 3.
[77] *House Journal, 1870–1871*, p. 82.

astating interest payments which had accumulated with successive defaults, following that of the Alabama and Chattanooga. By an agreement negotiated in the Spring of 1873, the railroad companies, through an Act known as the "$4,000 a mile law," agreed to turn in their $16,000-a-mile bonds, and to receive back $4,000-a-mile straight state bonds, thus reducing the State liability by 75 percent.[78] In December of 1873, Governor Lewis stated that all of the roads involved had filed notice of their acceptance of the Act.[79]

It is strange that but little attention has been given to the effect of the Panic of 1873 upon the course of Reconstruction in the South. The failure of Jay Cooke removed from the scene, not only a heavy investor in Southern railroads, but also an "angel" of the Republican Party in the section; and left supreme in the field of these investments the combined forces of the Drexels and the rising Junius S. Morgan. While these circumstances may be of speculative interest here, they are worthy of study.

The majority of the Alabama and Chattanooga bonds had passed into the hands of a "group of English capitalists."[80] The accumulation of defaulted interest payments reached a peak in 1873, in the financial panic of that year. Even the L.&N. was completely prostrated. An operating deficit of $568,362 for the entire system in 1873 was laid at the doors of the South and North. "The prostration of the iron industries has greatly retarded the development of the rich mineral resources along the lines of that road, which had been greatly relied upon for supplying it with a profitable business."[81] The result was that the L.&N. went into bankruptcy and the ownership of the line passed finally and completely from whatever local capitalists had shared in its major control before, into the hands of eastern and European bankers.

The financial crisis made the election of 1874 of paramount importance to the persons involved, who saw an opportunity to rescue from the general wreckage whatever salvage might be had. Industrial conflict, accordingly, was sharply focussed in political conflict. The

---

[78] *Commercial and Financial Chronicle,* May 17, 1873, Vol. 16, No. 11, p. 659; December 13, 1873, Vol. 17, No. 442, p. 803.
[79] Ibid., p. 180.
[80] *Commercial and Financial Chronicle,* Vol. 16, No. 398.
[81] *Commercial and Financial Chronicle,* Vol. 19, No. 487, p. 423; Armes, op. cit., p. 252.

strictly racial and sectional interpretation of the period by Fleming is likely to suggest that all of the corruption visible in Alabama was an outcome of Black Republican thievery.[82] We may say that the basic economic issue of the campaign of 1874 in Alabama was to determine which of the financial interests involved would be able to make the best possible settlement with a state government bankrupted by the earnest efforts of both. Certain facts add piquancy to the general notion that Reconstruction in Alabama was a tightly drawn struggle between Virtue, as represented by the Democrats, and Vice, as represented by the Republicans.

Henry Clews, an associate of Jay Cooke, and a heavy investor in Southern issues, was among the most prominent of the bankers holding the Alabama railroad bonds which lay in the scale of battle.[83] Clews boasted of having negotiated Dix's nomination as Governor of New York, which, he believed, made Grant's renomination certain.[84] His interest in Alabama, he said, was motivated by a noble-hearted impulse "to help the South and to help develop its resources."[85] He added, almost as an after-thought, that he had considered Alabama as the most profitable place for investment on account of its manifest industrial advantages over the North in the years immediately after the War.[86] Writing of the "repudiation" of Alabama issues owned by him, after the final victory of the Democrats, he laid it to "political manipulation."[87] In addition to investments in State issues, Clews was associated with Samuel Noble and William D. "Pig-Iron" Kelley in financing the Oxford Iron Works at Anniston, which lay along the right-of-way of the Alabama and Chattanooga, and was a director of the Selma and Gulf Railroad (projected to run from Selma to Pensacola), advertised as forming "the most practicable route from the coal fields and valuable deposits of iron from Alabama, to the harbor of Pensacola."[88]

The election of 1874 determined the fate of the Republican Party

---

[82] Fleming, op. cit., pp. 583 ff.
[83] Henry W. Clews, *Fifty Years in Wall Street* (New York: Irving Publishing Co., 1908), pp. 254 ff.
[84] Ibid., p. 302.
[85] Ibid., p. 254.
[86] Ibid.
[87] Ibid.
[88] Armes, op. cit., p. 180; Kelley, *The Old South and the New,* passim; *Poor's Manual, 1870–1871,* p. 408.

in Alabama. George Houston, poetically represented in Democratic literature and in Fleming's accounts as "The Bald Eagle of the Mountains," and as the defender of "White Supremacy," was elected by a large majority.[89] Neither the campaign literature nor Fleming referred to his close cooperation and participation in the Sloss and L.&N. enterprises. Almost too innocently, Fleming states that: "The campaign fund was the largest in the history of the State; every man who was able, and many who were not, contributed; assistance also came from Northern Democrats, and Northern Capitalists who had investments in the South or *who owned part of the legal* bonds of the State."[90] As the "legality" of the bonds had not been determined at the time when these gentlemen made their contributions, the discrimination seems doubtful. Obviously the "Northern capitalists" who contributed to the Democratic fund did so *in the hope that with Democratic victory the bonds they owned would be declared legal by the new government.*[91] Nordhoff, a witness whose verdict was uncompromisingly against the Republican regime, said that "where conspicuous financial jobbery took place (in railroad legislation) Democrats have, oftener than not, been parties in interest."[92] Let us not forget what has already been noted; that as a specific effect of the Panic of 1873, it was the misfortune of the Republicans to enter the election of 1874 a year after the house of Jay Cooke had drawn Henry Clews with it to failure.[93]

There is a final incident to this industrial epic that may or may not have had a connection with the end of Reconstrcution in Alabama in 1874, and in other states soon thereafter. On December 21, 1874, at Macon, Georgia, was formed what has been described as the "most efficient railroad pool in the United States, largely owing to the genius of Albert Fink as manager."[94]

Sharp competition first appeared after prostration by the Civil War,

[89] Fleming, op. cit., p. 793.
[90] Ibid., p. 792. Italics the author's.
[91] Italics the author's.
[92] Nordhoff, *The Cotton States in 1875*, p. 89.
[93] Clews, op. cit., passim.
[94] William Z. Ripley, *Railroads: Finance and Organization* (New York: Longmans, Green & Co., 1915), p. 584. Fink, it will be remembered, was the guiding hand in the early L.&N. penetration of Alabama, and in that formulating the merger between the South and North and the L.&N. that defeated the designs of the Russell Sage, Republican, Alabama and Chattanooga.

when it was soon discovered that there were more roads than available traffic. Agreements to restore and maintain charges alternated for a time with the most destructive rate wars. . . . Bankruptcy and ruin in railroad affairs were widespread. Permanent success was finally wrought out of such chaos by the first General Commissioner, who perfected an agreement in 1875 which proved lasting.[95]

The pool rejoiced in the innocent name of "The Southern Railroad and Steamship Company." It allayed competition, and facilitated the growth of several great systems where the highly individualistic small lines had flourished theretofore.[96] Coincident with the formation of this pool, it is interesting to note certain changes in the directorates of many of the Southern lines as reported for 1875–1876, and contrasted with the same lists for 1868–1869.[97] J. Pierpont Morgan, in 1875–1876, appears as a Director for several of the Alabama and Georgia lines, including the Mobile and Montgomery, an L.&N. affiliate.[98] Josiah Morris appears as a member of the directorate of the Mobile and Montgomery, the Western Railroad of Alabama (a Central of Georgia affiliate), and the South and North (L.&N. affiliate).[99] H. B. Plant, founder of the Plant system, appears as Director of the Western Railroad of Alabama.[100]

The election of Governor Houston in 1874 provided an opportunity for the settlement of the "debt" of Alabama, as pledged by the winning party. The debt settlement is supposed to have been framed by a State Senator, Rufus W. Cobb, "and others."[101] Cobb, according to a biographical sketch, "devised the plan of readjustment for the state debt which Governor Houston submitted to the legislature after elaboration. He was the friend and admirer of Governor Houston during his administration."[102] Cobb was also President of the Central Iron and Coal Works at Helena, which was subsidized by the L.&N.[103] In addition, he was a local attorney for the L.&N.[104]

[95] Ibid.
[96] Ripley, op. cit., p. 585.
[97] See *Poor's Raildoad Manuals* for given years, passim.
[98] *Poor's Railroad Manual, 1876,* p. 476.
[99] Ibid., pp. 476, 484, 671.
[100] Ibid., p. 484.
[101] Owens, *History of Alabama and Dictionary of Alabama Biography,* 3:357.
[102] Ibid.
[103] Ibid.; Armes, op. cit., pp. 17, 147.
[104] Owens, op. cit., 3:357.

Governor Houston began his administration with the expressed desire of settling the "debt." It should be kept in mind here that "debts" are either paid, or repudiated; and those who, following Fleming, state that the "Reconstruction Debt" in Alabama amounted to from $25 million to $30 million, need to ask themselves how a "debt" of this size, existing at the accession of Houston in 1874, could become a "debt" of less than $10 million through his adjustments without actual repudiation. Certainly the Alabama "debt" was adjusted; but there was no repudiation. It will appear in the following paragraphs that the Alabama "debt" of $25 million to $30 million was not, at any time, an actual "debt," but always a potential one; and that if it had been, or become, an "actual debt," the State would have owned all of the railroads endorsed by it as compensation for the "debt" assumed. The long-heralded triumph of Governor Houston's "debt settlement" actually will be seen to have consisted in relieving the State of its "potential debt," and the railroads of the threat of State foreclosure on mortgages held by it, on grounds highly advantageous to the railroads; or, at least, to those railroad systems with which the leadership of the Alabama Democracy was on a fairly intimate basis.

As his "debt commissioners" Governor Houston appointed Levi W. Lawler, T. B. Bethea, and himself as *ex-officio* chairman. T. B. Bethea does not appear as a director or stockholder in any published records of these facts.[105] Levi W. Lawler was reported in 1868[106] and 1870 as a director of the Selma, Rome, and Dalton,[107] a competing road to the Alabama and Chattanooga; Peter Hamilton, listed with Rufus Cobb as one of the men responsible for the debt settlement in preliminary negotiations, is recorded as a Mobile and Ohio (an L.&N. subsidiary) director in 1868,[108] and in 1870–1871.[109] Houston was a director of the Nashville and Decatur (an L.&N. affiliate) in 1868[110] and 1870;[111] his law partner, Luke Pryor, whom he followed to

---

[105] In *Affairs of Southern Railroads,* or in successive *Poor's Manuals.*
[106] Ibid., p. 384.
[107] Ibid., 1871, p. 393.
[108] *Poor's Manual, 1869,* p. 104.
[109] Ibid., 1871, p. 268.
[110] Ibid., 1869, p. 266.
[111] Ibid., 1871, p. 114.

Washington as United States Senator from Alabama, was a director of the South and North (an L.&N. subsidiary) in 1870[112] and in 1875.[113]

The Report of the Debt Commissioners prefaced an analysis of the nature of State obligations by saying that the "direct and contingent indebtedness of the State is $30,000,000."[114] For political purposes, these obligations had been talked about during the campaign as though they were a "direct" debt; and the historians have not distinguished between the two classes. As suggested above, the greater part of this "debt" was *"contingent";* that is to say, it would become a direct debt only in the event that the State foreclosed its mortgages upon the railroad property, leaving the State in debt, indeed, to bondholders, to the amount of the endorsements and loans, but at the same time possessed of the valuable railroad properties as compensation.

The Debt Commission divided the said "indebtedness" into four classes. Class I was defined as including:

> . . . *bonds issued or loaned to railroad companies (consisting) of bonds bearing five, six, and eight percent interest; bonds issued for temporary loans; bonds hypothecated with and sold by the New York Guaranty and Indemnity Company, on account of a temporary loan; bonds hypothecated with and sold by agencies appointed by the United States District Court, in bankrupt cases; State obligations, bearing eight percent interest; State Certificates, known as "Patton money"; Trust funds, and some small claims against the State.*[115]

This class of indebtedness amounted to $11,677,470, including $1,050,000 of unpaid interest. The great portion of this debt had accumulated prior to Republican rule in 1868; when this party had taken over control in 1868, the State bonded debt was $6,848,400, with $2,494,654.87 of additional state funds which had been dissipated, but still involved the state in interest payments.[116] Obligations in Class I which might be laid to "Reconstruction extravagance" therefore accounted for approximately one million of the total.

112 *Affairs of Southern Roads,* p. 122.
113 Ibid., 1875, p. 671.
114 *House Journal, 1875–1876,* p. 192.
115 Ibid., p. 193.
116 *Poor's Railroad Manual, 1869–1870,* p. 470.

Class I debts were "settled" by a refunding operation by which the state was granted a lower rate of interest and the cancellation of past due interest payments.[117]

Class II amounted to $1,156,000. They represented the liability of the State for railroad endorsements compromised under the law of 1873, in Governor Lewis' administration, when the railroads had exchanged $4,000-a-mile bonds for the prior bonds valued at $18,000-a-mile. By this means the State had, by 1874, reduced its liability by retiring $5,103,000 worth of endorsed bonds.[118]

Class II debts were "settled" by exchanging endorsement bonds for one-half of their face value; in other words, admitted the Commission, the "State accepted a clear loss of one-half." The roads so favored were the (James Sloss–George Houston–Luke Pryor) L.&N. affiliate, the South and North; the Grand Trunk; and the Savannah and Memphis.[119]

Class III debts are called by Fleming "the worst of all."[120] They totalled $2,573,093. These obligations included $600,000 of claims rendered by the South and North,[121] of which Governor Houston's law partner, Luke Pryor, was a director,[122] and in which, as we have seen, the omni-present James W. Sloss had been from the first a prominent figure. Governor Houston himself had been a director of the affiliated L.&N. company, the Nashville and Decatur, in 1868[123] and in 1870.[124] The South and North claims were actually L.&N. claims, since the company was a subsidiary of the greater line.

Regarding these claims, the Debt Commission, of which, it will be remembered, Governor Houston was Chairman, stated:

> It is not our province to make any suggestion in regard to the claim of the South and North. . . . They are not connected in any way with the bonded debt of the State, and do not come within the scope of our investigation and adjustment.[125]

---

[117] *House Journal, 1875–1876*, p. 194.
[118] Ibid., p. 195.
[119] Ibid., pp. 195–196.
[120] *Op. cit.*, p. 581.
[121] *House Journal, 1875–1876*, p. 196.
[122] *Poor's Railroad Manual, 1875–1876*, p. 671.
[123] Ibid., 1868–1869, p. 266.
[124] Ibid., 1870–1871, p. 393.
[125] *House Journal, 1875–1876*, pp. 196–197.

But this $600,000 had been included in the "debt" as originally claimed by the Democrats, and as quoted by later historians. To disregard it was one of the simpler devices for "settlement" and "reduction" adopted by the Debt Commission.

The Commission dealt less kindly with $1,464,689 of obligations which involved the banking house of Henry Clews & Company. Clews, we have observed, was a banking associate of Jay Cooke,[126] and in Alabama had investments at Anniston in the Oxford Iron Works along with Samuel Nobel, erstwhile trader-between-the-lines, and William D. "Pig-Iron" Kelley.[127] Clews' interests had been with the Alabama and Chattanooga, the Russell Sage, Republican sponsored road that was intent on invading the Alabama Mineral District from the direction of Chattanooga as the L.&N. was similarly bent on tapping this region from the North.

Mr. Clews' autobiography states simply, but eloquently, that the Debt Commission was motivated by "political manipulations" in disposing of his claims.[128] This was their solemn pronouncement regarding the Clews obligation:

> *The State is liable only for the amount of the debt which was due to Clews and Co., amounting to about three hundred and ten thousand dollars, with interest. This amount is all that we recommend to be arranged by the State; and as to which of the claimants it belongs we do not undertake to decide.*[129]

It was in this manner that another million of the "debt" was settled.

Class IV "debts" amounted to $14,641,000. They consisted of endorsed bonds on the basis of $16,000 a mile which had not been compromised under the $4,000-a-mile law. The total obligation, on inspection by the Commission, was scaled down to $11,597,000,[130] excluding $3,024,000 in loans due from the Alabama and Chattanooga and the Montgomery and Eufaula with unpaid interest.[131] The "scaled down" figure of $11,597,000 included $5,300,000 worth of endorsements at $16,000-a-mile for the Alabama and Chattanooga, $3,474,000

[126] See p. 333, above.
[127] See p. 334, above.
[128] *Fifty Years in Wall Street*, p. 255.
[129] *House Journal, 1875–1876*, pp. 197–199; ibid., *1876–1877*, pp. 252–254.
[130] *House Journal, 1875–1876*, p. 199.
[131] Ibid.

worth of unpaid interest, and a $2 million loan from the State to the Alabama and Chattanooga.[132]

It has been pointed out above that Governor Lindsay, Democrat, had thrown the Alabama and Chattanooga into the hands of the State in 1871.[133] Extensive litigation had resulted, the bondholders, most of whom were English, claiming that the State had deliberately wrecked the road.[134] Considering the fact that Clanton, whom Lindsay appointed as one of the receivers, was also Executive Chairman of the State Democratic Committee, as well as a leading figure in the competing L.&N. affiliates, the complaint had at least plausibility. The Debt Commission compromised the claims of the English bondholders by (a) paying them $1 million thus disposing of the alleged nine million dollars of indebtedness charged against the State in this connection,[135] and (b) transferring to the owners of the railroad's first mortgage bonds more than a half million acres of land, in the heart of the rich mineral region, and which later became the scene of extensive industrialization in Alabama.[136]

The remaining items of endorsement, involving the Montgomery and Eufaula, the East Alabama and Cincinnati, the Selma and Gulf, the Selma, Marion and Memphis, and the New Orleans and Selma, were in litigation at the time of the Committee Report. The Commission stated that the action of the Court would probably result in nullifying the purported liability of the State, and that the interests of the bondholders would best be served by "their acceptance of a transfer of the lien of the State created by statute, and giving to the State a full discharge from those pretended claims against it."[137] In other words, the "Debt" Commission itself denominated as "pretended claims" large amounts which it afterward proudly claimed to have "settled," and which historians have accepted as the "Alabama Debt."

The final report of the Debt Commission stated that: "the volume of

---

132 Ibid.
133 See page 330, above.
134 (No author), *The Hill Country of Alabama, U.S.A.; or, the land of rest* (London Published for the English Committee of Bondholders, 1878), pp. 95–96.
135 *House Journal, 1875–1876*, p. 191.
136 Ibid., See also *The Hill Country of Alabama*, pp. 95–96.
137 *House Journal, 1875–1876*, p. 202.

indebtedness of the State, including State obligations, will be reduced to about $9,500,000 *exclusive of trust funds*."[138] Since the Commission had begun its first report by stating that the debt amounted to more than $30 million, this immense reduction was hailed as a triumph of Democratic honesty over Republican extravagance. It has been so regarded by practically all historians. More interesting still, the myth of an immense debt of $30 million, crushing the people of Alabama for two generations, has persisted along with the paradoxical belief that the Democratic Party, immediately on its return to power, rescued the State from an immense load of debt. To all intents and purposes, the debt existed for purposes of Democratic propaganda in the election of 1874; it ceased to exist in 1875–1876 for the purpose of showing Democratic honesty; but it has always existed to show how great was the ruin wreaked upon the State by the Republican, Reconstruction government.

Fleming's conclusion to a discussion of the debt situation remains in evidence as *the* perfect document:

> *There was not an honest white person who lived in the State during Reconstruction, nor a man, woman or child, descended from such a person, who did not then suffer or does not still suffer from the direct results of the carpet-bag-financiering. Homes were sold or mortgaged; schools were closed, and children grew up in ignorance; the taxes for nearly twenty years were used to pay interest on the debt then piled up. Not until 1899 was there a one-mill school tax (until then the interest paid on the Reconstruction debt was larger than the school fund),[139] and not until 1891 was the state able to care for the disabled Confederate soldiers.[140]*

Knight states that one of the reasons for the backwardness of Alabama in education was the fact that "upon Alabama was heaped a debt of $18,000,000."[141] Cubberley states, similarly, that the Recon-

[138] Ibid., pp. 53, 255.
[139] The Brookings Institution, in a recent study of the Alabama financial structure, pointed out that the reason Alabama had an archaic tax limit for schools was because of a strangle-hold upon state government by planters and industrialists, who had engrafted this limitation in the state constitution of 1875. See *Taxation of the State Government of Alabama* (Montgomery: Wilson Printing Co., 1932), vol. 4, pt 3, p. 47.
[140] Op. cit., pp. 585–586.
[141] Edgar W. Knight, *Education in the United States,* p. 468.

struction government caused backwardness in the schools through "wasting of resources."[142]

These statements may be seen to be exaggerated and incorrect, especially when they lay blame for immense "debts" upon "Negro," "Republican" regimes in Alabama. There was no "Negro" government; no such debts were left after Reconstruction; and what debts were created resulted from the activities of various capitalists working through both Republican and Democratic Party channels. The debt settlement of 1876 left the residual obligations of the State Government, including both bonded debt and the various trust funds for which the State was responsible, at approximately $12 million. It has been shown, above, that these same obligations in 1868, when the Reconstruction government took control, amounted approximately to $9,500,000.[143]

What is true is that in the negotiations leading up to the refunding of the debt, the holders of various State obligations drove a hard bargain with the Debt Commission regarding future tax policy. The Constitutional Convention of 1875 was in session while the debt negotiations were being held, and the articles adopted on taxation and finance were dictated by the arrangement with the bondholders. Considering their financial affiliations, it can be readily imagined that Governor Houston and his fellow-committeemen were all too eager to comply. On October 16, 1875, the Convention was reported on the verge of complete repudiation;[144] a combination of Black Belt Conservatives, not in the "ring," with hill country "radicals," were all for making trouble for the "debt" commission and its mission. The Committee on Taxation of the Convention reported that they had advised with General L. W. Lawler and Colonel T. B. Bethea, two of the three debt commissioners. These men were sanguine that the "debt" could be "reduced" from $30 million to $10 million through their negotiations, and advised the Convention to limit State tax levies to a maximum impost of .0075 on the dollar. If this were done, the debt commissioners believed that

---

[142] Ellwood P. Cubberley, *Public Education in the United States,* (Cambridge: The Riverside Press, Houghton Mifflin Co., 1924), p. 435.
[143] See page 338, above.
[144] *Commercial and Financial Chronicle,* Vol. 21, No. 534, September 18, 1875, p. 276.

Capital, seeing that our debt is reduced and our taxing power limited, will seek investment in our cheap lands, and population, always following capital, will fill up our waste places. . . . Capital (will see) that our property will enhance in value.[145]

In a letter written by the debt commissioners to the bondholders, dated December 30, 1875, it is revealed that the latter had made various suggestions regarding ways in which the expenses of the State could be cut, so as to allow payment of interest due on State obligations. One method suggested was to cut the size of appropriations made to the schools.[146] A second was to save money by cutting down the expenses of feeding prisoners.[147] In fact, the two fundamental anti-social social weaknesses in Alabama's state government to comparatively modern times, i.e., poor schools and the convict lease system, were specifically suggested by the bondholders as possible sources of needed revenue.[148]

During debate, in the Alabama House, on a proposed tax bill, the estimate of the Debt Commission was taken as a guide for the House Committee. The Debt Commission estimated a total income of $1,066,000 would derive from a seven and one-half mill levy. State expenses were estimated at

State Government	$400,000
Interest, Trust Fund	100,000
Appropriation, School	100,000
Interest, Univ. Fund	24,000
Interest, A.&M. Bonds	20,280
Interest, State Obligations	54,000
Total	$798,000

This would leave $241,720 to pay interest on the various debts.[149]

---

[145] *Journal of the Constitutional Convention of the State of Alabama of 1875* (Montgomery: W. W. Screws, State Printer, 1875), pp. 35–36.
[146] *Commercial and Financial Chronicle, January 29, 1876,* Vol. 22, No. 553, p. 110.
[147] Ibid.
[148] Governor Houston and his successor, Governor Cobb, who, as suggested above, were closely associated with James W. Sloss, turned the convict system from a liability into a profitable source of revenue for the State. See pages 321 and 322, above.
[149] *House Journal, 1876–1877,* pp. 254–256; *Commercial and Financial Chronicle,* February 12, 1876, Vol. 22. No. 555.

The refunding arrangement operated so that on several classes of obligations the interest began five years from the date of settlement, while on others interest was set at a low figure for the first few years.[150] The only provisions made for the support of schools were (a) the "Interest on the Trust Fund"; this meant that the interest upon the fictitious literary fund which had been dissipated in the failure of the State bank twenty years before, would be appropriated by the Legislature yearly to the support of the schools; and, (b), a yearly appropriation of $100,000 from the State Treasury.[151] The Constitution imbedded in the organic law of the State a fixed state tax levy maximum. This, together with the graduation of interest payments to increase over a period of years, and the Constitutional prohibition of local taxation for schools, effectually estopped any major increases in appropriations for schools so long as the Constitution of 1875 remained in force.[152]

Conclusion

The story of Reconstruction, as viewed in the foregoing pages, admittedly needs elaboration; it concerns itself unduly neither with whites, nor with blacks; with the State Legislature, nor with the Senate; with carpetbaggers, nor with scalawags; nor even with the senators, congressmen, governors, legislators, and other factotums usually accorded major attention.

Our story has sought to identify great social and economic forces whose working in Alabama during Reconstruction gives to the period the quality of inevitable, inexorable pressure and response, action and reaction. These forces are none the less significant because they lack tangible form, and frequently defy exact statistical description.

We have seen that the land—Mother Earth—attracted and repelled different social and economic classes of white migrants, and so molded the shape of institutions, and the ecology of their distribution. We have seen, further, that man-made institutions could become the source of attitudes which reciprocally reinforced the strength of the institution. The geography of Alabama determined the boundaries of

150 Ibid.
151 *House Journal, 1875–1876*, p. 204.
152 See *Brookings Institution Report*, op. cit.

the plantation system of cotton culture, and, together with the source of the migrants, defined the structure of chattel slavery in the State. The institution of chattel slavery in turn required the development of an elaborate set of mental attitudes bulwarking its structure. Social and economic classes among white persons depended for their form upon the nature of the land and the nature of the institution of Negro slavery, as well as upon "natural" principles of economic stratification. Each of these diversifying factors affected the institutions maintained, and, consequently, the attitudes derivative from them.

The natural endowment of the State with resources for an industrial civilization attracted capital bent on exploiting this mineral wealth. Our perspective enables us to perceive that accumulations of capital, and the men who controlled them, were as unaffected by attitudinal prejudices as it is possible to be. Without sentiment, without emotion, those who sought profit from an exploitation of Alabama's natural resources turned other men's prejudices and attitudes to their own account, and did so with skill and a ruthless acumen. Meanwhile, there were men of sentiment who had a mixed vision of another kind of social structure—the Northern Humanitarians, the landless whites and the landless Negroes. Reconstruction in Alabama, during its first stages, was affected by nineteenth-century Humanitarianism, as it was finally determined by nineteenth-century capital expansion and exploitation. A decadent and paralyzed agrarian structure founded on chattel slavery, in combination with political and economic forces working on a nation-wide scale, witnessed the defeat of the Humanitarian ideal and the triumph of the capital investor. Since, politically, Humanitarianism, as it had power to affect the government of the South, died with Thaddeus Stevens in 1868, Reconstruction after that date may be signalized as a struggle between different financiers. The panic of 1873, and the collapse of one of the contestants as a result, paved the way for the general peace that came in the period from 1874 to 1876.

In this retrospect such institutions as the Louisville and Nashville Railroad, the Alabama and Chattanooga Railroad, the Union League (considered as an instrument of Northern capital), the banking houses of the Cookes, of Russell Sage, of the Morgans and the Drexels, loom more significantly in Alabama Reconstruction than do the time-honored figures of the history books. Such personalities as James W. Sloss, Josiah Morris, Albert Fink, Henry Clews, Jay Cooke, William Kelley, Luke Pryor, Russell Sage, and V. K. Stevenson, assume larger proportions than all of the governors and legislators of whom such full account has been taken in the past.

We may even be tempted to conclude that the Carpetbaggers, the Scalawag, "Nigger domination," and even the Ku Klux Klan were not the principal heroes, or the villains, of the Reconstruction period in Alabama.

IV JUDGMENTS AND REFLECTIONS

The Reconstruction era left many intensely-felt residues of meaning in the historical memory of Americans. For large numbers of Southerners, the effort to impose black suffrage and an equality of rights upon their defeated section was felt to be an experience of political vindictiveness that justified their continued alienation from the institutions and values of the prevailing part of America. Conservative Northerners look upon the attempt to force a policy of equal rights upon the South as a tragic error, while liberal Northerners regard the outcome of Reconstruction as another proof of the tragic flaws in the American liberal tradition. Black Americans look upon the failure of Reconstruction as evidence of the ineluctable racism of white Americans.

Professional historians, because their training requires them to be critical of all efforts to sanctify judgments of the past, try to find a special kind of historical truth in at least two ways: (1) by taking account of the different voices that speak for the meaning of the past; (2) by trying to see the complexities of human behavior as part of a larger social movement in time. Such critical tests should guide us in our reading of the following reflections about the significance of Reconstruction in a larger framework of American history. And as we make our final critical judgments about the significance of Reconstruction we should confront such questions as: Why was Reconstruction an apparent failure? What were the weaknesses of radical policy? What were the achievements of the radicals for their own time and for the future?

C. Vann Woodward
SEEDS OF FAILURE IN THE RADICAL RACE POLICY

C. Vann Woodward's numerous works and articles have established him as a foremost authority on Southern political and social life in the post-Civil War period. The irony as well as the tragedy of Reconstruction history have frequently engaged his attention and comment. The following essay explores the implications of some of the ambiguities that lay at the heart of radical policy.

The Republican leaders were quite aware in 1865 that the issue of Negro status and rights was closely connected with the two other great issues of Reconstruction—who should reconstruct the South and who should govern the country. But while they were agreed on the two latter issues, they were not agreed on the third. They were increasingly conscious that in order to reconstruct the South along the lines they planned they would require the support and the votes of the freedmen. And it was apparent to some that once the reconstructed states were restored to the Union, the Republicans would need the votes of the freedmen to retain control over the national government. While they could agree on this much, they were far from agreeing on the status, the rights, the equality, or the future of the Negro.

The fact was that the constituency on which the Republican congressmen relied in the North lived in a race-conscious, segregated society devoted to the doctrine of white supremacy and Negro inferiority. "In virtually every phase of existence," writes Leon Litwack with regard to the North in 1860, "Negroes found themselves systematically separated from whites. They were either excluded from railway cars, omnibuses, stage coaches, and steamboats or assigned to special 'Jim Crow' sections; they sat, when permitted, in secluded and remote corners of theatres and lecture halls; they could not enter most hotels, restaurants, and resorts, except as servants; they prayed in 'Negro pews' in the white churches. . . . Moreover, they

From *American Counterpoint: Slavery and Racism in the North-South Dialogue* by C. Vann Woodward, by permission of Little, Brown and Co. Copyright © 1964, 1966, 1968, 1969, 1970, 1971 by C. Vann Woodward.

were often educated in segregated schools, punished in segregated prisons, nursed in segregated hospitals, and buried in segregated cemeteries." Ninety-four percent of the Northern Negroes in 1860 lived in states that denied them the ballot, and the 6 percent who lived in the five states that permitted them to vote were often disfranchised by ruse. In many Northern states, discriminatory laws excluded Negroes from interracial marriage, from militia service, from the jury box, and from the witness stand when whites were involved. Ohio denied them poor relief, and Indiana, Illinois, and Iowa had laws carrying severe penalties against Negroes settling in those states. Everywhere in the free states, the Negro met with barriers to job opportunities and in most places he encountered severe limitations to the protection of his life, liberty, and property.[1]

One political consequence of these racial attitudes was that the major parties vied with each other in their professions of devotion to the dogma of white supremacy. Republicans were especially sensitive on the point because of their antislavery associations. Many of them, like Senator Lyman Trumbull of Illinois, found no difficulty in reconciling antislavery with anti-Negro views. "We are for free white men," said Senator Trumbull in 1858, "and for making white labor respectable and honorable, which it can never be when negro slave labor is brought into competition with it." Horace Greeley the following year regretted that it was "the controlling idea" of some of his fellow Republicans "to prove themselves 'the white man's party,' or else all the mean, low, ignorant, drunken, brutish whites will go against them from horror of 'negro equality.' " Greeley called such people "the one-horse politicians," but he could hardly apply that name to Lyman Trumbull, nor for that matter to William H. Seward, who in 1860 described the American Negro as "a foreign and feeble element like the Indians, incapable of assimilation," nor to Senator Henry Wilson of Massachusetts, who firmly disavowed any belief "in the mental or the intellectual equality of the African race with this proud and domineering white race of ours."[2] Trumbull, Seward, and Wilson were the front rank of Republican leadership and they spoke the mind of the Middle West, the Middle Atlantic states, and New

[1] Leon Litwack, *North of Slavery: The Negro in the Free States, 1790–1860* (Chicago, 1961), pp. 91–97.
[2] Quoted in ibid., 92, 269–272.

England. There is much evidence to sustain the estimate of W. E. B. Du Bois that "At the beginning of the Civil War probably not one white American in a hundred believed that Negroes could become an integral part of American democracy."[3]

⟨When the war for Union began to take on the character of a war for Freedom, Northern attitudes toward the Negro, as demonstrated in the previous chapter, paradoxically began to harden rather than soften. This hardening process was especially prominent in the Middle Western states where the old fear of Negro invasion was intensified by apprehensions that once the millions of slaves below the Ohio River were freed they would push northward—this time by the thousands and tens of thousands, perhaps in mass exodus, instead of in driblets of one or two who came furtively as fugitive slaves. The prospect filled the whites with alarm and their spokesmen voiced these fears with great candor. "There is," Lyman Trumbull told the Senate, in April 1862, "a very great aversion in the West— I know it to be so in my state—against having free negroes come among us."[4] And about the same time, John Sherman, who was to give his name to the Radical Reconstruction acts five years later, told Congress that in Ohio "we do not like negroes. We do not disguise our dislike. As my friend from Indiana [Congressman Joseph A. Wright] said yesterday, the whole people of the northwestern States are, for reasons whether correct or not, opposed to having many negroes among them and the principle or prejudice has been engrafted in the legislation of nearly all the northwestern States."[5]⟩

⟨So powerful was this anti-Negro feeling that it almost overwhelmed antislavery feeling and seriously imperiled the passage of various confiscation and emancipation laws designed to free the slave. To combat the opposition Republican leaders such as George W. Julian of Indiana, Albert G. Riddle of Ohio, and Treasury Secretary Salmon P. Chase advanced the theory that emancipation would actually solve Northern race problems. Instead of starting a mass migration of freedmen northward, they argued, the abolition of slavery would not only put a stop to the entry of fugitive slaves but would drain the

[3] W. E. B. Du Bois, *Black Reconstruction in America, 1860–1880* (New York, 1935), p. 191.
[4] Quoted in Jacque Voegeli, "The Northwest and the Race Issue, 1861–1862," *Mississippi Valley Historical Review* 50 (1963): 240.
[5] *Congressional Globe,* 37th Cong., 2d sess. (April 2, 1862), p. 1495.

Northern Negroes back to the South. Once slavery were ended, the Negro would flee Northern race prejudice and return to his natural environment and the congenial climate of the South.[6]

The official answer of the Republican party to the Northern fear of Negro invasion, however, was deportation of the freedmen and colonization abroad. The scheme ran into opposition from some Republicans, especially in New England, on the ground that it was inhumane as well as impractical. But with the powerful backing of President Lincoln and the support of western Republicans, Congress overcame the opposition. Lincoln was committed to colonization not only as a solution to the race problem but as a means of allaying Northern opposition to emancipation and fears of Negro exodus. To dramatize his solution, the President took the unprecedented step of calling Negro leaders to the White House and addressing them on the subject. "There is an unwillingness on the part of our people," he told them on August 14, 1862, "harsh as it may be, for you free colored people to remain with us." He told them that "your race suffer very greatly, many of them by living among us, while ours suffer from your presence. . . . If this be admitted, it affords a reason at least why we should be separated."[7]

The fall elections following the announcement of the Emancipation Proclamation were disastrous for the Republican party. And in his annual message in December the President returned to the theme of Northern fears and deportation. "But it is dreaded that the freed people will swarm forth and cover the whole land?" he asked. They would flee the South, he suggested, only if they had something to flee from. *"Heretofore,"* he pointed out, "colored people to some extent have fled North from bondage; and *now,* perhaps, from both bondage and destitution. But if gradual emancipation and deportation be adopted, they will have neither to flee from." They would cheerfully work for wages under their old masters "till new homes can be found for them in congenial climes and with people of their own blood and race." But even if this did not keep the Negroes out of the North, Lincoln asked, "in any event, can not the north decide for itself,

---

6 Voegeli, 240–241.
7 Roy P. Bassler, ed., *The Collected Works of Abraham Lincoln,* 9 vols. (New Brunswick, 1953), 5:371–372.

whether to receive them?"[8] Here the President was suggesting that the Northern states might resort to laws such as several of them used before the war to keep Negroes out.

During the last two years of the war Northern states began to modify or repeal some of their anti-Negro and discriminatory laws. But the party that emerged triumphant from the crusade to save the Union and free the slave was not in the best political and moral position to expand the rights and assure the equality of the freedman. It is difficult to identify any dominant organization of so-called "Radical Republicans" who were dedicated to the establishment of Negro equality and agreed on a program to accomplish their end. Both Southern conservatives and Northern liberals have long insisted or assumed that such an organization of radicals existed and determinedly pursued their purpose. But the evidence does not seem to support this assumption. There undoubtedly *did* emerge eventually an organization determined to overthrow Johnson's policies and take over the control of the South. But that was a different matter. On the issue of Negro equality the party remained divided, hesitant, and unsure of its purpose. The historic commitment to equality it eventually made was lacking in clarity, ambivalent in purpose, and capable of numerous interpretations. Needless to say, its meaning has been debated from that day to this.

The Northern electorate that the Republicans faced in seeking support for their program of reconstruction had undergone no fundamental conversion in its wartime racial prejudices and dogmas. As George W. Julian told his Indiana constituents in 1865, "the real trouble is that *we hate the negro*. It is not his ignorance that offends us, but his color."[9]

In the years immediately following the war every Northern state in which the electorate was given the opportunity to express its views on issues involving racial relations reaffirmed, usually with overwhelming majorities, its earlier and conservative stand. This included the states that reconsidered—and reaffirmed—their laws excluding Negroes from the polls, and others that voted on such questions as office holding, jury service, and school attendance.

[8] Ibid., 535–536.
[9] George W. Julian, *Speeches on Political Questions* (New York, 1872), p. 299.

Throughout these years, the North remained fundamentally what it was before—a society organized upon assumptions of racial privilege and segregation. As Senator Henry Wilson of Massachusetts told his colleagues in 1867, "There is today not a square mile in the United States where the advocacy of the equal rights of those colored men has not been in the past and is not now unpopular."[10] Whether the Senator was entirely accurate in his estimate of white opinion or not, he faithfully reflects the political constraints and assumptions under which his party operated as they cautiously and hesitantly framed legislation for Negro civil and political rights—a program they knew had to be made acceptable to the electorate that Senator Wilson described.

This is not to suggest that there was not widespread and sincere concern in the North for the terrible condition of the freedmen in the South. There can be no doubt that many Northern people were deeply moved by the reports of atrocities, peonage, brutality, lynchings, riots, and injustices that filled the press. Indignation was especially strong over the Black Codes adopted by some of the Johnsonian state legislatures, for they blatantly advertised the intention of some Southerners to substitute a degrading peonage for slavery and make a mockery of the moral fruits of Northern victory. What is sometimes overlooked in analyzing Northern response to the Negro's plight is the continued apprehension over the threat of a massive Negro invasion of the North. The panicky fear that this might be precipitated by emancipation had been allayed in 1862 by the promises of President Lincoln and other Republican spokesmen that once slavery was abolished, the freedmen would cheerfully settle down to remain in the South, that Northern Negroes would be drawn back to the South, and that deportation and colonization abroad would take care of any threat of Northern invasion that remained. But not only had experiments with deportation come to grief, but Southern white persecution and abuse combined with the ugly Black Codes had produced new and powerful incentives for a Negro exodus while removal of the shackles of slavery cleared the way for emigration.

The response of the Republican Congress to this situation was the Civil Rights Act of 1866, later incorporated into the Fourteenth

10 *Congressional Globe,* 40th Cong., 3d sess. (Jan. 28, 1869), p. 672.

Amendment. Undoubtedly part of the motivation for this legislation was a humanitarian concern for the protection of the Negro in the South, but another part of the motivation was less philanthropic and it was concerned not with the protection of the black man in the South but the white man in the North. Senator Roscoe Conkling of New York, a member of the Joint Committee of Fifteen who helped draft the Civil Rights provisions, was quite explicit on this point. "Four years ago," he said in the campaign of 1866, "mobs were raised, passions were roused, votes were given, upon the idea that emancipated negroes were to burst in hordes upon the North. We then said, give them liberty and rights at the South, and they will stay there and never come into a cold climate to die. We say so still, and we want them let alone, and that is one thing that this part of the amendment is for."[11]

Another prominent member of the Joint Committee who had a right to speak authoritatively of the meaning of its racial policy was George Boutwell of Massachusetts. Addressing his colleagues in 1866, Boutwell said:

> *I bid the people, the working people of the North, the men who are strug-*
> *gling for subsistence, to beware of the day when the southern freedmen*
> *shall swarm over the borders in quest of those rights which should be*
> *secured to them in their native states. A just policy on our part leaves the*
> *black man in the South where he will soon become prosperous and happy.*
> *An unjust policy in the South forces him from home and into those states*
> *where his rights will be protected, to the injury of the black man and the*
> *white man both of the North and the South. Justice and expediency are*
> *united in indissoluble bonds, and the men of the North cannot be unjust*
> *to the former slaves without themselves suffering the bitter penalty of*
> *transgression.*[12]

The "bitter penalty" to which Boutwell referred was not the pangs of a Puritan conscience. It was an invasion of Southern Negroes. "Justice and expediency" were, in the words of a more famous statesman of Massachusetts, "one and inseparable."

The author and sponsor of the Civil Rights Act of 1866 was Sen-

---

[11] Alfred R. Conkling, *The Life and Letters of Alfred R. Conkling, Orator, Statesman, Advocate* (New York, 1889), p. 277.
[12] Quoted in Benjamin B. Kendrick, ed., *The Journal of the Joint Committee of Fifteen on Reconstruction* (New York, 1914), pp. 341–342.

ator Lyman Trumbull, the same man who had in 1858 described the Republicans as "the white man's party," and in 1862 had declared that "our people want nothing to do with the negro." Trumbull's bill was passed and, after Johnson's veto, was repassed by an overwhelming majority. Limited in application, the Civil Rights Act did not confer political rights or the franchise on the freedmen.

The Fourteenth Amendment, which followed, was even more equivocal and less forthright on racial questions and freedmen's rights. Rejecting Senator Sumner's plea for a gurantee of Negro suffrage, Congress left that decision up to the Southern states. It also left Northern states free to continue the disfranchisement of Negroes, but it exempted them from the penalties inflicted on the Southern states for the same decision. The real concern of the franchise provisions of the Fourteenth Amendment was not with justice to the Negro but with justice to the North. The rebel states stood to gain some twelve seats in the House if all Negroes were counted as a basis of representation and to have about eighteen fewer seats if none were counted. The Amendment fixed apportionment of representation according to enfranchisement.

There was a great deal of justice and sound wisdom in the Fourteenth Amendment, and not only in the first section conferring citizenship on the Negro and protecting his rights, but in the other three sections as well. No sensible person could contend that the rebel states should be rewarded and the loyal states penalized in apportionment of representation by the abolition of slavery and the counting of voteless freedmen. That simply made no sense. Nor were there many, in the North at least, who could object to the temporary disqualification for office and ballot of such Southern officeholders of the old regime as were described in the third section. The fourth section asserting the validity of the national debt and avoiding the Confederate debts was obviously necessary. As it turned out these were the best terms the South could expect—far better than they eventually got—and the South would have been wise to have accepted them.

The tragic failure in statesmanship of the Fourteenth Amendment lay not in its terms but in the equivocal and pusillanimous way it was presented. Had it been made a firm and clear condition for readmission of the rebel states, a lot of anguish would have been spared that generation as well as later ones, including our own. Instead, in equivocal deference to states rights, the South was requested to approve instead of being compelled to accept. In this I think the moderates were wrong and Thaddeus Stevens was right. As W. R. Brock put it, "The onus of decision was passed to the Southern states at a moment when they were still able to defy Congress but hardly capable of taking a statesmanlike view of the future."[13] It was also the fateful moment when President Johnson declared war on Congress and advised the South to reject the Amendment. Under the circumstances, it was inevitable that the South should reject it, and it did so with stunning unanimity. Only thirty-two votes were cast for ratification in all the Southern legislatures. This spelled the end of any hope for the moderate position in the Republican leadership.

After two years of stalling and fumbling, of endless committee work and compromise, the First Reconstruction Act was finally adopted in the eleventh hour of the expiring Thirty-ninth Congress. Only after this momentous bill was passed, was it realized that it had been drastically changed at the last moment by amendments that had not been referred to or considered by committees and that had been adopted without debate in the House and virtually without debate in the Senate. In a panicky spirit of urgency, men who were ordinarily clear-headed yielded their better judgment to the demand for anything-better-than-nothing. Few of them liked what they got, and fewer still understood the implications and the meaning of what they had done. Even John Sherman, who gave his name to the bill, was so badly confused and misled on its effect that he underestimated by some 90 percent the number who would be disqualified from office and disfranchised. And this was one of the key provisions of the bill. It was, on the whole, a sorry performance and was far from doing justice to the intelligence and statesmanship and responsibility of the men who shaped and passed the measure.

One thing was at least clear, despite the charges of the Southern enemies and the Northern friends of the act to the contrary. It was not primarily devised for the protection of Negro rights and the provision of Negro equality. Its primary purpose, however awkwardly

[13] W. R. Brock, *An American Crisis: Congress and Reconstruction, 1865–1867* (London, 1963), p. 149.

and poorly implemented, was to put the Southern states under the control of men loyal to the Union or men the Republicans thought they could trust to control those states for their purposes. As far as the Negro's future was concerned, the votes of the Congress that adopted the Reconstruction Act speak for themselves. Those votes had turned down Stevens' proposal to assure an economic foundation for Negro equality and Sumner's resolutions to give the Negro equal opportunity in schools, in homesteads, and full civil rights. As for the Negro franchise, its provisions, like those for civil rights, were limited. The Negro franchise was devised for the passage of the Fourteenth Amendment and setting up the new Southern state constitutions. But disfranchisement by educational and property qualifications was left an available option, and escape from the whole scheme was left open by permitting the choice of military rule. No guarantee of proportional representation for the Negro population was contemplated, and no assurance was provided for Negro officeholding.[14]

A sudden shift from defiance to acquiescence took place in the South with the passage of the Reconstruction Act of March 2, 1867. How deep the change ran it would be hard to say. The evidence of it comes largely from public pronouncements of the press and conservative leaders, and on the negative side from the silence of the voices of defiance. The mood of submission and acquiescence was experimental, tentative, and precarious at best. It can not be said to have predominated longer than seven months, from spring to autumn of 1867. That brief period was crucial for the future of the South and the Negro in the long agony of Reconstruction.

Southerners watched intently the forthcoming state elections in the North in October. They were expected to reflect Northern reactions to Radical Reconstruction and especially to the issue of Negro suffrage. There was much earnest speculation in the South. "It may be," said the Charleston *Mercury*, "that Congress but represents the feelings of its constituents, that it is but the moderate mouthpiece of incensed Northern opinion. It may be that measures harsher than any . . . that confiscation, incarceration, banishment may brood over

[14] G. Selden Henry, "Radical Republican Policy Toward the Negro During Reconstruction, 1862–1872" (Ph.D. dissertation, Yale, 1963), pp. 204–217.

us in turn! But all these things will not change our earnest belief—
that *there will be a revulsion of popular feeling in the North.*"[15]

Hopes were aroused first by the elections in Connecticut on April
1, less than a month after the passage of the Reconstruction Act.
The Democrats won in almost all quarters. The radical *Independent*
taunted the North for hypocrisy. "Republicans in all the great states,
North and West, are in a false position on this question," it said. "In
Congress they are for impartial suffrage; at home they are against
it." In only six states outside the South were Negroes permitted to
vote, and in none with appreciable Negro population. The *Independent* thought that "it ought to bring a blush to every white cheek in
the loyal North to reflect that the political equality of American citizens is likely to be sooner achieved in Mississippi than in Illinois—
sooner on the plantation of Jefferson Davis than around the grave
of Abraham Lincoln!"[16] Election returns in October seemed to confirm this. Republican majorities were reduced throughout the North.
In the New England states and in Nebraska and Iowa, they were
sharply reduced, and in New York, New Jersey, and Maryland, the
party of Reconstruction went down to defeat. Democrats scored
striking victories in Pennsylvania and Ohio. In Ohio, Republicans
narrowly elected the Governor by 8,000 votes but overwhelmed a
Negro suffrage amendment by 40,000. In every state where the voters
expressed themselves on the Negro suffrage issue, they turned it
down.

Horace Greeley read the returns bluntly, saying that "the Negro
question lies at the bottom of our reverses. . . . Thousands have
turned against us because we purpose to enfranchise the Blacks. . . .
We have lost votes in the Free States by daring to be just to the
Negro."[17] The *Independent* was quite as frank. "Negro suffrage, as
a political issue," it admitted, "never before was put so squarely to
certain portions of the Northern people as during the late campaigns.
The result shows that the Negro is still an unpopular man."[18] Jay
Cooke, the conservative financier, wrote John Sherman that he "felt

[15] Charleston *Mercury,* quoted in *DeBow's Review* 36 (September 1867): 250.
[16] *Independent,* April 4, 18, 1867.
[17] Quoted in ibid., Nov. 21, 1867.
[18] Ibid., Nov. 14, 1867.

a sort of intuition of coming disaster—probably growing out of a consciousness that other people would feel just as I did—disgust and mortification at the vagaries into which extremists in the Republican ranks were leading the party."[19]

To the South, the Northern elections seemed a confirmation of their hopes and suspicions. The old voices of defiance and resistance, silent or subdued since March, were lifted again. They had been right all along, they said. Congress did not speak the true sentiment of the North on the Negro and Reconstruction. President Johnson had been the true prophet. The correct strategy was not to seek the Negro vote but to suppress it, not to comply with the Reconstruction Acts but to subvert them. The *New York Times* thought that "the Southern people seem to have become quite beside themselves in consequence of the *quasi* Democratic victories" in the North, and that there was "neither sense nor sanity in their exultations."[20] Moderates such as Governor James W. Throckmorton of Texas, who declared he "had advocated publicly and privately a compliance with the Sherman Reconstruction Bill," were now "determined to defeat" compliance and to leave "no stone unturned" in their efforts.[21]

The standard Southern reply to Northern demands was the endlessly reiterated charge of hypocrisy. Northern radicals, as a Memphis conservative put it, were "seeking to fasten what they themselves repudiate with loathing upon the unfortunate people of the South." And he pointed to the succession of Northern states that had voted on and defeated Negro suffrage.[22] A Raleigh editor ridiculed Republicans of the Pennsylvania legislature who voted 29 to 13 against the franchise for Negroes. "This is a direct confession, by Northern Radicals," he added, "that they refuse to grant in Pennsylvania the '*justice*' they would enforce on the South. . . . And this is Radical meanness and hypocrisy—this their love for the negro."[23]

There was little in the Republican presidential campaign of 1868 to confute the Southern charge of hypocrisy and much to support it.

---

[19] Jay Cooke to John Sherman, Oct. 12, 1867, John Sherman Papers #28298, Library of Congress.

[20] *New York Times*, Oct. 19, 1867.

[21] J. W. Throckmorton to B. H. Epperson, Dec. 19, 1867, Epperson Papers, University of Texas Archives.

[22] Memphis *Avalanche*, Nov. 10, 1867.

[23] Raleigh *Daily Sentinel*, March 11, 1868.

The Chicago Platform of May on which General Grant was nominated contained as its second section this formulation of the double standard of racial morality: "The guaranty by Congress of equal suffrage to all loyal men at the South was demanded by every consideration of public safety, of gratitude, and of justice, and must be maintained; while the question of suffrage in all the loyal [i.e., Northern] States properly belongs to the people of those States." Thus Negro *dis*franchisement was assured in the North along with enfranchisement in the South. No direct mention of the Negro was made in the entire platform, and no mention of schools or homesteads for freedmen. Neither Grant nor his running-mate Schuyler Colfax was known for any personal commitment to Negro rights, and Republican campaign speeches in the North generally avoided the issue of Negro suffrage.

Congress acted to readmit seven of the reconstructed states to the Union in time for them to vote in the presidential election and contribute to the Republican majority. In attaching conditions to readmission, however, Congress deliberately refrained from specifying state laws protecting Negroes against discrimination in jury duty, officeholding, education, intermarriage, and a wide range of political and civil rights. By a vote of 30 to 5, the Senate defeated a bill attaching to the admission of Arkansas the condition that "no person on account of race or color shall be excluded from the benefits of education, or be deprived of an equal share of the moneys or other funds created or used by public authority to promote education. . . ."[24]

Not until the election of 1868 was safely behind them did the Republicans come forward with proposals of national action on Negro suffrage that was to result in the Fifteenth Amendment. They were extremely sensitive to Northern opposition to enfranchisement. By 1869, only seven Northern states had voluntarily acted to permit the Negro to vote, and no state with a substantial Negro population outside the South had done so. Except for Minnesota and Iowa, which had only a handful of Negroes, every postwar referendum on the subject had gone down to defeat.

As a consequence moderates and conservatives among Republicans took over and dominated the framing of the Fifteenth Amendment and very strongly left their imprint on the measure. Even the

[24] Edward McPherson, ed., *The Political History of the United States . . . During . . . Reconstruction* (Washington, 1871), pp. 337–341.

incorrigibly radical Wendell Phillips yielded to their sway. Addressing other radicals, he pleaded, ". . . for the first time in our lives we beseech them to be a little more *politicians* and a little less *reformers.*" The issue lay between the moderates and the radicals. The former wanted a limited, negative amendment that would not confer suffrage on the freedmen, would not guarantee the franchise and take positive steps to protect it, but would merely prohibit its denial on the grounds of race and previous condition. Opposed to this narrow objective were the radicals who demanded positive and firm guarantees, federal protection, and national control of suffrage. They would take away state control, North as well as South. They fully anticipated and warned of all the elaborate devices that states might resort to—and eventually did resort to—in order to disfranchise the Negro without violating the proposed amendment. These included such methods—later made famous—as the literacy and property tests, the understanding clause, the poll tax, as well as elaborate and difficult registration tricks and handicaps. But safeguards against them were all rejected by the moderates. Only four votes could be mustered for a bill to guarantee equal suffrage to all states, North as well as South. "This amendment," said its moderate proponent Oliver P. Morton, "leaves the whole power in the State as it exists, now, except that colored men shall not be disfranchised for the three reasons of race, color, or previous condition of slavery." And he added significantly, "They may, perhaps, require property or educational tests."[25] Such tests were already in existence in Massachusetts and other Northern states, and the debate made it perfectly apparent what might be expected to happen later in the South.

It was little wonder that Southern Republicans, already faced with aggression against Negro voters and terribly apprehensive about the future, were intensely disappointed and unhappy about the shape the debate was taking. One of their keenest disappointments was the rejection of a clause prohibiting denial or abridgment of the right of officeholding on the ground of race. It is also not surprising that Southern white conservatives, in view of these developments, were on the whole fairly relaxed about the proposed Fifteenth Amendment.

[25] Quoted in Henry, "Radical Republican Policy Toward the Negro," p. 255.

The shrewder of them, in fact, began to realize that the whole thing was concerned mainly, not with the reconstruction of the South, but with maneuvers of internal politics in the Northern states. After all, the Negroes were already fully enfranchised and voting regularly and solidly in all the Southern states, their suffrage built into state constitutions and a condition of readmission to the Union.

Were there other motives behind the Fifteenth Amendment? The evidence is somewhat inferential, but a recent study has drawn attention to the significance of the closely divided vote in such states as Indiana, Ohio, Connecticut, New York, and Pennsylvania. The Negro population of these states was small, of course, but so closely was the white electorate in them divided between the two major parties that a small Negro vote could often make the difference between victory and defeat. It was assumed, of course, that this potential Negro vote would be reliably Republican. Enfranchisement by state action had been defeated in all those states, and federal action seemed the only way. There is no doubt that there was some idealistic support for Negro enfranchisement, especially among antislavery people in the North. But it was not the antislavery idealists who shaped the Fifteenth Amendment and guided it through Congress. The effective leaders of legislative action were moderates with practical political considerations in mind—particularly that thin margin of difference in partisan voting strength in certain Northern states. They had their way, and they relentlessly voted down all measures of the sort the idealists, such as Senator Sumner, were demanding.[26]

For successful adoption the amendment required ratification by twenty-eight states. Ratification would therefore have been impossible without support of the Southern states, and an essential part of that had to come by requiring ratification as a condition of readmission of Virginia, and perhaps of Mississippi and Georgia as well.[27]

The Fifteenth Amendment has often been read as evidence of renewed notice to the South of the North's firmness of purpose, as proof of its determination not to be cheated of its idealistic war aims, as a solemn rededication to those aims. Read more carefully,

---

[26] William Gillette, *The Right to Vote: Politics and the Passage of the Fifteenth Amendment* (Baltimore, 1965), passim.
[27] Ibid., p. 92.

however, the Fifteenth Amendment reveals more deviousness than clarity of purpose, more partisan needs than idealistic aims, more timidity than boldness.

Signals of faltering purpose in the North, such as the Fifteenth Amendment and state elections in 1867, were not lost on the South. They were assessed carefully and weighed for their implications for the strategy of resistance. The movement of counterreconstruction was already well under way by the time the amendment was ratified in March 1870, and in that year, the reactionary movement took on a new life in several quarters. Fundamentally it was a terroristic campaign of underground organizations, the Ku Klux Klan and several similar ones, for the intimidation of Republican voters and officials, the overthrow of their power, and the destruction of their organization. Terrorists used violence of all kinds, including murder by mob, by drowning, by torch; they whipped, they tortured, they maimed, they mutilated. It became perfectly clear that federal intervention of a determined sort was the only means of suppressing the movement and protecting the freedmen in their civil and political rights.

To meet this situation, Congress passed the Enforcement Act of May 30, 1870, and followed it with the Second Enforcement Act and the Ku Klux Klan Act of 1871. These acts on the face of it would seem to have provided full and adequate machinery for the enforcement of the Fifteenth Amendment and the protection of the Negro and white Republican voters. They authorized the President to call out the army and navy and suspend the writ of habeas corpus; they empowered federal troops to implement court orders; and they reserved the federal courts' exclusive jurisdiction in all suffrage cases. The enforcement acts have gone down in history with the stereotypes "infamous" and "tyrannical" tagged to them. As a matter of fact, they were consistent with tradition and with democratic principle. Surviving remnants of them were invoked in recent years to authorize federal intervention at Little Rock and at Oxford, Mississippi. They are echoed in the Civil Rights Acts of 1957 and 1960, and they are greatly surpassed in the powers conferred by the Civil Rights Act of 1964 and the Voting Rights Act of 1965.

Surely this impressive display of federal power and determination, backed by gleaming steel and judicial majesty, might be assumed to have been enough to bring the South to its senses and dispel forever the fantasies of Southern intransigents. And in fact, historians have in the main endorsed the assumption that the power of the Klan was broken by the impact of the so-called Force Bills.

The truth is that, while the Klan was nominally dissolved, the campaign of violence, terror, and intimidation went forward virtually unabated, save temporarily in places where federal power was displayed and so long as it was sustained. For all the efforts of the Department of Justice, the deterioration of the freedman's status and the curtailment and denial of his suffrage continued steadily and rapidly. Federal enforcement officials met with impediments of all sorts. A close study of their efforts reveals that "in virtually every Southern state . . . federal deputy marshals, supervisors of elections, or soldiers were arrested by local law-enforcement officers on charges ranging from false arrest or assault and battery to murder."[28]

The obvious course for the avoidance of local passions was to remove cases to federal courts for trial, as provided under a section of the First Enforcement Act. But in practice this turned out to be "exceedingly difficult." And the effort to find juries that would convict proved often to be all but impossible, however carefully they were chosen, and in whatever admixture of color composed them. The most overwhelming evidence of guilt proved unavailing at times. Key witnesses under intimidation simply refused to testify, and those that did were known to meet with terrible reprisals. The law authorized the organization of the *posse comitatus* and the use of troops to protect juries and witnesses. But in practice the local recruits were reluctant or unreliable, and federal troops were few and remote and slow to come, and the request for them was wrapped in endless red tape and bureaucratic frustration.[29]

All these impediments to justice might have been overcome had sufficient money been made available by Congress. And right at this crucial point, once again, the Northern will and purpose flagged and failed the cause they professed to sustain. It is quite clear where the blame lies. Under the new laws, the cost of maintaining courts in the most affected districts of the South soared tremendously,

[28] Everette Swinney, "Enforcing the Fifteenth Amendment, 1870–1877," *Journal of Southern History* 28 (May 1962): 210.
[29] Ibid., pp. 210–211.

quadrupled in some. Yet Congress starved the courts from the start, providing only about a million dollars a year—far less than was required. The Attorney General had to cut corners, urge economy, and in 1873 instruct district attorneys to prosecute no case "unless the public interest imperatively demands it." An antiquated judicial structure proved wholly inadequate to handle the extra burden and clear their dockets. "If it takes a court over one month to try five offenders," asked the Attorney General concerning 420 indictments in South Carolina, "how long will it take to try four hundred, already indicted, and many hundreds more who deserve to be indicted?" He thought it "obvious that the attempt to bring to justice even a small portion of the guilty in that state must fail" under the circumstances. Quite apart from the inadequacy and inefficiency of the judicial structure, it is of significance that a majority of the Department of Justice officers in the South at this time, despite the carpetbagger infusion, were Southern-born. A study by Everette Swinney concludes that "some marshals and district attorneys were either sensitive to Southern public opinion or in substantial agreement with it." The same has been found true of numbers of federal troops and their officers on duty in the South.[30] Then in 1874 an emasculating opinion of the Supreme Court by Justice Joseph P. Bradley in *United States v. Cruikshank et al.* cast so much doubt on the constitutionality of the Enforcement Acts as to render successful prosecutions virtually impossible.

There is also sufficient evidence in existence to raise a question about how much the Enforcement Acts were intended all along for application in the policing of elections in the South, as against their possible application in other quarters of the Union. As it turned out, nearly half of the cost of policing was applied to elections of New York City, where Democratic bosses gave the opposition much trouble. Actually the bulk of federal expenditures under the Enforcement Acts was made in the North which leads one student to conclude that their primary object from the start was not the distraught South under reconstruction, but the urban strongholds of the Democrats in the North.[31] Once again, as in the purposes behind the Fifteenth

[30] Ibid., pp. 212–216.
[31] Robert A. Horn, "National Control of Congressional Elections" (Ph.D. dissertation, Princeton, 1942), pp. 143, 154–155, 183–187.

Amendment, one is left to wonder how much Radical Reconstruction was really concerned with the South and how much with the party needs of the Republicans in the North.

Finally, to take a longer view, it is only fair to allow that if ambiguous and partisan motives in the writing and enforcing of Reconstruction laws proved to be the seeds of failure in American race policy for the earlier generations, those same laws and constitutional amendments eventually acquired a wholly different significance for the race policy of a later generation. The laws outlasted the ambiguities of their origins. While the logic that excuses and vindicates the failures of one generation by reference to the successes of the next has always left something to be desired. It is, nevertheless, impossible to account fully for such limited successes as the Second Reconstruction can claim without acknowledging its profound indebtedness to the First.

W. R. Brock
THE WANING OF RADICALISM

W. R. Brock is an English scholar engaged in the study of American history and, therefore, is presumably freer of many of the emotional attitudes toward their past that beset American historians. His book on Reconstruction was written in order to study the behavior of American politicians and the American political system in a time of crisis because he believed that such a time would reveal some crucial things about American institutions and ideas. The following selection contains Professor Brock's concluding reflections about the outcome of Reconstruction and the meaning of that outcome for the United States and the modern world.

It is comparatively easy to explain the waning of Radicalism in terms of personal failure, evaporating enthusiasm, the urgent demands of business, and the tendency of all political organizations to fall into the hands of professionals. It is easy also to see how the

From *An Amercan Crisis, Congress and Reconstruction, 1865–1867* by W. R. Brock, pp. 284–304. Reprinted by permission of The Macmillan Company of Canada, Macmillan London and Basingstoke, and St. Martin's Press, Inc.

challenge of the new age, with its manifest problems of the relationship between private business and public authority, had a divisive
effect upon the Radicals—turning Kelley into a fanatical protectionist,
Schurz into a free trader, Butler into a Greenbacker, and Donnelly into
an agrarian radical—while drawing together the main body of Republicans around the citadel of American capitalism. But the break-up
of Radicalism may also reflect more profound weaknesses in the position which it maintained.

It has been argued that much of the Radical success was explained
by the pressures from below which drove cautious politicians even
further than they had intended, and that this pressure must be explained in ideological terms and not as the product of mere interest
groups. The ideology had expressed in abstract but attractive terms
certain propositions about man in society which, for a moment in time,
seemed to epitomize the aspirations of the Northern people. Racial
equality, equal rights and the use of national authority to secure both
were living ideas in the Reconstruction era as they have since become, in some quarters, in the mid-twentieth century. For the first
time these concepts were cast in the form of a political program which
could be achieved; but their success depended upon the response
which they aroused from the Northern people. After Reconstruction
the ideas persisted but failed to rouse the same enthusiasm; their
formal acceptance was a very different thing from the popular emotion which could push them forward despite the usual obstacles to
policies which disturb complacency and refuse to let men rest in
peace. The question remains whether the slackening of the pressure
behind the Radical ideology should be explained by rival distrac-
tions and changing interests or by a weakness in the ideology itself.
Examination will show that the generalities of the Radical ideology—
so attractive at first sight—could not stand pressure. The weapons
bent and broke in the hands of those who used them.

A belief in racial equality has never won universal assent and to
the majority of men in the mid-nineteenth century it seemed to be
condemned both by experience and by science. The literal equality
between men of obviously different physiological characteristics was
an abolitionist invention and it rested upon emotional conviction
rather than upon rational proof; the comparison between intelligent
Negroes and retarded poor whites proved little because the civiliza-

tion of a few blacks did not redeem the mass from docile ignorance and the degradation of some whites did not detract from the high standards of the majority. The abolitionist argument was based largely upon pure a priori statements or upon experience with fugitive slaves; a mass of argument could be produced against the one, while the defiance of the occasional runaway did not prove that the mass of his fellows were not fitted by nature for a subordinate position. The behavior of the Negro was obviously different from that of the whites and, though those who knew him best granted him some admirable traits, they would also maintain that he was sadly deficient in the capacity for industry, thrift, self-reliance, enterprise, sexual restraint and the whole galaxy of virtues esteemed by nineteenth-century civilization. The abolitionist argument that the Negro appeared "inferior" because he had lived in slavery for generations failed to carry weight because no free Negro society could be found to prove the proposition. Moreover there was an added complication in the mixed ancestry of so many of those who, like Frederick Douglass, were quoted as evidence of innate Negro intelligence. This is not the place to enter upon the tangled problem of racial characteristics; it is sufficient to state that in the later nineteenth century racial equality was a hypothesis which was generally rejected. It was not accepted in the North any more than it was in the South and even abolitionists were anxious to disclaim any intention of forcing social contacts between the races and all shied away from the dread subject of racial amalgamation.[1] An initial weakness of the Radical ideology was therefore its dependence upon a concept which was not self-evident, lacked scientific proof, and offended popular susceptibilities.

The usual weakness of equalitarian theory lies in demonstrating that people ought to be treated as equals in spite of natural inequalities, and this difficulty is acute when dealing with people of different races. While it is possible to argue, among men of the same race, that it is necessary to treat men as though they were equal, it is far harder to do so in the face of popular prejudice that men of a

---

[1] Cf. L.C. *Stevens Papers,* Stevens to Kelley, 6 Sep. 1866. "A good many people . . . are disturbed by the practical exhibition of social equality in the arm-in-arm performance of Douglass and Tilton. It does not become radicals like us to particularly object. But it was certainly unfortunate at this time."

different race are marked at birth as "inferior." The conventional Republican argument was that men were unequal in capabilities but equal in rights, and in the American context this proposition rested mainly upon an appeal to the preamble of the Declaration of Independence; but the assertions of the Declaration were not "self-evident" to most white Americans when applied to Negroes. Moreover there were some particular difficulties in equalitarian theory when applied to a mass of people, concentrated in a single region, and occupying from time out of mind a subordinate position in society. Equality demands protection of the weak against the strong and positive law to afford it; but it usually involves the assumption that given certain legal rights the due process of law will enable men to maintain their equality. With the Negroes this assumption could not be made: what was required was protection, maintained by enforceable law, at every point where the power of the dominant race was likely to impinge upon the weaker. With tradition, economic power, prejudice, social custom and, in most Southern districts, numbers all entrenched on one side, protection could not be provided merely by changing the law and leaving its administration to the local authorities and courts. The concept of Negro equality demanded interference with the processes of local government on a scale never before contemplated in America or in any other nation. Would the Northern majority be prepared to exert continuously this kind of pressure and provide this kind of protection? In the answer to this question lay the second great weakness of the Radical ideology.

Further difficulties lay in the complexities which sheltered behind the simple word "equality." Whatever the moral arguments the Negro was not, and could not be in the immediate future, an equal to the white man in economic life, in competition for the scarce educational facilities of the South, or in winning public office. Racial equality would have to be an artificial creation imposed upon Southern society; the Negro would have to have guarantees which were not given to the white man, and the quest for equality would demand unequal incidence of the law. No other minority required special legislation to ensure equal status in the courts, or the care of a Federal bureau, or the use of force to protect the right to vote. Negro equality implied that something must be taken from the whites, and this was explicit in two features of Radical policy: confiscation and disqualification. Stevens never wavered in his belief that Negro democracy must have an economic basis in Negro landownership; confiscation and redistribution were therefore cardinal points in his program. Yet the most passionate advocates of equality could not persuade the Republican majority to embark upon such a disturbance of property. Negro democracy would also be a sham if the former ruling class retained its grasp upon local and national office, and disqualification was necessary. This policy succeeded because it was supported by Northern fear of restored Southern domination at Washington, but it proved to be the most vulnerable and perhaps the least wise aspect of Reconstruction. Both confiscation and disqualification demonstrate the formidable difficulties which attend the imposition of equality upon a society in which it did not exist, and in which the beneficiaries of equalitarian policy were too weak, socially and economically, to stand upon their own feet. The price of equality was revolutionary change, vigilance and constant pressure, and who would pay the price when enthusiasm grew cold and the suspicion grew that the Negroes were not yet ready to exercise rights which could not be secured without the coercion of their fellow citizens.

It is in this context that the work of John A. Bingham assumes great significance. In his fight for the civil rights clause of the Fourteenth Amendment he cut equal rights free from Negro protection and made them national. The later perversion of this clause to protect the rights of corporations tended to obscure the significance of a measure which protected all citizens and all persons under the jurisdiction of the States, but once the importance of nationalized right was recognized the Fourteenth Amendment grew in stature. Conversely the Fifteenth Amendment was weak from the outset because it linked suffrage with race; it was a law for Negro enfranchisement and could be enforced only so long as some people had an interest in doing so. If the Fifteenth Amendment had declared in unequivocal terms that all males over the age of twenty-one who were citizens of the United States had the right to vote it might have been recognized as a cornerstone of democracy and attracted popular support. As it was the Fifteenth Amendment enacted "impartial" suffrage which meant that the states could impose any qualification they chose provided that it was not based on race; this meant that the white majority of the nation had no particular interest in its enforcement.

Beyond the major problem of equality by enforcement lay the vast and ramifying difficulty of definition. Was equality indivisible or if divisible which aspects were essential? The three classic definitions of equality—*in* the eyes of God, *under* the law, and *of* opportunity— each carried different implications. Equality in the eyes of God might well be an excuse for inequality on earth: Dives and Lazarus had both lived under the judgment of God, both received their deserts after death, and their inequality on earth was dramatic but irrelevant to their condition in eternity. Equality in the eyes of God implied some limitation upon the principle of subordination for it had been an essential part of the abolitionist case that the children of God should not be treated as less than human beings, but it provided no definition of the place of man in society. Many pious Northerners saw no inconsistency between Christian conviction and racial discrimination, and the brotherhood of man in Christ was no barrier to the belief that equality on earth was no part of God's purpose. It was therefore necessary to supplement the Christian concept of equality in eternity with the purely secular arguments for equality on earth.

Equality under the law had deep roots in the Anglo-Saxon tradition but in its mother country it had not proved incompatible with aristocratic privilege, an established Church, denial of suffrage to the masses, and the exploitation of low paid labor. The guarantee of equal status in the courts was a great and important addition to the rights of Negroes, but it would not of itself create a political and social revolution. Beyond the formal guarantee of equality under the law lay the intractable question of who should administer the law. The legal rights of Negroes might be recognized in Southern courts but they were likely to be strictly interpreted; one could be confident that the white Southern judge would administer the law scrupulously, but between the Negro and equal justice stood the white Southern jury. Equality under the law was a grand sweeping theory, without which no other form of secular equality was possible, but it did not erase the notion that the Negro was an inferior man to whom only a grudging recognition was extended. It might be argued that, once the groundwork of legal equality had been laid, the progress towards equality in other fields would follow, yet one might doubt the certainty of this hypothesis. It was only in 1867 that the British Parliament was to decide after centuries of equality under the law that the agricultural laborer was entitled to a vote, and millions of simple Englishmen still went unlettered to their graves.

Equality of opportunity seemed to be a more positive demand. If the racial barrier could be removed from access to education, occupation and public office the Negro would have the right to compete on equal terms with the whites in most of the fields to which his aspiration might lead him. Yet equality of opportunity implied inequality of achievement and in the South its immediate result might be the confirmation of white supremacy. If the Negro was to be given a real chance of equal achievement he must be given positive aids which were not given to the white man, and one was brought back once more to the basic problem of equalitarian theory: that positive government was required to correct habitual inequality. This led on to the political difficulty that, in the climate of nineteenth-century opinion, sustained and purposeful government intervention was unpopular and improbable. The comparatively modest aims of the Freedmen's Bureau aroused intense hostility in the South and many doubts in the North; any further attempt to translate the commitment to equality into governmental responsibilities might wreck the whole structure of Reconstruction, yet without this the purpose of equalitarian Radicalism could not be achieved.

Many Republicans contended that it was unnecessary to embark upon the troubled sea of racial equality if one could stop in the safe haven of guaranteed rights. The Negro was a man, and as a man he had certain inalienable rights; if these could be secured the vexed question of equality could be deferred or perhaps dismissed. This theory of inalienable right had better prospects than any theory of equality. American tradition had long accepted as its cornerstone the idea of man as an atom in society, entitled to do all that was within his power provided that it did not impinge upon the rights of others. But American tradition had usually failed to recognize the fact that rights were not "inalienable," that the exercise of legal rights depended upon the consent of the majority, or that some rights of some men could always be denied by the sovereign power of the people. In Reconstruction Americans were brought face to face with the problem of free men whose "rights" were denied by the local majority and could be secured only by external coercion. Moreover the whole attitude of Americans towards rights had been governed by their implicit acceptance of the idea of checks and balances. The rights of the people were a check upon the enlargement of authority, and to give some rights to some people at the expense of others had been damned by association with the idea of privilege. What was the intrinsic difference between rights conferred upon a chartered monopoly and rights conferred upon a weak minority? This conundrum had always been implicit in American political discourse but Reconstruction made it explicit.

Even if these pitfalls could be avoided there remained the knotty problem of which rights should be protected and how they could be distinguished from rights which were unprotected. The Declaration of Independence referred to the rights of life, liberty and the pursuit of happiness, but these were *among* the inalienable rights and not an exclusive list; and even if one stopped short at the classic three the pursuit of happiness was so elastic an idea that it was little guide to an enumeration of rights which could be protected by law. There were three main attempts to distinguish the categories of right and to determine which could, and which could not be protected. The first was the distinction between civil rights and political rights, the second between those which were fundamental and those which could be left to the discretion of political authorities, and the third was that between public and private rights. The first proposal made by Thaddeus Stevens—that all laws, state and national, should apply equally to all persons—attempted to cut through this maze of difficulties. Later Sumner was to express the same idea when he said "Show me . . . a legal institution, anything created or regulated by law, and I will show you what must be opened equally to all without distinction of color."[2] This was the true Radical argument. It recognized that private prejudice could not be legislated out of existence, but maintained that discrimination could be prohibited in every activity touched by the law. Stevens and Sumner would have left people to do what they liked in their homes or in private associations, but they would have outlawed discrimination at the polls, in

[2] C.G. 42.2.242.

public places, on public transport, and in education. Sumner even hoped to add churches, cemeteries and benevolent institutions to this list. He resisted the argument of "separate but equal" by asserting that "Equality is where all men are alike. A substitute can never take the place of equality."[3] At the other end of the Republican spectrum was Lyman Trumbull who said the "civil rights" (which should be guaranteed by law) were "the right to his liberty, to come and go as he pleases, have the avails of his own labor, and not to be restricted in that respect." In other respects the legal rights of Negroes must depend upon the discretion of their political sovereign for these were "all matters of privilege." This attempted to treat the Negro as a free man without treating him as an equal man, and Trumbull even regarded the right to serve on a jury as one of these matters of privilege.[4]

Before the Reconstruction controversy ended moderate Republicans including Trumbull himself, had moved significantly nearer to the Radical view of rights which ought to be guaranteed, but there remained a distinct cleavage between those who believed that wherever the law flowed it should carry with it equality of right, and those who believed that one soon reached a frontier at which a "right" became a "privilege" and could be withheld at the discretion of the legal sovereign. The extreme Radical position was unequivocal and relatively uncomplicated, but would require a large invasion of the traditional areas of State authority; the "moderate" position was clouded with difficulties of definition and separation but in the nature of things it was more likely to appeal to the majority of men who disliked sweeping logic and preferred to believe that the minimum of effort would produce the best results. Under the circumstances the best which the Radicals could obtain was probably the imprecise but traditional phrases which Bingham wrote into the Fourteenth Amendment. The "privileges and immunities" of citizens of the United States, "the equal protection of the laws," and "due process of law" were all expressions which could mean as much or as little as lawyers were prepared to read into them. They did not prevent the Supreme Court from legalizing segregation but they also provided ammunition for the Court's later attack upon segregation. It is pos-

3 Ibid.
4 Beale, ed., *Diary of Gideon Wells*, 2:489–490.

sible that Bingham's first suggestion, which would have given to Congress the responsibility for initiating measures to protect rights, would have obviated some of the difficulties inherent in judicial legislation; but Congress, even more than the Court, would be unwilling to act until there was sufficient public interest to support action. Once the Northern majority had refused to accept the principle that wherever the law operated race must be forgotten, and had accepted the distinctions between rights which were rights and rights which were privileges, the whole idea of equality under the law was lost. Natural right became neither more nor less than the right which the majority was prepared to recognize and to protect.

Charles Sumner realized the dangers inherent in the attempt to split up the rights of man into various categories, and devoted the closing years of his life to a struggle for a measure which would have embodied the Stevens principle of equal incidence of national and State laws on all citizens. When he was accused of occupying the time of the Senate with arguments over access to hotel rooms or the exclusion of Negroes from benevolent institutions he replied that "Every question by which the equal rights of all are affected is transcendent. It cannot be magnified. But here are the rights of a whole race, not merely the rights of an individual, not merely the rights of two or three or four, but the rights of a whole race."[5] A year after Sumner's death Congress enacted some of the provisions of the bill for which he had fought and guaranteed to the Negroes equal rights in hotels, places of public entertainment, and public transport, but did nothing about education. In 1883 the Supreme Court found this Act invalid on the ground that it was intended to protect "social" and not "civil" or "political" rights. In 1896 the Supreme Court upheld a State law requiring segregated facilities on railroads, and the tide of Radicalism which had once lashed so furiously against the ramparts was at its lowest ebb. Only a bold man could have predicted that the stone which the builders rejected was to become a cornerstone of liberal orthodoxy in the second half of the twentieth century.

The Radical solution to the dilemma of rights which were natural but which could only be secured by artificial means was Negro

5 C.G. 42.2.243.

suffrage. With the vote the Negro would be equipped to protect his own rights, and there were Jeffersonian echoes in the idea that the cultivator of the soil would not only defend his personal rights but also act as a repository for political virtue.[6] The voting Negro would protect himself against injustice and the Union against its enemies, but this concept of suffrage as a protective device proved inadequate when Reconstruction governments were compelled to assume the tasks of modern administration in a region where the best government had always been that which governed least.[7] So long as the vote was merely protective the ignorance of the Negro was not a relevant argument because a poor man could understand what had to be defended as well as the best educated; but when Negro suffrage became the basis for an economic and social revolution guided by positive government it was relevant to ask whether the former slave was yet equal to his responsibilities.[8]

The Radicals argued the case for Negro suffrage in the context of nineteenth-century liberal thought, and they can hardly be blamed for not having transcended the ideas of their age. Moreover they were inhibited by the political circumstances in which they had to operate. It was hard enough to convince Northern public opinion that Negro suffrage was safe and just without complicating the

[6] Henry Wilson observed (C.G. 39.2.43) that "I do not believe the country has suffered much from 1789 to this time on account of the ignorance of voters; it has suffered far more from the character of voters. The people of the country, the laboring men of the nation, desire proper legislation. They are for just, equal and humane laws. They are patriotic, and they have generally proved it; and you often find them by the hundreds and by the thousands voting nearer right than many of the most intelligent men in the country who have personal ends to accomplish. . . . We hear a good deal of the evils of ignorant suffrage. . . . The country has suffered far more during the last twenty years from the selfish conduct and unpatriotic conduct of intelligent men."

[7] A curious by-product of the protective theory was seen when Senator Pomeroy spoke up for female suffrage. Senator Williams argued that "to extend the right of suffrage to negroes in this country I think is necessary for their protection; but to extend the right of suffrage to women is not necessary for their protection."

[8] It was not long before the question was asked even in sound Republican circles. Cf. G. F. Hoar (C.G. 42.2.1872): "Both parties in this House agreed that the condition of the governments of the South . . . was due to the fact that, in reconstructing those States, you had based their governments upon their ignorance. The criticism is just, in part. You did, Republican statesmen, in reconstructing those States, found their government upon their ignorance. You could not do otherwise. The education of those States had proved itself unfit to govern. . . . The mistake you made was this: that you failed to see that the power to establish government on the will of the people, which you asserted, was in the nature of things inseparable from the power to require the education of the whole people."

question. In the summer of 1866 a Radical member of the Reconstruction Committee told Congress that "we may as well state it
plainly and fairly, so that there shall be no misunderstanding on the
subject. It was our opinion that three-fourths of the States of this
Union (that is of the loyal States) could not be induced to vote to
grant the right of suffrage, even in any degree or under any restriction, to the colored race."[9] Between this time and the passage of the
Fifteenth Amendment a remarkable change took place in public
opinion, but in order to foster it the Radicals were forced to rely less
and less upon appeals to abstract justice and more and more upon
the utility of the Negro vote to the party and to the Union. This stress
led them to pass lightly over the tasks which Negro democracy might
be called upon to perform, and to treat their votes merely as a coun-
terweight in the political balance of the nation.

Radicals themselves hesitated at times over the problem of the
vote. Was it one of the inalienable rights, or was it, as everyone
else said, a political right which could be granted or withheld at the
discretion of the political sovereign? Among the conservative Republicans, and particularly among the better educated, there was genuine
hesitation about mass democracy, and if they turned one eye towards
the Negroes of the South they turned the other to the foreign-born
city vote which formed the electoral basis of Boss Tweed's New York
ring. Reformers could join hands with the merely fearful in urging
the case for universal literacy tests, and old Know-Nothings could
make common cause with new Republicans against universal suffrage. Yet literacy tests which would exclude the mass of the Southern Negro people, and could be manipulated by the ruling State
authorities, were useless as a political solution in the South, and
Radicals were pushed from their early caution on the suffrage question to an outright avowal of belief in universal suffrage. In a letter
written for communication to a Republican meeting in New York in
January 1868 Thaddeus Stevens insisted that the right to vote was
inalienable, and put natural right ahead of the argument from utility,
but he went on to stress the other arguments in favor of universal
suffrage.

[9] C.G. 39.1.2766.

True, I deemed the hastening of the bestowal of that franchise as very essential to the welfare of the nation, because without it I believe that the Government will pass into the hands of the loco-focos, and that such an event will be disastrous to the whole country. With universal suffrage I believe the true men of the nation can maintain their position. Without it whether their suffrage be impartial or qualified I look upon the Republic as likely to relapse into an oligarchy which will be ruled by coarse Copperheadism and proud Conservatism. I have never insisted that the franchise should be unjustly regulated so as to secure a Republican ascendancy but I have insisted and do insist that there can be no unjust regulation of that franchise which will give to any other party the power if the Republicans are true to themselves and do not fall into their usual vice of cowardice. The Republicans once beaten into a minority by the force of Negro prejudice will never again obtain the majority and the nation will become a despotism.[10]

Six months before his death Stevens explained that after long reflection he had "finally come to the conclusion that universal suffrage was one of the inalienable rights intended to be inserted in (the Declaration of Independence) by our Fathers at the time of the Revolution and that they were prevented from inserting it in the Constitution by slavery alone."[11] His reflection owed more to the exigencies of contemporary politics than to a knowledge of history, but there is no need to doubt the sincerity of his conclusion. Universal suffrage was the logical and complete answer; "impartial" suffrage was not. With Stevens dead, however, there was no one with the same influence who could put the case so clearly and the Fifteenth Amendment enacted impartial and not universal suffrage. The Radicals failed in the first instance because they did not or could not spell out what Negro democracy was to do, and the second instance because they could not resist the modification of the right to vote which let in literacy tests, grandfather clauses, and poll taxes.

Paradoxically some of the Radical arguments for Negro suffrage tended to rebound. The idea that the vote would enable the Negro to protect himself provided an excuse for nonintervention, and for the belief that the Southern question could now be treated as a local question. In 1880 James G. Blaine, writing in the *North American*

---

[10] L.C. *Stevens Papers,* Stevens to F. A. Conkling, 6 Jan. 1868.
[11] Ibid., Stevens to J. H. Forney, 11 Mar. 1868.

Review, justified the grant of Negro suffrage by saying that "had the franchise not been bestowed upon the Negro as his shield and weapon for defense, the demand upon the General Government to interfere for his protection, would have been constant, irritating and embarrassing. Great complaint has been made for years past of the Government's interference, simply to secure to the colored citizen his constitutional right. But this intervention has been trifling compared to that which would have been required if we had not given suffrage to the negro."[12] It was thus easy to infer that having instituted Negro suffrage as an automatic regulator of the Southern political mechanism Northerners could turn their eyes away from what actually went on in the South. To be fair one should add that when Blaine wrote the extensive disenfranchisement of the Negroes had not taken place, and that in some districts he could vote freely provided that he voted for the Democratic ticket.

It is not suggested that equal participation by the Negro in Southern politics would have been automatically secured if the Radicals had succeeded in establishing the suffrage as an "inalienable right," but an unequivocal statement that all adult males had the right to vote would have been easier to enforce and more difficult to evade. Nor is it suggested that universal suffrage would have done anything to solve the vexed and unexamined question of what the Negro was to do with his vote. What is suggested is that the Fifteenth Amendment was a weak compromise which failed to achieve the Radical aims and, in the long run, helped to discredit that freedom of State action which moderates wished to preserve. Under the Reconstruction Acts all "loyal" males had voted; the Fifteenth Amendment allowed States to retreat from that position while the belief that the suffrage was secured on equitable terms allowed the Northern majority to relax pressure at the point where it was most needed. The keystone of the Radical arch proved too weak to hold up the edifice. In a sense Negro suffrage was premature—though it could have been written into the law at no other time—but this was only in part the result of Negro immaturity. Beneath the surface of the suffrage question lay larger problems of the role of government in a demo-

---

[12] James G. Blaine, *Political Discussions,* p. 278. From an article in the *North American Review,* 1880.

cratic State and these American society as a whole was unwilling or unready to contemplate. By 1880 *The Nation,* which had earlier given somewhat lukewarm support to Negro suffrage while insisting that it should be impartial and not universal, was emphasizing that the *quality* of voters should be the primary consideration.[13] For the intelligentsia who had, for the most part, thrown their influence behind Radical Republicanism, the great national problem was no longer the protection of Negro rights but the defense of public morality, social respectability and economic orthodoxy against demagogues, bosses, agitators, agrarian Radicals, and mass ignorance.

It has been argued in the preceding pages that an essential weakness in the Radical program lay in its demand for national intervention to secure equality and protect rights, exercising a power which was unfamiliar and depending upon the support of public opinion which might well be apathetic or even hostile to its objectives. The arguments for enlarged national power were made clearly and forcibly, and there was no failure on the part of the Radicals to realize that their policy demanded the use of national authority not only on a greater scale than ever before but also upon new principles. The idea which had been presented in Sumner's "Freedom National" speech of 1852 had germinated and grown until it was possible to see the nation newly based upon equal right and abandoning the divided sovereignty of the past. "It certainly seems desirable," said the moderate Luke Poland in 1866, "that no doubt should be left as to the power of Congress to enforce principles lying at the very foundation of all Republican government if they be denied or violated by the States."[14] This was a constant theme of the Republican party and one which brought forth the most bitter cries of anguish from their opponents. "The time was," said one Democrat in 1869, "when the suggestion of grave doubts of constitutional warrant would cause the advocates of pending measures to hesitate, to reflect. . . . Innovation and reform, however specious and desirable, were rejected

---

[13] *The Nation* always opposed the idea that suffrage was a natural right. It gave some pious advice about thrift ("Every deposit in a savings bank is worth ten votes") but in spite of its preoccupation with educational tests it refused to support a National Education Bureau or Federal aid for Southern education.

[14] In a particularly able and temperate defense of congressional policy. C.G. 39.1. 2961–4.

at once and finally unless clearly sanctioned by constitutional authority."[15] Six years later another Democrat expressed the common view of his party when he charged that Republican interpretation of the Constitution "freed from all verbiage and ambiguity . . . amounts simply to the assertion of a supreme power in Congress over every subject that concerns the life, liberty and property of any person within the United States; in other words over everything that is the subject of the law."[16] The detached observer may well ask what was wrong with the exercise of such power, and why the national government should not remedy the deficiencies of the States. The Radicals did not wish to scrap the Constitution, but they thought that its failure in 1861 demonstrated the need for greater flexibility in interpretation and greater concentration of power at the center. This may appear to have been not unreasonable, but by and large the Democrats have had the best of the argument, and modern historians have echoed their criticisms though approving an extension of national authority during the New Deal which went far beyond the wildest expectations of the Radicals. It remains to ask why the concept of strong national government, which has proved so attractive to so many men in the twentieth century, did not gather the support which might have sustained it during the later nineteenth century.

Some of the explanations are obvious. The weight of tradition was against strong national government, and the word "centralism" was bogey enough to frighten large numbers of people who would not stop to ask what was being centralized, by whom, and for what purpose. Increased national authority might put power into the hands of those who were distrusted by the would-be reformers, and the professional politician might be the beneficiary from an attempt to provide the national government with a moral purpose. Roscoe Conkling had a telling point against the opponents of "centralism" when he said that "Every civilized government may protect its citizens in the uttermost ends of the earth, but when the United States interposes to check murders, and burnings, and barbarities at which humanity shudders, perpetrated by thousands, and overawing all local authority, it is suddenly discovered that we are in danger of

---

[15] C.G. 40.3.642 (Eldridge of Kentucky).
[16] A. G. Thurman, speech at Mansfield, Ohio, 31 July 1875.

'centralism.' "[17] Yet for many people the argument against "centralism" was epitomized in the fear that it might increase the power of men like Roscoe Conkling; they could not ignore the fact that his vehemence against civil service reformers was as great as that against the perpetrators of Southern atrocities.

In their presentation of the case for national power the Radicals were inhibited by conventional American and nineteenth-century political thought. While the old Whigs, whose ideas they inherited, had believed in more positive action by the national government than their Democratic opponents, they had never thought of writing a blank cheque for government intervention. What they wanted was Federal responsibility for the performance of certain economic functions defined by the economic interests concerned, and since that time the concepts of *laissez-faire* had tended to narrow the sphere of action which business interests were likely to prescribe for government. Northern intellectuals who were attracted by the political aims of Reconstruction were precisely those who were equally attracted by the utopian elements in *laissez-faire*, by the theory of natural harmony, and by the faith in betterment through individual enterprise. The government was therefore being asked to "secure the blessings of liberty" at the very time when it was being asked to contract its responsibility for "promoting the general welfare," and the hope of securing civil justice for the Southern Negro was not coupled with the expectation of securing social justice for the Northern farmer and worker. Thus the Radicals' concept of national power was too wide to satisfy conservative men but not wide enough to gather support from the nineteenth-century movements of protest.

Even if the concept of national power had not suffered from these inherent weaknesses it would still have had a precarious hold upon the nation. Radical Reconstruction declared certain principles of national responsibility but it did nothing to create the institutions of government which could give these principles a permanent place on the national stage. The Freedmen's Bureau was such an institution but even its friends recognized that its life must be limited. The Fourteenth Amendment left the door open for Congress to make laws

[17] Speech at the Cooper Institute, New York, 23 July 1872.

which would enforce the civil rights clause, but it did not make it mandatory for Congress to do so and the assumption was that the law would be self-enforcing through the existing machinery of government and courts. The initiative remained with the traditional instruments of government—with the President, with the judges and with the States themselves—and no new instruments of government were brought into being. One can contrast this with the experience of the New Deal with its proliferation of governmental agencies; when enthusiasm receded the administrative achievement remained, and many Americans (ranging from highly paid government servants to the very poor) had acquired a vested interest in these new institutions. When Radical enthusiasm withered away it left behind it no such institutional bulwarks, and when the Freedmen's Bureau expired there remained no new government departments, no new government agencies, and no administrative doctrine to carry out those obligations to citizens of the United States of which so much had been heard.

The arguments which have been presented in the preceding pages have attempted to show why the ideology of Radical Republicanism, which appeared so powerful during the crisis of Reconstruction, failed to gather that momentum which could have carried it forward in the years which followed. It is of course exceedingly improbable that the Radicals of the Reconstruction period could have conceived their problems in any other way or that they could have gone on to produce the ideas and institutions which would have corrected the weaknesses in their edifice. Radicalism shared the weaknesses of all liberal bourgeois movements of the nineteenth century, and it would have required a far more profound revolution in thought and action to make them view their situation through the eyes of twentieth-century liberals. In their equalitarian sentiments, in their realization that individual rights might be incompatible with local self-government, and in their attitude towards national power they were prophets of the future; yet they remained children of their age and were bound by its assumptions and inhibitions. And even if their vision occasionally transcended these limitations they were unlikely to persuade the majority of their countrymen that the revolution which they had initiated ought to proceed to further innovation. The failure of Radicalism is thus a part of the wider failure of bourgeois liberalism to solve the problems of the new age which was drawing; but having said this it is important to remember that if the Radicals shared in the weaknesses of their age they also had some achievements which were exceptional.

First among civilized nations the United States had met the problems of a bi-racial society, and first among civilized nations they had committed themselves to the proposition that in such a society human beings must have equal rights. If the definition of "rights" was confused the idea that they must be recognized was clear. The civil rights clause of the Fourteenth Amendment was in many ways unsatisfactory, but it contained explosive material which could shatter the lines of racial discrimination. The United States had committed themselves to the statement that suffrage should be color-blind, and if the phrasing of the Fifteenth Amendment invited evasion the principle which it enunciated would outlive attempts to defeat it. Americans may well differ upon the wisdom of these equalitarian ideas, but it is impossible to deny their importance for the future. The Fourteenth and Fifteenth Amendments could have been enacted only during the period of Reconstruction, and without them the subsequent history of the United States would have been very different. Not least important has been their effect upon the Negro race in America, for the knowledge that the goals of Negro aspiration are already written into the Constitution has had the powerful consequence of turning American Negroes aside from thoughts of revolution. In his quest for equality the Negro appeals to established national law and not against it, and one of the most striking developments of twentieth-century history has been the failure of Communists among a people who had many reasons for disaffection. The constitutional amendments had an equally powerful effect upon Northern thought. If Northern opinion, in the later years of the nineteenth century, was not prepared to implement the principles of the amendments, they were not removed from the Constitution and were to become the basis for further thought about the problem of race in America and in the world at large. It is possible to attribute the modern American hostility to "colonialism"—which so often embarrasses the European allies of the United States—to memories of the Revolution, to ingrained suspicion of Great Britain and to mere calculation about the changing balance of power in the world; but it is equally significant that during Reconstruction Americans rejected the idea that law should recognize the "inferiority" of non-European races. These are not unimportant consequences and may serve to lighten the gloom with which Americans have been accustomed to regard the crisis of Reconstruction.

The great failure of Radical Reconstruction lay in its attempt to remold Southern society. Hypothetical arguments may be produced to show that the attempt should never have been made, or that it was not made thoroughly enough, that too much or too little pressure was applied to the white people of the South; all that the historian can do is to record that the attempt as made did not produce the immediate results for which Radicals hoped. If it is believed that nothing should have been done the responsibility of the Radicals for having done something is clear; if it is believed that not enough was done it has been argued that moderate pressure not Radical initiative laid the ground for a Southern counter-revolution. Radicals argued at the outset that compromise and conservatism were not the principles with which to meet an unprecedented situation, and though one may blame them for their determination to have a revolution it is a little unfair to blame them for being forced to stop half-way. On the other hand if the revolution was going to stop half-way it is fair to blame the Radicals for insisting upon the alienation of the Southern ruling class whose support was vital for any compromise solution. It can be shown—and it is likely that the evidence will gather weight—that the Reconstruction governments in the South were not so bad as they have been painted in the Southern picture, but no amount of argument is likely to convince anyone that they were successful governments. This book has been concerned with the ideas and motives of Northern Reconstruction policy and not with the consequences of that policy in the South. It is true that the policy cannot be divorced from its consequences but motives cannot be judged from results. The authors of Reconstruction policy did not intend that it should perpetuate racial antagonism in Southern society, discredit color-blind democracy, and provide further ammunition for Southern attacks upon the North. They were not disunionists, as Andrew Johnson called them, but they believed that the old Union, containing elements which could not combine, must be reconstructed. They hoped that the preamble

FIGURE 6. A cartoon comment on Hayes' conciliatory policy toward the South: "Saved from Its Friend (?). Old Democratic Party (*slightly bewildered*): 'My Child! My Child! Oh dear! He's stolen my Child!' Columbia: 'Oh bless you, Sir! You've brought us together again!'" From *Harper's Weekly*, October 20, 1877, p. 828. (*Courtesy Boston Public Library, Periodical Department*)

to the Declaration of Independence should become the new formula for national existence, and they hoped to endow the national government with the power to ensure this result. These ideas were not negligible, absurd or unworthy. Their presentation was marred by a bitterness which was the legacy of war but was sometimes redeemed by the idealistic impulses which war had released. They left a record of failure in the South and permanent alterations in the law of a great nation. They faced intractable problems which still vex the modern world and they anticipated many of the assumptions with which men now tackle these problems. There was tragedy in the crisis of Reconstruction, but the tragic element transcends the particular circumstances of the postwar era and belongs to the whole condition of modern man.

George M. Frederickson
RACE AND RECONSTRUCTION

Among the most perceptive writings on American intellectual history during the Civil War era are those produced by George M. Frederickson. His probing studies of the ideas of American intellectuals and public men have exposed layers of consciousness largely neglected by previous historians. In the following selection, Professor Frederickson analyzes black images in the minds of white Americans during the Reconstruction period.

Shortly after the surrender of the Confederacy, Horace Greeley summed up the Northern belief, firmly established by that time, that the Negro would remain in his present location as a permanently distinct race: "*One* bugbear has already vanished—that which held up to view four millions of vagabond Negroes, overspreading the entire area of the Free States, begging, stealing and smelling . . . scarcely a handful have left the South. There they were born; there they have lived; there they mean to live and die."[1] This much now

From pp. 175–197 in *The Black Image in the White Mind* by George M. Frederickson. Copyright © 1971 by George M. Frederickson. Used by permission of Harper & Row, Publishers, Inc.

[1] New York *Tribune*, May 25, 1865.

seemed clear; but what would be the status of the blacks in the South and their relation to the white majority of that region?

One possible approach was discussed briefly during the summer of 1865 and then rejected. The idea was perhaps suggested by General William T. Sherman's famous Special Field Order Number 15, issued on January 16, 1865, which set aside the Sea Islands of South Carolina and Georgia and a coastal area for thirty miles inland for exclusive settlement by Negroes, who were given temporary "possessory" titles to the land.[2] If Sherman's order had been carried out on a permanent basis and if the area had been enlarged or the concept applied to other regions, the resulting separation of the black and white populations in the South would have drastically altered, for better or worse, the future history of the region. Fantastic as the idea may seem in retrospect, there was actually some support in 1865 for the notion that the North should seize its opportunity to remake the South by effecting a thoroughgoing geographical separation of the races. The principal exponent of this policy was the moderate Republican General Jacob D. Cox, who was running for Governor of Ohio. In a letter of July 9, 1865, Cox argued that Northern policy toward the freedmen should combine a respect for "the rights of man in the fullest and most literal sense" with a realistic recognition of "the real conflict of races." Accepting in principle the Radical Republican view that the Negro should be given political rights, Cox nevertheless said that "co-partnership in political privileges between races that will not amalgamate, only intensifies the strife between them, and invariably ends in a war which either exterminates, extirpates, or subjugates the weaker." His solution was separation of the races *within* the South, giving to the blacks the coasts of South Carolina and Georgia and the entire state of Florida, as an area in which they could enjoy political rights and all the other benefits of "a separate corporate existence." Cox reasserted his proposal in a public letter to a group at Oberlin College, more fully describing the racial antagonism that made separation necessary. On the basis of his own observations, Cox contended that the war had not only embittered the relations of the races in the South but had also brought to the surface "a rooted antagonism which makes

[2] *The War of the Rebellion: Official Records,* Series I, vol. 47, part 2 (Washington, 1895): 60–62.

their permanent fusion in one political community impossible." The whites despised the blacks and the blacks utterly distrusted the whites, Cox said, affirming "the permanence and durability" of "such prejudices and enmities of race" as then existed in the South.[3]

Cox's views received considerable attention in the Republican press. A fairly typical comment was that of the Springfield *Republican,* which accepted "the facts upon which General Cox bases his argument for the local separation" but argued that the scheme was impracticable because the government lacked the power to force the redistribution of population that Cox advocated. Even if the plan could be carried out, the *Republican* contended, racial antipathy would simply crop up in a new form when representatives from the new black states attempted to take their seats in Congress.[4] The Chicago *Tribune,* a leading Radical organ, was more sympathetic to Cox's proposal; but Horace Greeley's New York *Tribune,* also considered a Radical paper, rejected it out of hand as "utterly impracticable" and as based on an exaggerated notion of the strength of racial feelings.[5]

Greeley's response in the *Tribune* might have been anticipated. The previous January he had objected to Sherman's special order for black settlement in the Sea Island area because he believed it would deprive the ex-slaves of the elevating association with whites that was a necessary part of their tutelage. Southern blacks, he affirmed, "must, like their fellows at the North, take their chance as a part of the whole people, free from the wrongs and disabilities of slavery, and aided by contact with white civilization to become good citizens and enlightened men."[6] Although Senator Doolittle of Wisconsin made a proposal similar to Cox's in the fall of 1865, Greeley's approach triumphed in Republican thinking.[7] Southern resettlement on racial lines was rejected because it required a coercive power

---

[3] Letters to William Dennison, July 9, 1865, and to E. H. Fairchild et al., July 25, 1865, Cox Papers, Oberlin College Library.
[4] Springfield *Republican,* August 12, 1865; clipping in the Cox Papers, Oberlin College Library. The *Republican* misinterpreted Cox's plan; he did not propose admission of black-dominated areas to statehood but suggested rather that they be governed as territories.
[5] Undated clippings in the Cox Papers, Oberlin College Library.
[6] New York *Tribune,* January 30, 1865.
[7] LaWanda and John H. Cox, *Politics, Principle, and Prejudice: Dilemma of Reconstruction America* (Glencoe, Ill., 1963), p. 215.

greater than the government was thought to posse
much of the now discredited doctrines of the colo
did violence to the deep-seated belief that the black i
little progress on his own. An important additional co
raised in a letter to Cox from Postmaster General Wi..... Dennison,
who warned him that his proposal would be unacceptable to the
Radicals "not only because they believe the negro is fitted to exercise all the rights of the citizen where he is, but that his remaining
and exercising such rights, even to the extent of voting, is necessary
to make the Southern states loyal and desirable members of the
Union."[8]

Having rejected colonization, migration to the North, and racial
separation within the South, concerned Northerners were left with
the problem of how to influence the face-to-face relationship of the
freedmen and their former masters in such a way as to prevent the
de facto reenslavement of the blacks, something which according to
many observers was a real possibility in 1865 and 1866. The Northern
racial policy that took shape was most often described as an attempt
to implement "equality before the law" or "equal rights." Among
Republicans, all but the most conservative—those who sided with
President Johnson in the struggle that soon developed between
Congress and the President—came to the conclusion in the months
after the war that the government should guarantee some sort of
fundamental equality to Southern Negroes, and a growing number
were beginning to say that this should include the right of suffrage.
Behind the complex events that led to Radical Reconstruction, one
of the underlying factors was this strong conviction on the part of an
apparent majority in the North that the freedmen must be granted
certain rights and protected in their exercise, in order to preserve
the fruits of victory and pay the debt owed the Negro for his aid in
saving the Union.

It should be recognized from the outset, however, that this commitment to equality was often limited or conditioned by an underlying
set of values that were not consistently egalitarian. "Equality before
the law" was compatible in theory with a very conservative kind of
society; in England it had been formally guaranteed for centuries

[8] William Dennison to Cox, July 19, 1865, Cox Papers, Oberlin College Library.

.nout conflicting with an institutional pattern which sanctioned flagrant forms of political and social inequality.[9] In October, 1865, the *Nation,* edited by the transplanted Englishman E. L. Godkin, described Northern Reconstruction aims in the following terms: "What we do seek for the negro is equality before the law, such as prevails between a Parisian water-carrier and the Duc de Rohan, or between a London cabman and the earl of Derby. This accomplished, we propose to leave him to make his own social position."[10] The *Nation* was obviously thinking in terms of a concept of equality that did not rule out vast disparities in the wealth, power, and status of individuals or groups. The statement was also in harmony with current *laissez-faire* concepts of the role of government and clearly implied that it was not the function of public agencies to elevate any group by extending aid and advantages that were not available to others and which went beyond the mere recognition of legal equality.

Such influential attitudes tended to place a priori limitations on what could be done to improve the situation of Southern blacks. A minority of humanitarians had argued from the beginning of their work among the freedmen during the war that a long period of special care and guardianship would be required before their charges could be expected to compete economically with the whites, but their views were out of tune with the dominant *laissez-faire* ideology.[11] In the course of providing an influential blueprint for Reconstruction measures, the Freedman's Inquiry Commission recommended the setting up of a Freedmen's Bureau to extend special help to the ex-slaves, but concluded that "all aid given to these people should be regarded as a temporary necessity. . . . The sooner they shall stand alone and make their own unaided way, the better both for our race and theirs." The best response to Southern white efforts to treat the freedmen in "an unjust and tyrannical manner" was not "special laws or a special organization for the protection of the colored people, but the safeguard of general laws, applicable to all

[9] See W. R. Brock, *An American Crisis: Congress and Reconstruction,* 1865–1867 (London, 1963), p. 289.
[10] *Nation* 1 (October 19, 1865): 491.
[11] For an illuminating discussion of the conflict among wartime humanitarians on the question of special assistance for blacks vs. a strict laissez-faire approach, see Willie Lee Rose, *Rehearsal for Reconstruction: The Port Royal Experiment* (Indianapolis, 1964), Chapter Eight.

against fraud and oppression." The commission predicted that once the Negro was given his basic rights he "will somewhere find, and will maintain, his own appropriate social position."[12]

The constant use of the singular to describe the Negro's future "position" suggested that Negroes *as a group* would inevitably find a definite social niche, rather than being fully integrated and dispersed as individuals up and down an interracial status hierarchy. Some representatives of Northern benevolence strongly implied or openly predicted that this "natural" group situation would be at or near the bottom of society. The Reverend Jared Bell Waterbury, writing for the American Tract Society, opined that "the two races are, it seems probable, to dwell side by side for years to come," noted that "amalgamation is not desirable," and concluded that "it may seem best they should dwell together in the relation generally of proprietors and laborers." Of course it would be the whites who would generally be the employers and "the blacks the employed." "Hence . . . even with strenuous efforts for their improvement the African must still acknowledge the superiority of the Saxon race."[13] The Reverend Horace James, Superintendent of Negro Affairs in North Carolina in 1864, maintained in 1865 that the blacks were "a nation of servants," who would "always make the most faithful, pliable, obedient, devoted servants that can enter our dwellings." "In the successive orders or ranks of industrial pursuits," James pointed out, "those who have the least intelligence must needs perform the more menial services, without respect to color or birth. Give the colored man equality, not of social condition, but equality before the law, and if he proves himself the superior of the Anglo-Saxon, who can hinder it? If he falls below him, who can help it?"[14]

James's approach to the Southern Negroes amounted to a willingness to see them find their natural level, which, it was strongly suggested, was that of a servant class. Thus "equality before the law" could readily be translated as *de facto* inequality in a "naturally" stratified social system. Such a view was common even among those Northerners who seemed most favorably disposed to the cause of

[12] *War of the Rebellion: Official Records*, Series II, vol. 4, 382, 370.
[13] The Reverend Jared Bell Waterbury, D.D., *Southern Planters and the Freedman* (New York, n.d. [probably 1865]), pp. 41–42.
[14] Reverend Horace James, *Annual Report of the Superintendent of Negro Affairs in North Carolina* (Boston, 1865), p. 46.

Negro rights. Many, however, avoided the positive implication of racial inferiority made by Waterbury and James and spoke merely of equal rights as a fair "test" of racial differences. In 1866 the *American Freedman,* organ of the Freedmen's and Union Commission (another major endeavor for relief and education of Southern blacks), candidly described such a relationship between equality of opportunity and possible differences in racial capacity: "The wisest and best friends of the freedmen do not aver that the African race is equal to the Anglo-Saxon. Neither do they admit any racial inferiority. They simply assert that the negro must be accorded an opportunity for development before his capacity for development can be known." Until such time "as both races shall enjoy the same rights, immunities, and opportunities . . . the white man's claim to superiority rests on a very shadowy foundation." The only fair way to determine the social position of the Southern blacks, the *American Freedman* concluded, was "untrammeled development of their native character" to "determine their place in society. Their specific gravity will fix their true level."[15]

Such thinking was characteristic of those committed to work among the freedmen and also part of the intellectual rationale for Congressional Radicalism. In February 1866, Representative Ignatius Donnelly of Minnesota, then a militant Radical Republican, gave a speech on Negro rights in which he acknowledged the likelihood of the Negro's inferiority and inability to compete successfully with whites: "If he is, as it is claimed, an inferior being and unable to compete with the white man on terms of equality, surely you will not add to the injustice of nature by casting him beneath the feet of the white man." If, after a fair trial, the Negro "proves himself an unworthy savage and brutal wretch, condemn him, but not till then."[16] The following year, Thaddeus Stevens, the most powerful and dedicated of the Radicals in the House of Representatives, threw down the gauntlet before white supremacists in a somewhat similar fashion. (in 18

---

[15] *American Freedman* 1 (April, 1866): 3.
[16] *Congressional Globe,* 39th Cong., 1st sess., pt. 1, 589. In a speech given in the preceding Congress, Donnelly had indicated that he believed that Negroes were indeed inferior. After arguing that blacks deserved a chance of achieving "the fullest development of which they are capable," he added that he would not "rate them above or even equal to our proud, illustrious and dominant race" (quoted in Voegeli, *Free but Not Equal,* p. 178).

After defending absolute equality of rights, Stevens advised "any who are afraid of the rivalry of the black man in office or in business" to "try to beat their competitor in knowledge or in business capacity, and there is no danger that his white neighbors will prefer his African rival to himself."[17]

Such statements suggested that some of the most egalitarian Northerners were willing to surrender the Southern blacks to a *laissez-faire* competitive process without ensuring that the freedmen had any real prospect of reaping the same rewards as the whites. It is not fair, perhaps, to include Stevens among this group, because in 1865 he proposed the confiscation of land and its distribution among the ex-slaves but little support developed, even among Radicals, for this proposal—it was too obviously a violation of "the rights of property" and a departure from the competitive ideal.[18] The operative Northern concept of equality was in fact doubly flawed in its application to the Negro: it gave prior sanction to social and economic inequalities which were likely to result from what was in fact —if not in theory—an unfair competition; and, in addition, it was compatible with a residual or hypothetical belief in racial inequality. The idea that equal rights led to equal opportunities was obviously not applicable to a people just released from slavery, but the prevailing belief in the probability of racial inferiority provided an ideological escape valve, a ready explanation for future Negro failures which would not call the bourgeois ideology of "self-help" and "equal opportunity" into question.

Some of the callousness implicit in the notion that a race degraded by slavery and suspected to be biologically inferior should simply be given its formal rights and then forced to compete in a capitalistic free-labor society was manifested in the postwar comments of Horace Greeley, who became known as a principal advocate of "the root hog or die" approach to the Negro problem. "Freedom and opportunity—these are all that the best Government can secure to White or Black," Greeley wrote. "Give every one a chance, and let his behavior control his fate. If negroes will not work, they must starve

---

[17] *Congressional Globe*, 39th Cong., 2d sess., pt. 1, p. 252.
[18] On the fate of Stevens's confiscation proposal see Hans L. Trefousse, *The Radical Republicans: Lincoln's Vanguard for Racial Justice* (New York, 1969), pp. 320, 322, 369.

or steal; and if they steal, they must be shut up like other thieves. If there be any among them who fancy that they, being free, can live in comfort without work, they have entered a school in which they will certainly and speedily be taught better." Greeley ended by indicating that all that needed to be done was to "clear away the wreck of slavery, dispel the lingering fear of a return to it, and we may soon break up our Freedmen's Bureaus and all manner of coddling devices and let negroes take care of themselves."[19]

Such an ideology helped shape Northern Reconstruction policy, as it developed in 1866 and 1867, by establishing limits beyond which the North was unwilling to go in its effort to aid and protect the Southern blacks. The Freedmen's Bureau was gradually weakened and phased out after 1866 and was replaced by "the safeguard of general laws," as provided by the Civil Rights Act of 1866 and the Fourteenth Amendment. But attempts to guarantee the Negro's equality before the law by Congressional action or amendments to the Constitution proved insufficient to protect him from the threat of oppression by Southern whites. Basic to the decision to go beyond such measures to a Reconstruction based on Negro suffrage was the growing conviction that Negroes must be given the vote to protect them against the extralegal efforts of "disloyal" whites to deny them the benefits of equality.

Negro suffrage came about despite the fact that only a small minority in the North had been in favor of such a step before 1866. Few Northern states at that time allowed Negroes to vote. Some leading Republicans still accepted the traditional belief that there was a distinction between such basic "rights" as the right to acquire property, receive equal treatment in the courts, and have free access to the professions, and "the privilege" of suffrage, which was supposedly given or withheld in accordance with the interests of the community.[20] Arguments against Negro suffrage could range from the blatantly racist claim that blacks were inherently unfit for self-government to the more reasonable argument that a people recently freed from bondage and almost entirely illiterate was not yet prepared for the responsibilities of full citizenship. What made Negro suffrage in the South acceptable to the North by 1867 was not a profound

[19] New York *Tribune*, May 25, 1865.
[20] See Brock, *American Crisis*, pp. 112, 291–292.

belief in the black man's capacity for intelligent citizenship but the political necessities of restructuring the Union under Northern or Republican hegemony. More precisely, it was the refusal of Southern whites to submit fully and in the proper spirit to minimal Northern demands which gave vital impetus to the movement to extend voting rights to the blacks.

Although there had been some disposition at the end of the war to give the ex-rebels a chance to show their loyalty to the Union, the behavior of the new Southern state governments in taking advantage of the vacillating and permissive Reconstruction policy of President Johnson to enact "black codes"—which, in the opinion of many Northerners, virtually reestablished slavery—and to elect ex-Confederate leaders to state and national office, conveyed to the North the impression that the overwhelming majority of Southern whites remained hostile to the Union.[21] The Negro, on the other hand, whatever his shortcomings, was at least "loyal." Increasingly persuasive as a guide to policy was the view that Representative George S. Boutwell of Massachusetts put forth in July, 1865: "Under all circumstances, a majority, a confessed majority of the South have shown themselves the enemies of this country. . . . On the other hand, the black man, despised, down-trodden, with no reason to cheer or bless the flag of the Republic, has led and guided and cheered the soldier, has enlisted in the armies of the Republic, has fought for the integrity of the nation and the safety of freedom."[22] In January, 1866, Representative Josiah Grinnell of Iowa echoed the sentiments of most Republicans when he said, "I will never prefer a white traitor to a loyalist black."[23] But it was Carl Schurz who provided what was perhaps the fullest and most eloquent statement of the basic argument that would soon become overpowering when he recommended Negro suffrage to President Johnson in the fall of 1865:   *(see p. 23 h.book, C. Schurz)*

In all questions concerning the Union, the National debt, and the future social organization of the South, the feelings of the colored man are

---

[21] See Eric L. McKitrick, *Andrew Johnson and Reconstruction* (Chicago, 1960), for a full discussion of the South's failure to meet Northern expectations of how defeated rebels should behave. McKitrick places a great deal of blame for this revival of Southern intransigence squarely on Andrew Johnson, who, he contends, misled the South about Northern attitudes.

[22] Address reprinted in the *Liberator*, August 4, 1865.

[23] *Congressional Globe*, 39th Cong., 1st sess., pt. 1, 223.

naturally in sympathy with the views and aims of the National Government. While the Southern white fought against the Union, the negro did all he could to aid it; while the Southern white sees in the national government his conqueror, the negro sees in it his protector; while the white owes to the National debt his defeat, the negro owes to it his deliverance; while the white considers himself robbed and ruined by the emancipation of the slaves, the negro finds in it the assurance of future prosperity and happiness. In all the important issues the negro would be led by natural impulse to forward the ends of the government, and by making his influence, as part of the voting body, tell upon the legislation of the states, render the interference of the National authority less necessary.[24]

Many Republicans who came to endorse Negro suffrage on such grounds did so with obvious misgivings. After a tour in the South in which he found much evidence of white intransigency and little disposition to give the freedmen even their most obvious rights, the journalist Whitelaw Reid argued that black suffrage was a necessity even though the Negroes are "not such material as, under ordinary circumstances, one would now choose for the duties of American citizenship."[25] Representative James A. Garfield of Ohio, who eventually supported Negro suffrage for pragmatic reasons, confessed privately in July, 1865, that he had "a strong feeling of repugnance when I think of the negro being made our political equal and I would be glad if they could be colonized, sent to heaven, or got rid of in any decent way. . . . But colonization has proved a hopeless failure everywhere."[26]

There were of course Republican Radicals like Charles Sumner who sincerely welcomed Negro suffrage because they saw it as fulfilling the egalitarian philosophy of the Declaration of Independence, but it is significant that at the time of the passage of the Reconstruction Act only six Northern states allowed blacks to vote. Between 1865 and 1868 there were a number of state referenda on black suffrage, most of which were decisively rejected by Northern voters. Understandably, then, some Republican politicians who advocated Negro suffrage in the South hesitated to commit their party to a

[24] Carl Schurz, "Report on the Condition of the South," in *Speeches, Correspondence, and Political Papers,* ed. Frederic Bancroft (New York and London, 1913), 1: 365–366.
[25] Whitelaw Reid, *After the War: A Southern Tour, May 1, 1865, to May 1, 1866* (Cincinnati and New York, 1866), p. 580.
[26] Garfield to Jacob D. Cox, July 26, 1865, Cox Papers, Oberlin College Library.

campaign to give ballots to Negroes in all the Northern states. This double standard was embodied in the Republican platform of 1868, which made a distinction between the necessity of federally imposed black voting in the South and the right of Northern states to determine their own suffrage requirements. After the election the Republicans took a bolder position and secured the passage of the Fifteenth Amendment, which effectively enfranchised Northern blacks. But a recent study of the origins of the Fifteenth Amendment suggests that its enactment resulted more from hardheaded political calculation than from ideological fervor. It would appear that Republicans anticipated a real political advantage from the black vote in states that generally saw a close contest with the Democrats.[27] It seems likely, therefore, that the decisive factor which provided the necessary support for black enfranchisement was not a popular commitment to racial equality but a belief that Republican hegemony and the restoration of the Union on a safe and satisfactory basis could be accomplished only by subordinating racial prejudices to political necessities.

Whatever the motivation of Radical Reconstruction and however inadequate its programs, it was a serious effort, the first in American history, to incorporate Negroes into the body politic. As such, it inevitably called forth bitter opposition from hard-core racists, who attempted to discredit radical measures by using many of the same arguments developed as part of the proslavery argument in the prewar period.

The new cause was defined as "white supremacy"—which in

[27] See, C. Vann Woodward, "Seeds of Failure in Radical Race Policy," *New Frontiers of American Reconstructon,* ed. Harold M. Hyman (Urbana, Ill., 1966), pp. 137–143; and William Gillette, *The Right to Vote: Politics and the Passage of the Fifteenth Amendment* (Baltimore, 1965), passim. Gillette contends that a principal reason the Republican leaders determined after the election of 1868 to enact the Fifteenth Amendment was that they sought to garner a Northern black vote that might be decisive in close elections. This thesis has been disputed by LaWanda and John H. Cox in their article "Negro Suffrage and Republican Politics: The Problem of Motivation in Reconstruction Historiography," *Journal of Southern History* 33 (August 1967): 303–330. The Coxes base their argument for Republican idealism, as opposed to political expediency, largely on the fact that the Republicans did not, as it turned out, benefit much from the new black vote. But this result does not actually refute Gillette's well-supported contention that many Republican leaders advocated the amendment because they *anticipated,* rightly or wrongly in the perspective of historical hindsight, that Negro suffrage would give them a vital political advantage.

practice allowed Southern whites to reduce the freedmen to an inferior caste, as they had attempted to do by enacting the "Black Codes" of 1865. To further this cause in 1868, Van Evrie simply reissued his book *Negroes and Negro "Slavery"* with a topical introduction and under the new title *White Supremacy and Negro Subordination.*[28] Nott also entered the Reconstruction controversy. In an 1866 pamphlet he reasserted the "scientific" case for inherent black inferiority as part of an attack on the Freedmen's Bureau and other Northern efforts to deal with the Southern race question. "If the whites and blacks be left alone face to face," he wrote, "they will soon learn to understand each other, and come to proper terms under the law of necessity."[29]

Edward A. Pollard, a Richmond journalist and prewar fire-eater, also attacked Northern Reconstruction proposals on racial grounds. His book *The Lost Cause Regained,* published in 1868, contended that "the permanent, natural inferiority of the Negro was the true and *only* defense of slavery" and lamented the fact that the South had wasted its intellectual energy on other arguments. Before the war, Pollard had advocated a revival of the slave trade because it would deflate the pretensions of uppity house servants and town Negroes by submerging them in a flood of humble primitives; he now endorsed Van Evrie's thesis that white democracy depended on absolute black subordination, and concluded his discussion of Negro racial characteristics by asserting that the established "fact" of inferiority dictated "the true *status* of the Negro."[30] Other propagandists of white supremacy, North and South, joined the fray. A writer named Lindley Spring attacked Radical Reconstruction in 1868 with a lengthy discourse on the benighted and savage record of blacks in Africa; and a Dr. J. R. Hayes excoriated the proposed Fifteenth Amendment in 1869 with a rehash of all the biological "evidence" for Negro incapacity.[31]

Inevitably, the pre-Adamite theory of Dr. Samuel A. Cartwright

---

[28] John H. Van Evrie, *White Supremacy and Negro Subordination* (New York, 1868).
[29] Josiah C. Nott, *The Negro Race: Its Ethnology and History* (Mobile, 1866), p. 27.
[30] E. A. Pollard, *The Lost Cause Regained* (New York, 1868), pp. 114–115, 128; and *The Southern Spy, or Curiosities of Negro Slavery in the South* (Washington, 1859), pp. 37–40.
[31] Lindley Spring, *The Negro at Home* (New York, 1868); Dr. J. R. Hayes, *Negrophobia on the Brain, in White Men . . .* (Washington, D.C., 1869).

and Jefferson Davis was trotted out. In 1866 Governor Benjamin F. Perry of South Carolina made it the basis of a defense of white supremacy; and in 1867 a Nashville publisher named Buckner Payne, writing under the pseudonym "Ariel," revived a controversy among racists by expounding the doctrine at some length in a pamphlet entitled *The Negro: What Is His Ethnological Status?*[32] Payne not only asserted that the Negro was "created before Adam and Eve" as "a *separate* and *distinct* species of *the genus homo,*" but also argued that it was because some of the sons of Adam intermarried with this inferior species, related, as it was, to the "higher orders of the monkey," that God had sent the flood as a punishment for human wrongdoing. Like almost all the racist respondents to Reconstruction, he contended that Negro equality would lead inevitably to amalgamation, and that miscegenation, in addition to resulting in the debasement of the white race, would bring on catastrophic divine intervention: "The states and people that favor this equality and amalgamation of the white and black races, *God will exterminate. . . .* A man can not commit so great an offense against his race, against his country, against his God, . . . as to give his daughter in marriage to a negro—a *beast. . . .*"[33]

Most of the propagandists who attacked Radical measures on extreme racist grounds had a prewar record as apologists for slavery, but Hinton Rowan Helper attracted the greatest attention because of his fame or notoriety as an ante-bellum critic of slavery. As we have seen, Helper had never concealed his anti-Negro sentiments. A letter of 1861 summed up his philosophy: "A trio of unmitigated and demoralizing nuisances, constituting in the aggregate, a most foul and formidable obstacle to our high and mighty civilization in America are Negroes, Slavery, and Slaveholders. . . .

> *Death to Slavery!*
> *Down with the Slaveholders!*
> *Away with the Negroes!*"[34]

[32] John W. De Forest, *A Union Officer in the Reconstruction,* ed. James H. Croushore and David M. Potter (New Haven, 1948), p. 117; "Ariel" [Buckner H. Payne], *The Negro: What Is His Ethnological Status?* (Cincinnati, 1867); see also Wood, *Black Scare,* pp. 6–7.

[33] "Ariel," *The Negro,* pp. 21–22, 23, 26–27, 47–48.

[34] Letter to "W," June 5, 1861, printed in Helper, *Nojoque; A Question for a Continent* (New York, 1867), pp. 252–253.

Having done justice to the first two imperatives in *The Impending Crisis,* Helper turned after the war to the third. His *Nojoque,* published in 1867, may have been the most virulent racist diatribe ever published in the United States. It contemplated with relish the time when "the negroes, and all the other swarthy races of mankind," have been "completely fossilized." To speed up the divinely ordained process of racial extermination, Helper proposed as immediate steps the denial of all rights to Negroes and their complete separation from the whites. All this of course went in the teeth of the emerging Reconstruction policies of what had been Helper's own party, and throughout the book he excoriated "the Black Republicans" for departing from the attitudes of the prewar period, a time when Republicans had billed themselves as "the white man's party." His heroes were "White Republicans" like Secretary of State Seward and those few Republicans in the House and Senate who had remained loyal to President Johnson and joined the Democrats in efforts to prevent Federal action on behalf of Negro equality.[35]

The active politicians—mostly Democrats—who opposed Radical Reconstruction were quite willing to resort to racist demagoguery, although they generally avoided the excesses of polemicists like Payne and Helper. President Johnson, for example, played subtly but unmistakably on racial fears in his veto messages of 1866; and later, in his third annual message to Congress, he put his views squarely on the line:

> ... it must be acknowledged that in the progress of nations negroes have shown less capacity for self-government than any other race of people. No independent government of any form has ever been successful in their hands. On the contrary whenever they have been left to their own devices they have shown an instant tendency to relapse into barbarism. . . . The great difference between the two races in physical, mental, and moral characteristics will prevent an amalgamation or fusion of them together in one homogeneous mass. . . . Of all the dangers which our nation has yet encountered, none are equal to those which must result from the success of the effort now making to Africanize the [Southern] half of our country.[36]

Equally blatant were the Northern Democratic Congressmen who

---

[35] Helper, *Nojoque,* pp. 207, 236, 298–299, and Chapter V, passim.
[36] Cox and Cox, *Politics, Principle, and Prejudice,* p. 213; quotation from Kenneth Stampp, *The Era of Reconstruction, 1865–1867* (New York, 1965), p. 87.

made speeches against Radical measures which appealed directly to the prejudices of white workingmen. As Representative John W. Chanler of New York put it, in attacking an 1866 proposal to give the vote to Negroes in the District of Columbia: "White democracy makes war on every class, caste, and race which assails its sovereignty or would undermine the mastery of the white working man, be he ignorant or learned, strong or weak. Black democracy does not exist. The black race have never asserted and maintained their inalienable right to be a people, anywhere, or at any time."[37]

In addition to such crude appeals to "white democracy," Democratic spokesmen in Congress provided detailed and pretentious discourses on the "ethnological" status of the Negro, drawn from writers like Nott and Van Evrie. The most notable of such efforts was the speech Representative James Brooks of New York delivered on December 18, 1867, in opposition to the First Reconstruction Act. "You have deliberately framed a bill," he accused the Radicals, "to overthrow this white man's government of our fathers and to erect an African Government in its stead. . . . The negro is not the equal of the white man, much less his master; and this I can demonstrate anatomically, physiologically and psychologically too, if necessary. Volumes of scientific authority establish the fact. . . ." Brooks then proceeded "in the fewest words possible to set forth scientific facts." He discoursed at length on "the hair or wool of the negro," on "the skull, the brain, the neck, the foot, etc.," and on the perils of miscegenation. In considering the last topic, he conceded that "the mulatto with white blood in his veins often has the intelligence and capacity of a white man," but added that he could not consent to suffrage for mulattoes because to do so would violate the divine decree "that all are to be punished who indulge in a criminal admixture of races, so that beyond the third or fourth generation there could be no further mulatto progeny." Having covered black and brown physiology, Brooks went on in standard racist fashion to portray Negro history as a great emptiness.[38]

In general such anti-Negro arguments were simply ignored by the proponents of Radical Reconstruction, who, by and large, tried to avoid the whole question of basic racial characteristics. But Brooks's

[37] *Congressional Globe,* 39th Cong., 1st sess., pt. 1, 217.
[38] *Congressional Globe,* 40th Cong., 2d sess., pt. V, 70–71.

speech, perhaps the most thorough presentation of the racist creed
ever offered in Congress, could not go unanswered. In a brief reply,
Thaddeus Stevens dismissed Brooks's views as contradicting the
Biblical doctrine of the unity of mankind. Resorting to sarcasm and
impugning Brooks's loyalty, Stevens agreed that Negroes were indeed "barbarians," because they had "with their own right hands,
in defense of liberty, stricken down thousands of the friends of the
gentleman who has been enlightening us today." Disregarding
Brooks's point about the "intelligence and capacity of mulattoes,"
Stevens proposed to match Frederick Douglass against Brooks in an
oratorical contest.[39] A more serious and extended reply to Brooks
was made from the Republican side of the aisle by John D. Baldwin
of Massachusetts. Baldwin's speech is significant because it clearly
reveals both the strengths and weaknesses of the Radical position
on race as a factor in Reconstruction.

In the first place, Baldwin contended, Brooks's argument was
largely a non sequitur; for "the question presented in these discussions is not a question concerning the equality or the inequality of
human races . . . it is a question concerning human rights. It calls
on us to decide whether men shall be equal before the law and have
equality in their relations to the Government of their country." Races,
like individuals, might indeed differ in their capacities, but this should
not affect their fundamental rights. In reply to Brooks's claim that
miscegenation would result from equality, Baldwin suggested that it
was much more likely to result from degradation such as had occurred under slavery, a system which provided a "fatal facility" for
"the mixture of races." As for Brooks's position on political rights,
it meant in effect that all Negroes should be excluded from suffrage
while "even the most ignorant and brutal white man" should be allowed to vote: "If he should propose to guard the ballot by some
exclusion of ignorance or baseness, made without regard to race or
class, candid men would listen to him and discuss that proposition."
But Brooks was propounding, according to Baldwin, a concept of
white privilege and "divine right" completely incompatible with the
American egalitarian philosophy. Eventually Baldwin touched gin-
gerly on the question of inherent racial differences and conceded the

[39] Ibid., pt. 1, 267.

point that the races were not alike, but argued that "it is quite possible that we shall find it necessary to revise our conception of what constitutes the superiority of race." The prevailing conception, he noted, had resulted from an admiration for the ability to conquer and dominate; but were such aggressive qualities "really the highest, the most admirable development of human nature?" Pointing to the recent rise of a higher regard for the gentler, more peaceable virtues, Baldwin suggested "that each race and each distinct family of mankind has some peculiar gift of its own in which it is superior to others; and that an all-wise Creator may have designed that each race and family shall bring its own peculiar contribution to the final completeness of civilization. . . ." Although he did not discuss directly how the racial character of whites and Negroes differed, he was clearly invoking the romantic racialist conceptions that had long been popular among Radicals and abolitionists.[40]

At first glance it would appear that Baldwin's speech constituted an adequate response to the racist critique of Radical Reconstruction, despite his avoidance of Brooks's specific physiological, anatomical, and historical arguments. It was indeed "rights" that the Radicals were attempting to legislate and not the identity of the races. But if, as Baldwin conceded, the races had differing "gifts"— with the whites holding a monopoly of the kind of qualities that led to dominance and conquest—then the competitive "test" of racial capabilities that the Radicals envisioned as resulting from their program would, to follow their own logic, lead inevitably to white domination, even without the support of discriminatory laws. Furthermore, their tendency to accept the concept of innate racial differences and their apparent repulsion to intermarriage were invitations to prejudice and discrimination on the part of those whites—presumably the overwhelming majority of Americans—who were less likely to respond to romantic appeals to racial benevolence than to draw traditional white-supremacist conclusions from any Radical admissions that blacks were "different" and, in some sense, unassimilable.

A few Radicals and abolitionists had early and serious doubts about the efficacy and underlying assumptions of the Reconstruction Acts

[40] Ibid., pt. 2, 456–458.

of 1867 and 1868. They suspected that quick readmission of Southern states into the Union under constitutions providing for Negro suffrage and the disfranchisement of prominent ex-Confederates would not by itself give blacks a reasonable opportunity to develop their full capacities and establish a position of genuine equality. Some understanding of this problem had been reflected in the land confiscation proposals of men like Thaddeus Stevens and Wendell Phillips. But it was the Radicals who worked for extended periods among the freedmen in the South who gained the fullest awareness of what needed to be done beyond what most Congressional proponents of Radical Reconstruction thought was necessary. Charles Stearns, an abolitionist who attempted to establish a cooperative plantation in Georgia as a step toward Negro landownership, attacked the notion that legal and political rights were all that was required to give the black man a fair, competitive position. In *The Black Man of the South and the Rebels*, published in 1872, Stearns denounced Greeley's philosophy of "root hog or die," arguing that even a hog could not root without a snout. In his view, provisions for land and education, far beyond anything that was then available to the blacks, were absolutely essential. Arguing that "the black man possesses all the natural powers that we possess," he pointed out that the blacks had not yet recovered from the degrading effects of slavery and were unable, even under Radical Reconstruction, to compete successfully or maintain their rights in the face of a bitterly hostile Southern white population.[41]

Albion W. Tourgée, an idealistic "carpetbagger" who settled in North Carolina and became a judge under its Radical regime, was an eloquent and persistent spokesman for the same point of view. Tourgée, who eventually made his experiences and perceptions the basis of a series of novels, sensed from the beginning that the Radical program, as it finally emerged from Congress, constituted a halfhearted commitment to Negro equality which was doomed to fail in the long run. In a letter to the *National Anti-Slavery Standard* in October, 1867, he announced his opposition to the "Plan of Congress" that was taking shape. "No law, no constitution, no matter how cunningly framed," he wrote, "can shield the poor man of the

[41] Charles Stearns, *The Black Man of the South and the Rebels* (New York, 1872), p. 16, and passim.

South from the domination of that very aristocracy from which rebellion sprang, when once states are established here. Anarchy or oligarchy are the inevitable results of reconstruction. Serfdom or bloodshed must necessarily follow. The 'Plan of Congress,' so called, if adopted, would deliver the free men of the South, bound hand and foot to their old-time, natural enemies." The Southern Republican Party, Tourgée was saying, was composed largely of impoverished blacks and lower-class whites. Even if assured of temporary political dominance by the disfranchisement of ex-Confederates, these men would soon find themselves at the mercy of the large landowners, who were in a position to apply economic pressure and undo the reforms of Reconstruction. With rare realism, Tourgée argued in effect that political power could not be maintained on the basis of suffrage alone but must be bolstered by adequate economic and social power—and this was precisely what Southern Republicans lacked.[42]

Tourgée's predictions of course came true. As the North looked on, manifesting an increasing reluctance to interfere—a growing desire to wash its hands of the whole matter—Southern white "redeemers" toppled one Radical government after another between 1870 and 1877 and established white-supremacist regimes. Southern Radicalism, supported largely by black votes and ruling through shifting and unstable alliances of Northern "carpetbaggers," Southern white "scalawags," and emergent black spokesmen, had no chance of withstanding the economic, political, and paramilitary opposition of the white majority. In his 1879 Reconstruction novel, *A Fool's Errand*, Tourgée provided an acute assessment of what the Northern leadership had done and why it failed to achieve its original objectives:

> After having forced a proud people to yield what they had for more than two centuries considered a right,—the right to hold the African race in bondage,—they proceeded to outrage a feeling as deep and fervent as the zeal of Islam or the exclusiveness of the Hindoo caste, by giving the ignorant, the unskilled and dependent race—a race which could not have lived a week without the support or charity of the dominant one— equality of

---

[42] *National Anti-Slavery Standard*, October 19, 1867 (letter signed "Wenckar"). For an excellent account of Tourgée's career see Otto H. Olsen, *Carpetbagger's Crusade: The Life of Albion Winegar Tourgée* (Baltimore, 1965).

> *political right. Not content with this, they went farther, and by erecting the rebellious territory into self-regulating and sovereign states, they abandoned these parties to fight out the question of predominance without the possibility of national interference, they said to the colored man in the language of one of the pseudo-philosophers of that day, 'Root, hog, or die!'*[43]

The Negro never had a chance in this struggle, as the entire novel makes clear. His ignorance and poverty made him no match for the white conservative forces.

What Tourgée and a few others—notably Representative George W. Julian of Indiana—would have preferred as a plan of Reconstruction was a comparatively long-term military occupation or territorial rule of the South, which would have guaranteed "Regeneration before Reconstruction." This "territorial tutelage" would have lasted for an indeterminate period, perhaps as long as twenty or thirty years —long enough to give the North a chance to prepare the freedmen for citizenship through extensive programs of education and guidance, presumably including some form of economic assistance, while at the same time working for a diminution of the racial prejudice and "disloyalty" of the whites.[44] But such an approach was rendered impossible both by pressures which impelled Republican politicians to seek readmission of loyalist-dominated Southern states to the Union in time for the election of 1868 and by the underlying social and racial attitudes that have been described. According to the dominant "self-help" ideology, no one, regardless of his antecedents, had a claim on society for economic security or special protection, or was entitled to a social status that he had not earned through independent struggle and hard work; the just penalty for laziness, inefficiency, or vice was severe social and economic deprivation, and it was becoming an open question at this time whether society's

[43] Albion W. Tourgée, *A Fool's Errand*, ed. John Hope Franklin (Cambridge, Mass., 1961), p. 137.
[44] See Tourgée's defense of this approach in the *Anti-Slavery Standard*, Oct. 19, 1867. See also George W. Julian's House speech of January 28, 1867, on "Regeneration before Reconstruction," in his *Speeches on Political Questions* (New York, 1872), pp. 348–360; and Brock, *American Crisis*, pp. 188–190. Julian's proposal for military rule of course became one element in the compromise plan that was actually put into effect, but its basic purpose was vitiated by the haste with which the Southern states were readmitted to the Union under new constitutions providing for Negro suffrage.

most abysmal "failures" should even retain their full right to participate in the political process. Having been provided with Federal laws
and Constitutional amendments which supposedly guaranteed his
legal equality, the black man was expected to make his own way
and find his "true level" with a minimum of interference and direct
assistance. When the Reconstruction governments foundered, many
in the North were quick to say that the blacks had had their fair
chance, had demonstrated their present incapacity for self-government, and could justifiably be relegated, for the time being at least,
to an inferior status.[45]

Tourgée probably understood better than anyone how tenuous
and conditional the Northern commitment to Negro equality had
been. His book *An Appeal to Caesar*, published in 1884, contended
that the Northern people

> *have always reflected the Southern idea of the negro in everything except
> as to his natural right to be free and to exercise the rights of the freedman.
> From the first [the North] seems to have been animated by the sneaking
> notion that after having used the negro to fight its battles, freed him as the
> natural result of a rebellion based on slavery, and enfranchised him to
> constitute a political foil to the ambition and disloyalty of his former
> master, it could at any time unload him upon the states where he chanced
> to dwell, wash its hands of all further responsibility in the matter, and leave
> him to live or die as chance might determine.[46]*

[45] The promulgation of such views in the North during the 1870s is described in
Victor P. De Santis, *Republicans Face the Southern Question—The New Departure
Years, 1877–1897* (Baltimore, 1959), pp. 44–45, 49–52.
[46] Albion W. Tourgée, *An Appeal to Caesar* (New York, 1884), p. 127.

Suggestions for Additional Reading

There are several recent works that provide excellent comprehensive accounts of the Reconstruction era: John Hope Franklin, *Reconstruction: After the Civil War* (1962); Kenneth M. Stampp, *The Era of Reconstruction* (1965); R. W. Patrick, *The Reconstruction of the Nation* (1967). David Donald's 1961 revision of J. G. Randall's *The Civil War and Reconstruction* has modified many points to take account of revisionist writing but much of Randall's earlier interpretation remains in the Reconstruction chapters.

For an understanding of the issues of historical interpretation concerning Reconstruction that have developed in recent decades one should see such articles as Howard K. Beale, "On Rewriting Reconstruction History," *American Historical Review* 45 (1940): 807–827; John H. Franklin, "Whither Reconstruction Historiography," *Journal of Negro Education* 17 (1948): 446–461; Bernard A. Weisberger, "The Dark and Bloody Ground of Reconstruction Historiography," *Journal of Southern History* 25 (1959): 427–447. Richard O. Curry, "The Abolitionists and Reconstruction: A Critical Appraisal," *Journal of Southern History* 34 (1968): 527–545 contains a provocative appraisal of recent writings on the role of abolitionists in radical Reconstruction.

Aspects of congressional Reconstruction are closely scrutinized in the books by W. R. Brock and LaWanda and John H. Cox that have excerpts in this volume. There is also a very detailed analysis of congressional Reconstruction politics in Eric L. McKitrick's *Andrew Johnson and Reconstruction* (1960). Also helpful is David Donald's *The Politics of Reconstruction* (1965). For special studies of the Reconstruction amendments see J. B. James, *The Framing of the Fourteenth Amendment* (1956), and William Gillette, *The Right to Vote, Politics and the Passage of the Fifteenth Amendment* (1965). Everette Swinney, "Enforcing the Fifteenth Amendment, 1870–1877," *Journal of Southern History* 28 (1962): 202–218 examines the unsuccessful attempts to enforce the right to vote. William S. McFeely, *General O. O. Howard and the Freedmen*, provides a good analysis of the failures of the Freedmen's Bureau, and J. E. Sefton, *The United States Army and Reconstruction* (1967) is a significant study of the role of the army in carrying out the Reconstruction policy.

Many of the studies of individual states of the South during the Reconstruction period were done in the first decades of the twentieth century by scholars who were influenced by William A. Dunning of Columbia University. These include such books as: John S. Reynolds, *Reconstruction in South Carolina, 1865–1877* (1905); J. E. de Roulhac Hamilton, *Reconstruction in North Carolina* (1914); William W. Davis, *Civil War and Reconstruction in Florida* (1913); Hamilton J. Eckenrode, *The Political History of Virginia During Reconstruction* (1904); Edwin C. Wooley, *The Reconstruction of Georgia* (1901); C. Mildred Thompson, *Reconstruction in Georgia, Economic and Political, 1865–1872* (1915); James W. Garner, *Reconstruction in Mississippi* (1901); Thomas S. Staples, *Reconstruction in Arkansas* (1923); John R. Ficklin, *History of Reconstruction in Louisiana Through 1868* (1910); Charles M. Ramsdell, *Reconstruction in Texas* (1910).

For later studies of the Reconstruction process in the Southern states which revise the earlier assessments of radical governments, see Francis B. Simkins and Robert H. Woody, *South Carolina During Reconstruction* (1923); Roger Shugg, *Origins of Class Struggle in Louisiana* (1939); Thomas B. Alexander, *Political Reconstruction in Tennessee* (1950); Alan Conway, *The Reconstruction of Georgia* (1966). Richard N. Current, *Three Carpetbag Governors* (1967), and Jonathan Daniels, *Prince of Carpetbaggers* (1958), are useful for the role of carpetbaggers. Thomas B. Alexander links scalawaggery to larger patterns of Southern politics in his article "Persistent Whiggery in the Confederate South, 1860–1877," *Journal of Southern History* 27 (1961): 305–329. Warren Ellem's "Who were the Mississippi Scalawags?" *Journal of Southern History* 38 (1972): 217–240 uses quantitative methods to demonstrate that Mississippi scalawags were most numerous in areas of ante-bellum Whiggery. For special studies of the role of black freedmen see W. E. B. Du Bois, *Black Reconstruction in America* (1935); Samuel D. Smith, *The Negro in Congress, 1870–1901* (1940); Vernon L. Wharton, *The Negro in Mississippi, 1865–1877* (1947); Otis Singletary, *Negro Militia and Reconstruction* (1957); Joel R. Williamson, *After Slavery: The Negro in South Carolina During Reconstruction* (1966).

Studies of the politics of "redemption" are available in Garnie W. McGinty, *Louisiana Redeemed: The Overthrow of the Carpetbag Rule, 1876–1880* (1941); Stanley Horn, *The Invisible Empire: The Story of the Ku Klux Klan, 1866–1871* (1939). On the waning of radicalism in national politics see C. Vann Woodward, *Reunion and Reaction: The Compromise of 1877 and the End of Reconstruction* (1951); Rayford Logan, *The Negro in American Life and Thought: The Nadir, 1877–1901* (1954); Patrick W. Riddleberger, "The Radicals Abandonment of the Negro During Reconstruction," *Journal of Negro History* 45 (1960): 88–102; Richard B. Drake, "Freedmen's Aid Societies and Sectional Compromise," *Journal of Southern History* 29 (1963): 175–186. Harold M. Hyman, ed., *New Frontiers of the American Reconstruction* (1966) contains the papers of an illuminating symposium on the meaning and outcome of Reconstruction (participants: Harold M. Hyman, Alfred H. Kelley, John Hope Franklin, August Meier, Harry Bernstein, W. L. Morton, C. Vann Woodward, Russel B. Nye). *The Radical Republicans and Reconstruction, 1861–1870* (1967) also edited by Harold Hyman is a fine collection of source documents for the period, but one should also consult Walter L. Fleming, *Documentary History of Reconstruction,* 2 vols. (1906–1907) for source materials on the Southern states.

5 6 7 8 9 10